White Queen Psychology and
Other Essays for Alice

White Queen Psychology and Other Essays for Alice

Ruth Garrett Millikan

A Bradford Book
The MIT Press
Cambridge, Massachusetts
London, England

This book was set in Sabon by Asco Trade Typesetting Ltd., Hong Kong, and printed and bound in the United States of America.

First printing.

Library of Congress Cataloging-in-Publication Data

Millikan, Ruth Garrett.
  White Queen psychology and other essays for Alice / Ruth Garrett Millikan.
      p.   cm.
  "A Bradford book."
  Includes bibliographical references and index.
  ISBN 0-262-13288-5
  1. Cognition—Philosophy. 2. Biopsychology. I. Title.
  BF311.M535   1993
  153.4—dc20   92-24024
                                                            CIP

For Don, with thanks

Contents

Preface

When the references cited at the ends of your papers begin to contain more of your own articles than of anyone else's, it is time to write a book. Or there is an easier way: just bind all the papers under one cover. Here, then, is a collection of articles, some old and some new. They are all outgrowths of *Language, Thought, and Other Biological Categories* (MIT Press, 1984), referenced here as *LTOBC*, and they all deal either with themes in the philosophy of cognition or with the biological theory that I believe should underlie the study of cognition. Rather than being strung together in a linear argument, they overlap and criscross, but in such a way as to result, I hope, in a pretty strong fabric. Because each was written to stand alone at least for a brief moment, there are underlying themes that recur, sometimes numerous times, with varying emphases. These overlaps should serve to underline and strengthen what I take to be most fundamental to the biological way of viewing cognition.

But why are the essays "for Alice"? Partly because of her special role in chapter 14, after which this volume is named. But there is another reason too. Everybody but *everybody* said that *LTOBC* was a *hard* book. That took me by surprise. I hadn't even supposed myself capable of writing a conceptually difficult book, and I had worked very hard on the exposition. But on thinking it over and talking it over, I slowly began to see the point. *LTOBC* was one long uninterrupted argument, with no intermissions, no recapitulations, and worst of all, with no explanation of its bearing on problems in the forefront of contemporary literature. The essays in this volume carry some of the themes from *LTOBC* considerably forward, but they all take their departure from problems with which the contemporary audience is familiar. As such, they constitute a sort of introduction, after the fact, to *LTOBC*. Alice, as we know, is not an ordinary child. She is an exceptionally bright and versatile one. The essays are not for Alice, then, because they are elementary. But I have worked hard (with varying success, I think) to make them as easy as possible. Compared to *LTOBC*, they are almost "popular essays." And there are fourteen chances here for Alice to start over, should she get stuck.

My special debts with regard to individual chapters° are acknowledged in footnotes. Thanks to John Troyer, who helped me also with the painful task of reading final proofs. And I would like to give very heartfelt thanks to all the members of my department at the University of Connecticut for creating such a warm climate for its women and such a generous and supportive atmosphere for scholarship. It is a rare pleasure to feel that one's colleagues are genuinely pleased and excited when one or another's article is accepted in a good journal or when one or another is invited to give a talk at an interesting place. It is rare too, I imagine, actually to find it fun to go to department meetings and department seminars because there is so much good-humored laughter there!

Acknowledgments

This book was prepared while I was a fellow at the Center for Advanced Study in the Behavioral Sciences, where financial support was provided by the National Endowment for the Humanities, grant no. RA-20037-88, and the Andrew W. Mellon Foundation.

"In defense of proper functions" first appeared in *Philosophy of Science* 56, no. 2 (1989): 288–302, and is reprinted here with the kind permission of *Philosophy of Science*.

Chapter 2 contains a short excerpt from "An ambiguity in the notion 'function'," *Biology and Philosophy* 4, no. 2 (1989): 172–176, copyright 1989 by Kluwer Academic Publishers and reprinted by permission.

"Thoughts without laws" first appeared in the *Philosophical Review* 95, no. 1 (1986): 47–80, and is reprinted here with the kind permission of the *Philosophical Review*.

"Biosemantics" first appeared in the *Journal of Philosophy* 86, no. 6 (1989): 281–297, and is reprinted here with the kind permission of the *Journal of Philosophy*.

"On mentalese orthography, part 1" first appeared in *Dennett and his critics*, ed. Bo Dahlbom (Blackwell, 1993) and is reprinted here with the kind permission of Basil Blackwell.

"Compare and contrast Dretske, Fodor, and Millikan on teleosemantics" first appeared in *Philosophical Topics* 18, no. 2 (1990): 151–161, and is reprinted here with the kind permission of *Philosophical Topics*.

"Explanation in biopsychology" first appeared in *Mental Causation*, ed. J. Heil and A. Mele (Oxford University Press, 1993) and is reprinted here by permission of Oxford University Press.

"Metaphysical antirealism?" first appeared in *Mind* 95, no. 4 (1986): 417–431, and is reprinted here by permission of Oxford University Press.

"Truth rules, hoverflies, and the Kripke-Wittgenstein paradox" first appeared in the *Philosophical Review* 99, no. 3 (1990): 323–353, and is reprinted here with the kind permission of the *Philosophical Review*.

"Naturalist reflections on knowledge" first appeared in *Pacific Philosophical Quarterly* 65, no. 4 (1984): 315–334, and is reprinted here with the kind permission of *Pacific Philosophical Quarterly*.

"The myth of the essential indexical" originally appeared in *Noûs* 24, no. 5 (1990): 723–734, and is reprinted here by permission of Oxford University Press.

White Queen Psychology and
Other Essays for Alice

Introduction

What is a mental representation? It is convenient to divide classical answers into three types: picture theories, causal and/or informational theories, and what I call "PMese theories" ("PMese" is Wilfrid Sellars's term for symbolic logic, from, I suppose, *Principia mathematica*). Each of these three theories of representation, if taken bare, runs into exactly the same problem, namely the problem of accounting for cognitive errors: misperceptions, false beliefs, confused concepts, bad inferences, unrealized intentions, and so forth. Each founders over the distinction between the facts of cognition and the norms of cognition. Call this the normativity problem. The underlying theme of the essays in this volume is that all of the basic norms applying to cognition are biological norms. Correct cognition, like healthy digestion and successful reproduction, is not what happens always or on the average. Correct cognition is what has accounted for the survival in the species of the complex mechanisms that are, at least occasionally and perhaps under ideal conditions, responsible for it. Let me begin by characterizing each of the three classical approaches to understanding mental representation in order to show at what point each runs into the normativity problem. I then say just a word to indicate how introducing biological norms helps with this problem. With this help, each of the three theories turns out to play an important role in the solution to the problem of what mental representation is.

1 Picture Theories

Picture theories of representation are based on the view that representations are like what they represent. More formally, a rule of projection or isomorphism, roughly in the mathematical sense, is what relates a representation to what it represents. This rule of projection is a function that maps members from a whole domain of representations onto their respective representeds. Any projection rule defines at least a formal similarity between the items in its domain and its range. Picture theorists thus propose that the defining relation between representation and represented depends on likeness, either likeness of an ordinary sort or perhaps likeness of a very abstract, formal mathematical sort. For example, the classical British empiricists tended to hold crude picture theories of how "ideas" represent, taking the likeness to be quite an ordinary sort of likeness, whereas Wittgenstein in the *Tractatus* held a picture theory of how thoughts that or beliefs that represent, taking the likeness to be structural likeness of a very abstract, formal character.

According to what can be called "pure" picture theories, the fact that the represented is *like* the representation is what *constitutes* the relation between representation and represented; that is all it consists in. *Pure* picture theories are thus easily criticized by pointing out that there is an infinite number of kinds of likeness. Everything is like everything else in one respect or another, indeed, in many respects. Thus the question arises, Which of these kinds of likeness constitutes the relation between representation and represented, and why? Clearly, *something* more must be added to make a picture theory viable.

A second failing of pure picture theories not so often commented on is that they seem not to leave room for misrepresentation. If representing something is picturing it, then representing it wrongly should be picturing it wrongly. Presumably, picturing it wrongly would be picturing it with something that was not a likeness of it according to the given rule. But if representing it *at all* depends upon the designated likeness relation holding between it and its reprsentation, representing it wrongly would then be indistinguishable from not representing it at all. For example, suppose that what makes my drawing a drawing of my cat is that it resembles my cat in accordance with a certain rule of projection onto two dimensions from the actual three-dimensional shape of my cat. Then if my drawing in fact fails to accord with my cat by this rule, it will turn out *not* to be picture of my cat. Perhaps it will be a picture of someone else's cat, perhaps of someone's in Tibet, that it does happen to resemble. But what it cannot be is a *bad* picture of my cat, because it won't be a picture of my cat at all. If the "of" or "being-about" relation is no more and no less than a certain likeness relation, then when the likeness fails, being about should fail as well. Thus the distinction between nonrepresenting and wrongly representing threatens to collapse.[1] Nor can it be repaired by requiring rough likeness for representing at all and exact likeness for correctly representing, for then my bad drawing of a cat will be about lots of people's cats at once, all those it roughly resembles. Some of these cats it may indeed resemble exactly by the rule, but surely it will not on that account be a good picture. An adequate picture theory of mental representation would have instead to ground the relation between representation and represented in such a way that only truth and falsity, and not representing itself, depends upon whether there is something onto which the representation maps by the designated rule.

What, then, makes a two-year-old's picture a picture of a cat? It is surely not its likeness to the cat, even though it may in fact be like the cat in accordance with some arcane projection rule. What makes it a picture of the cat is the two-year-old's intention in drawing it. She intended it to be like a cat. This works fine with two-year-olds and crayoned pictures, but an act of intending cannot be what hooks a *thought* onto its object. Intending requires thought, and thus would require one to have a *prior* thought of the intended object, which would lead to a regress. Now consider a camera. A camera does not, of course, intend to produce a likeness. Rather, it is an instrument that is *designed* to produce likenesses in accordance with a certain sort of projection rule. And a camera can fail in this: its lense can be scratched or aberrant, the film can be warped, the lighting conditions can be abnormal for its use, so that the picture comes out wrong, even unrecognizable. Take one more step now. We design a camera

---

1. Though it has many variations, there is exactly one classic solution for this problem, and it is not even remotely satisfactory. That is to postulate as the *immediate* correspondents of all respresentations, or all complex representations, not flesh-and-blood representeds but shades: objectified concepts or ideas, *Tractarian* senses, Fregean thoughts, propositions, possibilities, and so forth. Each of these shades is nothing more nor less than just something for representations to map onto or picture when they don't map onto anything real. If representing is picturing, in the minimal sense of mapping onto, but there is nothing real that the representation maps onto, it must map onto something unreal.

to produce representations, in accordance with certain rules of projection, by a certain method of physical interaction with the represented. Might not evolution have designed our brains to produce representations, in accordance with certain highly abstract rules of projection, by certain methods of physical interaction with what is represented? Could it be that evolutionary design is what hooks a percept or a thought onto the state of affairs it represents? This is the point I will argue.

2   Causal/Informational Theories

Contemporary causal and/or informational theories of mental representation have at least two sources of inspiration. That thoughts are of their causes is a classical view, best known, perhaps, from Descartes and Locke, who wished to know which of our thoughts are like their causes, their causes being supposed to be what they are thoughts of. The second model for causal/informational theories is the natural sign, an object or event type that is a reliable indicator of another type of object or event, due perhaps to a causal connection between the two. Thus lion spoor is a sign of a lion having passed by because lion spoor are found only when lions have passed by. Similarly, on this view, the photograph of a cat represents a cat not because it is like a cat but because things of its type are never seen except when cats have been about to cause them. Sometimes proponents of causal/informational theories hold that a mental representation represents whatever it is that it never occurs without, just as lion spoor represents lions because it never occurs without lions. Sometimes they hold that it represents whatever it covaries with or "tracks," just as the "on" light on an appliance represents whether the appliance is on because it covaries with or tracks when the appliance is off and when on. Mixed causal/informational and picture theories of representation are, of course, also possible and have been held under the label "reliability theories." Here the "picturing" part of the theory is just "compositionality"; the projection rules are Tarskian. According to such theories, what a representation represents is what it maps onto and at the same time reliably indicates.

Both Jerry Fodor and Fred Dretske, two committed causal/informational proponents, have emphasized that such theories have to face a normativity problem: the problem of "misrepresentation" (Dretske 1986) or "the disjunction problem" (Fodor 1987, 1990). Misrepresentation or false representation is, after all, exactly the occurrence of a representation without co-occurrence of its represented. Thus if the night is dark, skunks rather than cats can cause (mistaken) beliefs about cats. Does it follow that thoughts about cats are really thoughts about cats-or-skunks, since cat-or-skunk is all that they reliably indicate? A possible solution is to suppose that there are some special conditions under which there actually occurs the ideal dependency or covariation needed to define what represents what and that misrepresentation occurs only when these conditions are absent. Indeed, quite a lot of effort has gone into trying to delimit such a set of conditions under the label, for example, of "normal conditions."

Rather than attempting to specify a set of special content-determining conditions under which, by definition, whatever is perfectly indicated by a thought or percept is what is represented by it, suppose that we take seriously that indicating correctly is a biological *norm* for our cognitive-perceptual systems. Mental representations do not occur without their representeds so long as our perceptual-cognitive systems are operating *correctly*, i.e., in the way that has accounted for their survival in the species. Mental representations are accompanied by their appropriate representeds when these systems produce inner structures that map the environment in accordance with specified projection rules in the manner that accords with their design. One can determine which conditions are normal for the correct operation of these systems *only* by *first* specifying how these systems were designed to work, what projection rules they were designed to instantiate, what methods they were designed to use to effect the mappings. By itself this suggestion does not provide a definition either of representation or of representational content. But it explains how—through confusion of a biological norm with a simple disposition or fact—causal/informational theories achieve their initial plausibility.[2]

2. For a more accurate statement of the relation between causal/informational theories of representation and the one advocated here, see especially chapter 4.

3   PMese Theories

The PMese theory of mental representation is the classical theory of the twentieth century. It was inspired by the idea of a purely formal system, a system consisting of initially uninterpreted physical characters manipulated by rules operating over their physical forms. This idea was first applied in an attempt to understand, within a classical empiricist frame (with reference to theories of the origin of ideas), how "theoretical" terms in science, terms for things not observable, acquire meaning. The result was then generalized to apply to ordinary observation terms. These were taken to bear roughly the same relation to sense data or sense-data terms that theoretical terms had been taken to bear to observation terms.

The symbols in a purely formal system, it was thought, derive their meaning solely from the formal rules that govern their manipulation. For example, a formal symbol for "and," say "&," may derive its meaning from the following rules: (1) if one has written down the shape "p & q," one may then write down the shape "p," (2) one may also then write down the shape "q," and (3) if one has written down "p" and written down "q," one may then write down "p & q." That a symbol might derive its meaning from the rules of inference governing it, rather than the rules of valid inference being derived from prior meanings of the terms, was an entirely new idea, and all was swept before it. According to this new approach, the data of sense are not *copied* to produce mental representations, as supposed by British empiricists and phenomenalists. Rather, the data of sense are responded to with thoughts or sentences under the breath or inner symbols in a rule-governed way, just as the axioms and hypotheses in a formal system are responded to in a rule-governed way. The inner representations that result are in turn responded to by rule, to produce more inner representations and then output responses, the meanings of the inner representations being created through this rule-governed process. For example, the meaning of one's mental representation "cat" is derived from such sources as that thinking "cat" is a result of certain kinds of retinal stimulations; that thinking "is a cat" produces thinking "is an animal," "is a mammal," "likes fish," and so forth; that thinking "I wish to pet a cat," when accompanied by catish retinal stimulations, produces reaching gestures; and so forth. To be caught up in such a system of rules is what it *is* for something to be an inner representation with a meaning. Thus the mid-twentieth-century vision emerged of thought as a "theory" in the Quinean, Sellarsian sense. According to the PMese theory, inner representations are by their very nature things that are "calculated over" (Fodor) or that are "interanimated" (Quine).

PMese theories of mental representation are not necessarily at odds with picture theories. They are based on the claim that the role in a system of a certain kind—the most common idiom is "conceptual role" or "causal role"—determines representationhood and also representational content. But this might be so precisely because the role determines that there is a relevant picturing or mapping relation (likeness) between mental representings and the world. Sellars thought so, that the inference patterns executed in one's head are isomorphic to certain patterns in the world and that this is what produces mental "representing."[3] Quine, on the other hand, famously said that, no, there is no determinate or unique mapping of any relevant kind from PMese-theory representations to the world, and hence that picturing reality or corresponding to reality cannot ground or be what reference and truth are about.[4] Mixed causal/PMese theories are also possible and have been held under the label "dual aspect semantics" (e.g., Block 1986).

The normativity problem arises for PMese theories in a very direct way. If the actual inference dispositions that a thinker has are partial or full determinants of the meanings of the representations calculated over during inference, rather than the meanings of the representations determining which inferences are the valid ones, how can any invalid inferences occur? Or, to turn to input dispositions, since the dispositions that the thinker actually has to respond with inner symbols to the data of sense are determinants of the meaning of those very symbols, how can mistakes in recognizing occur?[5]

3. According to Sellars, "representing" is a relation between language and world, although "meaning" and "referring" are not.
4. Besides, as Quine saw it, the picture theory would require introducing "creatures of darkness" into our ontology—propositions and possible men in the doorway—shadows for *mis*representations to map onto. See note 1.
5. Of course, if one is a Quinean holist, one believes that there is no such thing as a mistake that determinately concerns just a particular perception, belief, or inference. There are no particular correspondence relations to the world that

4   Solving the Normativity Problem

One popular contemporary way to try to solve the normativity problem is to hope that if we add up several loose constraints on what a person's inner representations mean, none of which taken singly could account for normativity, together they will do the trick. This is meant somehow to yield tighter constraints and a best fit all around, and thus *pretty* determinately to fix the meanings of mental representations. If that is the reader's inclination, then she will find it best to read the second half of the last chapter of this book first, for there I try hardest to show how vain such a hope is.

Sellars took an answer to the normativity problem from Wittgenstein. According to Sellars, inference norms come from community; inference rules are just internalized rules of the public language game. I do not think that thought is a social construction, nor do I believe that language use is governed by rules of the sort envisioned by Wittgenstein. Our language is in deep respects just like any other animal's communication system, its forms embodying analogues of evolutionarily stable solutions to coordination problems. Its functions derive from what its forms—words, syntactic structures, and so forth—do for speakers and hearers so that they continue to be reproduced by speakers and consistently understood by hearers. These things are discussed in *LTOBC*, chaps. 1–4, and are not touched on in this book.

My purpose in this book is to clarify, defend, and show some of the implications of a biological solution to the normativity problem. Picturing, indicating, and inference are equally involved in human representing, but as biological norms rather than as mere dispositions. It is not the facts about how the system *does* operate that make it a representing

---

make thinking a productive enterprise. Rather, error is supposed to consist just in the emergence here or there of contradictions. But it is not clear on such a view what contradictions *are* beyond something one finds unpleasant and tries to get rid of. Or if one takes the view that the content of thought is determined not just by input and inference dispositions but also by behavioral output dispositions, then error would seem to consist roughly in the whole system of thought failing to produce the good life. Without invoking correspondence of some sort, the problem of how to tell good reasoning from good digestion and good sex looms large.

system and determine what it represents. Rather, it is the facts about what it would be doing if it were operating according to biological norms. When functioning properly, a mental representation[6] co-occurs with its represented, pictures what it represents, and (if it is of the right, rather sophisticated sort) participates in appropriate inferences.

Roughly indeed, the idea is this. Cognitive systems are designed by evolution to make abstract pictures of the organism's environment and to be guided by these pictures in the production of appropriate actions. This may involve deriving additional pictures by combining old ones in accordance with certain principles (inference, reasoning). It may also involve the formation of goal representations, pictures that guide the organism to produce or avoid what they picture (imagining, fearing that, desiring, intending). In the human case, biological design includes very general principles in accordance with which concepts are formed from appropriate sensory input, including input from perception through language. Forming adequate concepts is learning to represent or map in thought what *is* the same again *as* the same. On this ability are built the abilities to make judgments, then appropriate inferences, and also the abilities to acquire appropriate desires and get them fulfilled. Like anything *else* the organism does, this all takes place in a highly principled way when it works, but, of course, it does not always work, or if it does, not always smoothly.

The basic plan for this sort of solution to the normativity problem is laid out in *LTOBC*. This book does not in any way supplant that volume but rather rests upon it at numerous pivotal points. To put it straightforwardly, this book is designed to be read independently and, I hope, far more easily than *LTOBC*, but it is not designed to be criticized apart from the foundations laid in *LTOBC*. In the first two chapters I discuss and defend the theory of biological function needed for the project, and I defend the claim that our brains are adaptations for thinking, indeed, adaptations for thinking in the very ways in which we presently do think. I then clarify and defend a theory of mental representation. Implications for the science of psychology follow: that psychology is not at root a science involving laws, that explanations in psychology are unlike explanations in the physical sciences, that it in-

6. "Indicative" ones, anyway.

escapably is a deeply ecological science dealing with how the organism interacts with its wider environment.

Next in chapters 10 and 11 comes discussion of some worries dear only to philosophers (thank goodness). I show that the "realism" involved in the flatfooted correspondence views of representation and truth put forth here withstands antirealist critiques. By substituting a theory of biological competence for the standard reliance on dispositions in the construction of theories of meaning and truth, I provide a theory of understanding language that undercuts the verificationist's moves against realism. In chapter 12, I open the possibility of a naturalist treatment of the nature of knowledge based on a biologically rooted theory of competence.

Chapter 13, "The Myth of the Essential Indexical," was originally part of chapter 14, "White Queen Psychology," but was torn out at the late Hector-Neri Castañeda's request to appear in (what he knew would be) his last special issue volume of *Noûs*, on reference. Who but Castañeda would have sought out and insisted on publishing in his own journal, moreover, on adding his own complimentary remarks to, a paper that attacked one of his best known and favorite ideas? (I do not mean to imply that he agreed with me.) "White Queen Psychology" is a diatribe against meaning rationalism, as was the Epilogue of *LTOBC*. My desire is to kill meaning rationalism *dead*, and then beat on it. Perhaps I will succeed in raising one or two more doubts about it. Reasoning, I insist, is done in the world, not in one's head. Logical possibility (known a priori) is impossible. And the only hope for intentional psychology is to embrace its biological roots.

1

In Defense of Proper Functions

Several years ago I laid down a notion that I dubbed "proper function" (*LTOBC*) which I have since relied on in writing on diverse subjects. I have never paused to compare this notion with other descriptions of "function" in the literature or to defend it against alternatives. That may seem a large oversight, amounting even to irresponsibility, and I wish to take this opportunity to remedy it.

It does not seem to be so much the details of the definition of "proper function" that need defense as its basic form or general plan, which looks to the *history* of an item to determine its function rather than to the item's present properties or dispositions. At any rate, it is this historical turn in the definition that I propose to defend. To understand this defense, you will not need to know the details of the definition I have given. Let me just say this much about it.

The definition of "proper function" is recursive. To put things very roughly, for an item A to have a function F as a "proper function", it is necessary (and close to sufficient) that one of these two conditions should hold. (1) A originated as a "reproduction" (to give one example, as a copy, or a copy of a copy) of some prior item or items that, *due* in part to possession of the properties reproduced, have actually performed F in the past, and A exists because (causally historically because) of this or these performances. (2) A originated as the product of some prior device that, given its circumstances, had performance of F as a proper function and that, under those circumstances, normally causes

I am grateful to John Troyer, Peter Brown, and Jonathan Bennett, and to the members of the philosophy departments at Dartmouth and at Johns Hopkins, for helpful comments on earlier drafts of this essay.

F to be performed by *means* of producing an item like A. Items that fall under condition (2) have "derived proper functions", functions derived from the functions of the devices that produce them. Because the producing devices sometimes labor under conditions not normal for proper performance of their functions, devices with derived proper functions do not always have normal structure, hence are not always capable of performing their proper functions—a fact, I claim, that is of considerable importance.

This disjunctive description is extremely rough and ready. To make it work, "reproduction" must be carefully defined, the kind of causal-historical "because" that is meant carefully described, "normal conditions" defined, and various other niceties attended to. (The full description of proper functions consumes two chapters of *LTOBC*.) But this rough description should make clear what I mean by saying that the definition of "proper function" looks to history rather than merely to present properties or dispositions to determine function. Easy cases of items having proper functions are body organs and instinctive behaviors. A proper function of such an organ or behavior is, roughly, a function that its ancestors have performed that has helped account for proliferation of the genes responsible for it, hence helped account for its own existence. But the definition of "proper function" covers, univocally, the functions of many other items as well, including the functions of learned behaviors, reasoned behaviors, customs, language devices such as words and syntactic forms, and artifacts. Moreover, if my arguments in *LTOBC* are correct, explicit or conscious purposes and intentions turn out to have proper functions that coincide with their explicit or conscious contents. I have built a naturalist description of intentionality on the notion "proper function" (*LTOBC* and chapters 3, 4, and 11 herein).

I do have an excuse for having delayed my defense of the notion "proper function." The fact is that it is not crucial for the uses to which I have put the notion, whether or not its definition is merely stipulative or, if it is not merely stipulative, in what sense it is not. The point of the notion "proper function" was/is mainly to gather together certain phenomena under a heading or category that can be used productively in the construction of various explanatory theories. The ultimate defense of such a definition can only be a series of illustrations of its usefulness, and I *have* devoted considerable attention to such illustrations (*LTOBC* and chapters 3, 4, 7, 11, and 12 herein). However, although it makes no material difference for the uses to which I have put the definition whether it is or is not merely stipulative, I believe that it is *not* merely stipulative, and that it is clarifying to understand the sense in which it is not. Besides, even if "proper function" were to be taken as a merely stipulative notion, the best way to understand it, though not to evaluate it, would surely be to see how it compares with other notions of function that have been described in the literature.

Some writers on function, teleology, and related matters have been explicit that they were attempting to provide conceptual analyses of certain idioms in current usage. For example, Andrew Woodfield states at the outset of his book *Teleology* (1975) that his project is to provide necessary and sufficient conditions for application of various kinds of sentences containing "in order to" and equivalent phrases. Many other writers simply take for granted that the project is conceptual analysis. To give a germane example, Larry Wright (1976, 97), Christopher Boorse (1976, 74), Ernest Nagel (1977, 284), and Bigelow and Pargetter (1987, 188) each argue against an account of biological function that presupposes evolution by natural selection on the grounds that Harvey didn't know about natural selection when he proclaimed the discovery of the heart's function, or that evolutionary theory would have to be conceptually true to play any such role in the definition of function.[1] Such criticisms are valid only if the project is analysis of the *concept* of function.

Now I firmly believe that "conceptual analysis," taken as a search for necessary and sufficient conditions for the application of terms or as a search for criteria for application by reference to which a term has the *meaning* it has, is a confused program, a philosophical chimera, a squaring of the circle, the misconceived child of a mistaken view of the nature of language and thought. (Not to appear opinionated, but this prejudice is painstakingly defended in *LTOBC*, chaps. 6, 8, and especially 9, so I have, I think, a right to it.) Still, I think that Woodfield and

---

1. Karen Neander's "Teleology in biology" (manuscript), from which I originally got the page references in the above passage to Wright, Boorse, and Nagel, contains a brilliant defense of the "etiological" account of function while remaining within the tradition of conceptual analysis.

Wright, especially, have done good jobs of putting large portions of the area of this particular circle into a square, whether or not they have used only compass and rule in doing so. That is, theories of meaning to one side, each has done a fine job of collecting and systematizing various things that, without doubt, often *are* in the backs of people's minds when applying notions like "in order to" and "function," a fine job of spelling out analogies that commonly lubricate our transitions with these terms from one sort of context to another. Luckily there is no need to compete with Woodfield and Wright. My purpose, my program, is an entirely different one from that of conceptual analysis. An indication of this is that I do need to assume the truth of evolutionary theory in order to show that quite mundane functional items such as screwdrivers and kidneys are indeed items with proper functions. It is true, of course, that ordinary persons make no such assumption when attributing functions to these items, nor does my thesis imply that they do.

It is traditional to contrast three kinds of definition: stipulative, descriptive, and theoretical. Descriptive definitions are thought to describe marks that people actually attend to when applying terms. Conceptual analysts take themselves to be attempting descriptive definitions. Theoretical definitions do something else, exactly *what* is controversial, but the phenomenon itself, the existence of this kind of definition, is evident enough. A theoretical definition is the sort the scientist gives you in saying that water is HOH, that gold is the element with atomic number 79, or that consumption was in reality several varieties of respiratory disease, the chief being tuberculosis, which is an infection caused by the bacterium *Bacillus tuberculosis*. Now I do have a theory about what theoretical definitions are, a theory about how the theoretical definition of "theoretical definition" should go. Unfortunately, this theory rests upon a theory of meaning that rests in turn on the notion "proper function," the very notion under scrutiny. But assuming that you at least countenance the *phenomenon* of theoretical definition, let me say that my definition of "proper function" may be read, roughly, as a theoretical definition of function.[2] It may be read as a theoretical definition of

---

2. More accurately, the definition is intended to express the "sense" of this notion rather than describing its "intensions," where "sense" and "intensions" are interpreted as described in *LTOBC*. That is, according to my theoretical defini-

function in the context "The/a function of ____ is ____" (the function of the heart is to pump blood), though *not* in the context "____ functions *as* a ____" (the rock functions as a paperweight). The definition of proper function may also be read as a theoretical definition of "purpose."

Now jade turned out to be either of two compounds, nephrite or jadite, these being chemically quite distinct, and there are two quite different kinds of acidity and several alternative ways to count genes, if current chemical and genetic theories are correct. Similarly, there would be no reason to suppose *in advance* that "has a function" must correspond to a unitary nondisjunctive kind. But my claim is that "has a function" *does* as a matter of fact correspond, in a surprising diversity of cases, to having a *proper* function. Further, the various properties, the various analogies, which are influential in leading us to speak of quite diverse categories of items as having "functions" are properties or analogies that are characteristically *accounted for* by the fact that these items have coincident *proper* functions. It does not follow, nor is it my claim, that there are no *logically* possible cases in which analogy might lead us to speak of an item's function when the item in fact had no proper function. Nor does it follow that every *logically* possible case in which an item has a proper function is a case we would recognize offhand as a case of having a function. The technique of testing a definition by a search through possible worlds, by ingenious construction of fictional counterexamples, is not appropriate for theoretical definitions. There are also logically (or at least conceptually) possible worlds in which water does not turn out to be HOH.

A particularly glaring example of the failure of my definition to cover logically possible cases that strike many as legitimate cases of having purpose or function is the example of accidental doubles. According to my definition, whether a thing has a proper function depends on whether it has the right sort of history. Take any object, then, that has a proper function or functions, a purpose or purposes, and consider a double of it, molecule for molecule exactly the same. Now suppose that this double has just come into being through a cosmic accident resulting in the sudden spontaneous convergence of molecules which, until a

---

tion of "theoretical definition," what a theoretical definition analyzes is (Millikanian) sense.

moment ago, had been scattered about in random motion. Such a double has no proper functions because its history is not right. It is not a reproduction of anything, nor has it been produced by anything having proper functions. Suppose, for example, that this double is your double. Suddenly it is sitting right there beside you. The thing that appears to be its heart does not, in fact, have circulating blood as a proper function, nor do its apparent eyes have helping it to find its way about as a proper function, and when it scratches where it itches, the scratching has no proper function.

Contrast this historical notion of proper function with any description of function that makes reference only to *current* properties, relations, dispositions or capacities of a thing. Contrast it, for example, with any of the various contemporary descriptions that have been offered of purposive behavior as goal-directed, or with descriptions of purposiveness as involving negative feedback mechanisms, or of the purposive as that which tends toward the "good" of some creature, or contrast it with Jonathan Bennett's (1976) description of purposive action in terms of dispositions to act given dispositions to "register" situations in which "instrumental predicates" apply, or with Robert Cummins's (1975, 1983) description of the function of an item within a system admitting of a functional analysis. According to each of these conceptions of function, if anything has a function, of course its double must have a function too, the same function. To many this seems an obvious truth, one that any respectable theory of function should entail. So in the cases of your double's heart, eyes and scratchings, all of these contemporary definitions seem to be *headed* in the right direction, my definition in the wrong direction. What am I to say about that?

What I'm going to say, rather brazenly, is that such cases are like the case of fool's gold, or better, since the case is fictional, like the case of Twin Earth water. Perhaps lots of people have taken fool's gold for gold, people in perfectly good command of their language. And if suddenly transplanted to Twin Earth, you would take XYZ to be water. Similarly, even though many people would be prone to say it did have a purpose, that apparent heart in your double's body really would not have a purpose. It would merely display enough *marks* of purposiveness to fool even very sophisticated people. Without any question, there has never in fact existed anything within several orders of magnitude of the complexity of your fictional double, anything that was as neatly engineered to further its own survival and reproduction, that did not also have a history of the right sort to bestow upon its various parts the relevant proper functions. Nor do there *in fact* exist complicated goal-directed items, or items displaying complicated negative feedback mechanisms, or items that do anything like "registering" situations, or items with interesting Cummins functions, that do not *in fact* have corresponding proper functions. Having the *right sorts* of current properties and dispositions is in point of *fact*, in *our* world, an infallible index of having proper functions. If you like, it is criterial, as criterial, say, as the red of the litmus paper is of acidity. But it is not turning litmus paper red that *constitutes* acidity, nor is it having the right sort of current properties and dispositions that *constitutes* a thing's having a purpose. To the degree that each of these contemporary descriptions in terms of current properties or dispositions is successful, each describes only a *mark* of purposiveness, not the underlying structure.

The definition of "proper function" is intended as a theoretical definition of function or purpose. It is an attempt to describe a unitary phenomenon that lies behind all the various sorts of cases in which we ascribe purposes or functions to things, which phenomenon normally *accounts for* the existence of the various analogies on which applications of the notion "purpose" or "function" customarily rest. My claim is that actual body organs and systems, actual actions and purposive behaviors, artifacts, words and grammatical forms, and many customs, etc., all have proper functions, and that these proper functions correspond to their functions or purposes ordinarily so called. Further, it is *because* each of these has a proper function or set of proper functions that it has whatever marks we tend to go by in *claiming* that it has functions, a purpose, or purposes.[3]

3. Suppose that there really is a planet on which something as complex and apparently functional as your double is created by accident. I don't mean to rest my case wholly on the overwhelming unlikelihood of such an event. Similarly, there *may* be some very queer circumstances under which litmus paper turns red in a neutral environment. Then the "criteria" commonly used to determine purposiveness or acidity are fallible indices, but the natural phenomena that correspond to these notions remain the same. For a theory of the relation of intension to extension that supports this kind of claim, see *LTOBC*, Millikan 1986, and chapters 4 and 11 herein.

I have said that the definition of "proper function" is intended to explain what it is for an item to *have* a function or purpose, but not what it is for an item to function *as* something. Robert Cummins (1975, 1983) has given us a definition of function that is probably best construed as a theoretical definition, but a theoretical definition of "function as," in some contexts of use, rather than of "function" meaning purpose. Cummins's project is to explicate what "contemporary natural scientists" are describing when they offer a certain kind of explanation of the performance of an item within the context of a system. Very roughly, what these scientists do, according to Cummins, is to explain why the system as a whole has the capacity to do some complex or sophisticated task by appealing either to its capacity or to the capacities of its parts to do a series of simpler tasks which add up, flow-chart style, to the original complex capacity. Cummins calls this kind of explanation "functional explanation" and claims that the various elementary capacities appealed to in such explanation correspond to "functions," within the system, of the elements having these capacities.

This notion of function is a highly illuminating one. But it does not correspond, nor does Cummins take it to correspond, to that basic sense of "function" that hooks function to purpose. For example, according to Cummins's definition, it is arguably the function of clouds to make rain with which to fill the streams and rivers, this in the context of the water-cycle system, the end result to be explained being, say, how moisture is maintained in the soil so that vegetation can grow. Now it is quite true that, in the context of the water cycle, clouds function to produce rain, function *as* rain producers; that *is* their function in that cycle. But in *another* sense of "function," the clouds have no function at all, because they have no purpose.

Cummins explicitly waves aside all reference to "purposes" and all "appeals to the intentions of designers and users" in describing a thing's function, at the same time acknowledging that such appeals are, of course, made in many contexts in which we apply the term "function" (Cummins 1975 [1980], 185). By Cummins' definition, in order to *have* a function an item must actually *function* in a certain way, function *as* something or other, or at least must have a disposition or capacity so to function: "if something *functions as* a pump in a system . . . then it must be capable of pumping" (p. 185, emphasis mine). But it is of the essence of purposes and intentions that they are not always fulfilled. The fact that we appeal to purposes and intentions when applying the term "function" results directly in ascriptions of functions to things that are not in fact capable of performing those functions; they neither function as nor have dispositions to function as anything in particular. For example, the function of a certain defective item may be to open cans; that is why it is called a can opener. Yet it may not function *as* a can opener; it may be that it won't open a can no matter how you force it. Similarly, a diseased heart may not be capable of pumping, of functioning *as* a pump, although it is clearly its function, its biological purpose, *to* pump, and a mating display may fail to attract a mate, although it is called a "mating display" because its biological purpose is to attract a mate.

There is another way of viewing the definition I have given of "proper function," which throws the spotlight not on purpose but on *function categories*. Every language contains nearly innumerable common nouns and noun phrases under which things are collected together in accordance *not* with current properties, activities or dispositions, but in accordance with function. For example, consider the categories thermometer, can opener, heart, kidney, greeting ritual, mating display, fleeing behavior, stalking behavior, adverb, noun, indicative mood sentences, and word for green. Anything falling in one of these categories is what it is, falls in the category it does, by reference to function. One way to focus on the problem that the definition of "proper function" is designed to solve is to ask how items that fall under function categories are grouped into types.

Now an obvious fact about function categories is that their members can always be defective—diseased, malformed, injured, broken, disfunctional, etc.—hence unable to perform the very functions by which they get their names.[4] Nor will it do (as a surprising number of people have done) merely to point out that the typical or normal items falling in a function category actually do or can perform the function that defines the category. The problem is, how did the atypical members of the

4. Defective sentences and words? The easy examples are mispronunciations. For example, the child that pronounces "sin" like "thin" *mispronounces* the word "sin." She does not correctly pronounce the word "thin."

category that cannot perform its defining function *get* into the same function category as the things that actually can perform the function? Besides, it is not always true that typical items falling in a function category perform that function. It is quite possible, for example, that the typical token of a mating display fails to attract a mate and that the typical distraction display fails to distract the predator.

Nor is mere similarity to other items that perform a certain function either necessary or sufficient, by itself, to bring an item under a function category. No matter how similar a piece of driftwood is to an oar, this similarity does not, by itself, make it into an oar. No matter how similar the mating display of one fish may be to the aggression display of another, this does not make the mating display into an aggression display. And no matter how similar the scratches that the glacier left on the rock are to a token of the English word "green," they do not thereby compose a token of a word for green. Also consider: exactly what rules would articulate the *kind* of similarity to functioning members of a category the non-functioning members should have? For example, exactly *what* sorts of (current) properties must an item have in common with some functioning token or other of a can opener in order to count as a "can opener that doesn't work"? The question is absurd on its face. Indeed, a thing that bears no resemblance to any can opener previously on earth—suppose it has been designed in accordance with a totally new principle—may still *be* a can opener, and may be one despite the fact that it doesn't work. Remember the train brake that Christopher Robin made that "worked with a string sort of thing"? "It's a very good brake, but it hasn't worked yet," said Christopher. What's amusing about that is not that Christopher claims it's a brake but that he claims it's a very *good* brake.

There is a tendency, I think, to believe that the phenomenon of defective members of function categories is a superficial phenomenon, that it is only by some sort of extension or loosening up of basic criteria in accordance with which things are placed in function categories that defective members are admitted as members at all. But note how different the notion "defective" is from, say, the notion "borderline case" or the notion "case only by courtesy." Monographs may be only borderline cases of books, or may be books only by courtesy, but surely monographs are not *defective* books. The notion "defective" is a normative notion. The problem is, what makes the defective item fall under a *norm*? Surely not just that it *reminds* one of things that do serve a certain function, so that it makes one wistful.

That members of function categories can be defective is coordinate with purposes being things that may not get fulfilled. Function categories are *essentially* categories of things that need not fulfill their functions in order to have them. Just as the characteristic mark of intentionality is that intentional items can be false, unsatisfied, or seemingly "about" what does not exist, so the characteristic mark of the purposive, of that which has a function, is that it may *not* in fact fulfill that purpose or serve that function. For example, your randomly created double exhibits no purposive behaviors and has no purposive parts because there is no way that any of his/her states or parts could be *defective* or might *fail*. That creature of accident, wonderful as he or she may be, falls under no norms.

The intimate connection between function category and purpose and the essential connection of these with norms, hence with possible failure, is easily obscured, however, when we turn to the analysis of purposive *behaviors*. This is because the vast majority of our categorizations of behaviors, the vast majority of our simple descriptions of behaviors, employ success verbs rather than verbs of trying. We tend to categorize behaviors according to the purposes they actually *achieve*. Indeed, we often ignore purpose altogether, classifying behaviors in accordance *merely* with effects of these behaviors, whether purposive effects or not. For example, I can bump you with my elbow either purposefully or by accident. On the other hand, merely trying to bump you and failing doesn't count as bumping at all. Of course verbs of trying do exist in the language. Consider "fleeing," "stalking," "fishing," "hunting," "looking," "bidding for attention," and, of course, any ordinary action verb prefaced by "trying to." *These* action categories are function categories, defined by reference to purposes rather than achieved effects. What makes a behavior fall into one of *these* categories?

The question is seldom tackled head on. Rather, investigators typically begin with the question, "What makes purposive behavior purposive?" (or, say, "goal directed?") and then take as their *paradigms* of purposive behavior not trying behaviors but behaviors described, as it is most natural to describe behaviors, by success verbs. Only later do they attempt to loosen up or stretch the model they have already built for successful purposive behaviors to cover the unsuccessful cases (if they ever recognize these cases at all). The result is that unsuccessful trying behavior is described as though it were a loose or borderline case of purposeful behavior, purposive only by courtesy. Or purposiveness is described as though it admits of degrees, the distinction between the purposive and the nonpurposive appearing to need drawing at an arbitrary place. Let me give an example.[5]

Early in his discussion of goal-directed behavior, Wright tells us that

successful teleological behavior, directed behavior that actually achieves its goal, provides us with the best paradigm; it gives us the sort of case from which all others can be seen as natural derivatives. (Wright 1976, 37)

Soon after, Wright gives us the following formula:

S does *B* for the sake of *G* iff:
(i) *B* tends to bring about *G*
(ii) *B* occurs because...it tends to bring about *G*. (P. 39)

Context makes it clear that this formula is a modification of a simpler formula covering only successful purposive behavior and containing "does bring about" in place of the looser "tends to bring about." Wright comments that the phrase "tends to bring about" in his formula "represents the entire 'family'" of which other members are "is the type of thing that brings about" (compare: is similar to items that *do* function to bring about—the wistfulness again), "is required to bring about," "is in some way appropriate for bringing about" (1976, 39), etc. (Later Wright seems to imply that "might easily be mistaken for something that would bring about" may have to be included in this "family" too [1976, 49]. A loosening up indeed!) The unpacking that Wright then produces of "*B* occurs because it tends to bring about *G*," in this context, is dispositional. What he describes under this heading is a strong *correlation* between behaviors to which *S* is disposed and behaviors that "tend to bring about *G*." His claim is that the existence of such a cor-

5. I have a special reason for using Wright's views as my foil in the following paragraphs. Various published remarks to the contrary, there is no overlap at all between Wright's analysis of function and mine. A reason for the confusion, I believe, is Wright's peculiar usage of the term "etiological," which does *not*, in his vocabulary, make reference to causes or origins (see below and, for example, note 7).

relation, *taken alone*, licenses us to inter, or to say, that the behavior occurs *because* of the tendency. This "because," it is important to notice, is *not* a causal-historical "because," but a special teleological "because."

Now suppose that we set aside problems that may arise with other members of the "tends to bring about" family. And suppose that we set aside questions about the reference class within which the statistics for "tends to" are to be gathered. (More about that in a moment.) We must still answer these questions. First, how *strong* a correlation must there be between what *S* is disposed to do and behaviors that "tend to bring about *G*" for us to attribute purposiveness to *S*? Second, how *strong* does a tendency have to be to count as a tendency, to count as helping to strengthen the correlation? And how would one decide either of those questions but arbitrarily? This kind of *intrinsically* fuzzy and arbitrary distinction between the purposeful and the purposeless—quite different, notice, from admission of borderline cases between clear paradigms—is just wrong. It not only is bad theory; it is not good conceptual analysis, not an accurate reflection of how most people *think* of purposiveness. But where writers acknowledge at all that purposive behavior may fail, this kind of fuzzy result is typical.[6]

Because investigators have assumed that the paradigm cases of purposive behavior are cases of successful behavior, they have been led to give descriptions of purposiveness that are variations on dispositional themes; to give one example, led to locate purposiveness in mechanisms, such as feedback mechanisms, which will produce dispositions to reach some goal or state. True, Wright takes the dispositions that evidence a behavior as being purposive to license a peculiar sort of inference to a peculiar sort of *explanation*, namely, the behavior occurs *because* of its tendency to lead to the goal. But Wright gives this kind of "because" or "on account of" no explication besides saying that it *is* the kind of "because" we make inferences to when we discover dispositions of the sort he describes. Possibly something like this is correct on the level of con-

6. According to my own definition of "proper function," borderline cases do exist. These are always cases either of *derived* proper functions or of functions of members of "higher-order reproductively established families" (*LTOBC*, chap. 1), and it is not the failure of the functional device itself but a partial failure of its producer that results in the vagueness.

ceptual analysis. But on the level of *theory*, it leaves us with no useful distinction between an animal's having the right dispositions, and its having them in accordance with the right explanation, no useful distinction between the dispositions that count as *evidence* for teleological structure, and that which they evidence—the teleological structure itself.[7] My position, by contrast, is that although discovery of the sorts of mechanisms and/or dispositional structures that Wright and other theorists describe usually does license inference (inductive yet empirically certain inference) to a peculiar sort of explanation, this explanation is a straightforward *historical* explanation. Things just don't turn up with inner mechanisms or with dispositions like that unless they have corresponding proper functions, that is, unless they have been preceded by a certain kind of history. Moreover, being preceded by the right kind of history is *sufficient* to set the norms that determine purposiveness; the dispositions themselves are not necessary to purposiveness.

My claim has been that accounts of purpose or function in terms of present disposition or structure run afoul exactly when they confront the most central issue of all, namely, the problem of what failure of purpose and defectiveness are. But what leads me to conclude that *historical* analysis is what is needed instead? The fact that a historical analysis *works*, of course. The historical analysis I have given does cover all of the actual cases in which we ascribe functions to things. But prior to that, there is a strong clue that suggests that a good look at the historical dimension is needed for this kind of analysis.

Notice that talk of functional mechanisms and of dispositions that characterize purposive items is always talk accompanied implicitly by *ceteris paribus* clauses. My desk lamp has a disposition to give off light when its switch is depressed, but not of course when unplugged, when under water or when at 1,000 degrees Fahrenheit. The mouse may have

---

7. Wright's discussion of goal-directed behavior differs in this respect from his analysis of the functions of body organs. In the case of body organs, he reads the "because" in "X is there because it does (results in) Z" (1979, 81) more like a causal "because" but still not as a causal-historical "because." Wright says that the formulation "because X does Z" does *not* reduce to "because things like X have done Z in the past" (pp. 89–90). Rather, we are asked to accept that X might be there *now* because it is true that *now* X does or Xs do result in Z. How the truth of a proposition about the present can "cause" something else to be the case *at present* is not explained.

a disposition to take measures that will remove it from the vicinity of the cat, but not if under water, at 1,000 degrees Fahrenheit, in the absence of oxygen, while being sprayed with mace, or just after ingesting cyanide. Indeed, there are thousands of stressful conditions under which the mouse might be placed, which would extinguish its escaping behavior; you merely have to be sadistic enough to think of them. Nor can we plead that the mechanism must be under conditions such that it operates "properly" for "operating properly" is merely operating as it is "supposed" to operate, that is, in accordance with its design or purpose.

Increasingly I find in the literature on purpose (and on various subjects connected in one way or another with the related phenomenon of intentionality) handwaving, when things get rough, toward the relevant *ceteris paribus* clauses under the heading "normal conditions." On pain of circularity, "normal conditions" cannot mean "conditions under which the thing operates properly." What, then, *are* "normal conditions"? Are they average conditions? Where? Not throughout the universe, surely, for the average conditions there are being in nearly empty space at nearly absolute zero. Average conditions on earth? Conditions on earth have varied enormously throughout its history and they vary from place to place.

More central, note that what count as normal conditions for mouse behavior, shark behavior, robin behavior, earthworm behavior, and tapeworm behavior are quite different. Being underwater *is* a normal condition for shark behavior. The dispositions that express goal-directedness toward, say, obtaining food are dispositions defined against quite different background conditions in the cases of the various species.

Are normal conditions for a mouse, perhaps, just conditions that mice, on the average, are in? Then if we tossed all mice but Amos into outer space, our listing of Amos's "dispositions under normal conditions" would have to change, the main one left to him being, I suppose, to explode.

Perhaps normal conditions under which Amos' dispositions are to be described are those under which his design is optimal for survival and proliferation? But *those* conditions include living in a world without cats. Also, of course, the wonder drug that prevents cell aging must be in Amos's water just as oxygen must be in his air. If Amos happens to be diabetic, someone who is disposed to administrator insulin must be available; if Amos is neurotic, some useful reward must be found for his neurotic behavior.

To explain what "normal conditions" are is surely going to take us on an excursion into history. At the very least, we must make a reference to something like conditions in which mice have *historically* found themselves, or better, found themselves when their dispositions actually aided survival. And if a listing of Amos's relevant dispositions depends on an implied reference to his species, then the question of what makes him fall into the category "mouse" needs to be raised. But the question of Amos's species is itself a question that diverts us through history. Mice must be born of mice. Consider: if a seeming mouse were born of a fish, what would set the "normal conditions" for manifestation of its relevant disposition?

But a more telling question, perhaps, than, Why look at history when trying to describe what functions and purposes are? is the question, Why *not* look at history? Why is there so much resistance to looking at history? There is a univocal answer to this question, I believe, and bringing it into the light of day proves very instructive.

We take consciously intentional action to be a paradigm of purposiveness. And that is correct; it *is* one paradigm (among others). But the idea that a consciously intentional action could have the purpose it does *not* by reference to anything merely present, let alone anything present in *consciousness*, runs strongly against the grain. Indeed, it runs against one of the most entrenched beliefs of both philosophers and laymen. This is the belief that the consciousness of one's own intentions is an *epistemic* consciousness, that is, in the case of one's own explicit intentions at least, what one intends is *given*, simply and *wholly* given, to consciousness. But, the thought goes, historical facts, certainly facts about one's evolutionary history, clearly are not simply *given* to consciousness. Hence what one's explicit conscious intentions are could not possibly depend on facts about one's history. Q.E.D.

The belief that the intentional contents of one's explicit intentions are "given" to consciousness is just one strand of a tangle of entrenched beliefs which I have called "meaning rationalism" (*LTOBC*). Meaning rationalism, in its various forms, has gone unquestioned in the philosophical tradition to such a degree that, to my knowledge, no arguments have ever been adduced to support it. However, a large portion of Wittgenstein's *Philosophical investigations* is devoted to an attempt to *dispel* the notion that what one intends, especially when one intends to follow a rule, is given in what appears before consciousness. And a considerable portion of the Wilfrid Sellars corpus is built on the motif that *nothing* is, epistemically, given to consciousness. More recently Hilary Putnam (1975b) and then Tyler Burge (1979) have argued that what one means by a word is not, certainly not always, determined by the contents of one's head, but by relations *between* one's head and the world. But it is hard to see how *any* relation between one's head and the rest of the world could be a relation that is simply and wholly given to consciousness. If these philosophers are right and meaning something or intending something or purposing something depends on relations *not* packed inside an epistemic consciousness, then why are historical relations not as good candidates for this position as any other relations?

2

Propensities, Exaptations, and the Brain

1 Introduction

The term "proper function" was introduced into *LTOBC* for theoretical use, and its definition was stipulated.[1] As I argued in chapter 1 above, I do believe that the phenomena the definition picks out underlie purposiveness in the most general sense, but I also wish to reemphasize that the uses for which the definition was developed do not depend upon this. Its point was to capture a certain similarity that I took to be important among items falling in biological categories, language categories, cognitive categories, purposive-action categories, artifact categories, and certain kinds of cultural categories. The interest was in the phenomena themselves rather than in traditional ways of classifying the phenomena. It was probably unwise to use the term "biological category" as an informal substitute for "proper-function category"—a use that appears, of course, right in the title of *LTOBC*—for this has given the false impression that my aim was to capture biologists' usage. On the contrary, I do not consider biological examples of proper functions to be more central than any others. In fact, the proper functions of language forms play a very much larger role in *LTOBC* than the proper functions of forms studied by biologists.

There are, however, two themes in the recent literature on biological function that do speak directly to my concerns. I required a history of selection behind my "proper functions." Bigelow and Pargetter (1987)

Special thanks to Bill Lycan, Peter Godfrey-Smith, and Brian Smith, for comments on an earlier draft.
1. To my knowledge, at least, it does not occur as a noun in the literature prior to *LTOBC*. My intention was to contrast a thing's "proper" or *own* function with functions imposed on it or accidental to it.

argue, however, that *biological* functions are best defined by reference to propensities for selection rather than a history of selection. If Bigelow and Pargetter were right, then I should have to rethink whether propensities would serve my purposes as well. This would be especially urgent because many have found the least digestible part of my position on intentionality to be the insistence that, since intentionality rests on proper function, which rests in turn on selective history, intentionality is not fully constituted within the present moment of thought or consciousness. I argued in the last chapter that a crippling defect of any definition that looks for function in current dispositions rather than history is that such definitions cannot ground the notion of malfunction. They cannot account for function categories that contain malfunctioning members. Especially important, no such notion of function could ground an understanding of the nature of cognitive mistakes, inadequate concepts, mistaken beliefs, false sentences, unhealthy desires, impotent desires, unfulfilled directives, and so forth. But there are other arguments against the propensity view of biological function that may be more persuasive. I will argue that the propensity theory is, in fact, entirely *empty*, and hence clearly useless for *anyone's* purposes.

The second theme has been introduced by evolutionary biologists themselves (Gould and Lewontin 1979, Gould and Vrba 1982). It has been suggested that human cognitive capacities may not rest directly on a history of natural selection at all but may have resulted from other evolutionary contingencies. Now it is absolutely central to my position on intentionality, and on many related matters, that cognitive categories be definable by reference to proper functions of the cognitive systems. Again it seems that I should reexamine whether proper functions, as I defined them, will in fact do the theoretical work I intend. My conclusion will be that, given a minor and congenial change in the original definition of "proper function," only a creationist could seriously dispute that our contemporary cognitive functions are proper functions of the human cognitive systems.

2 The Rationale for the Definition of "Proper Function"

Let me begin by explaining why I introduced the notion of selection into the definition of "proper function" in the first place. This will also give me an opportunity to review some of the main features of the definition of "proper function" as given in *LTOBC*.

My first thoughts about function ran parallel to lines now familiar from Larry Wright's work (1973, 1976).[2] An item has a function if it is there because of something it can do. But I had in mind a "because" that was strictly causal.[3] If it is to be causal, the "because there is something it can do" must be an elliptical reference to something past and to something once actually done, since neither present capacities nor unmanifested capacities can be causes of present things. Moreover, in the cases of biological functions, functions of words and other language devices, and functions of behaviors learned by trial and error, it seemed clear that it was not the functional item itself but some past item like it that had been responsible for causing the item to be there by doing the thing we call its function. (I was not concerned here about reasoned behaviors and artifacts, because I had in mind that the functions of these items were derived in a more roundabout way. They were derived via a prior function of the biological mechanisms that produced the reasoned intentions that in turn produced these items. See *LTOBC*, chap. 2) The simplest idea, then, would be to define a thing's function as what something like it once did that helped cause it to be, to be where it is, or to be as it is.

The difficulty with this simple move is that the stages of anything that cycles will fit. It is true that this sort of definition of function may at first look plausible for biological functions (though I will soon argue that it has fatal flaws). Each individual animal can be taken to represent one turn of a cycle as it develops from embryo stage to adulthood, then reproduces. Moreover, to have a biological function would seem to re-

2. I am embarrassed to say that I was not at the time acquainted with Wright's work. Chaps. 1 and 2 of *LTOBC* were written last, in considerable haste, and with shockingly little preparation.
3. Wright carefully specifies that his "because" can refer to reasons as well as causes (e.g., 1973, 157), and he makes extensive use of this freedom, for example, in talking about the functions of goal-directed systems (see chapter 1 above). I think readers have a tendency to forget that in the early 1970s it was not yet taken for granted that reasons can be, let alone that they always are, causes. Davidson had to fight very hard to let any reasons be causes. Readers also tend to forget that the basic meaning of "etiology," a term on which Wright relies extensively, is not the medical use. The wider use of "etiology" makes reference to either reasons or causes. See *Webster's Third New International Dictionary*.

quire at least sometimes being part of such a cycle (e.g., the utility of the sickle-cell anemia gene in sometimes preventing malaria, hence death, before reproduction). Aging and death, though these occur with perfect regularity, are not true parts of this cycle unless they manage to contribute in some way to reproduction or maintenance of another generation. Nor, failing this contribution, do they have biological functions. They are just necessary excretions. So far so good. But the stages of an idling motor; the positions, vector velocities, and accelerations of the planets; the various stages in the earth's water cycle; and so forth will also have functions by this definition. Several of Boorse's (1976) examples against Wright's analysis of function fit this form, for example, the break in the gas hose that sustains itself by leaking gas that overcomes the man who came to fix it. Even more simple, on this analysis, the top apples in the barrel would seem to have the function of being eaten, for they wouldn't be on top if yesterday's top apples hadn't already been eaten. What, then, to do?

I did two things. First, I required the way in which the functional item was produced from its ancestor or ancestors to involve reproduction or copying of its functional features. Minimally, the way in which the ancestor is responsible for the functional item being there must be such that, had those properties of the ancestor that accounted for its ability to perform the function been different along certain dimensions, the progeny (the ensuing turns of the cycle) would have differed accordingly.[4] That takes care of the idling motor, the earth's water cycle, the break in the hose (the break in the hose is not its own ancestor), and the top apples in the barrel. For example, the property of being top apple, and hence the one eaten, is not passed from top apple to top apple by copying. Nor is one piston's firing a copy of the last. But tokens of words and syntactic forms are copied from earlier tokens of the same types, customs are copied from previous exemplifications of the same customs, behaviors learned by trial and error are copied over, and so forth, which is just what we want.

---

4. I warn you that this is a very sloppy rendition of the discussion of functions in *LTOBC*. For example, in *LTOBC*, I explain that the progeny of animals are not in fact reproductions of them in this sense. The full definition of "proper function" has to be complicated by first defining the intermediary notion "reproductively established family," which I am not introducing here.

This move doesn't, however, take care of the positions, vector velocities, and accelerations of the planets, for these *are* copied from one another. Within quite a large latitude, had the earth been in a different place going at a different speed in a different direction last year, this placement and vector velocity would have reproduced itself this year. (The year would have had a different length, of course.) Simply cycling through reproductions, no matter how complex the cycle, doesn't intuitively seem to be having a function in any reasonable sense. And there is a more significant problem that it does also not take care of. To see this, we need to examine biological functions more carefully, to which I now turn.

3   The Importance of Selection

In the biological case there is reproduction.[5] Might one define biological function, then, as anything done by a thing's biological ancestors that contributed to the cycle of conception, development, and reproduction, leading eventually to its formation? If the answer is no, then we have a clear and important case in which cycling, including reproduction, is not enough for the wanted functions. The general form of the argument is this. You cannot require of a biological function that its performance have been a necessary link in the chain from *every* previous generation to *every* next generation in the lineage of a functional item. At the other extreme, however, surely it is not enough that one ancestor in the lineage of a reproduced item should have contributed just once in history to reproduction or development of the line by effecting this "function." Nor can one draw some arbitrary line between these two extremes, for it is just not so that having a function or not having it is such a wishy-washy distinction for the biologist. I don't mean to suggest that there are no borderline cases of biological function. But surely having versus not having a function is not on a seamless continuum such that it doesn't matter *at all* where between the extremes one draws a line. The place the line is naturally drawn, I concluded, is where natural selection draws it. Only if an item or trait has been *selected* for reproduction, *as over against other traits, because* it sometimes has a certain

5. More accurately, one has reproductively established families. See note 4.

effect does that effect count as a function. Notice that selection is involved in the other cases of function we wish to cover as well. It is because of a *correlation* (over negative as well as positive cases) with a function that behaviors learned through trial and error are reproduced, and because of a *correlation* (over negative as well as positive cases) with a function that linguistic forms and certain customs are reproduced. But the position of the earth, I take it, was never selected for.

Now for the details of the argument. Suppose that the fish in my aquarium have built into them various mechanisms to help them detect and escape from predators but that since there are no predators in my aquarium, my fish reproduce without these mechanisms being used. Surely it does not follow that when these mechanisms recur in my fishes' progeny, they no longer have biological functions. It is easy to miss this sort of point if one concentrates on physiological functions. For a great many physiological functions, such as gross heart function or gross kidney function, do have to be performed in every generation for the life cycle to continue. But there are lots of other functions that don't have to be performed in every generation. Lots of camels, for example, never really use their humps. And many house cats don't need their mouse-catching proclivities. Indeed, unleashing these proclivities results only in roundworms. Wherever the need for a particular function is highly contingent on environmental circumstance, functions cannot be understood as necessary steps in getting from generation to generation.

One way to think of the cycle of reproduction is to analyze it into a set of functions defined as Cummins (1975) defines functions. A Cummins function is the contribution that an aspect or portion of a system makes toward the capacities of the larger system of which it is a part. "Functional explanations," in Cummins's sense, explain how a complex system as a whole has the capacity to do some complex or sophisticated task by appealing either to its capacity or to the capacities of its parts to do a series of simpler tasks that add up, flow-chart style, to the original complex capacity. Cummins calls these simpler tasks the "functions" of the parts or aspects. An item has a Cummins function only relative to some chosen supersystem of which it is currently being considered to be a part. For example, it may be that the leaves on certain deciduous trees have quite a different function relative to the growth and reproduction cycles of the trees than relative to the local ecosystem, or relative to the whole biosystem. Since there is no limit to the numbers and kinds of things that can be looked upon as being systems or parts of systems, having or not having a Cummins function is not an absolute matter in the way that having a purposive function is. And Cummins functions do not, of course, depend in any way upon the histories of the items having them. On the other hand, an obvious candidate to think of treating as a system having parts with Cummins functions is the cyclical system that is the development and reproduction of an individual animal insofar as it repeats the pattern of its ancestors' development and reproduction and passes the potential for this pattern on to its progeny. To put this differently, a very salient complex capacity to be explained would seem to be the capacity to survive, develop to adulthood, and reproduce. One way to think about the question of whether biological function can be defined without reference to natural selection, then, is to ask whether the notion of having a Cummins function within the system that is the growth and reproduction cycle for a given animal is or is not a well-defined notion. If it is, then perhaps we need make no reference to selection in defining biological function.

Cummins functions are charted by flow charts or the equivalent. Flow charts typically contain lots of if-thens. They chart what is done or what happens on this or that contingency, and what is done or happens next given this or that outcome of previous response. In this respect, they might be good means of modeling growth and reproduction cycles. They could allow for the animal and the animal's parts to perform a wide variety of alternative actions or tasks, depending upon environment and circumstance. But the difficulty is to draw a distinction between those iffy things that happen during the growth and reproduction cycle of an animal that are unfoldings of the system and those that occur outside the confines of the system. Which happenings on the way from conception to reproduction represent performances within the system under analysis and which are merely accidental?

To take the classic example, how many of my ancestors' survivals and reproductive successes must be attributable in part to the good eyesight produced by eyeglasses they wore before my nose acquires the supporting of eyeglasses as one of its biological functions? How many of my ancestors have to have been saved from death due to exposure by the clothes they hung on their shoulders before my shoulders have clothes suspension as one of their functions? How many babies in my ancient lineage have to have been saved by their capacity to go into instant hibernation when dropped into cold water for this capacity to have a biological function in my progeny? How many fetuses have to have been saved by the mother's morning sickness from accidental poisoning for morning sickness to have a function.[6] How many teenagers in my lineage have to have lucked out rather than mucked up during their teen rebellions for my kids' dispositions to teen rebellion to have biological functions? How many have to have been luckily saved from auto accidents by their love of *fast* speeds (surely that can happen too) before love of speed acquires a function? I plead that questions of this sort make no sense at all. Whether something has a function is not a matter of how often it has accidentally helped out in the movement from generation to generation. Anything whatever might occasionally have done that. It is a matter of whether it was selected to help out in this way.

That is why actually having been selected for, actually having affected the constitution of the gene pool of a deme or species, must play a role in the notion of biological function. The functional trait must be one that is there in *contrast* to others that are *not* there, because of historic difference in the results of these alternative traits. It must be tied to genetic materials that were selected from among a larger pool of such materials because of their *relative* advantageousness. The difference between merely luckily or accidentally cycling through successive generations and having genuinely functional traits whose biological *purpose* is to contribute to such cycling lies in whether these traits were once selected from among other once extant traits due to their superior capacities to continue the cycle. Graphically, whether my shoulders have as a biological function to hold up my clothes depends not on what proportion of my ancestors used their shoulders that way to advantage but on whether there were once shoulderless people who died out because they had nothing to hang their clothes on. And whether my kids' teen rebellions have a function depends on whether there were once non-

6. It has recently been proposed that morning sickness has the function of saving fetuses from subtle poisons that wouldn't hurt the mother but would hurt the fetus.

rebellious kids who failed because of this to produce as many progeny on average as rebellious kids and whether these contrasting traits were such as to be reliably passed on genetically.[7] (For important qualifications to these very crude statements, see section 7 below.)

4 Why Not Propensities?

Notice that a perfectly parallel argument rules out mere *propensities* to perform Cummins functions in the growth and reproduction cycle as criteria for biological function. A propensity theory of biological function will have to turn to potential not just for cycling but for *selection* if it is to get started at all. Unfortunately, however, the notion of potential for selection is a notion without substance, as I will now attempt to show.

Bigelow and Pargetter tell us that "something has a (biological) function just when it confers a survival enhancing propensity on a creature that possesses it" (1987, 192). Later they speak of a "survival enhancing propensity" as roughly equivalent to a "propensity for selection" (p. 194). I take it the idea is something like this. A trait that enhances or would enhance survival is one where, on average over the *actual* individuals in the species, having it would produce a more fit individual than not having it. There is a reference here to counterfactuals, to what the fitness values of various individuals that have the trait would have been if they hadn't had it, to what the fitness values of various individuals that don't have the trait would be if they did have it.

Unfortunately, exactly in this sort of context, counterfactuals are notoriously indeterminate in truth value. If a given individual with a certain trait were *not* to have it, what would this individual have instead? There is no such thing, for example, as being simply *not mo-*

7. Mark Bedau (1991) complains that if one defines "biological function" by reference to natural selection in the sort of way I have defined "proper function," one lets in certain kinds of clay crystals as items having biological functions. His assumption seems to be that the "biological" part of the notion of biological function should fall out of the given analysis of function, whereas my project has been to give a much broader definition of "function" under which biological functions fall as one among other varieties of functions, so if crystals can have functions, as well as learned behaviors, artifacts, words, customs, etc., that is fine by me. Similarly, no one seems to doubt that viruses can have their own nasty little functions, but whether they are life forms is a matter of dispute.

nogamous. Is the individual then to be celibate? Or homosexual? Or polygamous? If polygamous, how many wives does he juggle? How does he employ them? What do others in the community do about it? Are they monogamous, for example? Suppose that you didn't have a nose. Well, would you have gills instead? Or maybe a trunk? Or just two holes? A closed flap over the two holes so that you must breath through your mouth? What would you do without eyes? Well, you might have radar in front, or bats' ears. There is really *no sense at all* to the question of how much, if at all, your monogamy, your nose, or your eyes "enhance" your fitness, without first on answer to the question, *Enhances it over what?* The notion of superior fitness, as actually used in evolutionary biology, is a well-defined notion only because it is *never* taken to attach to any trait in a vacuum or absolutely but rather is understood only relative to alternative traits *actually found in the population*. A moment's reflection shows that this is indeed the only way to unpack the "enhanced" in "enhanced fitness" so as to lend it any substance.

But if that is the way one must anchor the notion "enhanced propensity for survival," then no trait can be said *currently* to enhance this propensity unless it fails to be universal in the species, that is, unless it has *current* competitors. On this reading, for example, not only is it not the function of noses to support eyeglasses, but noses have no functions at all, unless the current population contains a portion of genetically noseless people who have, on average, fewer progeny than the rest of us. There seems to be only one sensible way out of this dilemma. Count as a function not just what a trait is currently being selected for; if it is not currently, not this week, under any selection pressures from specific alternative traits, count what it *was* selected for. A trait's biological function is what it actually did—did most recently—that accounts for its current presence in the population, as over against *historical* alternative traits no longer present.[8]

---

8. Bigelow and Pargetter seem to think that no such historical notion of function can enter into functional explanations without making these explanations tautological. That is surely a confusion. To say that trait *t* has function *f* is to say that *t* had a history during which it was selected for doing *f*. So if you want to know why current members of a species have *t* the answer is, very simply, *because t has the function f*, that is, because *t was* selected for because it *did f*. Of course, *f* was not the function of the very first *t* tokens selected, even though

My suggestion, then, is that in the first instance (second instances are described in chap. 2 of *LTOBC*), items have functions when their being there depends on reproduction from ancestors having similar traits, these traits having been causally efficacious in helping to produce these items, and these traits having been selected at some point in this history for their capacity to make this kind of contribution. That is pretty rough. I tried to be more accurate in *LTOBC*. Notice that this kind of definition does not require that natural selection itself be a *cause* of any functional trait.[9] The question of whether natural selection causes the emergence of traits is not at issue. It is enough if it preserves traits against competitors. The requirement on a certain kind of cause of the functional item's being there is fulfilled by the cycling, not the selection. But cycling is not enough. Copying and selection are required as well.

5 The Attack on Adaptationism

So much for the philosophers. Now for the challenge from certain biologists who claim that human cognitive functions may not have been selected for. The challenge stems mostly from misunderstandings of the nature and force of these biologists' claims. But the following passage, written by two of the most eminent of contemporary evolutionary biologists, does have a threatening look:

The brain, though undoubtedly built by natural selection for some complex set of functions, can, as a result of its intricate structure, work in an unlimited number of ways quite unrelated to the selective pressure that constructed it. . . . Current utility carries no automatic implication about historical origin. Most of what the brain now does to enhance our survival lies in the domain of exaptation—and does not allow us to make hypotheses about the selective paths of human history. (Gould and Vrba 1982, 13)

---

they did *f* and that is why they were selected. They were not selected "because they had functions" but because they did *f*. Compare the following: Some fires have occurred because people lit them. These tokens of lightings subsequently became causes of fires. The fires occurred because the *lightings* occurred; they did not occur 'because they had causes.'"
9. I mention this because Cummins (1975) and Sober (1984b) claim that natural selection is never a cause of traits. I think this is an error, but it doesn't matter for the definition of "proper function." The condition of being "on account of a correlation" in *LTOBC* may be read as referring to a certain broad kind of explanation rather than always to a cause.

Let me fill in the background behind this (quite singular) statement so that we can understand and evaluate it.

There has been much discussion recently among biologists and also philosophers of biology concerning ways that various structures and traits of animals can originate other than by direct natural selection (begin with Gould and Lewontin 1979; Lewontin 1984; Gould and Vrba 1982; Sober 1984b, 1987). Some of these ways we can immediately dismiss as not relevant to the question of human *cognition*, so let me do that first.

There is, first, random genetic drift, whereby sampling errors, rather than utility to its bearers, are responsible for fixation of some trait in a population. This can happen with traits that have in themselves no large differential effect on fitness.

Second, there is pleiotropy, whereby irrelevant or even deleterious traits become fixed because they ride close to advantageous genes on the chromosome or are accidental byproducts of genetic structures that also produce advantageous traits. Presumably, pleiotropy could also produce accidentally advantageous traits, traits that had a minor positive effect on fitness but an effect so small that it did not happen actually to help in selection of the trait.

Third, there is allometry, whereby the proportional size of various parts of an animal's body are determined by developmental considerations producing differential growth rates for various tissues not necessarily related to utility. This third principle can be generalized. It is clear that possible developmental paths are limited in definite though not yet well understood ways, so that it may often be hard or impossible to grow one trait without either simultaneously growing certain other traits or radically changing major features of the structural design of the animal.

Last, there are what Gould and Lewontin (1979) labeled "spandrels." Clearly, it is a bad error to make "the assumption that all traits, *arbitrarily described*, are adaptive" (Lewontin 1984, 242, emphasis mine). The hollow of your armpit, your chin, the match between the length of your hand and the distance from the end of your nose to the top of your ear do not, as so described, have functions. Nor, perhaps, do your knee-jerk reflexes, your dislike of the sound of fingernails scratching the blackboard, or your love of sparkley, colored lights. Like the spandrels of San Marco, the funnel shaped interstices between the great arches of San Marco's dome into which the artists poured wonderfully fitting mosaics, these traits may well be accidental byproducts of design.

Now if one makes the assumption, as some sociobiologists seem to have done, that various fairly complex human behaviors may either distort and crash through, or bypass entirely, more general cognitive channels—think of knee jerks—then I suppose there might be certain human behavioral tendencies that resulted directly from drift, pleiotropy, or allometry. Maybe the intense aversion to wood in the mouth apparently inherited by certain members of my family has its origin there. And it is practically analytic that there are such things as human behavioral spandrels. Surely my aversion to highways whose designations begin with a capital I, as so described, is a spandrel, as is my tendency to point my eyelashes at my toes whenever a puff of air is blown into my eye. Nor should we assume that just because a trait looks to us like an *obvious* unit to describe, such as a tendency in males to bond, that it isn't a spandrel. In this connection, it is important to note that sociobiology has been a central and often quite proper target of the antispandrelists. The interest here, however, is not in specific behaviors, whether or not these are arbitrarily described, but in general cognitive capacities, such as the capacities to develop concepts, to form empirical beliefs, and to reason.

What Gould and Vrba actually suggest is not that such capacities might be spandrels but that they might be "exaptations," a notion I will discuss immediately. The general form of the argument against such capacities' resulting from drift, pleiotropy, or allometry, and against their being mere spandrels, has recently been reviewed by Pinker and Bloom (1990, especially pp. 708–712 and 766–767). Clear signs of a selectionist origin include complexity of design, with "heterogenous structure" producing a "unity of function" that can be "stated independently and more economically than description of the structure" and that is "special because it is improbable for systems lacking that organization which are otherwise physically similar to it," and special because it specifically benefits the organism that has it. When you are ready to speculate that the human eye got there by genetic drift, pleiotropy or whatever, then you may play the same game with cognition. But Pinker and Bloom remind us of Darwin's observation that we don't find even relatively simple structures lying about that benefit only *other* organisms, such as horses wearing naturally grown saddles. Why not if drift, pleiotropy, and so forth are actually capable of creating such structures as eyes and cognitive systems? These random designers surely wouldn't be selective about *whom* they benefitted with their products. Why, then, are there no computing systems or TV sets, ready for our immediate use, growing on trees or elephants?

6   Exaptations

What, then, is this "domain of exaptations" that Gould and Vrba wish to invoke to explain brains? "Exaptation" is their coinage, but it is a good term that has caught on. Gould and Vrba distinguish what they call "exaptations" from what they call "adaptations," a term that must itself be mildly disciplined to serve this purpose. An adaptation is "any feature that promotes fitness and was built by selection for its current role" (Gould and Vrba 1982, 6). Exaptations are "characters... evolved for other uses (or for no function at all), and later 'coopted' for their current role" (p. 6). Gould and Vrba quote Darwin:

> The sutures in the skulls of young mammals have been advanced as a beautiful adaptation for aiding parturition, and no doubt they facilitate, or may be indispensable for this act; but as sutures occur in the skulls of young birds and reptiles, which have only to escape from a broken egg, we may infer that this structure has arisen from the laws of growth, and has been taken advantage of in the parturition of the higher mammals. (Darwin 1859, 197)

These sutures in the skulls of young mammals are exaptations.

One possible story about the origin of bird wings goes like this: Early terrestrial ancestors of birds grew feathers for warmth. These feathers were subsequently lengthened and shaped for catching insects, then modified for flight. And now, in some species, the wings are held up as a "mantle" casting a shadow over the water so that the wading birds can see to catch minnows. If the wings have not been modified by selection for the purpose of fishing, they are pure exaptations for this function. At each earlier transitional stage they were first exaptations ("preadaptations") but were later modified or "postadapted" to become "secondary adaptations" for the new use. "Any coopted structure (an exaptation) will probably not arise perfected for its new effect. It will therefore develop secondary adaptations for the new role" (Gould and Vrba 1982, 12).

There are certain rodents whose cheeks seem (as Gould puts it) to have got turned inside out during development, whereupon they started to be used as external pouches for transporting provisions (Gould 1980). The inverted cheeks were exaptations for transporting food. There are sea turtles that crawl up on land once a year and laboriously dig deep holes in the sand in which to lay their eggs, clumsily using their flippers for this task. They haven't got anything else to use, but it seems clear that the flippers are designed only for swimming. They are clumsy exaptations for digging.

Gould and Vrba say that only adaptations have "functions." Exaptations instead have "effects." They are aware, of course, that this restriction on the term "function" is stipulative and not just a reflection of general biological usage. Do exaptations have *proper* functions?

First let me ask Gould and Vrba a question, indeed, the classic question. Are noses an exaptation for supporting eyeglasses? We seem here to be right back to the dilemma of section 3, there being no principled way to distinguish between exaptations and any accidental uses that one or a dozen exemplifications of a trait accidentally serve for their bearers. Examples such as the use of inverted cheeks for pockets or the use of flippers for digging occur in every generation, in every turn of the growth and reproduction cycle. But surely Gould and Vrba would not wish to exclude important new uses of a trait just because, due to circumstance, they sometimes skip a generation before being exemplified again. Why then are the mouths of dogs not exaptations for bringing newspapers in for a reward? "Exaptation" is surely strangely open-ended for a term of science if no modification whatever of the organism is required to accompany an exaptation.

Notice, however, that in the cases of the flippers and inverted cheeks, it's not true that no change in the organism has occurred. It is not that each new infant rodent, having explored its body and discovered inverted cheeks, says to itself, "How convenient! Just the right sort of thing to carry my lunch in." The behavior that uses the inverted cheeks is wired in. And so it is with the turtles. The method of digging is adapted to the flippers. We cannot imagine that the turtles would dig the same way, with the same motions, if they had hands. Nor can we suppose their digging to be controlled as our digging would be, by a general purpose controller that adapts on the spot to the flippers (compare scuba divers). Indeed, isn't this exactly why the "co-opted" uses of the inverted cheeks and the turtles' flippers are of interest to the evolutionary biologist, in a way that noses supporting eyeglasses and dogs using their mouths to bring in the newspaper are not?

Once we have noticed this, however, another problem surfaces. On Gould and Vrba's account, the flippers of the turtle do not count as having digging as one of their functions because the flippers developed first and the mechanisms responsible for the digging behavior were only later adapted to the flippers. But if this is to be our way of assigning functions, shouldn't we also say that it is not the function of wings to help the bird fly but only of certain specified *parts* of wings to do so? The feathers, for instance, would seem not to have as one of their functions to help the bird fly, because they were developed for insulation. Nor does the trait of having a pair of wings rather than only one wing have helping the bird to fly as a function. Indeed, the trait of having a *pair* of wings would seem to have no function at all, because the original point of bisymmetry, assuming there was one, surely had nothing to do with any current uses of the wings. Indeed, I'm afraid it will turn out, on this sort of analysis, that very few aspects of any current animals are functional. Nearly every trait will turn out to be merely an exaptation.

7   Proper Functions and Brains

I now have three suggestions to make concerning proper functions. If proper functions are understood as I will propose, there will remain, I submit, no possible question that normal perceptual and cognitive function for contemporary humans is a *proper* function of their brains.

First, I suggest that we fill in the odd large gap that Gould and Vrba have left between adaptation and exaptation. An adaptation, they say, is a trait "*built*" by selection" for its current role, while an exaptation was only "co-opted" for its current role. But by far the main job of selection is not "building" at all but day to day *maintenance* of the gene pool. What selection does day to day is not to alter population profiles but steadily to throw out the deleterious junk that would otherwise collect in the gene pool due to drift and a raft of minor mutations. Some times this kind of selection is called "selection against" and distinguished from "selection for," which alone is thought to cause evolution. The logic of the two kinds of selection, however, is precisely the same. Both merely separate traits to be kept from traits to be thrown out, thus simultaneously selecting both for and against. Nor does any kind of selection cause evolution in the sense of literally "building" new traits. The proportion of the population that already has a trait being selected for is what determines whether the selection is causing evolution or merely maintaining the status quo. There is no difference in the selection process itself. What should we say, then, of the trait that was originally selected for one role but has long been actively *maintained* for another? As I understand "selection," such a trait has surely been "selected for" its new function. If the logic of the process is the same, the term for the process should surely be the same. Its new function is what in *LTOBC*, I called its "most proximate proper function," such functions usually being the only functions of interest to any but the paleontologist.

On this reading, surely a very large proportion of Gould and Vrba's exaptations will have those functions for which they have been co-opted as *proper* functions. Turning to brains, these will have normal human perception and cognition as proper functions if *either* these abilities were once selected for *or* they have for some time been actively maintained in the species. It seems undeniable that normal perception and cognition, as we find these operating in a majority of present-day humans, have in one or both of these senses been selected for during the history of the species. Only in a society that spends on each retarded child many multiples of what it spends for a normal school child could it possibly be overlooked that retardation has historically been a severe life-threatening handicap. And so for other disturbances of normal cognitive function, such as schizophrenia. The only conceivable doubt that might be introduced here is whether modern humans really do exhibit use of the *same* cognitive capacities that ancient humans did—a point that I will turn to momentarily. The skeptic would need to argue here that not only ancient man but also classical man, medieval man, and Enlightenment man had no life-preserving need for the cognitive functions we find normally in play in humans today. It would be interesting to see the argument.

My second suggestion concerning the notion of proper function is to make things neater by altering its definition in the following way. In *LTOBC*, I defined what I called a "Normal explanation for proper performance" of a functional trait. Take any trait that has a proper function. Look to its history. Pick out every occasion on which one of its ancestors actually performed that proper function, and look to see how that ancestor did it. What environmental conditions did it rely on to succeed in this performance? What other cooperating organs, behaviors, or traits, either of the animal itself or of other organisms nearby, have to be mentioned in explaining how that function was performed? Derive from this—I think that there is no question that one usually can—a general explanation, or perhaps a couple of alternative general explanations, that cover all or very nearly all of these individual historical cases. That explanation is the Normal explanation for performance of that proper function by that trait. Suppose now that in giving the Normal explanation for performance of one of the proper functions of one trait of an organism, one has to mention as a Normal condition for this performance the presence and action of some other reproduced structure or trait of the organism. Let us count the contribution of this second structure or trait to the proper performance of the first as one of the second structure's proper functions.

If we count proper functions that way, the sea turtles' flippers will have digging as one among their proper functions, since they must be mentioned in explaining how the hole-digging programs in the turtles' nervous systems Normally work. And so for the rodents' inverted cheeks. The biwinged construction of the bird and its feathers will have as one of their proper functions to help the bird fly, and in mantling birds, the wings will also have the function of mantling. But no mention of the dog's mouth need be made in giving a Normal explanation of how the general learning mechanisms in the dog that are responsible for its newspaper-retrieving behavior have historically worked. The explanation for how these mechanisms Normally work is on a far more general or abstract plane. Similarly for the use of your nose to support your eyeglasses. No genetic changes have occurred in your ancestry that rest for their utility upon the specific fact that noses support eyeglasses. Your ability and disposition to rest your eyeglasses on your nose is merely one more application of certain far more general or abstract tool-using abilities that normal humans have possessed for countless generations.

What follows concerning the human brain is that, no matter for what functions it was designed or recently maintained, for any aspect of its current function to be a *proper* function, it is sufficient that there have been some modification of humans built upon this current use, for example, modification of the vocal tract, the speech-perception apparatus, the memory system, and so forth. Being "built" by natural selection is sufficient for proper function, being maintained by natural selection is independently sufficient, and having been utilized by other structures built or maintained by natural selection is also independently sufficient for proper function. It is hard to see how modern human cognition could fail to be caught in one or more of these nets.

The third point about proper functions that I wish to clarify concerns the level of abstraction used in describing them. This point is parallel to that made just above about the abstractness of the plane upon which Normal explanation rests in the case of the dog programs responsible for bringing in the newspaper and the human programs responsible for placing one's glasses on one's nose. Recall the words of Gould and Vrba on brains: "The brain...can, as a result of its intricate structure, work in an unlimited number of ways quite unrelated to the selective pressure that constructed it." Later they comment on "the myriad and inescapable consequences of building any computing device as complex as the human brain" (Gould and Vrba 1982, 14). It is well to remember here that Gould and Vrba are authorities not on brains or cognition but only on paleontology and evolutionary biology. The image they invoke seems to be the rather outdated one of the brain as universal Turing machine, flexibly programmed to serve first one then another function. It certainly doesn't fit well with the rapidly growing evidence that the brain is a highly differentiated organ containing numerous structures with highly specialized functions.[10] Nor does it fit with contemporary developments in cognitive science that emphasize the difficulty of building a cognitive system that will perform a myriad

10. Evidence from brain-damaged patients, evidence from invasive studies of animal brains, recent evidence from PET studies (positron emission tomography), and evidence from the great diversity of cognitive styles and capacities found among normal humans.

of intertwined functions competing against one another for urgency in real time and that relies heavily and continuously on interaction with the structure of the environment in order to do so.[11] But more to our purposes here is the question of what it would *mean* to say that the brain was "working in ways quite unrelated to the selective pressure that constructed it."

Sober, in *The nature of selection*, (1984b), poses the following question:

A *Drosophila* population is subject to high-temperature stress. It gradually evolves a thicker skin, which is selectively advantageous because it insulates. Later on, the environment is changed and the temperatures are now very low. The thickened skin it evolved before remains advantageous. Is the thickened skin an adaptation merely for *high* temperature tolerance, or is it an adaptation for *generalized* temperature tolerance? (1984b, 209)

Sober argues for the second alternative on grounds very like those I would like to give. I would say that so long as both the effect of the thickened skin and the normal explanation for production of this effect can be described in a univocal way over all the instances, these are all performances of the same proper function. This is the principle in accordance with which the stomach's function is to digest proteins, starches, sugars, etc., not just a disjunct of more specific food items with which ancient or nineteenth-century man happened to be acquainted. Similarly, your eyes do not take on a new function when they see jet-liners, TV commercials, and Rubik cubes for the first time.

In accord with this, it is quite likely that there has been no change whatever in the functions performed by the human cognitive systems in the last 100 thousand years or so. For there is no reason whatever to suppose that the general principles in accordance with which primitive man developed concepts, acquired beliefs and desires, and combined them to yield purposive action were any different than those whereby modern children do so. There is no reason that I can see to postulate any recent changes in the use of the brain.[12]

11. For a lucid discussion, see Clark 1989, chap. 4.
12. For elaboration, see chapter 11, sections 5 and 6.

3

Thoughts without Laws

Thirty years ago, Wilfrid Sellars introduced the thesis that our ordinary talk about thoughts and other "private episodes" is not in the first instance inner observation talk (nor logical construct talk) but *theory* talk (Sellars 1956).[1] At that time his position was unintuitive, hard to understand, highly controversial—and wonderfully refreshing. One effect was to cast new light on the weaknesses and strengths of both introspective psychology and traditional behaviorisms in such a way as to give "aid and comfort" (as Sellars likes to say) to a newly emerging psychology, a psychology that wished to explain behavior by postulating inner episodes of a sort that might eventually be described physiologically. It is marvelous how wanting to think a thesis true can lift it straight from the nether region of the unintuitive, difficult, and problematic to the heights of the clear, distinct, and obvious. At the present time, a premise shared by many who agree on little else is that ordinary talk about thoughts and other "private episodes" constitutes a sort of folk theory, a primitive science of psychology, the purpose of which is to predict and explain behavior. To attack this premise (for example, Stich 1983) is definitely to swim upstream.

Of course to say that folk psychology is a primitive theory designed to explain behavior does not tell us very much that is positive unless

I am much indebted to Stephen Crain for a very careful and constructive reading of the first draft of this essay. Comments on a later draft by Alexander Rosenberg, Barry Loewer, Adam Morton, and an unknown referee for the *Philosophical Review* were also helpful.
1. Sellars held that in the second instance private episodes are observed entities. They can be directly observed by those who have them. But observation terms, for Sellars, are merely terms applied without inference and do not necessarily denote anything real.

accompanied by suitable remarks about what theories are. Sellars did accompany his thesis with such remarks, with an explicit endorsement of a dominant sort of theory of theories current in the 1950s and still current, in the relevant respects, today. This theory of theories has taken various forms, but its core is always the same: theoretical terms are defined by the place they have in a system of postulated *laws* connecting the entities and properties for which they stand with other entities and properties postulated by the theory and with happenings among items outside the domain of the theory proper; the purpose of the theory is to explain and regularize patterns in phenomena outside of the domain of the theory proper by reference to the postulated entities, properties, and laws. In the case of folk psychology, the theoretical items would be mental properties and states, the phenomena to be explained and regularized would be behaviors, given the external situations in which they occur. Given this theory of theories, to say that folk psychology was a theory was to say that the items to which folk psychology refers—beliefs, desires, visual images, etc.—are essentially law-governed items, that is, they are law-governed items if they exist at all, if the folk theory is true. To say *that* was indeed to say something positive, even something cheerful. For it was to suggest that a genuine nomological science of psychology might be built from the materials of folk psychology suitably trimmed and trained.[2]

Now the idiom of folk psychology is shot through with references to items that are, in Brentano's sense, "intentional," items that are "about" other things or "of" other things: beliefs about whales, fears of falling, recognitions of faces, etc. To put this another way, these items have "semantic content," or just "content." Granted that having content is an essential character of many folk-psychological entities, these entities being indeed differentiated or individuated in part in accordance with content, it seemed to be implied that both the intentionality and the specific contents of these intentional items must correspond to the kinds of lawful causal interactions these had with one another, with the environment, and with behavior. This view meshed nicely with popular views

---

2. I am going to argue that Sellars was wrong in thinking that folk psychology is a theory *in this particular sense.* But the basic thesis of "Empiricism and the philosophy of mind" is in no way affected by this. The article is a landmark in twentieth-century philosophy.

derived from the sprawling tradition of philosophical analysis (for example, verificationism) about the nature of meaning hence, spilling over, of the content of mental terms. According to these views (I am putting things very crudely here), meaning is given by showing what a term implies and/or what implies it and, ultimately, what its proper connections are with sensory data. All that was needed now, it seemed, was to map logical implications onto causal interactions among the contentful entities of folk psychology, thus exposing the *way* in which these entities "meant" things, were intentional, had content.

But in the last ten years or so various arguments have accumulated to the effect that the content of an inner intentional item, say a belief, is not a direct function of its causal role (for example, Putnam 1975b; Burge 1979, 1982; Stich 1983). This is the same as to say that doubt has been cast on the thesis that folk psychology is a "theory" in the sense described by Sellars, or at least upon the thesis that it might be a *true* theory of this kind. I will not rehearse these arguments here, for it is not my purpose to evaluate them. Instead, I wish to examine the relevance of the suspicion that folk psychology is not a theory in Sellars's sense to the question of the relation between folk psychology and a mature scientific psychology or "cognitive science."

It seems to be widely assumed that if folk psychology is not a true theory of the kind Sellars described, then folk psychology cannot be used as a footing for construction of cognitive science. To put this differently, it is assumed that either ascribing semantic content to inner states of people is, implicitly, claiming and claiming truly that people have items or states in them that obey specified kinds of nomological laws *or* that ascription of content to inner states has no role of importance at all to play in a mature cognitive science. For example, Stich (1983) and the Churchlands (P.M. 1979, 1981; P.S. 1980) deny the first half of this disjunct, hence embrace the second; Burge (1984) has recently denied the second half hence attempted to reclaim the first.[3] My claim will be that folk psychology is not a rudimentary nomological theory but that it need not be to play a crucial role in the development of cognitive science. Folk-psychological items or states are not defined

___

3. Burge (1984) suggests that it is only "individualistic" interpretations of intentional state attributions that fail to explain behavior nomologically.

by reference to laws, not even to rough statistical laws.[4] Similarly, ascribing content to inner psychological states does not involve postulating any laws. Yet cognitive science could not possibly get on with its tasks without ascribing content to inner psychological states. At the same time I will explain how folk psychology, despite the fact that it postulates no laws and despite the fact that we seldom know very many *details* about the intentional states of other people, still enables us to do a great deal of explaining and a certain amount of fallible predicting of human behavior.[5]

1   Biological Categories, Proper Functions, and Normal Conditions

Psychology, no matter how it is done, necessarily *is* a branch of physiology, hence biology. Human physiology is the study of how the various parts and systems that make up a human work, that is, of what they do and of how they go about doing it. Psychology studies what mental tasks are and how they are performed, on the assumption, of course, that there *are* some special systems (material or nonmaterial) that work in accordance with special principles and do special kinds of tasks that fall, sensibly, into a distinguishable field for study—study of the "mental."

Now consider: how does physiology differ from, say, organic chemistry? Of course, these disciplines study different kinds of bodies or systems. Physiology studies whole human bodies and middle-sized parts and even extremely small parts of bodies; organic chemistry studies systems that are incredibly small, the systems that are organic molecules. But the fundamental difference is that the organic chemist and the physiologist wish to understand how the systems they study work in rather different senses of "work."

To know how an organic molecule "works" is to understand how the

4. More accurately, the only plausible *reconstruction* that I can see of folk psychology makes no reference to laws. For example, I will try to show that the categories of folk psychology correspond to categories that are best explained in terms of evolutionary theory. But, of course, folk psychology makes no explicit reference to evolutionary theory.
5. Many details supporting the position for which I will argue are given in *LTOBC*. The emphasis there was on language. Here I will focus more sharply on thought, painting in the necessary background with broad intuitive strokes.

system it comprises holds itself together as a system; what kinds of forces will destroy it and why; what the products of such destruction or decomposition will be; and what kinds of larger systems it can become a part of, when, and why. In this sense of "works" there is no such thing as *not* working, or as not working well or not working right; whatever the organic molecule does is part of its "working." For example, if the system flies apart, the result is not a molecule that is failing to work but some other molecule, molecules or particles. The human body, on the other hand, is a kind of system that does not necessarily work or work right or well. Correlatively, failure to work or to work right or well does not automatically transform a human body into something else (mummies are human bodies too). The objects that physiologists study—human bodies, circulatory systems, red blood cells, etc.—fall in a different kind of ontological category than do organic molecules. Call these categories "biological categories."

Biological categories are carved out not by looking at the actual structure, actual dispositions, or actual functions of the organ or system that falls within the category but by looking at (or speculating about) its history.[6] A heart, for example, may be large or small (elephant or mouse), three-chambered or four-chambered, etc., and it may *also* be diseased or malformed or excised from the body that once contained it, hence unable to pump blood. It falls in the category *heart*, first, because it was produced by mechanisms that have proliferated during their evolutionary history in part because they were producing items that managed to circulate blood efficiently in the species that contained them, thus aiding the proliferation of that species. It is a *heart*, second, because it was produced by such mechanisms in accordance with an explanation that approximated, to some undefined degree, a Normal explanation for production of such items in that species and bears, as a result, some resemblance to Normal hearts of that species. By a "Normal explanation" I mean the sort of explanation that historically accounts for production of the majority of Normal hearts of that species. And by a "normal heart," I mean a heart that matches, in relevant respects, the majority of hearts that, during the history of that

6. How biological categories are carved out is described much more exactly in *LTOBC*, chaps. 1, 2.

species, managed to pump blood efficiently enough to aid survival and reproduction. In like manner, every body organ or system falls in the biological or physiological categories it does due to its historical connections with prior examples of kinds that have served certain functions or, typically, sets of functions. So whether or not it is itself capable of serving any of these functions, every organ or system is associated with a set of functions that are biologically "proper" to it, functions that have helped account for the survival and proliferation of its ancestors. I call these functions "proper functions" of the organ or system.[7]

Associated with each of the proper functions that an organ or system has is a Normal explanation for performance of this function which tells how that organ or system in that species has historically managed to perform that function. For example, there are a number of proper functions that *can* be performed by certain systems of the human body, given the presence of appropriate lithium compounds in the bloodstream but that were *historically* performed using calcium. The Normal explanations for how these functions are performed make reference to the presence of calcium in the blood rather than lithium. Similarly, the heart of a person who wears a pacemaker to assure that the electrical signals sent to the heart muscles are properly timed does not pump blood in accordance with a fully Normal explanation. (I am capitalizing "Normal" so that it cannot be read to mean merely average. As we will soon see, what is Normal is not always statistically average; indeed, sometimes it is quite unusual.)

Not only body organs and systems but also various states and activities of these organs and systems have proper functions. Consider a chameleon. Its skin contains a system whose job is to arrange pigmented matter in such a way that the chameleon will match whatever it is sitting on at the moment. Obvious further proper functions of this system are to arrange that the chameleon will be invisible to predators hence will avoid being eaten. If we look at any particular color pattern that characterizes any particular chameleon at a particular time, we can

---

7. The notions "proper function," "Normal constitution," "Normal explanation for proper performance," and "Normal conditions for proper performance" are given explicit definitions in *LTOBC*, chaps. 1, 2.

say what the proper functions of this pattern are, even though it is possible (though unlikely) that no chameleon has ever displayed just this particular kind of pattern before. The proper functions of the pattern are to make the chameleon invisible and to prevent it from being eaten—functions that it derives from the proper functions of the mechanism that produced it. The Normal explanation for performance of this function is that some predator comes by, glances toward the chameleon, but does not see it because it matches what it sits on, hence goes past without eating the chameleon.

Of course, if no predator comes by, this color state of the chameleon cannot perform its proper function—or not in accordance with a Normal explanation. Lots of states (tokens) have proper functions they never get a chance to perform. Also, just as body organs and systems are sometimes diseased or malformed hence unable to perform their proper functions, so aberrant states and activities of a body or system can have proper functions that they would not be able to perform even under Normal conditions. Consider a chameleon that does *not* match what it sits on. This might have come about because the pigment arranging system of the chameleon was out of order. Or it might be because, although its pigment arranging system was perfectly healthy, the chameleon was in an environment that did not provide Normal conditions for operation of this system. (I don't know on what principles this system operates, but suppose that radiant energy in unusual wavelengths could confuse the system.) In either case, just as a thing that has been produced by mechanisms designed to make hearts is a heart with the proper function of pumping blood so long as it bears a resemblance to Normal hearts and was produced in accordance with an explanation that approximated a Normal explanation for production of hearts, so the chameleon's wrong color pattern (token) is a protective device or state with the proper function of preventing the chameleon from being eaten. And there is still a Normal explanation for performance associated with this function, though it is very unlikely to be realized. Chameleons' color patterns have historically prevented chameleons from being eaten because what the chameleons sat on matched the chameleons. So a Normal condition for proper performance of the color pattern is that there be something that the chameleon is sitting on that matches it. If this condition held, the color pattern could prevent the chameleon from being eaten in accordance with a Normal explanation. Suppose, for example, that some sympathetic soul places the sick chameleon on something it *does* match. The color pattern still has the same proper function, and *now* it might be performed in accordance with a Normal explanation. The entire history of this proper performance would not have been Normal of course, but from now on, things could proceed Normally.

Consider also a more complex case. There is a mechanism in worker honey bees that has as proper functions to produce, after the bee has spotted a new supply of nectar, a bee dance (a certain activity) that bears a certain mapping relation to the position of the nectar, hence to produce the flying of fellow worker bees in a certain direction, hence to get these bees to nectar, hence to get nectar into the hive. Each particular bee dance has as proper functions, derived from the proper functions of this mechanism, to cause worker bees to fly in a certain direction, hence to find nectar, etc. Now consider a particular bee dance, *Sacre du sucre*, danced by a particular bee at a particular time. In what direction is it the proper function of *Sacre du sucre* (the token) to propel the watching bees? First, towards nectar. But equally cogently, in the direction indicated by *Sacre du sucre*, for the mechanism by which bee dances have historically performed their proper functions is by propelling worker bees in a direction determined by a certain definite function (mathematical sense) of the orientation of the dance. Now suppose that something has gone wrong; *Sacre du sucre* was danced by mistake and does not in fact indicate the direction of any nectar. *Sacre du sucre* then has conflicting proper functions (1) to send the workers towards nectar and (2) to send the workers where the dance says to go, for instance, north-northwest. But there is no honey north-northwest. So not only can states and activities have proper functions without performing them and without even being capable of performing them, they can also have proper functions that, even if performed, would not contribute to performance of certain of their own *further* proper functions (or not, at least, in accordance with an uninterrupted Normal explanation; someone might, of course, be kind enough to place some nectar where the bees that complied with the incorrect dance were aiming).[8]

8. For more details about the derivation of the proper functions of states and

2 Psychology as a Branch of Biology

Now it seems reasonable that various states of the systems psychologists study have proper functions (which they may or may not get a chance to perform, or even be capable of performing, indeed, which it might sometimes even be pointless or opposed to their own more ultimate purposes for them to perform) that are derived from the proper functions of the mechanisms that produce them and that there are Normal explanations for performance of these functions. Thus, although it might be that a certain facet or state of one's cognitive system was unique in history—say one had a unique belief or a unique desire—still this state has a proper function or set of proper functions and these functions are associated with Normal explanations for their proper performance. There must, after all, be a finite number of general principles that govern the activities of our various cognitive-state-making and cognitive-state-using mechanisms and there must be explanations of why these principles have historically worked to aid our survival. To suppose otherwise is to suppose that our cognitive life is an accidental epiphenomenal cloud hovering over mechanisms that evolution devised with other things in mind.

Now to study how an entity as falling within a biological category "works" involves (1) understanding what functions are proper to it and to its constitutive systems, parts, and states and (2) understanding how these functions are Normally performed. It does not involve studying just anything at all that the entity might be disposed to do and any old way that one might induce it to do this. For example, the physiologist is not interested in such exotica as why the Normal heart makes just those peculiar sounds that it makes (nor in how one might induce it to make other sounds), for presumably these sounds have no proper functions.[9] But he *is* interested in how the body manages to maintain just that peculiar temperature that it maintains, this maintenance having, it seems, numerous proper functions. True, one thing that physiologists

---

about the Normal explanations for performance of these functions, see *LTOBC*, chaps. 2, 6–8.
9. Should current speculations that a mother's heart sounds help to synchronize her baby's body rhythms turn out to be correct, I would, of course, have to change the example.

study is diseases. But no parallel to such studies exists within the field of organic chemistry precisely because "disease" is defined with reference to, by *contrast* with, that which is functioning properly or that which is Normally constituted.

Imagine a physiologist trying to study the liver or the eye without having any idea what its proper functions are—what it is supposed to do. Clearly his first job will be to try to find out what it is supposed to do, what it is for it to "work." Until he has formed some kind of hypothesis about this there is no way of proceeding to a study of *how* it works. There is no way of knowing even *when* it is working, let alone working right or well, and no way of distinguishing the Normally constituted and properly functioning samples of its kind from those that are malformed, diseased, or malfunctioning. Nor is there any way of proceeding to a study of how it works without knowing something about the surrounding conditions upon which it Normally relies.

Similarly, it seems reasonable that the psychologist would need to begin with some understanding of what the proper functions of the systems he studies are, his concern being to understand the mechanisms whereby, and the conditions under which, these functions are Normally realized. The systems the psychologist studies differ from many of those the physiologist studies in that they are much more malleable. They are supposed to mold themselves over time and even to adapt themselves moment by moment in time so as to take account of the peculiar environment of the individual organism and its temporary position within that environment. They are designed to change their states or to produce new states with extraordinary frequency, even continually. But these states must still have proper functions, and there must be Normal versus abNormal ways in which they fulfill these functions if and when they do fulfill them. Only by beginning with some hypotheses about the functions of these systems and of their various states could a neurologist begin the work of searching for these systems and states in the brain and of describing *how* these systems and their various states Normally perform their respective functions. Surely there are an infinite number of ways that brain states might be classified or described if one did not care whether or not one was describing state types that had proper functions. But if one does care about this, the only way to begin is by having some hypothesis about what these functions are.

Now suppose that folk psychology were a theory in *this* sense: it postulates that there exist certain entities or states within the body—beliefs, desires, intentions, fears, etc.—that have certain proper functions. (What the defining functions of these states might be can be left open for the moment.) Then if folk psychology were *right*, it would surely be necessary for any developed scientific psychology to take account of these entities or states *as* folk psychology understands them, that is, as aspects of the body having certain proper functions. If I can make it plausible that the entities that folk psychology postulates are indeed defined by their proper functions, and make plausible that the proper functions with which folk psychology endows these entities very likely *are* had by some special parts or states of the body, that should be enough to show that cognitive science can probably use folk psychology as a starting point. The job of cognitive science would then be, in part, to explain what the Normal constitution of these psychological entities is and *how* they Normally perform their defining proper functions.

But I said I would argue that folk psychology is not a theory in the sense that Sellars defined—that it does not make reference to nomological laws, even to rough statistical laws, in defining the entities that it postulates. What then is the relation between having a certain proper function or proper functions and falling under laws?

3   Proper Functions versus Laws

Once the physiologist has in his hand a hypothesis about what the proper functions of a body part or system are, he can tackle the task of finding out *how* it performs these functions. His eventual aim is to describe the Normal constitution of the simplest component parts of the system in terms such that how the system functions can be understood by principles of physics, organic chemistry, etc. Along the way (and it's a very long way) he uses "functional analyses" in something like Cummins's (1975, 1983) sense.[10] That is, he divides the part or system into smaller and smaller parts and systems, describing the proper functions

---

10. It should be born in mind, however, that I have described proper functions in a way that, for certain purposes, differs significantly from Cummins's description of functions.

of each and how these combine to effect the proper function of the whole. At the same time (especially if he is interested in pathology) he examines what the Normal explanations and Normal conditions for performance of these functions are.

Now for the most part it is a proper function of some other parts or systems in the body to produce or to maintain the Normal conditions that a body part or system relies upon for performance of its functions. For example, very many body functions have as a Normal condition for performance that the body be at approximately 98.6 degrees Fahrenheit, and there are several organs or systems within the body whose job it is to see that this condition is maintained. For this reason it can often be assumed that insofar as a body part or system is itself healthy or Normally constituted and insofar as it is operating within a body the rest of which is passably healthy, it *will* perform its proper functions. So although physiology does not uncover universal laws applying to *all* examples of the systems that it studies, it can make some generalizations that hold for all healthy examples of such systems.

However, as we move from the body's interior to its periphery, we find exceptions to the rule that healthy parts of healthy bodies invariably perform their proper functions. At the periphery of the body, Normal conditions for proper performance of functions are often external conditions over which other body systems have no control. For example, one proper function of the sweat glands is to cool the body by evaporation of the water that they secrete. This proper function will fail to be performed through no fault of the body if the humidity is too high. The proper function of the eye-blink reflex is to prevent approaching objects from entering the eye. But it may be that this function usually fails to be performed, not because the reflex is not swift enough but because what triggered it was not in fact something that otherwise would actually have entered the eye. A proper function of the swimming mechanism in a human sperm is to get the sperm to an ovum. But only a minute proportion of these mechanisms actually perform this function, because of the paucity of human ova. Sometimes, then, devices have proper functions that have no tendency to correspond to laws or uniformities even when the constitution of these devices is perfectly Normal. This is because the Normal conditions for performance of a device's proper functions are sometimes optimal conditions rather than statistically average conditions or conditions the device is usually in. Many biological devices have survived because a critical yet small proportion of their number has performed useful functions or because a critical yet small proportion of their issue has done so.

Now the contentful entities or states that folk psychology postulates, those that exhibit intentionality, would seem to be par excellence things that ultimately serve us only via happenings at our peripheries and beyond. As our behaviors impinge on the world, the results effect more happenings in the world, and these return to impinge upon our bodies again. So it would not be surprising if some or all of the proper functions of these contentful entities or states, functions derived from the proper functions of the mechanisms that produced them, often failed to be performed. Then these proper functions would not correspond to laws or even, perhaps, to high probabilities and folk psychology, if it postulated these entities *as* things having certain proper functions, would not be a theory in anything like the sense described by Sellars.

Of course folk psychology might still be used to do quite a lot of explaining and a certain amount of very fallible predicting. Consider an analogy: "I wouldn't light my pipe over there; that's a smoke detector over your head." Smoke detectors can be out of order. Moreover, not all conditions are conditions under which they are designed to operate. (Perhaps they can be too cold, too wet, or too close to a magnet.) But one still knows that they are *liable* to go off when they encounter smoke, that they are more likely to do this than are other gadgets chosen at random. Even if smoke detectors were extremely fallible devices, requiring quite special conditions in order to work, still it would be reasonable to offer as an explanation of why one was beeping simply that it was a smoke detector in the presence of smoke. And it would be reasonable to take the precaution of not lighting one's pipe under smoke detectors.

Yet the relevance of folk psychology to cognitive science would not rest on its feeble ability to predict and explain. If the contentful entities of folk psychology have proper functions and if these functions are correctly understood by folk psychology, then folk psychology describes the "competence" (in one of Chomsky's senses) of certain devices inside us. It is then up to the neuropsychologist to look for devices that have this kind of competence; and to describe the processes by which, *under the right circumstances*, actual performances of these functions are effected.

4 Motions, Behaviors, and Actions

My job now is to make it plausible that folk psychology *is* a theory that attempts to explain actions by positing inner things or states having certain proper functions rather than things that obey certain laws. But first we must be clearer about what "actions" are, about *which* phenomena it is appropriate to ask a psychology, whether "folk" or "scientific," to explain (this section). And we must also be clearer about what can and what cannot be predicted or explained about the workings of a thing by knowing only that it has a certain proper function (section 5).

The happenings that either folk psychology or a developed scientific psychology could be expected to explain are strictly limited to those that occur in accordance with proper functions of the body's systems (or that occur as common aberrations of these functions—abnormal psychology). The systems that the psychologist studies are systems that produce, among other things, bodily movements and then effects beyond the body. So the psychologist interests himself in the etiologies of bodily motions and effects. But just as the physiologist does not care why the heart says "pit-a-pat," the psychologist does not interest himself in just any of these motions and effects. He is interested only in ones it is appropriate to describe as "behaviors" or as "actions." For how an animal's movements and their effects must be described so as correctly to fall under the heading "behaviors" or "actions" depends upon the proper functions of the mechanisms that produce them.

For example, an ethologist may study certain of a fish's movements under the heading "moving the tail from side to side" but not under the heading "moving the tail from north to south" or "undulating in front of a famous ethologist." This will be because he takes it that the side to side movement accords with a proper function, a competence, of certain mechanisms within the fish whereas the north to south direction of the movement and the fact that it occurs in front of a famous ethologist are accidental. Moving the tail from side to side is a genuine behavior of the fish; moving the tail from north to south and undulating in front of a famous ethologist are not behaviors of the fish.[11] The ethologist may also study these movements under the heading "swimming" because a proper function of these movements is to propel the fish through the water, and he may study other movements of the fish under the heading "mating display" because these movements are supposed to attract mates. He will not study either of these movements under the heading "predator display," although these movements may regularly attract predators, for attracting predators is not a proper function of either. Displaying itself to predators is not a behavior of the fish.

Similarly, the psychologist will not be concerned to explain how it happens that I flatten the forest-floor plants and scare the mice away as I pass through the woods unless he supposes that it is a proper function of my system, in its current state and environment, to produce these results (say I am leaving a trail on purpose and I am afraid of mice). If it is not a proper function of my system to produce these results, these happenings correspond neither to genuine actions nor to genuine behaviors of mine. Also, although "moving my right hand towards you," "handing you a dollar bill," and "paying back what I owe you" (all pointing to the same movement) may describe behaviors or actions of mine, "moving my right hand 20 inches northwest" and "handing you a picture of Washington" (still pointing to the same movement) are not likely to describe behaviors or actions of mine (compare Burge 1984; Dretske 1984). Hence it is not likely to be the business either of folk psychology or of scientific psychology to attempt to explain why I move my right hand 20 inches northwest or why I hand you a picture of Washington.

5   What Knowing about a Proper Function Does Not Tell Us

We have noted that knowledge of the main proper function or functions of a thing does not automatically yield knowledge of its inner workings. More interesting, it does not necessarily yield knowledge even of its grossest outer workings. To know that it is the job of a large unen-

---

11. I realize that I am forcing the notion "behavior" in this passage, forcing it to do some *work*. In the mouths of many students of behavior, the notion "behavior" is quite empty, meaning just a motion or some effect of the motion of an organism.

closed piece of machinery to ingest loose hay and disgorge neatly wired square bales of hay does not necessarily enable one to predict the motions event of its grossest parts as it performs this function. Similarly, turning an example of Daniel Dennett's on its head (Dennett 1978, chap. 1), knowing only that a chess-playing computer is designed to win chess games, I may guess that it will make allowable chess moves and also beat me at chess. But, contra Dennett, this does not tell me *how* it will go about the business of beating me. For this I would need, minimally, a more detailed functional analysis of the computer's capacities, perhaps a look at its program. Of course, I may be able to predict some of its moves just by seeing what it would *have* to do to beat me or probably would have to do to beat me—like interposing a bishop as the only possible means of getting out of check or of avoiding getting into an obvious trap. But unless I have watched it for awhile and discerned that it relies on such and such simplistic strategies, that is, guessed what some of its subsidiary proper functions are, for the most part I will have no idea exactly what move it will make next.

To summarize, if folk psychology were to attempt to explain actions by postulating that people contain inner items or states that have certain proper functions, then:

1. Folk psychology would not explain motions of people under random descriptions but would explain only genuine behaviors or actions of people (section 4 above).

2. Especially if the actions to be explained were at a remove from the body (for example, shooting rabbits) or fell under abstract descriptions (for example, paying you back what I owe you), folk psychology might explain these without at the same time explaining or predicting the exact "moves" that effected these actions (section 5).

3. It might be that the proper functions of the inner items or states that folk psychology posits very often failed to be performed, making retrospective explanation rather than prediction the major contribution of folk psychology to folk understanding (section 3 above).

6 Desires

"Desire" suggests a yearning. It suggests even that what is desired is not overlikely to come about. But focus instead upon the wider, more philosophical sense of "desire"—that in which "belief" and "desire" correspond to the traditional categories "cognition" and "volition," these two exhausting the realm of propositional attitudes. For example, in this sense of "desire," I desire whatever I intend, even though I may not yearn for but dread going through with this thing, and I desire whatever I adopt as an explicit goal.

Given this cover-all notion of desire, the most obvious proper function of every desire, it is reasonable to suppose, is to help cause its own fulfillment. For it is reasonable that *the mechanisms in us that manufacture desires* (not, of course, any specific desires) have proliferated because the desires they produce are sometimes (though by no means always) relevant to our flourishing and eventually reproducing, and because relevant desires have sometimes participated in processes that ultimately effected their fulfillment. (Reminder: very many biological devices seem to have survived because *sometimes* they were effective, because they performed well under optimal conditions.) If so, a proper function of the desire to eat is to bring it about that one eats; a proper function of the desire to win the local Democratic nomination for first selectman is to bring it about that one wins the local Democratic nomination for first selectman. That is, the descriptions that we give of desires are descriptions of their most obvious proper functions.[12] Hence, that desires (types) are distinguished or individuated (named) in accordance with content is as ordinary a fact as, say, that the categories "heart," "kidney" and "eye," as naming parts of both crayfish and people, are carved out by reference to *their* most obvious proper functions. A description of *all* of the proper functions of a human desire, like a description of all of the proper functions of a human heart, would have, of course, to say much more. It would contain a full functional analysis

---

12. One reader asked, concerning the desire that many have not to have children, whether a malfunction in motivational psychology is always responsible for such a desire. The answer depends on what you mean by "malfunction." If external conditions are not optimal, perfectly healthy systems sometimes produce states that have proper functions that are not in accord with their own ultimate purposes (see section 1). Do they then "malfunction"? Also, there is no reason to suppose that the design of our desire-making systems is itself optimal. Even under optimal conditions these systems work inefficiently, directly aiming, as it were, at recognizable ends that are merely roughly correlated with the biological end that is reproduction. For example, mammals do not, in general, cease efforts at individual survival after their fertile life is over, nor is it reasonable to suppose that this is only because of the invaluable services they offer to their grandchildren. Also see chapters 8, 9, and 11 herein.

telling exactly how the desire was supposed to effect its fulfillment. Or, more likely, it would tell how human desires in general Normally (not on the average) effect their fulfillments—the mechanisms and principles involved. (These mechanisms may be different for chimpanzees, if chimpanzees have desires, but possibly they are the same for all humans.)

Very often the proper functions in accordance with which desires are named are not performed. Indeed, perhaps most desires, like sperm, are born into a world in which conditions, outer and/or inner, are not Normal for their fulfillment. For example, like baby fishes that run into bigger fishes before practically any of their proper functions have been performed, many desires run into bigger opposing desires before they can even get underway, or they run into beliefs that imply the impossibility of their fulfillment. Still, to know that a person has a certain desire (especially if it is a goal or intention) is to have *some* hold on what he *may* in fact do.

Exactly *how* he will do it, if he does in fact do it, is, of course, another matter. *Do* we predict one another's exact moves? Or do we predict only that certain of one another's desires (for example, goals, intentions) are likely to be fulfilled—say, getting dinner inside one, getting a dozen eggs home, getting to class, getting the floor washed and the laundry done. What desires (goals, intentions) a person has we guess because they tell us ("I'll bring home some eggs," "I want to get to Boston this summer") or by generalizing from their past behavior (she almost never misses class) or by generalizing from the behavior of other people or of other similar people or by *verstehen*—by knowing what goals we would have if we were in the other's shoes. How likely a person is actually to fulfill a certain desire of his we guess in the same sort of way. (This likelihood roughly accords with the desire, then goal, then intention series.) When we do expect people to do things but then they don't in fact do them, often this can be explained by reference either to unexpected circumstances or to unexpected beliefs or counterdesires. But this kind of explanation does not fit the covering-law model of explanation. Like historical explanation, it is retrospective. It proceeds not by reference to initial conditions and laws but by telling what happened in sequence—telling that first this factor entered the scene, then that factor—so we can understand *how* it was that this happened.

Jerry Fodor (1980) has been considerably exercised (as he likes to say) by the (undoubted) fact that, knowing only that it is true *of* the girl next door that John wants to meet her, we cannot predict that John will exhibit next-door-directed behavior. For John may believe that this girl whom he wishes to meet languishes in Latvia. Fodor, following a long tradition, realizes that determinate prediction of a person's behavior, starting with knowledge of only certain of their beliefs and desires, is blocked by the fact that this behavior may always depend crucially on some other beliefs and desires about which one does not know. And, supposing the girl who lives next door to be Jane, of course it is true that the exact moves John makes in his attempt to meet Jane—indeed, whether he makes any such moves at all—will depend upon his other beliefs and desires. But a very straightforward (though extremely falli-ble) surmise still follows immediately from the fact that John desires to meet Jane (especially if this desire is a goal or an intention) and from this fact *alone*. Namely, eventually John *will* meet Jane (say, after he gets back from Latvia). For example, it is a lot more likely, given that he desires to meet *Jane*, that he will meet Jane at some point in his career than it is that he will meet any other girl randomly selected from the world's population. For functional devices (as a class) are more like-ly to perform their proper functions than to cause any other effects chosen at random. The intentional characterization of John, "He wants to meet...," where the blank space is filled in and read fully trans-parently, *does* give us a handle on what John might well do and certain-ly a handle by which we may later be able to explain why John did what he did do, though not a handle that fits into a deductive or nomo-logical scheme.

Further, from the fact that John desires to meet Jane, we can say something about *how* John's desire will probably get fulfilled, *if* it gets fulfilled. Folk psychology understands not only the main proper func-tions of desires but understands something about the functional analysis of the mechanisms that produce their fulfillment, that is, about the sub-sidiary proper functions of desires. John will gather relevant informa-tion and, using his desire as premise, make practical inferences on the basis of which he will act—that's how his desire will get fulfilled, if it gets fulfilled Normally.

Exactly *what* information might be used and *what* inferences might be made is not, of course, specified in saying what desires John has. For example, if both John and Bill want to meet Jane, the identity conditions in accordance with which they have the same desire make no reference to what information each has or might gather or to what inferences each might make. For them to have the same desire it is enough that each be in a state proper functions of which are (1) to meet Jane and (2) to accomplish this by use of appropriate information and inference. Hence an analysis of John's and Bill's concepts of Jane is of no interest here; no reference is made to how each thinks of Jane or how each would recognize Jane if he met her. The networks of inference dispositions that fill out John's and Bill's concepts, their internal wiring, their specific "input-output dispositions" are all irrelevant to whether or not they have the same desire.

But it is tempting to think that if only we did know all of John's beliefs and desires, we would be able to predict his moment-by-moment behavior, that, barring breakdowns of the cognitive systems, folk psychology does contain an implicit nomological theory after all. This theory, it is traditionally thought, is obtained by mapping the logical connections among John's beliefs and desires and between these and sensory data onto inference dispositions and "input-output" dispositions. Putting aside current arguments to the effect that the input-output-plus-inference dispositions that characterize a person's brain could not in fact determine the semantic contents of his beliefs nor vice versa (for example, Putnam 1975b; Burge 1979, 1982; Stich 1983), there is a quicker reason to reject this traditional view. It has long been recognized that strict mapping of logical implications onto inference dispositions is not possible since people do not always believe the logical consequences of their own beliefs. More recently it has been noticed (for example, Minsky 1981, Bach 1985, Dennett 1984) that if people did believe (in a nondispositional sense of "believe," that is, if they "core-believed," stored, or ground out) all of the consequences of their beliefs their heads would soon be filled with trash to the overflow mark and they would grind to a halt trying to make the simplest practical decisions. Clearly, the failure to make all of the inferences that one's beliefs entail is not just a result of malfunction or faulty design. If it is a subsidiary proper function of our beliefs and desires to participate in processes of inference, there must also be mechanisms in us that tell them when to engage in this pastime, that tell us when to run our inference-making systems and with which beliefs and desires. Just as logic tells us nothing about how to construct proofs but only how to check them for validity, so it tells us nothing about these mechanisms, hence nothing about any actual inference dispositions. In no sense, then, is folk psychology a Sellarsian theory.[13]

7 Beliefs

If that is the sort of postulated thing that the folk call a desire, what sort of thing is a belief? One of its proper functions is to participate in inferences in such a manner as to help produce fulfillment of desires. That much is obvious if my claim was correct that desires have as a subsidiary proper function to participate in practical inferences along with beliefs. But that much, taken alone, yields no information about how beliefs are named, about their type-identity conditions, hence no clue about what gives them specific semantic content. Beliefs are not typed (named) by telling *which* desires they are supposed to sponsor, nor, it seems plausible, do belief tokens have as proper functions to help fulfill one desire more than another. For similar reasons, although another proper function of beliefs is surely to participate in inferences to yield other beliefs, true ones, this proper function also yields no identity conditions for beliefs. What I will argue is that beliefs are not typed (as beliefs that p versus beliefs that q) in accordance with any particular proper functions that they have but in accordance with certain of the conditions that must obtain if they are to fulfill their proper functions (for example, helping to fulfill some-desires-or-other) *in accordance with a Normal explanation.*

A clue that suggests this thesis lies with the labels "true" and "false," with which the folk evaluate beliefs. Notice that these labels are not

---

13. It is true that folk psychology attributes to people belief in the straightforward logical consequences of their beliefs. But this is because the folk count mere propensities to core believe as beliefs. The point is that these propensities are not *laws*. Compare: "Dogs bite" attributes a propensity to dogs but not a law or a disposition—at least not if "disposition" makes reference to there being some definite conditions under which dogs always bite.

applied to desires or intentions. Philosophers seeking symmetries have espied one between "true" versus "false" applied to beliefs and "fulfilled" versus "unfulfilled" applied to desires and they have invented the neutral "satisfied" versus "unsatisfied" to cover both these contrasts. Certainly there is a symmetry between true beliefs and fulfilled desires, one that I will discuss in section 9 below. But there is also an important asymmetry: false beliefs are *defective*, whereas unfulfilled desires are not. There is nothing wrong with me or my desire if I desire to visit China yet circumstances prevent my ever getting there or I decide I want to do something else more. But there *is* something wrong with me or with my belief if I believe that China is west of Europe. "True" and "false" are normative terms; "fulfilled" and "unfulfilled" are merely descriptive.

If a false belief were one that was defective in the same sense in which we speak of other things within the body as being defective, then a false belief would be one that was not likely to serve all of its proper functions. And indeed, according to folk psychology, though false beliefs may participate in inferences in a Normal way, they *are* unlikely to end up helping one to produce any new beliefs that are true or helping one to fulfill any of one's desires. Or if they do do this, this will not happen *in accordance with any Normal explanation*. For example, if John falsely believes that Jane languishes in Latvia, his resulting trip to Latvia may help him to fulfill some desire or other, perhaps even his burning desire to find the love of his life, say Lara or Aino. Maybe he will even meet someone in Latvia who knows where *Jane* is. But this will be an accident, not, presumably, a result of the elegant self-programming of his well-designed nervous system. More explicitly, it will not be the result of his nervous system's operating in accordance with general principles that also explained how his ancestors' nervous systems programmed themselves and used these programs so as to help them to proliferate.

Yet surely John's belief that Jane languishes in Latvia might help him to arrive at some new true belief or to fulfill some desires or other in accordance with a Normal explanation *if only Jane languished in Latvia*. This suggests that the truth condition of a belief is a *Normal condition* for fulfillment of proper functions that lie beyond simply participating in inferences. That is, the truth condition of a belief is one of the conditions that must obtain if the belief is to fulfill any such functions in accordance with a Normal explanation. Turning this another way, apparently beliefs are named or described (typed) in accordance with certain of their Normal conditions for functioning properly. For example, if both John and Bill believe that Jane languishes in Latvia, the identity conditions in accordance with which they have the same belief make no reference to John's or Bill's *concepts* of Jane or of Latvia, no reference to how each would describe or recognize Jane or Latvia nor to any specific kinds of inferences they are disposed to make using their respective beliefs. What John and Bill have in common is only that each harbors in him something that is supposed to participate in inferences so as to help produce new true beliefs and help fulfill desires but that cannot perform these latter functions Normally—that is, in accordance with principles relied upon during evolutionary design of the cognitive systems—unless Jane does languish in Latvia.

Now a Normal condition for sweating to cause cooling of the body is that the humidity is less than 100 percent. But that the body sweats when the humidity is not less than 100 percent does not entail that the sweating itself is abNormal or that something is wrong with the body. So why should the absence of a Normal condition for proper performance of a belief imply that the belief is defective? Consider this analogy. If we say, using slightly more precision, that a proper function of the sweating is to help return the body to its Normal temperature, then we see that the body's being overheated is another Normal condition for the sweating's serving its function. And absence of *this* Normal condition when the body is sweating does suggest that something is wrong with the body. For though it is a proper function of the sweat glands to secrete sweat, this is so only if and when the body is overheated. Similarly, presumably it is a proper function of the belief-manufacturing mechanisms in John to produce beliefs-that-*p* only if and when *p*, for example, beliefs that Jane is in Latvia only if and when Jane is in Latvia and beliefs that it is raining only if and when it is raining. To turn this around, a belief that Jane is in Latvia is, and is *essentially*, a thing that is not Normally in John unless Jane is indeed in Latvia.

Notice, however, that if the body sweats when not overheated it does not follow that the sweat glands themselves are defective. More likely, they are working under abNormal conditions, say, stimulated by substances that are not Normally in the blood stream or that are not Normally there unless the body is overheated. Similarly, that John has a false belief need not indicate that his belief-manufacturing mechanisms are faulty. Indeed, it need not indicate that anything *in* him is abNormal (except the belief). Perhaps his belief-making mechanisms have been laboring under *external* conditions not Normal for performance of their proper functions. For example, perhaps Bill told John that Jane was in Latvia and John's experience has been that Bill is a very reliable person. Normally functioning belief-making mechanisms must often rely on the principle that past regularities can be projected into the future. But, of course, such mechanisms will then perform properly and Normally only under the condition that this principle holds in the particular case, and it doesn't always hold. John's belief-making mechanisms are no more infallible than are his sweat glands, even when nothing is wrong with either. Similarly, when John perceives things wrongly this is not always the fault of his perceptual systems. Sometimes Normal conditions for proper functioning of these systems are not met, as when the train on the track next to the Latvian express leaves the station but John's perception is that it is his train that is leaving instead. The Normal condition that is not met here—a condition that his perceptual systems were built to rely upon or that he has learned, in a Normal way, to rely on—is that the moving object move relative to a background visible to John. Clearly, this is a condition that is not inside John.

Because our belief-making systems are dependent for their proper operation upon numerous conditions for which the body's systems are not responsible, it is not surprising if many of the beliefs of perfectly healthy people are false. Possibly, the systems that it is psychology's job to investigate are unique with regard to the high incidence of abNormal or malformed states or parts that they contain. And perhaps because false beliefs are not abnormal states, not states that are unusual, it has been easy to overlook the fact that false beliefs are abNormal states. The search has been for a functional description applying to "the belief that *p*," where "*p*" describes some given content, it being supposed to be quite irrelevant whether the belief that *p* is true or false. But to expect to find no fundamental difference between descriptions of what true beliefs do and descriptions of what false beliefs do is as absurd as to expect to find no fundamental difference between what healthy livers do and what jaundiced livers do.

8   Independence of Beliefs and Desires: Rational Animals

I have argued that folk psychology postulates inner items (for example, structures or events or states or entities) that have certain proper functions and Normal conditions for proper performance of these functions rather than postulating items that have certain dispositions, that obey certain laws, or that are *defined*, say, by reference to certain computational programs. I have promised to argue that folk psychology is probably right—that likely there are inner items that have the functions and depend on the conditions that folk psychology postulates. In order to do this, it will be necessary to fill in more details than folk psychology offers about the nature of these inner items. First, however, let us milk folk psychology as dry as possible.

According to the folk, *human* beliefs and desires interact with one another during processes called "inferences," but it is not clear that animal beliefs and desires must do this. For example, consider a toad that is swallowing lead pellets as fast as you toss them at him. It is natural to say (whether literally or by extension is not relevant here) that the toad thinks the pellets are bugs. It is natural to say this even after one understands that this behavior is really the expression of a simple tropism or reflex over which no Normally malleable part of the toad has control, that there is no division of toad aspects or toad modes to correspond to the division between believing the pellets are bugs and wanting to eat bugs, in short, that nothing like practical inference is going on in the toad. We say that the toad thinks the pellets are bugs merely because we take it that the toad's behavior would fulfill its proper functions (its "purposes") Normally only if these were bugs *and* that this behavior occurs Normally (not necessarily normally) only upon encounter with bugs. Similarly, we may say of a lobster held firmly by the thorax that it is trying to, that it wants to, pinch us but can't reach, and we say of the toad that what it really wants is to eat bugs. That is, we attribute a desire to a primitive animal whenever it exhibits behavior that we take to have a certain proper function even though we may be certain that the animal is incapable of making inferences or uncertain whether it is capable of this.

But when we (the folk) turn to humans or to animals we take to be more like humans, say dogs and cats, we are not so indiscriminate. For example, we do not attribute a desire to prevent a foreign object from entering the eye either to you or to your dog just because the eye-blink reflex is triggered. What more, exactly, do we require for belief and desire in the case of humans? Folk theory is not precise on this matter, but at least these two theses can be mined from it.

1. In the human case, beliefs are separate entities from desires and nothing is both a belief and a desire. Contrast the belief of the toad swallowing lead pellets. His inner activity does not include separable states or features, one to correspond to his belief that the pellets are bugs, another to his desire to eat bugs. Or consider a bee doing a bee dance. The bee dance might be said to express either a belief that there is nectar at a certain location or a desire that fellow worker bees should go to that location or both. But it is unlikely that there is any distinction *within* the performing bee to correspond to the distinction between belief and desire—unlikely that the bee either believes or desires anything in the human way.

2. In the human case, beliefs and desires are things that can interact with other beliefs and desires to form new beliefs and desires. That is, beliefs and desires can participate in inference processes. Further, no strictures beyond relevance (some semblance of logic) determine which beliefs and desires may interact with which to form new beliefs and desires or help to produce actions; beliefs are not hooked to certain uses and unavailable for others. Contrast the toad's belief that these are bugs, which is fixedly hooked to its desire to eat bugs. If I believe that something is a beefsteak, I may well use this belief for some purpose other than to fulfill a desire to eat beefsteak, but the toad's belief has no such independence. Also contrast any behavior that is merely a response conditioned to a stimulus. The rat that has been conditioned to press a bar for food when the little green light goes on may be said to believe, when the light goes on, that if he presses the bar food will appear. But only if this belief could be unhooked from his desire to eat food and turned to other purposes (perhaps it could be) would it be like a human belief.

In short, according to folk theory, humans can collect information without having any particular uses for that information in mind, and they can have desires without knowing how to fulfill them. Surely there is no reason to challenge the folk on this point. Indeed, this sort of in-dependence between beliefs and desires, coupled with the ability to combine beliefs and desires in novel ways, is surely the essence of rationality. Thus, not only are human beliefs and desires entities the identity conditions for which make no reference to specific uses or to specific means of fulfillment (beyond that these means include infer-ence); they are free-floating entities the actual mechanics of which must be free from such specifics too. What kind of mechanics might accord with such a description of human beliefs and desires?

9 Inner Maps

On this matter, folk theory offers no guidance. But the philosophical tradition, reaching back at least as far as the wax impressions in Plato's *Theaetetus*, offers a theory that, though currently out of favor, does describe human beliefs and desires as quite independent things. The doctrine of modern computationalism that inner representations are representations in part because they are "calculated over"—because they do something like participating in inferences—is, I believe, peculiar to our times. The classical position was that inner representations are representations because they are *like* what they are *about*. According to this view, beliefs and desires are inner "impressions" or "images" or "pictures" of sorts: beliefs are pictures of what is or was or will be; desires are pictures of what will be if the desires produce their proper results. Thus beliefs and desires could be stored quite inde-pendently of one another, then brought out to interact during processes of inference.

This classical theory is easily parodied. Imagine blue and triangular brain states standing for blue and triangular things, beautiful brain states standing for beautiful things, etc. And imagine a little man inside the brain looking at these colorful brain states and interpreting them. For why would it matter whether or not the states were like what they represented unless someone needed to understand them? At one time Wittgenstein (1922) thought that the first part of this parody could be averted by thinking of the likeness between a thought and the "fact" it represented as a very abstract formal likeness—likeness in "logical form." Roughly, the idea was that something like mathematical mapping relations correlated the domain of thought with the world. But unfortunately, mathematical mapping relations are embrassingly legion (Wittgenstein 1953, Quine 1960, Putnam 1978b). An indefinite number of them can be defined that will correlate, in one way or another, any two domains of entities having much size or complexity. Which of these, which sort of abstract "similarity," is the kind, then, that makes inner representations represent?

Suppose we begin by considering a very familiar and nonmysterious example of a biological device that works by "picturing" something else: a bee dance. The bee dance represents the location of nectar that has been spotted by the dancing bee; it is "about" the location of nectar. At least, it is natural to say this. Bee dances seem to be like inner representations conceived of on the classical model though not on the contemporary model that requires inner representations to be "calculated over." Let me try to spell out exactly what is involved in this case of "representing."[14]

Assume that proper functions of a bee dance are causing watching bees to fly towards nectar, causing watching bees to find nectar, causing nectar to be gathered into the hive, etc. Then any bee dance *that serves its proper functions in accordance with a Normal explanation* (that part is important) is related in this way to other bee dances that do the same: transformations of the dance (say, rotate the axis of the dance 20 degrees clockwise) correspond one-to-one to transformations of the location of nectar relative to hive and sun (say, shift the nectar 20 degrees further west off a direct line between sun and hive). Thus, although the bee dance is not what one would ordinarily call "similar" to what it represents, it is a kind of map or picture *when all goes Normally.*

Now notice these things. First, which mapping rule (which transformation correlation) is the relevant one to mention, which rule determines what the dance represents, is quite obvious. This rule is determined by the evolutionary history of the bee. It is that in accordance with which the dance must map onto the world in order to function properly in accordance with a Normal explanation or, what is the same, in order that the mechanisms within watching bees that physi-

14. I am using the term "representation" in the usual way here, not in the technical sense used in *LTOBC*, where full-fledged "representations" are contrasted with mere "intentional icons." See also chapter 5 herein.

cally translate the dance pattern into a direction of flight should perform all of their proper functions (including getting the bees to nectar) in accordance with a Normal explanation. Second, although the dance can serve its proper functions only because it is a sort of map or abstract likeness of where the nectar is, there is no need for any little man inside the interpreting bee to know about this likeness. Interpreting bees just react to the dance appropriately, allowing it to guide them. Third, bee dances have the characteristic feature that Brentano associated with intentionality: unlike natural signs and natural information carriers, say photographs, they can be of or about something that does not exist. For when a bee dance is wrongly executed and does not map the location of any actual nectar according to B-mese rules, as long as it is still a B-mese well-formed formula, one can still say where there would have had to have been nectar for it to serve its proper functions Normally. One can say what its "truth conditions" are.

When all goes properly and Normally, the bee dance also maps onto the resulting direction of flight of watching bees and onto the place they end up after flight. It is not merely an "indicative" representation but also an "imperative" one. As an imperative representation, it has fulfillment conditions, these being different from its truth conditions in that they correspond to proper functions of the dance rather than to Normal conditions for performance of its functions. Like the toad's belief that these are bugs and his desire to eat bugs, these two aspects of the dance—the indicative and the imperative—cannot be torn apart. Bee dances express beliefs and desires in the sense in which toads have beliefs and desires. But it is pretty certain that they do not express beliefs and desires in the sense in which humans have these. Bees, as Bennett (1964) has observed, are not rational.

Now try this. Call the actual condition or state of affairs in the world that makes a human belief that is true to be true, or that makes a fulfilled desire to be fulfilled, its "real value" (this not to be confused with its truth condition or with its meaning: only beliefs and desires that are satisfied have real values) Then, adding what we have learned from folk psychology, having a real value is one condition that is needed in order that a human belief should help to fulfill desires or to help produce more true beliefs in accordance with a Normal explanation. And a real value to correspond to is one thing that it is a proper function of a desire to produce—to cause to be. Now postulate that the real value of a human belief or desire has a second characteristic: there are transformations (notice, not "aspects" or "parts") of the belief or desire that correspond one-to-one to transformations of its real value so as to produce other thought/real-value pairs in a systematic way. Notice how such transformations differ from the kind described by transformational grammars: they turn representations into other representations having different subject matter. For example, a transformation performed on the belief that x loves y might produce the belief that y loves x, the same transformation applied twice returning us to the original. The corresponding transformation of real value would operate on the state of affairs that is x's loving y to produce y's loving x. Possibly most of the transformations in accordance with which beliefs and desires map are substitution transformations, that is, they have the form, *substitute such-and-such into the what's-it-called place.* (In *LTOBC*, I argued that this is the most common kind of transformation in accordance with which language maps onto the world.) For example, the belief that John loves Aino may be a transformation of the belief that John loves Jane by the transformation rule *substitute the such-and-such mental structure* (the one naming Aino) *into the such-and-such* (direct object?) *place.* Perhaps this transformation corresponds to the transformation upon real value, *substitute Aino into the patient role.* In this way, we suppose, when all goes properly and Normally, beliefs and desires map onto real values in accordance with determinate rules.[15] And when a belief is not true or a desire is not fulfilled, still we can say what its real value would have had to have been for all to go properly and Normally, what its satisfaction conditions are, for these are determined by the same rules.

Thus folk psychology, embellished with something akin to the traditional notion that thoughts are like impressions or pictures, might be placed in the context of modern physiology to yield a theory of content

15. Notice that this is not a traditional way to describe the mapping of intentional items onto the world. It correlates *whole* beliefs with *whole* conditions or affairs in the world and correlates *transformations* of these with *transformations* of world affairs, rather than beginning by correlating mental "terms" with their referents, then building up to mental "sentences." The reasons for describing the mapping functions that correlate intentional items with their real values in this way are discussed in *LTOBC*, chap. 6.

for beliefs and desires, a naturalist theory of intentionality.[16] Such a theory would place few restrictions on or, to turn things around, would give little guidance to the physiological psychologist speculating a priori about what beliefs and desires are like physically. Structures, states, entities, and events are all things to which mathematical transformations can apply, and transformations are of many kinds (the most flexible being substitution transformations). So beliefs and desires might be "pictures" in a very abstract sense indeed. Still, to tell the scientist that he should search for some kind of picturing system in the brain, for mechanisms that can produce pictures of actual states of affairs (belief-producing mechanisms), for other mechanisms that can use pictures to produce corresponding states of affairs (desire-fulfilling mechanisms), and for mechanisms that allow these various pictures to interact with one another roughly as folk psychology says they do—that is to tell him what *problem* he is trying to solve. Obviously there is no way to begin an empirical investigation without some such guidance. One has to know what one is investigating!

10 Some Implications

Given this embellished folk theory, it would be easy enough to see how the human brain qua manipulator of symbols in accordance with their "forms" or "shapes" is the same as the brain qua "semantic engine"—as appraiser of meanings and author of truths.[17] Representations that the brain manipulates or calculates over are symbols at all—are things having a *significant* "shape" or "form"—only insofar as they are, first, semantic items, items that map onto the world when they succeed in

16. As for the prospect that contemporary functionalism will eventually explain intentionality (this to be carefully distinguished from explaining intelligence or smartness—see Fodor 1980 and Cummins 1983), one of the most clearheaded champions of this approach has recently said of it, ". . . hard to swallow. . . . Yet I think we had better try hard to swallow it, and digest it too, because, to echo Fodor, there just isn't any other definite proposal in the offing" (Cummins 1983, 90). This is followed by discussion of five unsuccessful functionalist recipes for intentionality and a rough suggestion for further culinary experiments. Surely, it would be indelicate for an unbeliever to interrupt this preparation for a last supper. Better just to place another definite proposal in the offing—as I have tried to do here and in *LTOBC*.
17. The "shapes" metaphor is Jerry Fodor's (1980). The term "semantic engine" is Daniel Dennett's (1981a).

performing their full proper functions Normally. Compare Dretske's concern (1983, 88): "I wonder what makes a structure's role a *conceptual/inferential* role. . . . It presupposes that the structures over which computations are being performed already have semantic content. Where did they get it?" But for beliefs and desires to function properly and Normally, they must participate in inference processes, that is, they must be calculated over or manipulated. And the *way* they are Normally manipulated must be sensitive to all the differences between them that are *significant* differences in "shape" or "form," that accord with differences in semantic content. Indeed, *that* these differences correspond to genuine differences in semantic content *depends* on the fact that these symbols are Normally manipulated differently, that is, on the fact that different manipulations accord with their subsidiary proper functions. How else could their more removed proper functions (re: desires) or Normal conditions for proper performance (re: beliefs) be different? Thus there is no distinction between the brain as symbol manipulator and as semantic engine.

Similarly, if beliefs and desires are maps of the sort I have described, the distinction that some have wished to draw between an inner representation and a propositional attitude, the latter construed as a relation to the representation of the person or system that has or processes the representation, is at best moot. Suppose that an inner representation were the sort of item that could be removed with tweezers and set under a microscope. Just as a beef heart that lies in the market is still a heart, the representation would still be a belief, desire, visual image or whatever it had been. Not that you could tell, just by inspecting it and seeing what it could do, that it was this. You would have to know or guess its history: that it came out of a body and that it was designed by evolution, or by learning systems that evolution had designed, to serve a certain kind of function. For example, an extracted belief would remain a belief because it would still be the sort of biological item that, in order to function properly and Normally, needed to be embedded in a system that used it in a very specific way, a way that required that it map *so* onto the world.

4

Biosemantics

Causal or informational theories of the semantic content of mental states which have had an eye on the problem of false representations have characteristically begun with something like this intuition. There are some circumstances under which an inner representation has its represented as a necessary and/or sufficient cause or condition of production. That is how the content of the representation is fixed. False representations are to be explained as tokens that are produced under other circumstances. The challenge, then, is to tell what defines certain circumstances as the content-fixing ones.

1

Note that the answer cannot be just that these circumstances are *statistically* normal conditions. To gather such statistics, one would need to delimit a reference class of occasions, know how to count its members, and specify description categories. It would not do, for example, just to average over conditions-in-the-universe-any-place-any-time. Nor is it given how to carve out relevant description categories for conditions on occasions. Is it "average" in the summer for it to be (precisely) between 80 and 80.5 degrees Fahrenheit with humidity 87 percent? And are average conditions those which obtain on at least 50 percent of the occasions, or is it 90 percent? Depending on how one sets these parameters, radically different conditions are "statistically normal." But the notion of semantic content clearly is not relative, in this manner, to arbitrary parameters. The content-fixing circumstances must be *non-arbitrarily* determined.

A number of recent writers have made an appeal to teleology here, specifically to conditions of normal function or well functioning of the systems that produce inner representations. Where the represented is R and its representation is "R," under conditions of well functioning, we might suppose, only Rs can or are likely to produce "R"s. Or perhaps "R" is a representation of R just in case the system was designed to react to Rs by producing "R"s. But this sort of move yields too many representations. Every state of every functional system has normal causes, things that it is a response to in accordance with design. These causes may be proximate or remote, and many are disjunctive. Thus, a proximate normal cause of dilation of the skin capillaries is certain substances in the blood, more remote causes include muscular effort, sunburn, and being in an overheated environment. To each of these causes the vascular system responds by design, yet the response (a red face), though it may be a natural sign of burn or exertion or overheating, certainly is not a representation of that. If not every state of a system represents its normal causes, which are the states that do?

Jerry Fodor (1986a) has said that, whereas the content of an inner representation is determined by some sort of causal story, its status *as* a representation is determined by the functional organization of the part of the system which uses it. There is such a thing, it seems, as behaving like a representation without behaving like a representation of anything in particular. What the thing is a representation of is then determined by its cause under content-fixing conditions. It would be interesting to have the character of universal I-am-a-representation behavior spelled out for us. Yet, as Fodor well knows, there would still be the problem of demonstrating that there was only one normal cause per representation type.

A number of writers, including Dennis Stampe (1979), Fred Dretske (1986), and Mohan Matthen (1988), have suggested that what is different about effects that are representations is that their function is, precisely, to represent, "indicate," or "detect." For example, Matthen says of (fullfledged) perceptual states that they are "state[s] that [have] the function of *detecting* the presence of things of a certain type" (1988, 20). It does not help to be told that inner representations are things that have representing (indicating, detecting) as their function, however, unless we are also told what kind of activity representing (indicating, detecting) is. Matthen does not tell us how to naturalize the notion "detecting." If "detecting" is a function of a representational state, it must be something that the state effects or produces. For example, it cannot be the function of a state to have *been* produced in response to something. Or does Matthen mean that it is not the representational states themselves but the part of the system which produces them which has the function of detecting? It has the function, say, of producing states that correspond to or covary with something in the outside world. But unfortunately, not every device whose job description includes producing items that vary with the world is a representation producer. The devices in me that produce calluses are supposed to vary their placement according to where the friction is, but calluses are not representations. The pigment arrangers in the skin of a chameleon, the function of which is to vary the chameleon's color with what it sits on, are not representation producers.

Stampe and Dretske do address the question what representing or (Dretske) "detecting" is. Each brings in his own description of what a natural sign or natural representation is, then assimilates *having the function of representing R* to being a natural sign or representer of *R* when the system functions normally. Now the production of natural signs is undoubtedly an accidental side effect of normal operation of many systems. From my red face you can tell that either I have been exerting myself or I have been in the heat or I am burned. But the production of an accidental side effect, no matter how regular, is not one of a system's functions; that goes by definition. More damaging, however, it simply is not true that representations must carry natural information. Consider the signals with which various animals signal danger. Nature knows that it is better to err on the side of caution, and it is likely that many of these signs occur more often in the absence than in the presence of any real danger. Certainly there is nothing incoherent in the idea that this might be so, hence that many of these signals do not carry natural information concerning the dangers they signal.

2

I fully agree, however, that an appeal to teleology, to function, is what is needed to fly a naturalist theory of content. Moreover, what makes a thing into an inner representation is, near enough, that its function is to represent. But, I shall argue, the way to unpack this insight is to focus on representation *consumption*, rather than representation production. It is the devices that *use* representations that determine these to be representations and, at the same time (contra Fodor), determine their content. If it really is the function of an inner representation to indicate its represented, clearly it is not just a natural sign, a sign that you or I looking on might interpret. It must be one that functions as a sign or representation *for the system itself*. What is it, then, for a system to use a representation *as* a representation?

The conception of function on which I shall rely was defined in *LTOBC* and defended in chapter 1 under the label "proper function." Proper functions are determined by the histories of the items possessing them; functions that were "selected for" are paradigm cases.[1] The notions "function" and "design" should not be read, however, as referring only to origin. Natural selection does not slack after the emergence of a structure but actively preserves it by acting against the later emergence of less fit structures. And structures can be preserved due to performance of new functions unrelated to the forces that originally shaped them. Such functions are "proper functions" too and are "performed in accordance with design."

The notion "design" should not be read—and this is very important—as a reference to innateness. A system may have been designed to be altered by its experience, perhaps to learn from its experience in a prescribed manner. Doing what it has learned to do in this manner is then "behaving in accordance with design" or "functioning properly" (*LTOBC* and chapters 3, 11 herein).

My term "normal" should be read normatively, historically, and relative to specific function. In the first instance, "normal" applies to explanations. A "normal explanation" explains the performance of a particular function, telling how it was (typically) historically performed on those (perhaps rare) occasions when it was properly performed. Normal explanations do not tell, say, why it has been common for a function to be performed; they are not statistical explanations. They

---

1. An odd custom exists of identifying this sort of view with Larry Wright, who does not hold it. See chapter 1. Genetic selection is not the only source of proper functions. See *LTOBC*, chaps. 1 and 2.

cover only past times of actual performance, showing how these performances were entailed by natural law, given certain conditions, coupled with the dispositions and structures of the relevant functional devices.[2] In the second instance, "normal" applies to conditions. A "normal condition for performance of a function" is a condition the presence of which must be mentioned in giving a full normal explanation for performance of that function. Other functions of the same organism or system may have other normal conditions. For example, normal conditions for discriminating colors are not the same as normal conditions for discriminating tastes, and normal conditions for seeing very large objects are not the same as for seeing very small ones. It follows that "normal conditions" must not be read as having anything to do with what is typical or average or even, in many cases, at all common. First, many functions are performed only rarely. For example, very few wild seeds land in conditions normal for their growth and development, and the protective colorings of caterpillars seldom actually succeed in preventing them from being eaten. Indeed, normal conditions might almost better be called "historically optimal" conditions. (If normal conditions for proper functioning, hence survival and proliferation, were a statistical norm, imagine how many rabbits there would be in the world.) Second, many proper functions only need to be performed under rare conditions. Consider, for example, the vomiting reflex, the function of which is to prevent (further) toxification of the body. A normal condition for performance of this function is presence, specifically, of poison in the stomach, for (I am guessing) it is only under that condition that this reflex has historically had beneficial effects. But poison in the stomach certainly is not an average condition. (Nor, of course, is it a normal condition for other functions of the digestive system.[3])

2. This last clarification is offered to aid Fodor ("On there not being an evolutionary theory of content," hereafter "NETC," unpublished), who uses my term "Normal" (here I am not capitalizing it, but the idea has not changed) in a multiply confused way, making a parody of my views on representation. In this connection, see also nn. 5 and 9.

3. "Normal explanation" and "normal condition for performance of a function," along with "proper function," are defined with considerable detail in *LTOBC*. The reader may wish, in particular, to consult the discussion of normal explanations for performance of "adapted and derived proper functions" in

If it is actually one of a system's functions to produce representations, as I have said, these representations must function as representations for the system itself. Let us view the system, then, as divided into two parts or two aspects, one of which produces representations for the other to consume. What we need to look at is the consumer part, at what it is to use a thing *as* a representation. Indeed, a good look at the consumer part of the system ought to be all that is needed to determine not only representational status but representational content. I argue this as follows. First, the part of the system which consumes representations must understand the representations proffered to it. Suppose, for example, that there were abundant "natural information" (in Dretske's, 1981, sense) contained in numerous natural signs all present in a certain state of a system. This information could still not serve the system *as* information, unless the signs were understood by the system, and, furthermore, understood as bearers of whatever specific information they in fact do bear. (Contrast Fodor's notion that something could function like a representation without functioning like a representation of anything in particular.) So there must be something about the consumer that *constitutes* its taking the signs to indicate, say, *p*, *q*, and *r* rather than *s*, *t*, and *u*. But if we know what constitutes the consumer's *taking* a sign to indicate *p*, what *q*, what *r*, etc., then, granted that the consumer's takings are in some way systematically derived from the structures of the signs so taken, we can construct a semantics for the consumer's language. Anything the signs may indicate qua natural signs or natural information carriers then drops out as entirely irrelevant; the representation-producing side of the system had better pay undivided attention to the language of its consumer. The sign producer's function will be to produce signs that are true *as the consumer reads the language*.

The problem for the naturalist bent on describing intentionality, then, does not concern representation production at all. Although a representation always is something that is produced by a system whose prop-

---

chap. 2 of that work, for these functions cover functions of states of the nervous system which result in part from learning, such as states of human belief and desire.

er function is to make that representation correspond by rule to the world, what the rule of correspondence is, what gives definition to this function, is determined entirely by the representation's consumers.

For a system to use an inner item as a representation, I propose, is for the following two conditions to be met. First, unless the representation accords *so* (by a certain rule) with a represented, the consumer's normal use of, or response to, the representation will not be able to fulfill all of the consumer's proper functions in so responding—not, at least, in accordance with a normal explanation. (Of course, it might still fulfill these functions by freak accident, but not in the historically normal way.) Putting this more formally, that the representation and the represented accord with one another so is a normal condition for proper functioning of the consumer device as it reacts to the representation.[4] Note that the proposal is not that the content of the representation rests on the function of the representation or of the consumer, on what these do. The idea is not that there is such a thing as behaving like a representation of X or as being treated like a representation of X. The content hangs only on there being a certain condition that would be *normal* for performance of the consumer's functions, namely, that a certain correspondence relation hold between sign and world, whatever those functions may happen to be. For example, suppose the semantic rules for my belief representations are determined by the fact that belief tokens in me will aid the devices that use them to perform certain of their tasks in accordance with a normal explanation for success only under the condition that the forms or "shapes" of these belief tokens correspond, in accordance with said rules, to conditions in the world. Just what these user tasks are need not be mentioned.[5]

4. Strictly, this normal condition must derive from a "most proximate normal explanation" of the consumer's proper functioning. See *LTOBC*, chap. 6, where a more precise account of what I am here calling "representations" is given under the heading "intentional icons."

5. In this particular case, one task is surely contributing, in conformity with certain general principles or rules, to practical inference processes, hence to the fulfillment of current desires. So, if you like, all beliefs have the *same* proper function. Or, since the rules or principles that govern practical inference dictate that a belief's "shape" determines what other inner representations it may properly be combined with to form what products, we could say that each belief has a *different* range of proper functions. Take your pick. Compare Fodor 1989 and "NETC."

Second, represented conditions are conditions that vary, depending on the *form* of the representation, in accordance with specifiable correspondence rules that give the semantics for the relevant *system* of representation. More precisely, representations always admit of significant transformations (in the mathematical sense), which accord with transformations of their corresponding representeds, thus displaying significant articulation into variant and invariant aspects. If an item considered as compounded of certain variant and invariant aspects can be said to be "composed" of these, then we can also say that every representation is, as such, a member of a representational system having a "compositional semantics." For it is not that the represented condition is itself a normal condition for proper operation of the representation consumer. A certain correspondence between the representation and the world is what is normal. Coordinately, there is no such thing as a representation consumer that can understand only one representation. There are always other representations, composed other ways, saying other things, which it could have understood as well, in accordance with the same principles of operation. A couple of very elementary examples should make this clear.[6]

First, consider beavers, who splash the water smartly with their tails to signal danger. This instinctive behavior has the function of causing other beavers to take cover. The splash means danger, because only when it corresponds to danger does the instinctive response to the splash on the part of the interpreter beavers, the consumers, serve a purpose. If there is no danger present, the interpreter beavers interrupt their activities uselessly. Hence, that the splash corresponds to danger is a normal condition for proper functioning of the interpreter beavers' instinctive reaction to the splash. (It does not follow, of course, that it is a usual condition. Beavers being skittish, most beaver splashes possibly occur in response to things not in fact endangering the beaver.) In the beaver-splash semantic system, the time and place of the splash varies with, "corresponds to," the time and place of danger. The representa-

---

6. These examples are of representations that are not "inner" but out in the open. As in the case of inner representations, however, they are produced and consumed by mechanisms designed to cooperate with one another; each such representation stands intermediate between two parts of a single biological system.

tion is articulate: properly speaking, it is not a splash but a splash-at-a-time-and-a-place. Other representations in the same system, splashes at other times and places, indicate other danger locations.

Second, consider honey bees, which perform "dances" to indicate the location of sources of nectar they have discovered. The tempo of the dance and the angle of its long axis vary with the distance and direction of the nectar. The interpreter mechanisms in the watching bees—these are the representation consumers—will not perform their full proper functions of aiding the process of nectar collection in accordance with a normal explanation unless the location of nectar corresponds correctly to the dance. So the dances are representations of the location of nectar. The full representation here is a dance-at-a-time-in-a-place-at-a-tempo-with-an-orientation.

Notice that, on this account, it is not necessary to assume that most representations are true. Many biological devices perform their proper functions not on the average but just often enough. The protective coloring of the juveniles of many animal species, for example, is an adaptation passed on because *occasionally* it prevents a juvenile from being eaten, though most of the juveniles of these species get eaten anyway. Similarly, it is conceivable that the devices that fix human beliefs fix true ones not on the average, but just often enough. If the true beliefs are functional and the false beliefs are, for the most part, no worse than having an empty mind, then even very fallible belief-fixing devices might be better than no belief-fixing devices at all. These devices might even be, in a sense, "designed to deliver some falsehoods." Perhaps, given the difficulty of designing highly accurate belief-fixing mechanisms, it is actually advantageous to fix too many beliefs, letting some of these be false, rather than fix too few beliefs. Coordinately, perhaps our belief-consuming mechanisms are carefully designed to tolerate a large proportion of false beliefs. It would not follow, of course, that the belief consumers are designed to *use* false beliefs, certainly not that false beliefs can serve all of the functions that true ones can. Indeed, if none of the mechanisms that used beliefs ever cared at all how or whether these beliefs corresponded to anything in the world, beliefs would surely be functioning not as representations but in some other capacity.

Shifting our focus from producing devices to consuming devices in our search for naturalized semantic content is important. But the shift from the *function* of consumers to *normal conditions* for proper operation is equally important. Matthen, for example, characterizes what he calls a "quasi-perceptual state" as, roughly, one whose job is to cause the system to do what it must do to perform its function, given that it is in certain circumstances, which are what it represents. Matthen is thus looking pretty squarely at the representation consumers, but at what it is the representation's job to get these consumers to do, rather than at normal conditions for their proper operation. As a result, Matthen now retreats. The description he has given of quasi-perceptual states, he says, cannot cover "real perception such as that which we humans experience. Quite simply, there is no such thing as *the* proper response, or even a range of functionally appropriate responses, to what perception tells us" (1988, 20).[7] On the contrary, representational content rests not on univocity of consumer function but on sameness of normal conditions for those functions. The same percept of the world may be used to guide any of very many and diverse activities, practical or theoretical. What stays the same is that the percept must correspond to environmental configurations in accordance with the same correspondence rules for each of these activities. For example, if the position of the chair in the room does not correspond so to my visual representation of its position, that will hinder me equally in my attempts to avoid the chair when passing through the room, to move the chair, to sit in it, to remove the cat from it, to make judgments about it, etc. Similarly, my belief that New York is large may be turned to any of diverse purposes, but those which require it to be a *representation* require also that New York indeed be large if these purposes are to succeed in accordance with a normal explanation for functioning of my cognitive systems.

3

We have just cleanly bypassed the whole genre of causal-informational accounts of mental content. To illustrate this, we consider an example of Dretske's. Dretske tells of a certain species of Northern Hemisphere bacteria which orient themselve away from toxic oxygen-rich surface water by attending to their magnetosomes, tiny inner magnets,

7. Dretske (1986, 28) and David Papineau (1987, 67ff.) have similar concerns.

which pull toward the magnetic north pole, hence pull down (1986). (Southern Hemisphere bacteria have their magnetosomes reversed.) The function of the magnetosome thus appears to be to effect that the bacterium moves into oxygen-free water. Correlatively, intuition tells us that what the pull of the magnetosome represents is the where-abouts of oxygen-free water. The direction of oxygen-free water is not, however, a factor in *causing* the direction of pull of the magneto-some. And the most reliable natural information that the magnetosome carries is surely not about oxygen-free water but about distal and prox-imal causes of the pull, about the direction of geomagnetic or better, just plain magnetic, north. One can, after all, easily deflect the magneto-some away from the direction of lesser oxygen merely by holding a bar magnet overhead. Moreover, it is surely a function of the magnetosome to respond to that magnetic field, that is part of its normal mechanism of operation, whereas responding to oxygen density is not. None of this makes any sense on a causal or informational approach.

But on the biosemantic theory, it does make sense. What the mag-netosome represents is only what its *consumers* require that it cor-respond to in order to perform *their* tasks. Ignore, then, how the representation (a pull-in-a-direction-at-a-time) is normally produced. Concentrate instead on how the systems that react to the representation work, on what these systems need in order to do their job. What they need is only that the pull be in the direction of oxygen-free water at the time. For example, they care not at all how it came about that the pull is in that direction; the magnetosome that points toward oxygen-free water quite by accident and not in accordance with any normal ex-planation will do just as well as one that points that way for the normal reasons. (As Socrates concedes in the *Meno*, true opinion is just as good as knowledge, so long as it stays put.) What the magnetosome repre-sents, then, is univocal; it represents only the direction of oxygen-free water. For that is the only thing that corresponds (by a compositional rule) to it, the absence of which would matter, the absence of which would disrupt the function of those mechanisms that rely on the mag-netosome for guidance.

It is worth noting that what is represented by the magnetosome is not proximal but distal; no proximal stimulus is represented at all. Nor, of course, does the bacterium perform an inference from the existence of the proximal stimulus (the magnetic field) to the existence of the represented. These are good results for a theory of content to have, for otherwise one needs to introduce a derivative theory of content for mental representations that do not refer, say, to sensory stimulations, and also a foundationalist account of belief fixation. Note also that, on the present view, representations manufactured in identical ways by different species of animal might have different contents. Thus, a certain kind of small, swift image on the toad's retina, manufactured by his eye lens, represents a bug, for that is what it must correspond to if the reflex it (invariably) triggers is to perform its proper functions normally, while exactly the same kind of small swift image on the retina of a male hoverfly, manufactured, let us suppose, by a nearly identical lens, represents a passing female hoverfly, for that is what it must correspond to if the female-chasing reflex it (invariably) triggers is to perform its proper functions normally. Turning the coin over, representations with the same content may be normally manufactured in a diversity of ways, even in the same species. How many different ways do you have, for example, of telling a lemon or your spouse? Nor is it necessary that any of the ways one has of manufacturing a given representation be especially reliable ways in order for the representation to have determinate content. These various results cut the biosemantic approach off from all varieties of verificationism and foundationalism with a clean, sharp knife.

4

But perhaps it will be thought that belief fixation and consumption are not biologically proper activities, hence that there are no normal explanations, in my defined sense, for proper performances of human beliefs. Unlike bee dances, which are all variations on the same simple theme, beliefs in dinosaurs, in quarks, and in the instability of the dollar are recent, novel, and innumerably diverse, as are their possible uses. How could there be anything *biologically* normal or abnormal about the details of the consumption of such beliefs?

But what an organism does in accordance with evolutionary design can be very novel and surprising, for the more complex of nature's creatures are designed to learn. Unlike evolutionary adaptation, learning is not accomplished by *random* generate-and-test procedures. Even when learning involves trial and error (probably the exception rather than the rule), there are principles in accordance with which responses are selected by the system to try, and there are specific principles of generalization and discrimination, etc., which have been built into the system by natural selection. How these principles normally work, that is, how they work, given normal (i.e., historically optimal) environments, to produce changes in the learner's nervous system which will further ends of the system has, of course, an explanation—the normal explanation for proper performance of the learning mechanism and of the states of the nervous system it produces.

To use a worn-out comparison, there is an infinity of functions which a modern computer mainframe is capable of performing, depending upon its input and on the program it is running. Each of these things it can do, so long as it is not damaged or broken, "in accordance with design," and to each of these capacities there corresponds an explanation of how it would be activated or fulfilled normally. The human's mainframe takes, roughly, stimulations of the afferent nerves as input both to program and to run it.[8] It responds, in part, by developing concepts, by acquiring beliefs and desires in accordance with these concepts, by engaging in practical inference leading ultimately to action. Each of these activities may, of course, involve circumscribed sorts of trial and error learning. When conditions are optimal, all this aids survival and proliferation in accordance with a historically normal explanation, one of high generality, of course. When conditions are not optimal, it may yield, among other things, empty or confused concepts, biologically useless desires, and false beliefs. But even when the desires are biologically useless (though probably not when the concepts expressed in them are empty or confused), there are still biologically normal ways for them to get fulfilled, the most obvious of which require reliance on true beliefs.[9]

8. This is a broad metaphor. I am not advocating computationalism.
9. A word of caution. The normal conditions for a desire's fulfillment are not necessarily fulfillable conditions. In general, normal conditions for fulfillment of a function are not quite the same as conditions which, when you add them and stir, always effect proper function, because they may well be impossible conditions. For example, Fodor (1989 and "NETC") has questioned me about the normal conditions under which his desire that it should rain tomorrow will perform its proper function of *getting* it to rain. Now the biologically normal way

Yet how do we know that our contemporary ways of forming concepts, desires, and beliefs do occur in accordance with evolutionary design? Fodor, for example, is ready with the labels "pop Darwinism" and "naive adaptationism" to abuse anyone who supposes that our cognitive systems were actually selected for their belief- and desire-using capacities (1987, "NETC"). Clearly, to believe that every structure must have a function would be naive. Nor is it wise uncritically to adopt hypotheses about the functions of structures when these functions are obscure. It does not follow that we should balk at the sort of adaptationist who, having found a highly complex structure that quite evidently is currently and effectively performing a highly complex and obviously indispensable function, then concludes, *ceteris paribus*, that this function has been the most recent historical task stabilizing the structure. To suspect that the brain has not been preserved for thinking with or that the eye has not been preserved for seeing with—to suspect this, moreover, in the absence of any alternative hypotheses about causes of the stability of these structures—would be totally irresponsible. Consider: Nearly every human behavior is bound up with intentional action. Are we really to suppose that the degree to which our behaviors help to fulfill intentions, and the degree to which intentions result from logically related desires plus beliefs, is a sheer coincidence, that these patterns are irrelevant to survival and proliferation or, though relevant, have had no stabilizing effect on the gene pool? But the only alternative to biological design, in my sense of "design," is sheer coincidence, freak accident—unless there is a ghost running the machine![10]

---

for such a desire to be fulfilled is exactly the same as for any other desire: one has or acquires true beliefs about how to effect the fulfillment of the desire and acts on them. Biologically normal conditions for fulfillment of the desire for rain thus include the condition that one has true beliefs about how to make it rain. Clearly this is an example in which the biological norm fails to accord with the statistical norm: most desires about the weather are fulfilled, if at all, by biological accident. It may even be that the laws of nature, coupled with my situation, prohibit my having any true beliefs about how to make it rain; the needed general condition cannot be realized in the particular case. Similarly, normal conditions for proper function of beliefs in impossible things are, of course, impossible conditions: these beliefs are such that they cannot correspond, in accordance with the rules of Mentalese, to conditions in the world. For more on this theme, see chapter 8.

10. For more details, see chapter 2 herein.

Indeed, it is reasonable to suppose that the brain structures we have recently been using in developing space technology and elementary-particle physics have been operating in accordance with the very same general principles as when prehistoric man used them for more primitive ventures. They are no more performing new and different functions or operating in accordance with new and different principles nowadays than are the eyes when what they see is television screens and space shuttles. Compare: the wheel was invented for the purpose of rolling ox carts, and did not come into its own (pulleys, gears, etc.) for several thousand years thereafter, during the industrial revolution. Similarly, it is reasonable that the cognitive structures with which man is endowed were originally nature's solution to some very simple demands made by man's evolutionary niche. But the solution nature stumbled on was elegant, supremely general, and powerful; indeed, I believe it was a solution that cut to the very bone of the ontological structure of the world. That solution involved the introduction of representations, inner and/or outer, having a subject/predicate structure and subject to a negation transformation. (Why I believe that that particular development was so radical and so powerful has been explained in depth in *LTOBC*, chaps. 14–19. But see also subsection "Negation and propositional content" below.)

5

One last worry about my sort of position is voiced by Daniel Dennett (1978a) and discussed at length by Fodor (1986b). Is it really plausible that bacteria and paramecia, or even birds and bees, have inner representations in the same sense that we do? Am I really prepared to say that these creatures too have mental states, that they think? I am not prepared to say that. On the contrary, the representations that they have must differ from human beliefs in at least six very fundamental ways.[11]

11. Accordingly, in *LTOBC*, I did not call these primitive forms "representations" but "intentional signals" and, for items like bee dances, "intentional icons," reserving the term "representation" for those icons, whose representational values must be identified if their consumers are to function properly. See the subsection "Acts of identifying" below.

Self-representing elements

The representations that the magnetosome produces have three significant variables, each of which refers to itself. The time of the pull refers to the time of the oxygen-free water, the locale of the pull refers to the locale of the oxygen-free water, and the direction of pull refers to the direction of oxygen-free water. The beaver's splash has two self-referring variables: a splash at a certain time and place indicates that there is danger at that same time and place. (There is nothing necessary about this. It might have meant that there would be danger at the nearest beaver dam in five minutes.) Compare the standard color coding on the outsides of colored markers: each color stands for itself. True, it may be that sophisticated indexical representations such as percepts and indexical beliefs also have their time or place or both as significant self-representing elements, but they also have other significant variables that are not self-representing. The magnetosome does not.

Storing representations

Any representation the time or place of which is a significant variable obviously cannot be stored away, carried about with the organism for use on future occasions. Most beliefs are representations that can be stored away. Clearly, this is an important difference.

Indicative and imperative representations

The theory I have sketched here of the content of inner representations applies only to indicative representations, representations which are supposed to be determined by the facts, which tell what is the case. It does not apply to imperative representations, representations which are supposed to determine the facts, which tell the interpreter what to do. Neither do causal-informational theories of content apply to the contents of imperative representations. True, some philosophers seem to have assumed that having defined the content of various mental symbols by reference to what causes them to enter the "belief box," then when one finds these same symbols in, say, the "desire box" or the "intention box," one already knows what they mean. But how do we know that the desire box or the intention box use the same representational system as the belief box? To answer that question we would have to know what constitutes a desire box's or an intention box's using one representational system rather than another which, turned around, is the very question at issue. In *LTOBC* and chapters 3 and 8, I develop a parallel theory of the content of imperative representations. Very roughly, one of the proper functions of the consumer system for an imperative representation is to help *produce* a correspondence between the representation and the world. (Of course, this proper function often is not performed.) I also argue that desires and intentions are imperative representations.

Consider, then, the beaver's splash. It tells that there is danger here now. Or why not say instead that it tells other nearby beavers what to do now, namely, to seek cover? Consider the magnetosome. It tells which is the direction of oxygen-free water. Or why not say instead that it tells the bacterium which way to go? Simple animal signals are invariably both indicative and imperative. Even the dance of the honey bee, which is certainly no simple signal, is both indicative and imperative. It tells the worker bees where the nectar is; equally, it tells them where to go. The step from these primitive representations to human beliefs is an enormous one, for it involves the separation of indicative from imperative functions of the representational system. Representations that are undifferentiated between indicative and imperative connect states of affairs directly to actions, to specific things to be done in the face of those states of affairs. Human beliefs are not tied directly to actions. Unless combined with appropriate desires, human beliefs are impotent. And human desires are equally impotent unless combined with suitable beliefs.[12]

Inference

As indicative and imperative functions are separated in the central inner representational systems of humans, they need to be reintegrated. Thus, humans engage in practical inference, combining beliefs and desires in novel ways to yield first intentions and then action. Humans also combine beliefs with beliefs to yield new beliefs. Surely nothing remotely like this takes place inside the bacterium.

12. Possibly, human intentions are simultaneously in both indicative and imperative moods, however, functioning to represent settled facts about one's future and also to direct one's action.

Acts of identifying

Mediate inferences always turn on something like a middle term, which must have the same representational value in both premises for the inference to go through. Indeed, the representation consumers in us perform many functions that require them to use two or more overlapping representations together and in such a manner that, unless the represesenteds corresponding to these indeed have a common element, these functions will not be properly performed. Put informally, the consumer device *takes* these represented elements to be the same, thus identifying their representational values. Suppose, for example, that you intend to speak to Henry about something. In order to carry out this intention you must, when the time comes, be able to recognize Henry in perception as the person to whom you intend to speak. You must identify Henry as represented in perception with Henry as represented in your intention. Activities that involve the coordinated use of representations from different sensory modalities, as in the case of eye-hand coordination, visual-tactile coordination, also require that certain objects, contours, places, or directions, etc., be identified as the same through the two modalities. Now, the foundation upon which modern representational theories of thought are built depends upon a denial that what is thought of is ever placed before a naked mind. Clearly, we can never know what an inner representation represents by a direct comparison of representation to represented. Rather, acts of identifying are our ways of "knowing what our representations represent." The bacterium is quite incapable of knowing, in this sense, what its representations are about. This might be a reason to say that it does not understand its own representations, not really.

Negation and propositional content

The representational system to which the magnetosome pull belongs does not contain negation. Indeed, it does not even contain contrary representations, for the magnetosome cannot pull in two directions at once. Similarly, if two beavers splash at different times or places, or if two bees dance different dances at the same time, it may well be that there is indeed beaver danger two times or two places and that there is indeed nectar in two different locations.[13] Without contrariety, no con-

---

13. On the other hand, the bees cannot go to two places at once.

flict, of course, and more specifically, no contradiction. If the law of noncontradiction plays as significant a role in the development of human concepts and knowledge as has traditionally been supposed, this is a large difference between us and the bacterium indeed.[14] In *LTOBC*, I argued that negation, hence explicit contradiction, is dependent upon subject-predicate, that is, propositional, structure and vice versa. Thus, representations that are simpler also do not have propositional content.

In sum, these six differences between our representations and those of the bacterium, or Fodor's paramecia, ought to be enough amply to secure our superiority, to make us feel comfortably more endowed with mind.

14. In *LTOBC*, I defend the position that the law of noncontradiction plays a crucial role in allowing us to develop new methods of mapping the world with representations.

5

On Mentalese Orthography, Part 1

"How then do I see the Golden Age? . . . First, there will be our old, reliable friend, folk psychology, and second, its self-consciously abstract idealization, intentional system theory. Finally there will be a well-confirmed theory at a level between folk psychology and bare biology, sub-personal cognitive psychology. We can now say a bit more about what it might be like: it will be 'cognitive' in that it will describe processes of information-transformation among content-laden items—mental representations—but their styles will not be 'computational'; the items will not look or behave like sentences manipulated in a language of thought" (Dennett 1987, 235).

"Processes of information-transformation" among "content-laden" "mental representations" but whose "styles are not computational," that do not "behave like sentences manipulated in a language of thought"—that is what I suspect too. But whether Dennett and I *really* agree depends on a number of other things, such as what "processes of information-transformation" would be, what "content-laden" means, what "representations" are, what "computation" or "manipulation" is, and what "sentences . . . in a language of thought" would be like, for a few!

The name "representation" does not come from scripture. Nor is there reason to suppose that the various things we daily call by that

Part 2 of this paper appears in Millikan 1993. I am much indebted to Bo Dahlbom and Bill Lycan for helpful comments on earlier drafts. This paper was prepared while I was a fellow at the Center for Advanced Study in the Behavioral Sciences, where financial support was provided by the National Endowment for the Humanities, grant no. RA-20037-88, and the Andrew W. Mellon Foundation.

name have an essence in common, or if they do, that anything people have in their heads could conceivably share it. What is needed is not to discover what mental representations *really are* but to lay down some terms that cut between interestingly different possible phenomena so that we can discuss their relations. In part 1, I will distinguish and label four different kinds of possible phenomena in the neighborhood of representation. First are "tacit suppositions". Then, each a subset of the last, there are "intentional icons," "inner representations," and "mental sentences." "Intentional icons" are "contentful." "Representations" participate in "processes of information-transformation"—I will call it "inference." But neither "mental sentences" nor any other "representations" are "computed" or, as I will say, "calculated over." This will be the burden of part 2 (Millikan 1993).

1 Tacit Suppositions

There are times when the design of an organism or one of its parts is so neatly specialized to mesh with some feature of its natural environment that one might almost "read" the environmental feature off the design. In such cases the design of the organism might also be said to "presuppose" the environmental feature; in the absence of that feature, the organism or part could not possibly function as designed. There are two kinds of instances in which it is particularly natural to think of such design features as "representing" environmental features.

The first is illustrated by biological clocks. In the case of diurnal clocks (diurnal circadian rhythms), for example, had the earth spun faster or more slowly, the biological clock inside the animal would have needed to be adjusted accordingly, so the clock rhythm is naturally thought of as "representing" the length of a day. Likewise, the color pattern of the Viceroy butterfly, which "mimics" that of the bad tasting Monarch, might naturally be said to "represent" the Monarch's design. Mechanisms in various species adjusted to respond to subtle distinguishing features of conspecifics, predators, or prey are often thought of as containing "representations" of these in the form of "templates" for recognition: had the features been different along certain dimensions, the templates would have had to differ accordingly. Similarly, the cerebral motor cortex is said to contain a "representation" of the hand, different but connected areas of the brain receiving input from corresponding different but connected parts of the hand. Had the hand had more digits, the brain would have needed more of these areas to correspond. All these cases have in common that a certain design feature of the organism seems to "map" onto a feature of its environment (or another feature of the organism) in this sense: had the environmental feature differed along certain dimensions, the design feature would have had to differ along isomorphic dimensions to effect the same coordination or adaptation in the same way.

The second representationlike phenomenon is illustrated by a well-known feature of Marr's theory of vision. According to Marr, the construction of a perceptual representation of an object in three dimensions, starting from retinal stimulation patterns, works on certain suppositions about the edges of objects, ambient light, and interactions between these. Some would say these assumptions were "tacitly represented" by the visual systems or in the operation of these systems. To generalize, any environmental feature that is not explicitly represented but must be presupposed for correct operation of an "inferencer"—a mechanism that, when working properly, derives new true representations from old true representations—is naturally thought of as "tacitly represented" by or through the operation of the inferencer (compare Dennett 1987, 216–217).

In both these kinds of cases, what is said to be "represented" may be false in some environments. The tacit assumptions of Marr's reconstructions, for example, can easily be falsified in the laboratory. Indeed, it is because of the obvious possibility of something like falseness that the word "representation" surfaces. In none of these cases, however, will I use the term "representation." What we have in each of these instances, I will say, is merely a system or part that requires certain conditions, under which it was designed to operate, in order to function properly in its normal way. Its structure fits these conditions, or is a function of them, because it has been adapted to them; it does not "represent" these conditions. Rather than "representing" these conditions, I will say that the system "presupposes them for its proper operation" and that they correspond to "tacit suppositions" of the system, suppositions that may sometimes be false.

2   "Content-Ladenness": Intentional Icons

A second group of items I call "intentional icons"—"intentional" as in "intentionality."[1] Intentional icons are akin to those structures mentioned above that map onto, or are isomorphic to, environmental features to which they are adapted. A difference, however, is that intentional icons are not built into the organism but acquired by the individual in response to the environment. Often, though not always, they are temporary adaptations to a temporary environment. They exhibit a dimension or dimensions of possible variance running parallel to possible variances in the environment. A rule of projection, in the mathematician's sense, maps the one onto the other. I call this rule the icon's "mapping rule." That the environment corresponds to the icon in conformity with this mapping rule is presupposed for proper operation of the system containing the icon.

But intentional icons are distinguished in two other ways as well. First, there must be a mechanism in the organism whose function is to produce the icon. And there must be a way that this mechanism, when successful, actually *effects* or brings it about that the icon maps onto the environmental feature.[2] For example, although various surface patterns occurring in the outer sense organs (say, vibrating ear drums) may systematically map certain patterns in the distal environment, these surface patterns are not intentional icons. This is because no biological mechanisms have as their functions to produce (as distinguished from merely receiving) these mappings. The patterns are merely natural signs. On the other hand, images on the retina of the eye are formed due to the structure of the eye lens. And the eye lens was designed by evolution for the purpose of bringing about systematic mappings between

1. In this essay I discuss only one of two kinds of "intentional icons" defined in *LTOBC* (also see chapter 8 below), namely, indicative intentional icons. Equally important are imperative intentional icons, but I will try to get by here without them.

2. This may or may not involve the feature's being a cause of the icon that maps it. For example, the orientation of the magnetosome in Dretske's favorite bacterium (Dretske 1986) is an intentional icon of the direction away from oxygen, but oxygen has nothing to do with the causes of its orientation (see chapter 6 herein). Similarly, intentional icons may map onto future features of the environment.

certain environmental structures and these images. The patterns are thus intentional icons; the lens is their "producer."

Second, there must be a mechanism (or mechanisms) in the organism that may use or be guided by the intentional icon in the performance of certain of its normal functions. When so guided, this user will function properly in the usual way only if the icon and the environment match by the relevant mapping rule. Thus, although there are mechanisms in the skin of a chameleon whose job is to make the color of its skin match the color of its surround, there are no other mechanisms in the chameleon that use these colors for guidance. The colors, then, are not intentional icons. On the other hand, we need not require that the guided mechanism reside in the same individual as the icon-producing mechanism. The production and the "consumption" of the icon may be accomplished by any mechanisms *designed*, biologically or in some other way, to cooperate on the iconing project. For example, the dances that honey bees execute to guide fellow workers to nectar are paradigm cases of intentional icons.

Intentional icons do not, as such or in general, carry "natural information."[3] Nor do they "covary" with or "track" what they icon. Their definition makes no reference to how likely or unlikely they are actually to correspond to their designated environmental features, nor to how likely these features are to get mapped by them. I have no idea how reliable bees are at dancing the right dances, dances bearing mapping relations to nectar that have historically led watching bees to the spot. Maybe bees are good at this, and maybe they're not. But if bee dances mapped nectar locations correctly only once in ten, surely the effect would still be better than if the workers hunted for nectar independently. And the dances would still be intentional icons. Rather than being natural information, the "content" of an intentional icon is described by telling what sort of structure or feature would have to be in the organism's environment for the icon to map onto by its mapping rule, for its consumer to use it successfully in the normal way, that is, the way that historically accounted for the interlocking design of producer, icon, and consumer.

3. In the sense of "natural information" defined in Dretske's *Knowledge and the flow of information* (1981).

To look ahead to the possibility that thoughts are intentional icons, notice that according to my story, the content of an intentional icon is neither a direct nor indirect function of the stimulations, empirical evidence, or prior thoughts that induce it. Its semantic value is determined by whatever mapping relation is in fact doing the work of successfully guiding the organism through its activities in its world when controlled by the representation. Or to be more accurate, I should refer not to how the organism is in fact guided but to the general principles in accordance with which it is *designed* to be guided—designed to make icons, perhaps also to *learn* to make icons (concept formation),[4] designed to combine icons in inference, and designed to be guided by icons in action. For, an organism's design, its "competence," may be very far from its actual performance. Quite special conditions are required for the correct performance of most biological devices.[5]

Intentional icons can be extremely simple devices harbored by extremely simple organisms. For example, consider simple signals, such as an animal's warning cry to its conspecifics. Count its time and place as being *part* of the signal. The time or place of the signal is now seen to map onto the time or place of the signaled event. Signal at time t_1 and place p_1 corresponds to danger at t_1 and p_1. If the signal is shifted over two miles and ahead three days, the danger needs to be shifted over two miles and ahead three days for the signal to do its work. So it is possible to consider even these simple devices to be varieties of intentional icons.[6]

That one can look upon even simple signals in this way should make it clear how extremely simple an organism might be that harbors intentional icons. And it should also make clear how very local or minimal may be the mirroring of the environment accomplished by an intentional icon. Why, then, do I dignify these icons with the title "intentional"?

4. See *LTOBC*, chaps. 9, 18, and 19.
5. This is why massive redundancy of function is the norm everywhere in the life world, as is early death rather than reproduction. For discussion, see chapter 9.
6. In *LTOBC*, I called these simple icons "intentional signals." Intentional signals usually indicate time or place with the *same* time or place, but one could imagine, say, an animal signal whose t_1 part (the now part) indicated danger five minutes from t_1 or winter within a month of t_1, or whose p_1 part meant *somewhere between p_1 and the food supply.*

How could anything exhibit intentionality that did not think? And how could anything think that did not make inferences, and hence that was not, at least to an approximation, rational? Is not rationality, as Dennett claims, "the mother of intention" (Dennett 1978c, 19)? The contemporary mood is so adverse to the idea of intentionality without reason that even perception, a faculty traditionally taken as continuous from us to the lowest animals, is sometimes thought to be intentional only insofar as it produces a disposition to judgment and inference (Armstrong 1968, Smart 1975, Shoemaker 1975).

The word "intentionality" was (re)introduced in modern times by Brentano for a quite definite purpose. Of course, the fact that Brentano intended "intentionality" to be the distinguishing mark of the mental doesn't help very much if we suspect that mentality comes in styles and degrees. But Brentano was more specific than that. He thought that what was funny about the mental was that it could be directed toward something that didn't exist. You can think about your vacation in Spain or about Saint Christopher even though perhaps neither of them was or will be. And that, or the closest thing to it, is just what can happen with intentional icons. The intentional icon can be such that even though there is no environmental feature onto which it appropriately maps, there still "should" be. That is, the icon will misguide its users exactly because there is no such environmental feature. In this respect, false intentional icons are just like false sentences. So I call them "intentional" and speak of them as having "intentional content."

It is not uncommon for an intentional icon normally to map in accordance with a definite rule of projection onto more than one environmental feature. Despite this, it is possible to define the content of an intentional icon with considerable determinacy if you do it in the following way. Consider the content to be that mapped feature to which the icon specifically adapts the *user(s)* of the icon. It is the feature that, if removed from the environment or incorrectly mapped, will guarantee failure for its *users*. It will guarantee failure, that is, if there occur no coincidental interventions, no helpful contingencies of a sort not historically normal for performance of the users' functions. Suppose, then, that in the normal case the bee dance maps not only onto the location of nectar but also onto the direction from which the dancing bee last approached the hive. Its content concerns the location of nectar, not the direction of the dancer's approach. This is because it is only if the location of nectar is mapped wrongly that the watching bees' normal reactions to the dance will fail to serve their proper functions, barring miraculous intervention. If the location of nectar is correctly mapped but in fact the dancing bee's last approach to the hive was from an unusual direction, this won't affect the success of the watching bees.

Consider another example, made famous by Fred Dretske (1986). The little magnetosome, the organ sensitive to magnetic fields, in certain Northern Hemisphere bacteria, pulls toward magnetic north, hence toward geomagnetic north, hence down, hence away from surface water, and hence away from oxygen, which is toxic to these bacteria. It thus guides them to safety. Considered as an intentional icon, the pulling of the magnetosome in a certain direction has just one intentional content. It intentionally icons the more oxygen versus less oxygen polarity, for it is being wrong about this that would guarantee its failure to perform its normal function. Note that it is not one of its *functions*, for example, to move the bacterium either down or toward geomagnetic north, any more than it is one of its functions to move it toward true north, toward molten rock, or toward snow (the arctic). None of these events figures in a causal chain that helps to *effect* its survival. Each is merely a usual correlate of performing its true biological function.

I have been emphasizing very simple intentional icons. But there are good reasons to suppose that animals exhibiting flexible behaviors achieve this flexibility by harboring correspondingly complex intentional icons. Dennett himself has provided the argument, most clearly, perhaps, in connection with the representation of rules rather than of states of affairs, but the idea is the much same.[7] Begin, he suggests, by considering an automatic elevator designed to "follow" one set of "tacit rules," or tacit suppositions (section 1 above), from 9:00 to 5:00 on weekdays and a different set during off-peak and weekend hours. To accomplish this, a clock switches it between two different hardwired control systems at the appropriate times.

We can imagine similar systems in animals . . . , for instance, an animal that is both aquatic and terrestrial, and when it is on the land it obeys one set of rules,

---

7. "Styles of mental representation," in Dennett 1987. See especially pp. 220–225. In my official terminology, representations of rules are "imperative intentional icons" (*LTOBC*, chap. 6).

and when it is in the water it obeys another. Simply *getting wet* could be the trigger for changing internal state from one set of rules to the other.

...But we could have more elaborate switching machinery, so that which system of rules was transiently tacitly represented depended on complex distal features of the environment.... Then there is no apparent limit to the specificity or complexity of the state of the world...that could be tacitly represented by the current state of such a system. [Note that Dennett's "tacitly represented" here is at best my "tacitly presupposed."]

...But as the number of possible different states...grows..., this profligacy demands...economies achieved via multiple use of resources. For instance, where the different states are variations on a theme..., it becomes useful—virtually mandatory—to...change states by *editing* and *revising*, one might say, instead of *discarding* and *replacing*. Economies of this sort require systematicity. (Dennett 1987, 223–224)

Now what is "systematic" accords with rules, in the sense that it is projectable to cover new cases. And what these rules govern must not be just changes in the inner states of the organism, so that they proceed in an orderly fashion. The rules must govern relations *between* these inner states of the organism and the relevant "complex distal features of the environment." Only if certain transformations performed on the one produce parallel transformations performed on the other will there be a point to the systematicity. But that is the same as to say that the states are intentional icons. "Systematicity" here just corresponds to the semantic productivity built into the notion of intentional icon.

In the above quoted passage Dennett goes on to warn that "the 'syntactical' elements of such systems are to be viewed first as having an entirely internal semantics..., 'referring'...not to things and events in the outer world" (1987, 224). I do not understand this restriction. If the rules that the animal must follow exhibit themes with multiple variations, presumably this is because the states of the world to which the animal needs to adapt exhibit themes with multiple variations. The transformations of the animal's interior surely must systematically correspond not just to other adjustments in the animal's interior but to transformations of its world. Perhaps this is why Dennett's phrase is qualified: "viewed *first*."

Consider, for example, quite mundane perceptual capacities. To be able to negotiate physical movement among the objects in its world, an animal must be prepared to deal with any of innumerable arrangements of objects surrounding it. For many sighted animals, these arrangements are mapped onto patterns of ambient light impinging on the moving animal and brought to a focus through a lens in the eye. A description of the rules by which variations (transformations) in the pattern of the light impinging on the animal correspond to variations in the arrangements of surrounding objects is exceedingly complex. But the mapping is there, and the animal uses it. It uses the pattern presumably by projecting it internally to become a pattern in the nervous system, which again maps onto the arrangement of external objects. Only in this way could movement be guided *according* to this arrangement, guided in part as a function of this arrangement. The rules in accordance with which this latter inner movement-controlling pattern maps onto the environment may be even harder to describe than the rules for the ambient light. To take a topical example, the rules by which the order or pattern within a large complex connectionist network in the brain maps onto the chunk of the world it represents might be nearly impossible for us to describe. "Brain writing" may indeed prove to be "illegible" to the outside observer.[8] But the inner patterning is surely there and as such constitutes an intentional icon having a productive semantics. Thus, whether or not it also produces a disposition to conception and inference, perception itself exhibits intentionality.

Moreover, surely this lesson carries over from perception to cognition generally. We are prepared to pack into our heads any one of an innumerable number of alternative "settings" for adapting us to whichever one of an innumerable number of ways the world might turn out to be. This could not possibly be done without system, without a productive inner semantics, without the use of intentional icons.[9]

3   "Processes of Information-Transformation": "Representations"

Yet surely we must agree with Dennett that having real *thoughts*, truly being believers, is somehow connected with being rational. In any event, there is surely an important distinction of kind that needs marking between simple intentional icons and human thoughts. Hormones running

8. Compare "Brain writing and mind reading," Dennett 1978a, 43.
9. On the necessity of a productive semantics or "articulateness" for inner representations, see also chapter 6.

in the blood stream can be intentional icons; surely they are not con-tinuous with thoughts. Indeed, perceptions that guide an animal in motion, though these may be complex and multidimensional, seem not necessarily, just as such, to be thoughts. In fact, there are without doubt a number of quite wide distinctions of kind between the simplest inten-tional icons and thoughts, just which distinctions and how many being, at the moment, a matter of rather free speculation. But one distinction that seems hardly speculative is exactly that between simple intentional icons and items that participate in processes of inference. To honor this distinction I have withheld the term "representation" until now.

I call "representations" only those intentional icons that have as one of their functions to participate in *mediate* inference. *Immediate* infer-ence, by contrast, is probably best assimilated to translation, which, of course, can be partial. Translating information from one iconic medium into another, say from retinal patterns to connectionist neural patterns, I am not considering to be inference. Nor am I interested in moves that distill more restricted information or more general information from that already given in some single icon. Paradigmatically, moves from *p* & *q* to *p* are not of interest here, nor are moves from "Fido barks" to "Something barks." What makes an intentional icon into a representa-tion is that one of its various jobs is to combine with *other* icons to pro-duce icons carrying *new* information.[10] It is this kind of "process of information-transformation among content-laden items" that defines "mental representations" (Dennett, as quoted at the beginning of this chapter).

Imagine a creature that carries about in its head intentional icons that are three-dimensional maps of various places it has been—not maps in

10. In the last section, in order not to complicate matters too much, I defined "intentional icon" in a manner including only what I prefer to call "indicative intentional icons" (*LTOBC*, chap. 6). Here I am making another simplification. "Representations," as I really prefer to use that term, are intentional icons that must be "identified" in order to perform some of their functions (see *LTOBC*). The act of identifying occurs whenever two icons of either kind that overlap in content are joined to produce either another intentional icon *or* action based on the two icons taken together. For example, granted that sight and touch yield intentional icons, the use together of the sight and feel of the same object to produce a coordinated manipulation of it involves an act of identifying, and hence involves visual and tactual "representations." (I discuss the act of identify-ing below, but only as it pertains to indicative icons and inference.)

three spatial dimensions, of course, but dimensions in some neurally realizable medium. It has a map of the locale in which it last found water, and another of the locale in which it last saw lions. On each of these maps its den is marked. Now imagine that it overlaps these maps, using its den as a pivot, and arrives at a third map showing the proximity of lions to the source of water. Reacting to this new map, it seeks a new source of water rather than going back to the lion-infested source on its map. Granted that in combining the maps in this way, the animal's brain was functioning in a way it was biologically designed to function, that is, the combining accorded with a "competence" of the animal, this would be a paradigm case of mediate inference. As is characteristic of all mediate inference, two vehicles of information have been combined, *using a middle term*, so as to produce a third vehicle containing new information. Accordingly, the maps are "representations."[11]

Soon I will argue that mental sentences, should these occur, would be intentional icons. But it seems quite reasonable that much of our active thinking, much of our inferring, may occur in media more like maps or models (in the lay sense) than like sentences. Such models would have to be very abstract indeed, the mathematical isomorphisms between representations and world structures being far from tangible. I have already suggested that certain very abstract patterns found in neural nets could be intentional icons. There is no reason why the results of superpositional storage of information in neural nets should not be considered to yield conclusions of inference. Whether superimposed information gets correctly stored in the same net with certain old information clearly depends on there being a semantic overlap on some level, there being what I am calling "middle terms."

There is also another way in which "inference," as I intend that term, might look quite unlike inference as we typically express it by presenting "arguments" in the form of a series of sentences. Intentional icons occurring in different representational media might be premises and/or premise and conclusion of a single inference. Suppose, for example, that

11. Can a bee, having watched dances of fellow bees showing nectar at two different locations relative to the hive, put these two dances together and fly directly from one of these locations to the other? In this unlikely event, bee dances would be representations.

by combining information contained in perception of an object *seen* to be in a certain place with information about that object as *felt* to be in that same place, one comes to believe, say, that a green apple is hard. Here the premises are percepts, and the conclusion is a thought, but the movement from premises to conclusion turns on a middle term, and it is inference. It is "information-transformation among content-laden items." The percepts involved in such a transaction would, accordingly, be representations.

It does not follow from this definition of "representation," however, that every creature harboring representations is rational. This is for at least two reasons. First, it is likely that many inferencers produce true conclusions from true premises by heavily relying on tacitly presupposed information about the organism's normal environment (section 2 above). This information would have to be made explicit in the premises of a correct logical reconstruction of the inference. "Rational" is another term that is pretty much up for grabs, its long philosophical history having hindered more than helped. But if we reserve it for a creature *capable*, at least, of explicit *valid* mediate inference, inference in which all information-bearing premises are explicit, then it may well apply, as Aristotle suggested, to just us.

The other reason that harboring representations does not imply rationality is that there is no cause to suppose that every creature capable of inference, in the sense described, is capable of recognizing the intrusion of *inconsistency* among its representations and prepared to respond to such intrusions in a productive way. From the definition of mental representation I have given, nothing follows about consistency. Nothing prohibits an organism from harboring as large a number of contrary or contradictory representations as it pleases, due either to malfunction inside the organism or unfavorable conditions outside. The ability to recognize and eliminate contradiction in inner representations is a distinct capacity not even hinted at in laying down the definition of representation. But having at least a lot of this capacity should surely be required as a condition on being fully "rational." (The conclusion of part 2 of this essay [Millikan 1993] entails that this capacity is not as unproblematic for humans as is generally supposed. Like the ability to make inferences, the ability to recognize contradiction depends upon recognizing middle terms or, as I will later put it, on being able to "coidentify" correctly. But in no case, I will argue, is that ability transparent. A creature that never had *any idea* when it had contradicted itself in thought, however, could hardly be accorded rationality.)

4 "Sentences...in a Language of Thought"

Many are prone to confuse the claim that representations "map" onto the world with advocacy of a "picture theory" of representation and hence to reject it out of hand.[12] "Compositionality," on the other hand, is all the rage. What is interesting about compositionality is that it allows new semantic entities to be made by rearranging the parts or aspects of old ones. For instance, it allows "Jane loves John" to be made out of "John loves Jane." You can, of course, think of this change as produced by rearranging the parts "loves," "John," and "Jane," but a more generalized way to think of it is as an operation, in the broad mathematician's sense, performed on "John loves Jane"—the same operation that, when performed on "The cat ate the mouse," produces "The mouse ate the cat," and so forth. Another kind of operations recognized by mathematicians is "substitute in" transformations, for example, "John loves Jane" may be transformed into "John loves the mouse" by the same "substitute in" move that transforms "Bill hits the nail" into "Bill hits the mouse." By other substitution operations we get from "John loves the mouse" to "The cat loves the mouse" and then to "The cat eats the mouse." Various introductions of the negative are also operations, ones that take us, for example, from "John loves Jane" to "John does not love Jane" or from "All John's money is invested in land" to "Not all John's money is invested in land."

12. For example, here is Fodor quoting Millikan 1991a: "'A second suggestion follows from the suggestion that representations are like maps.'... Yeah, well. The last time I looked, the consensus was pretty general that picture theories of meaning had hopeless semantic indeterminacy problems of their own. (The relevant considerations have been common currency at least since Wittgenstein's *Investigations*; for discussion see *Language of Thought*)" (Fodor 1991, 295). A discussion of the relevant considerations was also used to introduce the theory of intentional icons in *LTOBC*, chap. 5. According to picture theories, that the represented is mapped by the representation in accordance with a rule is what *constitutes* the representation-represented relation; that is all this relation consists in. I assume that the reader too is acquainted with "the relevant considerations" that doom this view.

Each of these various kinds of operations corresponds, of course, to a parallel operation on or transformation of the arrangements necessary in the world for the corresponding sentences to be true. ("Transformation" must be read here in the mathematical sense, of course. Transformations of arrangements in the world are not *changes*.) But where operations performed on representations correspond one-to-one to transformations performed on representeds, then (by the rule of proportion that $a:b$ as $c:d = a:c$ as $b:d$) there must also be a "mapping" in accordance with a rule of projection between the domains of representations and of representeds. That is, semantic compositionality just *is* one kind of "mapping." Thus, as I read it, Dennett's assurance that "certainly some sort of very efficient and elegant sort of compositionality accounts for the essentially limitless powers we have to perceive, think about, believe, intend. . . different things" (Dennett 1987, 149) is just one more voucher for intentional icons.[13]

Similarly, to turn to other fashionable words, suppose that semantic "generativity" or "productivity" or "learnability" require that semantic rules project from a relatively small number of cases to all cases. Then these require a "mapping" from representations to representeds.

It seems to follow that mental sentences are "representations" under the definition I have given. What else besides representationhood should we require of "mental sentences"? Sentences are usually thought of as composed of parts that can be strung together to contribute to the meaning of the whole and that can be recombined to yield different meanings. But how literally should we interpret "parts" and "strung together"? For example, consider the "sentences" in Sellars's "Jumblese," where a tall "T" stands for "Tom is tall" and a shaky "T" stands for "Tom is scared" and writing "T" on top of "B" stands for "Tom is taller than Bill." Do these count as sentences? I suggest that it would prove philosophically very dull not to count them. But I do suggest that we insist on subject-predicate structure. There must be possible transformations of the icon to correspond to other subjects having the same predicate, and there must be transformations to correspond to the same

13. Sometimes people require recursivity for "compositionality." I suspect that recursivity is neither a pervasive nor a particularly important aspect of thought. It is not infinite productivity but just productivity that matters.

subject having other predicates. Then bee dances are not sentences, for they have no subject terms, and a rabbit's danger thumps are not sentences, for they never predicate of a time and place anything other than danger. Let us require also that the icon be subject to a negation transformation. Then the alarm calls of the vervet monkeys are not sentences because, although the times and places of the calls vary with the times and places of predators (subject terms), and although there are different calls for different predators (predicate terms), the vervets' calls are never negated.[14]

5 Inner Representations and Ascriptions of Belief

I now offer a radical translation of the following words from Dennett:

I am as staunch a realist as anyone about those core information-storing elements in the brain, whatever they turn out to be, to which our intentional interpretations are anchored. I just doubt that those elements, once individuated, will be recognizable as the beliefs we purport to distinguish in folk psychology. (1987, 71)

Consider the relation between a bee dance showing nectar 15 degrees west of the line between the sun and the hive and the English sentence "There is nectar 15 degrees west of the line between the sun and the hive." If the bee dance is true, the sentence too has got to be true; the sentence is implied by the bee dance. The two maps—bee dance and sentence—cover in part the same content. But this content is mapped in the two cases by entirely different projection rules. The bee dance is an analogue icon, while the sentence is articulated by substitution transformations. The bee dance has one basic analogue rule for direction, transformations of the orientation of the dance corresponding to transformations of the angle of the nectar relative to the sun. The sentence transforms into sentences indicating other directions in various ways: by "6" substituting in for "5," for example, or "east" substituting in for "west." The sentence is subject to a negation transformation, whereas the bee dance is not. Indeed, no two bee dances are even contraries of one another. Any set of bee dances *might* be true all at once, nectar

14. The importance of the cooperating structures subject, predicate, and negation is examined in detail in *LTOBC*, chaps. 16–19.

being in all those places at once, lucky bees. Furthermore, the bee dance has, as it were, no subject term or terms. There are no transforms of it that indicate relations of things other than nectar to things other than the sun and the hive, or that indicate alternative kinds of relations between the sun and the hive.

In a similar way, the correctness of an ordinary map or diagram, chart or graph, may entail the truth of various sentences, yet the common content will be projected via rules that articulate it against quite different contrasting possibilities. The space of significant transformations surrounding such icon is different; each resides in what the early Wittgenstein would have called a different "logical space." Implication relations between nonpropositional icons and sentences can also go the other way. What a frog's eye tells a frog's brain may not imply any definite English sentence or sentences, but English sentences can be constructed that will imply the truth of what any particular frog's eye is currently telling its brain. And so with animal danger signals, the various cries of the vervet monkeys, and so forth. In each of these cases it seems reasonable to say that one icon implies what the other says, or implies part of what it says, but that it does not make this content explicit. One "implicitly" represents what the other "explicitly" represents. This accords, I believe, with Dennett's own terminology (1987, 216).

Granted all this, it might be that although there are no such things as mental sentences, still the contents expressed by public-language sentences correctly ascribing beliefs to a person are all implicit in, in the sense of immediately entailed by, that person's mental representations. This model does not require that a person be capable of articulating all their own beliefs in propositional form, either mentally or verbally. Nor does it require that a person have command of any propositional, i.e., sentencelike, representational system at all. Nor does this entail that all of a person's mental representations can be correctly described as beliefs or that all are of the kind that belief-desire talk makes an attempt to capture. Some might be like the icons in the frog's eye, that is, implied by representations with propositional structure but not having nearly that degree of structure themselves. But it might still be that "*core* information-storing elements in the brain" (emphasize "core")—though not "recognizable," "once individuated," as "the beliefs we purport to distinguish in folk psychology"—would strictly entail the belief-ascribing sentences through which we customarily filter their contents.[15]

This suggestion about beliefs has a consequence, however, that may be in conflict with Dennett's vision of the "intentional stance," in which belief-desire ascription floats entirely free of reference to representations inside. If correctly ascribed belief contents are entailed by the contents of real mental representations, then belief ascription will be involved in a reconstruction not of the *entire* behavioral pattern of an agent but only of parts. Inner representations have (by my definition) a potential effect upon action. But not all of a creature's actions need be representation-controlled, nor need all failures of the representation-forming and representation-using systems be failures to represent the right content. To start with obvious examples, surely knee jerks and reflex eye blinks are not to be accounted for by reference to beliefs and desires. Nor are such errors as tripping or spilling ones coffee. Similarly, I suggest, errors in comprehending a sentence or reading a map, errors in perception or (to take "perception" broadly) errors in recognizing ones true situation, quirks in ones expectations of and attitudes toward self or others—none of these are invariably accountable to mistaken beliefs or desires. For example, not all errors in giving change need be so accountable,[16] nor need such quirks as "having a thing about redheads."[17] In each of these cases it may be that the peculiarity is attributable to some glitch in the system not describable in intentional terms, not resulting from inner representation. I am not saying that the description in intentional terms may be indeterminate. Rather, these quirks may have no legitimate intentional descriptions at all.

To try to rationalize such happenings would be not just unhelpful but plain wrong. Similarly, if inner representations are as I have described them, rationalizing away apparent inconsistency will sometimes be just

15. I am assuming without argument a point on which Dennett and I agree. Creatures that have beliefs must make inferences. But in truth, this is only a decision on the usefulness of a certain terminology. I have a botanist friend who claims to be trying to condition her venus flytraps. She whistles and stamps and then touches their traps whenever she enters the greenhouse, and she says that they close at her touch because they believe she's a fly. This use of "believes" is not just possible but actual, and who is to say it's not literal?
16. Compare Stich 1981 and Dennett 1987, "Making Sense of Ourselves" and "Reflections: When Frogs (and Others) Make Mistakes."
17. See Dennett 1987, 148.

plain wrong. There may often be considerable ambiguity in the behavioral evidence for inconsistency, but the real *inner* facts of the matter, as common sense also requires, may remain entirely determinate.[18]

18. This is not intended as an argument for full determinacy of belief content. For example, malfunctions producing representations that are illegible to their own inner interpreters certainly cause indeterminacy. And so does sufficient disruption of the systems responsible for "coidentifying," discussed in part 2 (Millikan 1993) and in Millikan, forthcoming.

6

Compare and Contrast Dretske, Fodor, and Millikan on Teleosemantics

By "teleosemantics" is meant a teleofunctional account of what determines the semantic contents of inner representations.[1] One contrast among these three authors is that Millikan and Dretske adopt teleological accounts while Fodor rejects teleosemantics. But I can compare the teleosemantic view Fodor would have held had he not thought better of it, namely, the view he rejects in *Psychosemantics* (1987) and in *A theory of content* (1990). I will emphasize Millikan's view because it seems to be the most difficult—it has at least managed to trip some very competent commentators—and because I have studied it the hardest.

A central problem that teleosemantics is designed to solve concerns mental *mis*representation. It is not possible to accomplish a naturalistic analysis of the representation-represented relation by a single step describing only the relation that holds between the thinker's current states and dispositions and the thinker's environment when she or he harbors a *true* representation. This is because there are two kinds of nontrue representations to be accounted for: those that are not true and those that are not representations. The failure to hold of a single-step true-representation-to-world relation could account for only one of these kinds of failure. To understand false as well as true representation, apparently we must understand what *bare* representation is, and then what being true or false is, over and above bare representation. The problem for a naturalist is to do this without introducing ad hoc abstract objects, say unanalyzed meanings, senses, propositions, or possible states of affairs, as somehow ingredient in nature.

1. Thanks to Steven Wagner for the neologism "teleosemantics."

The teleosemanticist solves this problem by introducing teleofunctions into the analysis. On the dominant current analyses, these are functions that are not built out of current properties and dispositions but rest on historical relations. To have a teleofunction is to have emerged from a certain sort of history, one involving some form of selection. Because of this history, the teleofunctional item counts as being "designed to," or even less formally, "supposed to," have a certain structure, and as being "supposed to" perform a certain function. "If language device tokens and mental intentional states (believing that, intending to, hoping that) are members of proper function or 'biological' [i.e., teleofunctional] categories, then they are language devices or intentional states [representations] not by virtue of their powers but by virtue of what they are supposed to be able to do yet perhaps cannot do. For example, just as hearts and kidneys are sometimes diseased or malformed, so sentences and beliefs are sometimes false, and words and concepts are sometimes ambiguous and sometimes vacuous" (*LTOBC*, 17). The contrasts among the teleosemanticists concern how to employ the notion of a teleofunction in order to yield the notion of a representation of a state that is "supposed to" correspond in a certain way to the environment, even though it may not in fact correspond.

The first disagreement among our three authors concerns which are the mechanisms whose functions are relevant to mental semantics. According to Fodor's original plan, it is the representation-producing mechanisms that should be examined. To discover what the semantic content is of the representations these mechanisms produce, we should ask to what these representations correspond when the producing mechanisms operate under biologically ideal conditions. For example, granted that the conditions for perception are ideal, we should expect "That's a horse" to be tokened in Mentalese when and only when that's a horse. The problem with this suggestion, as Fodor notes in *Psychosemantics*, is that ideal conditions for making one sort of observation are not the same as ideal conditions for making another. For example, ideal conditions for seeing very small objects are different from ideal conditions for seeing very large objects. In general, what constitute ideal conditions for making a particular judgment depend upon the content of the judgment. The content of the judgment cannot, then, be derived from the ideal conditions without circularity. If the teleofunction of the representation producing devices is the relevant factor to explore, it seems that we must address this function more directly.

Dretske's teleosemantic proposal is to do just that. There are biological systems, he claims, that have as their functions to represent or "indicate" states of the environment. On a selectionist account of function, this means that they have been selected during evolutionary history "*because* they played a vital information-gathering role...essential...to the satisfaction of a biological need," or it means that they have been selected during a learning process for a similar reason.[2] A problem with this suggestion, one that Dretske highlights in "Misrepresentation" (1986) but soft pedals into a footnote in *Explaining behavior* (1988, 63), is that for typical cases it seems to yield *numerous* representeds corresponding to each inner representation. Dretske's key example concerns the magnetotactic systems of certain Northern Hemisphere bacteria. These systems contain tiny magnets that pull toward magnetic north, hence toward geomagnetic north, hence down, hence away from the surface of the water, hence toward regions of lesser oxygen, oxygen being toxic to these organisms. Which of these various things is it the function of the magnetosome to indicate? Dretske claims that the answer is indeterminate. For example, "this primitive sensory mechanism is, after all, functioning perfectly well when, under [a] bar magnet's influence, it leads its possessor into a toxic environment" (1986, 29), because it still correctly indicates magnetic north. Fodor's example of this same problem concerns the frog's (neural) fly detector. Surely, he claims, this mechanism is designed to detect small ambient black things and small shadows crossing the retina as much as to detect flies.[3]

As a corrective to the emphasis that others in the teleosemantic business have placed on the function of the representation producers, Millikan (chapter 4 herein) has recently been emphasizing the devices that use or "consume" representations. The official statement of Millikan's position, *LTOBC*, however, emphasizes producer and consumer equally. It also distinguishes the functions of these two from that of a third and quite different thing, the representation itself. The roles that these

2. Caution: Dretske (1988) claims to be agnostic on the question concerning the philosophical analysis of biological function talk.
3. Fodor (1990) claims it is also designed to detect flies-or-BBs, but that is a different matter. On this, see Millikan 1991a.

three items play are distinct but equally important for an analysis of mental semantics.

The indeterminancy problem that Dretske and Fodor encountered is solved by examining the role of the representation consumer with care. Representation consumers are devices that have been designed (in the first instances, at least) by a selection process to cooperate with a certain representation producer. The producer likewise has been designed to match the consumer. What the consumer's function is, what it is supposed to effect in responding as it does to the representations it consumes, could be anything at all. It may have numerous alternative functions. It may also be but one of many consumer systems that use representations made by the same producer. The consumer operates, of course, *after* the producer does, and a *full* explanation of how the consumer has historically managed to perform its function or functions—in Millikan's terminology, a full "Normal explanation for proper performance" of its function—would include that the *producer* first performed *its* function properly, and it would include an explanation of *how* the producer's function has historically been accomplished. A "most proximal Normal explanation for proper performance" of the consumer's function, on the other hand, is one that does not go into any events that occur in the production-consumption chain prior to the consumer's activities. It begins at the point at which the consumer enters the event chain and explains how, given certain initial surrounding conditions, given the consumer's normal structure or constitution, and given certain initial relations between consumer and environment, the consumer has historically produced the effects that are its functions. It explains in the briefest possible way that is still *complete* how the consumer does this for *just* those (possibly infrequent) cases when the consumer has succeeded. That is, the point is not to explain the frequency or infrequency of the consumer's successes, but to explain success in just those cases in which success occurs.

Now *that* sort of explanation will necessarily make reference to an initial relation among consumer, representation, and environment that is of interest to the teleosemanticist. For surely one relation that is strikingly implicated is the *coincidence* between the representation that the consumer confronts and a certain condition in the environment, namely, the condition that, consequent to the analysis, will be designated as the one the representation represents. Prior to analysis, this condition is picked out in accordance with a certain *rule* of correspondence having the following property: unless we assume that some actual condition in the world corresponds in accordance with this rule to the representation confronted by the consumer, we cannot account, *with any single explanation that covers historical instances of consumer successes generally*, for *why* the consumer produces the effect that is its function. In the case of the magnetosome, this crucial initial relation (this particular "Normal condition for proper performance" of the consumer) is that the magnet points toward lesser oxygen; in the frog case, that the firing of the detector is coincident with the presence of an edible bug. None of the other correspondences mentioned, as above, by Dretske or Fodor is relevant to *this* kind of explanation of the consumer's performance, hence none is relevant to the semantics of the inner representations consumed.

But now the question arises, What makes these hypothesized semantically relevant correspondences different from yet other correspondences that appear to figure with equal importance in "most proximate normal explanations" for performances of consumer functions? For example, surely the occurrence of the magnetosome's signal needs to be coincident with the presence of an immediate surround of water if its consumer is to perform properly, and the firing of the frog's bug detector needs to coincide with presence of a surround of air and presence of a stable platform under the snapping frog. This is where the function of the representation *producer* needs to be brought in. The representation producer has been designed by selection to produce representations for the consumer *that* correspond to conditions in the world *by* the rule of correspondence that figures in the most proximate normal explanation of the consumer's successes. To be very explicit, the producer's job is to produce not just a representation—graphically, a "shape"—but to produce a correspondence, a certain relation *between* "shape" and world. Obviously, if this is the producer's function, there must be a way that it sometimes *effects* this function. But the magnetotactic system does not help to *effect* that the tug of the magnet coincides with the presence of a surround of water, nor does the frog's bug-detection system help to *effect* that its firings coincide with the presence of a surround of air and presence of a frog-supporting platform. So it cannot be a *function* of these systems to produce these correspondences, hence these correspondences are not relevant to mental semantics.[4]

What, then, are the functions of representations themselves? It is not uncommon among teleosemanticists to suggest that a representation is something whose function is to represent, or to "indicate." To claim this is not necessarily to run in circles. A toggle reamer, after all, is something whose function is to ream toggles. But then we had better know what it is to ream a toggle and, similarly, what it is to represent or indicate something. (Let me drop the "or" and just say "indicate.") There are two sensible things that "indicate" might mean in this context.

Indicating might be, at least in part, a standing in a relation of correspondence to or coincidence with something thereby indicated. In that case, indicating would be not something that a representation *effects* but some way that it *is*, namely, standing in a certain relation. But functions are things *effected* by items having functions. To speak otherwise is to confound what is surely best kept separate. Besides functions, there are, after all, normal explanations both of the genesis of various biological items and of their proper operations, and there are normal conditions associated with both of these kinds of normal explanations. By reference to these various categories, everything that needs to be said can surely be said, and said clearly, without having to blunt the term "function." So if indicating is standing in a relation of correspondence, then it is not one of the *functions* of a representation to indicate anything. Rather, it is a function of a representation *producer* to *produce* a representation that indicates.

But there is another thing that indicating might be: it might be something done by the representation to the representation's consumer, namely, the representing of certain conditions *to* that consumer. Think of this act of representing as the effecting of a change of a certain sort in the consumer. In that case, the representation may be seen as having representing as a genuine function. Specifically, to represent circumstance *c* to consumer (interpreter) *i*, the representation effects a change in *i* that adapts *i*'s further activities to *c*, that is, modifies *i*'s activities

---

4. This is the answer to the puzzle about determinacy, given Millikan's account, which Cummins attempts to solve by introducing what he calls "basic factors" (1989, chap. 5).

so that *i*'s teleofunctions get performed in, or via mediation of, or despite, *c*.

After the smoke has cleared, it appears that Dretske and Millikan agree on at least two general points: that inner representations are produced by systems having as teleofunctions the production of true representations, and that misrepresentation occurs when these systems miss. Yet there is a strong contrast between their views on how to unpack "true representation" in the context of this analysis, that is, on the details of the job description that is written for representation producers.

Dretske begins with a story about natural signs, or "indicators," and then adds teleology to it. His story goes through several versions (1981, 1986, 1988), but should there be some inconsistencies among these, they do not affect the point at issue with Millikan. For Dretske, an "indicator" is not just an item that actually corresponds to or actually coincides with the affair it indicates. It is one the occurrence of which, as a *type*, makes entirely certain, or at the bare minimum highly likely, the existence of an affair of the *type* indicated. For example, the firings of the frog's bug detector cannot be indicators of bugs unless the probability that a bug is present is high given that the detector has fired. The job of a representation producer is to make indicators in this sense of "indicator," according to Dretske. Indicators made by such a producer are full-fledged, true "representations" (Dretske 1988). When the producer's product fails to coincide with what it should indicate, this product is a false "representation." (False representations do not "indicate" in Dretske's terminology.)

A problem with Dretske's view is that it is hard to see how it could be the function of any biological device literally to *effect* the production of one of his "indicators." To do so, the device would have to *effect* that certain statistics should hold. The frog's bug-detecting system, for example, would have to literally *effect* that the statistics on bugs versus BBs in its environment should be such that, when it fires, the chances favor a bug. But *that*, it surely cannot do. All it can *effect* is that coincident with a bug, there happens a firing. It can at most effect first one such coincidence and then later another.[5]

---

5. Insofar as it manages to effect such coincidences, it will, of course, *alter* the relevant statistics somewhat or, in some cases, greatly. But altering the statistics and effecting them whole are quite different things.

Millikan describes the function of the representation producer according. Its function is to produce representations, "shapes," that *correspond*, that is, correspond in the manner required by the representations' consumers in order that these consumers should function properly. If circumstances are not normal for the producer, that is, if circumstances are not as they have historically been when the producer has succeeded in its task, then, of course, the producer will almost undoubtedly fail. For example, the frog's bug-detecting apparatus fails whenever a BB shadow crosses the frog's retina. It fails to produce a true representation. But this apparatus cannot be held responsible for the likelihood versus unlikelihood of BBs. It cannot be held responsible for the statistics on its *rate* of success or failure.

But, you may object, is it not part of a representation producer's job to be reliable? Surely the bug detector wouldn't have been selected had it been too unreliable. The frog wouldn't then have had *this* kind of bug detector, but another kind. True, but *that* observation can be made of *any* item that has a function. No teleofunctional item is such that it would have been selected if it had been "too unreliable" about the performance of its functions. But this fact cannot turn being reliable into a part of the function of every teleofunctional item. Indeed, to reiterate, being reliable can't be the function of *any* teleofunctional item for the easy reason that no item *effects* its own reliability. Reliability always depends on the dependability of *external* factors, on the prevalence or rarity of normal conditions for proper performance.

There is a second point of importance here too. Consider: how unreliable is "too unreliable"? Sperm tails, as the Millikan litany goes, are overwhelmingly unreliable at performing their function of propelling the sperm to an ovum, but not, apparently, "*too* unreliable." Similarly, the food detectors built into goldfish are not, apparently, "too unreliable," despite the fact that a goldfish in a dirty bowl may spit back out all or nearly all of the particles these detectors have instructed it to ingest. Nor, apparently, are the danger signals that various species of animals employ "too unreliable," despite the fact that many, in all probability, are much more often wrong than right. What counts as "too unreliable" is a function of the costs incurred when representations turn out false versus the gains that are made when they turn out true and also of the costs when the animal *fails* to signal what should be signaled. These equations have different values for each kind of representation-producing mechanism.[6] Reliability, then, can be no part of the *definition* of representation any more than it is part of the definition of other kinds of teleofunction.

A third contrast among the teleosemanticists is the special emphasis that Millikan alone places upon the *articulateness* of all complete representations. Complete representations represent complete states of affairs. Complete states of affairs are, as such, articulated, though this articulation may sometimes be very simple, as in the case of the state of affairs constituted by a bug's being here now (rather than here then or there then or there now). A representation that represented something simpler than a state of affairs, one that represented, say, only an object or a property or a *type* of state of affairs (compare a propositional function), would make no *claim*, hence would fail to be true or false, to represent anything either correctly or incorrectly. It would be, or be similar to, a name, *saying* nothing at all. As Frege saw, only when placed in a completing context, such that along *with* this context it represents an articulate state of affairs, does a name truly represent anything.

Now it certainly is possible that an unarticulated representation should be *defined* for use on some special occasion to serve as the name of some state of affairs. It could be defined, that is, by someone who employs a prior articulated representation for this purpose. Thus Paul Revere's single lantern once named the state of affairs that was the British approaching on April 18, 1775, by land. But any such representation will have a use only *once* with any one interpreter. When it has been used once, it has been used *up*. A representational system consisting of just one inarticulate representation can represent just one state of affairs; hence it would have no reason to be perpetuated.

On the other hand, suppose that Paul Revere's signal had not inarticulately signaled the coming of the British by land for that day only but had articulately signaled their coming by land "tonight," the date of the signal standing for the date of the coming. In that case, the signal might be usable again, for the British might come again. But, to think more carefully, it would not in fact *be* the same signal that was used again

6. For a discussion of these equations, see Godfrey-Smith 1991, chap. 10.

but another signal, one with a different date, hence one that represented a different state of affairs. An articulate representation belongs to a *system* of representation, which *system* can be perpetuated. Conversely, barring an explicit convention such as Paul Revere's, set up especially for a single anticipated occasion, only an articulate representation can represent what has not been represented before. For example, only an articulate representation, such as one whose time and place represent that same time and place, can represent to the frog that a bug is here now.

Representation articulation, Millikan claims, is at root the same phenomenon as what is more fashionably termed "compositionality." The principle governing it is the principle of "projection" in the mathematical sense. Even the most primitive of representations ("intentional signals" and "intentional icons") are abstract "pictures," in the sense of *Tractatus logico-philosophicus*, or "maps," in the mathematician's sense, of what they represent. The most sophisticated of linguistic representations are articulate, are compositional, in accordance with the same basic principle as are the most primitive, though the rules of projection involved are, of course, far more complex.

The last contrast that I will mention among the teleosemanticists concerns the role that learning plays in defining the functions that determine mental semantics. Fodor does not seriously consider the possibility that representational capacities resulting from learning might be described in teleofunctional terms. He seems to assume that the only functions that could be relevant to mental semantics are functions derived directly from Darwinian natural selection during the evolution of a species. Representations involving concepts that are not innate, he takes it, could not possibly be treated by a teleosemantic analysis. "You can now see why Darwinian/teleological apparatus does no good," for "when the cognitive mechanisms are behaving as the forces of selection intended them to," "there is no Darwinian guarantee that a properly functioning intentional system ipso facto has the [learned] concept HORSE (to say nothing of the concept PROTON)" (Fodor 1987, 116–17).

Dretske (1988) handles this problem by assuming the classic position that learning is parallel to natural selection. He claims that a learning process may result in the selection or "recruitment" of (what was previously only) an internal *natural* indicator of some condition *c* in an (individual) animal's environment to serve as stimulus for a behavior that brings a reward when performed under c. When that happens, a *function* is bestowed on that indicator, the function of indicating. Dretske does not greatly elaborate this theme. I do not think, however, that it would be opposed to the spirit of his enterprise to extend the notion of behavior in this context to cover inner behaviors, such as thinking processes, and to extend the notion of a reward to cover inner rewards, such as the confirmation of one's beliefs or the avoidance of contradiction.

If Dretske were to allow that sort of extension, he would be moving closer to agreement with Millikan, who likened associative learning to natural selection. A special clause is built into her definition of "proper function" (teleofunction) in order to accommodate associative learning as one originator of proper functions (*LTOBC*, 24). Later the processes that result in the formation of theoretical concepts are described as involving something like trial and error learning for those (possibly rare) cases when concepts are not acquired through a public language. The trials and the rewards here are for the most part inner, with the law of contradiction playing a moderately traditional role. But Millikan adds a string to this bow that increases its range considerably. This is the doctrine of derived proper functions (*LTOBC*, chap. 2) in accordance with which certain kinds of teleofunctions that are built into an animal during evolutionary history interact with the environment of the individual animal to produce new teleofunctions, new biological purposes for these individuals, without the mediation of addional selection processes (*LTOBC* and chapters 3, 11 herein). That learning effects the creation of new teleofunctions is due very largely to this factor, even when learning works by trial and error, by generation and test. And, of course, there are important forms of learning that don't work this way.

The doctrine of adapted and derived proper functions has also another use in the explanation of how new mental teleofunctions are born. It explains how the teleofunctions of elements in a public language become translated into teleofunctions attaching to items in individual language learners' heads (*LTOBC*, chap. 9). I should like to say much more about the notions of adapted and derived proper functions, and about the multiple uses of these notions. But the examination hour is over. Perhaps I shall write my dissertation on this.

7

What Is Behavior? A Philosophical Essay on Ethology and Individualism in Psychology, Part 1

In a recent seminar in the department of biobehavioral sciences at my university a lively controversy suddenly emerged from a sleepy discussion of experimental results. "Grooming behavior"? Surely that was a contaminated description, not a straight description of the experimental data. The *behavior*, the datum, was that the animal "scratched itself," a description containing no speculations about function. The speaker did not agree. There is nothing amiss, indeed everything right, he insisted, in classifying behavior in accordance with function, and there was every reason to believe, in this case, that grooming was the function of the behavior.

Meanwhile philosophy of psychology is engaged in a debate that has, as I will try to show, the same roots. Will a mature cognitive psychology need to characterize its subjects in ways that make reference to how they are imbedded in their environments? Or will it be "individualistic," making reference only to what supervenes on the structures of individual bodies and brains? The individualists argue that the behavioral dispositions of a person clearly depend only on that person's *inner* constitution, and hence that there can be no need to refer to the individual's relation to the wider environment in order to explain them. The anti-individualists argue that it is impossible even to describe much of the behavior that it is psychology's job to explain without reference to the environment. For example, "Jane pointed to the red block" and "Jane said that she was ill" are surely descriptions of behaviors requiring explanation (Burge 1986a), yet the first makes reference to a block in the

Special thanks to the animal-behavior scientists Colin Beer, Matthew Kramer, and Ben Sachs for help with this chapter.

environment, the second to the role within her language community of the sounds Jane made. Siding with the individualists, my colleague in biobehavioral science mutters that these latter descriptions are surely descriptions of the hypothesized *functions* of Jane's behavioral outputs, not uncontaminated descriptions of the form of her behavior.

These controversies stem, I believe, from the same misunderstanding. The confusion concerns what "behavior" is in the sense that it is the behavioral scientist's job to explain it. Classical ethologists believed that, in principle, all the behaviors of an organism could be described by an ethogram prior to making any assumptions about the functions of these behaviors.[1] Classical animal behaviorists, who concentrated on learning theory, believed the same. A proper description of sensory input and behavioral output for any organism would be just whatever description was needed to formulate regularities or input-output laws for the system. This has also been the stance of psychological individualists. The difference between the latter two is mainly that the contemporary individualist looks for laws that refer to states of *inner* mechanisms regulating behavior as well as to input and output. Let me lay my cards down on the table straightaway by contrasting this classical position on behavior with what I believe behavior, in the relevant sense, actually is.

Any animal's activities can be described in a potentially infinite number of ways, and hence classified under any of a potentially infinite number of categories of form. Behavior, I will argue, is the *functional* form of an animal's activity. Other forms of the animal's activity are not relevant to behavioral science. As such, behavior obviously cannot be isolated and described prior to speculation about function; to offer a description of behavior is to offer a hypothesis precisely as to what *has* a function.

Furthermore, because the functions of behaviors are to make specific impacts on the environment, behaviors cannot be isolated and described apart from reference to the environment. Etiological explanations of behavior concern mechanisms that tailor the forms of behaviors to the structure of the environment and/or strategically place these behaviors

1. For a contemporary defence of this view, see Schleidt and Crawley 1980 and Schleidt 1985.

within the environment so as to have appropriate impact. Hence, explaining the operation of these mechanisms requires describing the relations their operations normally bear to the environment. To take a central example, in order to understand how beliefs, desires, and other intentional states enter into the explanation of behavior, we must understand what relations these states bear to the environment when they have been properly induced and are functioning in a way that is biologically normal.

In this chapter I will explain and defend the claim that behavior is functional form for the general case of ethology. In chapter 8, I will show how the truth of this claim entails that behaviors extend far out into the environment, and I will show why etiological explanations of behaviors cannot proceed without continual reference to this wider environment.

What, then, is behavior, the core subject of ethology? I am using "ethology" broadly here to cover animal-behavior studies generally, and I am including humans among the animals. A behavior is, I suggest, at least the following:

1. It is an external change or activity exhibited by an organism or external part of an organism.
2. It has a function in the biological sense.
3. This function is or would be normally fulfilled via mediation of the environment or via resulting alterations in the organism's relation to the environment.

Requirement 1 gives us a rough way to distinguish behaviors from physiological processes.[2] Notice that it allows things other than movements to be behaviors, things such as emission of sounds (vocalization, sonar), of pheromones, of light signals (fireflies), of electric shocks (electric fish); things such as changes of color (octopuses and chameleons), emitting heat (incubating), and so forth.

Requirement 2 is the central one. Most of this chapter will explain and defend it. It may help the reader, in looking ahead to the human case, to recall that the mechanisms responsible for human purposive actions have emerged from a history of natural selection and have

---

2. For a different tradition on the use of the term "behavior," see, as a paradigm, Engel 1986.

biological functions (see chapter 2). If human purposes are a species of biological purposes or proper functions, then human actions are behaviors in the sense described. This position will be clarified in part 2 of this essay (chapter 8).

Requirement 2 excludes from the class of behaviors such things, taken in themselves, as loss of heat, emission of odors, nonfunctional changes in pallor (turning red when one is hot), and galvanomic skin responses. Requirement 3 excludes such things, considered by themselves, as excretion of waste (e.g., sweating merely *as* excreting, breathing CO_2 into the atmosphere), getting a sun tan, getting calluses on one's hands, and shivering, for although these events or processes have functions, the performance of these functions is not mediated by the environment. That is, these activities do not effect changes in, or in relation to, the environment in order that the environment should give a return on the investment.

The simplest forms of behavior are not environmentally induced or influenced, or if they are, this influence is not functional. Put simply, the organism does not strategically *place* these behaviors in the environment. Thus we breath, the clam passes sea soup through its digestive tract, the barnacle waves its foot, and the jellyfish drags its tentacles. Each of these is a behavior with a function, but none is strategically placed in response to the environment. Perhaps the barnacle or the clam slows down its activity when the water gets too cold, but if so, this will not be a strategic deceleration but a mere byproduct of the organism's chemistry. Similarly, our breathing speeds up or slows down in response to our bodily needs, but not in direct response to the environment so as to place it correctly in the environment.

More interesting behaviors are those that are advantageously placed in the environment so that they occur, tend to occur, or occur more often than randomly, when the environment is ready to cooperate. They are placed so as to effect their functions through the mediation of the environment, when and where the environment is ready to mediate. It is on these latter kinds of behaviors that I will concentrate. Animal and human psychology might be distinguished within the somewhat broader field of ethology by the fact that psychology too concentrates on the latter behaviors, emphasizing mechanisms of control of behavior by or partly by the environment.

The behavioral scientist with whom I began this essay took it that "grooming behavior" was a description of behavioral "function" in a sense in which descriptions of function go beyond straight descriptions of the experimental data to incorporate illicit speculations of some kind. My project is to argue that there is no such thing as a minimal, antiseptic, or unprejudiced description of the data, the behavior, that it is the job of the behavioral scientist to explain. But first, it will be well to understand this fear of infection by function. There are, I believe, several overlapping historical sources of this fear.

If we look to the history of behaviorism, we find a strong concern that the data for psychology should be intersubjectively observable data, in contrast, specifically, to data collected by introspection. One of the things that was traditionally thought to be known by introspection and, when the chips were down, by introspection alone, was what one's intentions or purposes were in action. It apparently followed that no reference to an organism's purpose in behaving should be made when describing behavioral data. To describe behavior by reference to its purpose would be to describe it by reference to hidden, possibly occult, causes in the organism, causes that, at the very least, could not be directly observed. It would be to build "mentalistic" notions or at least assumptions about hidden variables into the very description of one's data.

Out of the tradition of ethology came a parallel concern about the dangers of anthropomorphism. It is all too easy to read motives into an animal's behavior by analogy with what one's own motives would be. For example, Lehner (1979) cautions us that in describing a dove's behavior "as 'escape flying behavior' we are assuming that the dove was responding to a stimulus from which it *wanted* to escape" (1979, 46). But it may well be that nothing parallel to the motives of humans are to be found in such animals at all; certainly the ethologist should be careful not to prejudge such motives. And even if a label such as "grooming behavior" does not carry the implication that the animal has grooming as a personal motive, still by initially labeling the behavior as grooming rather than merely scratching, one may be blinding oneself to the true functions involved or to the necessity of seeking hard evidence for the functions one thereby assumes. According to a famous quote from Konrad Lorenz, "It is an inviolable law of inductive natural science that it has to *begin* with pure observation, totally devoid of any preconceived theory and even working hypothesis. This law has been broken by one and all of the great schools of behavioral study" (1950, 232).[3]

Thus in the tradition of classical ethology, one begins the study of an animal by first constructing an ethogram.[4] The ethogram is a list of the units in the animal's behavioral repertoire, described, in the first instance, purely as a set of motor patterns. But it is sometimes recognized explicitly (more often implicitly) that progress cannot be made without also noting something about the context of occurrence of these motor patterns. For example, to describe a behavior as eating, jumping, bar pressing, or scratching is already to have moved beyond muscle contractions to the wider context of these. Indeed, Drummond (1981) argues that a complete description of a behavioral unit would include, besides "intrinsic properties" (e.g., motor patterns), also location, orientation, physical topography, and physical effects.

Drummond's inclusion of physical effects in a description of pure behavioral form is particularly interesting, since description of effects has been taken by others to be description of the function, as *opposed* to the form, of behavior. For example, Robert Hinde tells us that "there are two methods for describing behavior. One involves reference ultimately to the strength, degree and patterning of muscular contractions. . . . The other involves reference not to these changes but to their consequences" (1970, 10). On this Lehner (1979, 44–45) comments that the distinction between "empirical description—description of the behavior in terms of body parts, movements and postures—(e.g., baring the teeth)" and "functional description—incorporation of reference to the behavior's function—(e.g., bared-teeth threat)" is "nearly synonymous" with Hinde's distinction between describing muscle contractions and describing consequences of these. Similarly, Bastock (1967, 11) writes that "displays. . . are best defined in terms of their function. *Threat* displays tend to cause withdrawal on the part of the adversary; *appeasement* or *submissive* displays tend to reduce attacks" (taken from

3. Colin Beer and others call this "the doctrine of immaculate perception."
4. I am much indebted to Matthew Kramer for supplying me with a quick review of current literature on ethogram construction from chap. 4 of his dissertation (1989). The references in this and the next paragraph, except Hinde 1970 and Lehner 1979, were found through this source.

Purton 1978). Purton (1978) discusses what he considers to be the *mistake* of conflating functions with mere effects. My argument will be that *exactly the same considerations that distinguish functions from mere effects also distinguish behavioral forms from mere motions*, from incidental effluences of the organism, and from other incidental changes occurring on its surface. Nonfunctional activity forms have exactly the same status as do nonfunctional effects of behaviors. Neither is a proper subject matter or a part of the data that behavioral science must explain. Conversely, to distinguish those forms of motor pattern and other outputs of the organism that are proper data for behavioral science from those that are not is impossible without implicitly postulating the *existence* of some function or other for the output, if not always the specifics of the function.

Concerning the task of constructing an ethogram, the obvious questions have, of course, arisen about how to segment the motor patterns that an animal exhibits into chunks, how long these segments should be, and how similar to one another they must be in order to be grouped together as examples of the same behavior (Schleidt and Yakalis 1984). But the consensus seems to be that as ethologists become more familiar with the animal under study, this theoretical problem tends to subside, and practical agreement to emerge (Kramer 1989). I would like to convince you that the problem of how to segment motor patterns into chunks is in fact but the tiniest tip of a huge theoretical iceberg. The theoretical problem is theoretically huge. It is solved in practice only by either commonsensical or ethologically experienced implicit reference to function. Since common sense for the most part solves this theoretical problem, one can appreciate its magnitude only by withholding common sense. Please try not to flinch, then, as I proceed to rub your nose in the theoretical absurdity.

There is a tendency to think of the motions of an individual organism as constituting a straightforward set of manageable size. These are the "outputs" for individualist psychology, the items that must be explained as deriving from "inputs" to the sensory systems by references to the regulating mechanisms between. And a collection of these events, observed one by one and incorporated into a list, are supposed to constitute the basic data for ethology. The ethologist's initial problem is how to divide and classify these individual behaviors so as to put each relevant *type* on the list just once. The individualist has a similar problem, for she wishes to *explain* the movement events, and events can be explained only under types. There is no such thing as explaining, simply, "so-and-so's current movements"; movements must be explained under general principles, and hence under general descriptions. The problem that emerges, then, is not just how to divide and count behavioral events. It is that the number of possible descriptions that might be given of any *one* movement event is completely unmanageable. Please try to keep common sense under control while I belabor this point.

Consider, for starters, that motions can only be described relatively, through mention of spatial and temporal relations to chosen relata. Relative to *what* should a given motion be described so as to classify or to explain it? Should we try to explain why Amos the mouse moves away from the cat, toward the kitchen clock, toward the waiting broom, toward London, or toward the North Pole? Should we explain why Amos's eyes blinked just before a piece of dust struck his closed eyelids, when the clock said 2:37:08, just as Amos's whiskers twitched, or just as the end of Amos's tail passed the fifth blue square of the kitchen linoleum? Indeed, did Amos blink, or was it just that his upper eyelashes removed themselves, in an arc, away from his eyebrows, or moved to point at his navel or his nose or his toes? Should we explain why muscle cell no. 237 in Amos's right biceps contracted at the same time that muscle cell no. 153 in Amos's left ear relaxed, or why it contracted at the same time that muscle cell no. 863 in his right *triceps* relaxed? Or would it be better to explain how it happened that *all* of the muscle cells in his body happened to coordinate so as miraculously to convey him across the floor, rather than leave him in a twitching heap in the middle? We might *attempt* to explain any of these things, and, in principle we might succeed with enough physics and chemistry, and a full chemical-physical state description of Amos and of a big enough piece of the world around him at a certain very exact time. But surely it is not the job of any life science to explain Amos's motions under every one of the uncountable number of descriptions that can be given of them. Under what descriptions, then, *is* it the behavioral scientist's job to explain Amos's motions? What is the *principle* involved here? This, I take it, is the same as the question of which of these descriptions describe *behaviors* of Amos, rather than mere motions, behaviors being the concern of the behavioral life scientist.

Motions are not peculiar with regard to the infinity of their possible descriptions. Amos can make squeaks, chattering sounds, sneezes, coughs, choking sounds, or he can be silent—silent except that, if you listen closely, he makes breathing sounds and little thumping sounds with his feet (danger signals or just foot patter?) and also with his heart. Which of these sounds and which silences are subject matter for behavioral science? How should the sounds be described? By pitch, inflection, duration, periodicity, harmonic structure, rhythmic structure, amplitude, or pattern of repetitions? Consider the sounds that a human makes. Some of these, such as screams and laughs, can be described relatively crudely. Others, the speech sounds, need to be described in great detail and in accordance with principles of such subtlety that they are not yet fully understood. Still other sounds, such as sounds made while choking or urinating, sounds made by the heart, and normally those made in breathing, do not need to be described at all. Sometimes silences need to be described, and sometimes they do not. Given the infinity of possible descriptions of emitted sounds and interspersed silences, what determines the descriptions that are relevant to behavioral science?

Does one look, perhaps, for repeated behavioral units, for patterns that recur? That mice run away from cats, for example, is a recurrent phenomenon, that they run toward waiting brooms is not. But the heart says "pit-a-pat" with wonderful regularity, every mouse eyeblink is a momentary movement of its eyelashes away from its eyebrows, every mouse foot touching the floor makes a minuscule thump, and choking is a distinctive and reliably reproducible sound under the right stimulus conditions. Yet none of these are behaviors, not in the sense we seek. None of these is the behavioral scientist required to explain (though explanations may fall out of behavioral science, of course, if these mouse outputs are shown to be accidental byproducts of other outputs that *do* require explanation).

The structure of the theoretical problem here may be clarified by comparing it with the better recognized problem concerning which *effects* of an organism's bodily motion require explanation. Hinde (1970) and Drummond (1981) suggest including physical effects of an organism's movements as part of the description of the form of the organism's behaviors. Yet we know that not every effect of an organism's movement can be considered part of its behavior. One effect of Rattus-the-rat's current muscle contractions is that the bar in front of him is depressed. But a second is that the watching experimenter frowns or smiles, a third that an elongated shadow passes over the floor in front of the cage, a fourth that a food pellet enters his cage, a fifth that this pellet makes a rattle that alerts young Templeton in the cage next door, making his mouth water, and so forth. We know that it is not the job of the behavioral scientist to explain all of these happenings. The productions of these effects are not all behaviors.

In truth, very few things that an organism does are behaviors. "Doing" is a far more general notion than is "behaving." To "do," one need merely satisfy an active verb. Active verbs are for the most part noncommittal about whether or not what they describe is the realization of a function or purpose. In the case of a few verbs, for example, "fall," "trip," and "slip," function or purpose is definitely excluded. And there are a few verbs, for example, "hunt," "fish," "seek," "challenge," and "threaten," that tell *only* of function and not at all of form. Thus to know that an animal is hunting is to know that the function of its behavior is finding and/or catching, but it is not to know anything whatever about the form that this behavior takes. Hunting behaviors can be realized with walking behaviors, swimming behaviors, flying behaviors, eye movements, movements of the fingers through the yellow pages, or "mental movements" (hunting through one's memory for a name). To say that an animal hunts is to say nothing at all about either the form or the result of its behavior. But most verbs are just the opposite. They designate form or result and are noncommittal about function. For example, "He bumped me with his elbow" and "He stepped on my toe" are noncommittal about whether the doing was a function or purpose of his bodily movement or merely a result of it. It is even possible inadvertently to "sign a check," accidentally to "warn someone," or involuntarily to "raise one's arm," under prompting of a well-placed electrode. Indeed, one might even "say that one is not feeling well" without doing so purposefully. Perhaps one is asleep or reciting sentences in a foreign language. That is, each of these descriptions *can* be used as a description of the form or result of a doing that is not, however, a *behaving* in the sense that concerns behavioral science.

But I have been ignoring a loud clamor in the wings. The clamor is that *law*, not function, is what distinguishes those bodily motions, sounds, effects of these, and so forth, that it is the behavioral scientist's job to attend to. The motions to be explained must be described under whatever descriptions yield *laws* of behavior. For example, there are no *laws* of mouse behavior that determine mouse motions relative to kitchen clocks or the North pole, but likely there are laws that determine mouse motions relative to cats, or at least relative to the orientations on mouse retinas of catlike images. (By "laws" can be meant, of course, not only lawful dispositions of the whole mouse but also lawful dispositions of parts of inner mechanisms in the mouse, which laws add up, flow-chart style perhaps, to an explanation of the mouse's outer behavioral dispositions.) Similarly, if there is some law of behavior under which falls Rattus's pushing the bar down but none under which falls his causing an elongated shadow, then ipso facto that Rattus pushes the bar down is a behavior that it is the psychologist's job to explain, whereas that Rattus causes an elongated shadow is not. Indeed, the actual history of psychology suggests that the psychologist may be able to predict the bar-pressing effect in accordance with laws of rat psychology without being able to predict the bodily motions that cause the bar pressing, without, say, predicting whether Rattus will use both paws, the right paw, the left paw, or his nose to depress the bar. Some of the laws of rat psychology may be about behavior described just in accordance with effect, and hence not about bodily motions at all.

This classic move is premised, I believe, partly on a confusion between function and law. If one supposes that functions are in general lawfully performed, as opposed to being performed only under ideal conditions, then searching for functions is easily assimilated to searching for laws. Compare Bastock's assimilation, cited above, of the function category "threat display" to the category of "displays that tend to cause withdrawal on the part of the adversary." The move is based also on a misconception concerning science, on the belief that valid sciences always deal in laws. I discuss these two mistakes in chapter 9. Here I will try to show only that outputs that fall under laws are not always behaviors.

The chameleon has a disposition to turn brown when placed in a brown box. The mouse has a disposition to brown nicely when placed in an oven at 350 degrees Fahrenheit. The chameleon's color change exemplifies a law of behavior that it is the ethologist's job to study. Why does the mouse's color change not exhibit a law of behavior that it is the ethologist's job to study? Or if one prefers muscle contractions, why is it not a law of behavior that rigor mortis invariably sets in shortly after the ingestion of cyanide, or that muscle rigidity results from the right sort of encounter with tetanus. It has been demonstrated that male rats deprived of food for nine days copulate less frequently than rats not so deprived.[5] Was this the discovery of a behavioral law?

But perhaps you will object here that antecedents that break the system under study, antecedents that damage the organism, can't yield laws *for* or *of* the systems under study. For example, whether or not decrease in copulation after nine days of starvation is a rat behavior falling under a psychological law depends on whether the starvation does damage to the rat's insides so that it is no longer a proper subject for the study of rat psychology. But that objection is a cheating one. For what it *means* to say that the system broke down is exactly that it is not a function of the system or a byproduct of its functions to react in this way. The very subject matter of behavioral study, the *intact* animal, is defined by reference to proper or normal function. Behavioral dispositions are dispositions not just of any old chunk of warm matter but of a chunk having a normal constitution, where this is defined relative to its (historically defined) proper functions (chapters 1 and 2). Most of the dispositions of Amos and Rattus as chunks of matter are chemical and physical, not psychological. To find the psychological ones, we must make a necessary reference to the *functions* of Amos's and Rattus's dispositions.

To make this clearer, consider some lawful dispositions that may be realized without destroying the biological system. A strong enough electric shock administered to the body in one place contracts the muscles in another. Cockroaches become torpid when the temperature drops

5. Sachs 1965, as re-presented in Hinde 1970. In fact, Sachs's experiment was much more interesting than Hinde's discussion suggests. Even after nine days without food, rats mostly choose sex over food when offered both.

too low. A mild blow below the knee cap causes a kick. If spun around enough times in the same direction, children fall down. When a puff of air hits an open eye, it blinks. Which of these lawful consequences are behaviors? My suggestion is that the eye-blink reflex is the only one of these that is clearly a behavior. It is the only one, so far as we know, that has a function. The rest are probably "spandrels," results of the system's architecture that are accidental relative to its functional design (see chapter 2). Similarly, the eye-blink reflex is *properly* described as a blink or closing of the eyes, not as a movement of the eyelashes away from the eyebrows or toward the navel, nose, or toes, for only the covering of the eyes, as such, has a biological function. That the blinker's eyelashes move away from his eyebrows is a response that falls under laws, but it does not fall under behavioral laws.

I will also not accept as an objection that some behavioral scientists would call knee jerks or becoming torpid when too cold "behaviors." My claim is that if they believe that these happenings have no functions, then if they think about it carefully, they will see that they *shouldn't* call them behaviors, not with a capital "B." The impulse to call them behaviors rests on a confusion. It rests on the assumption that whatever an animal *does* is behavior. And it rests on a false belief about the data of science. It rests on the belief that not only must behavior, the basic data for the behavioral sciences, be observable but that it must also be observable, right on the surface, that it *is* behavior. I have been trying to show that this is not so, that there is no *surface* feature that distinguishes behaviors from other doings.

But now it will be asked, How can the behavioral scientist's initial *data*, what she is supposed to explain, be only forms of output that have functions when the fact that a form has a function is not an observable fact but a matter of theory? Well, how can the classical chemist's data, what she is supposed to explain, be only the behaviors of chemical elements and compounds and not also of mixtures when the fact that a substance is an element or compound and not a mixture is not an observable fact but only a matter of chemical theory? The philosophy of science has matured a great deal since it helped to give birth to behaviorism. Not only have anxieties about speculating on the contents of little black boxes been dispelled; so have anxieties about infecting ones data-gathering with theory. If there is agreement on anything among current philosophers of science, it is on this: what the data for a given branch of science are and how those data must be described so as to connect with theory are matters that are adjusted along with theory and cannot be finally settled in advance. Theoretical science is, in this respect, always a bootstrapping operation.

Of course, it is true that ethologists spend much time putting down in their field notebooks descriptions of behaviors whose functions they do not yet understand. They make a point of trying to describe behaviors in ways that do not prejudge the issue of *specific* function. This practice makes eminent sense. In no science is it good to jump to conclusions. But the fact that the ethologist's preliminary field notes often turn out to be *useful* attests not to the fact that the behavioral data for ethology are recognizable prior to theory. It attests to the soundness of the traditions behind such data collecting and to the perspicacity of the trained field worker in separating out descriptions that are *likely* to be descriptions of functional forms from those that are unlikely to be. Thus it is that as ethologists become more familiar with the animal under study, the theoretical problems about how to "chunk" and classify behaviors tend to subside, and practical agreement to emerge (Kramer 1989).

This is not the place to explore the rich question by what signs and symptoms the ethologist discerns that a certain behavioral unit is bound to have some function or other. But it is very often true that the ethologist rightly perceives this long in advance of entertaining any specific hypothesis about what that function is. On the other hand, it is also true that the ethologist can sometimes be badly mislead. It is not always obvious what it is that an animal is doing that constitutes its true behavior. Reflect, for example, that few but trained linguists can even hear all the salient distinctions among sounds in human languages unrelated to their own, but these distinctions are crucial if one wishes to describe verbal behaviors. Similarly, Colin Beer (1975, 1976) tells an involved story about difficulties in discovering where the true behaviors lie within the vocalizations and within the "facing away" behaviors of laughing gulls. "In spite of the technical advances in data collecting and data processing . . . , one still has to start out with selection of one out of an infinite number of possible descriptive strategies, in accordance with whatever one's wits and experience offer as the best bet" (Beer 1973, 54).[6]

I have urged that the behavioral scientist's job is not to study just the properties of a chunk of living matter but to study the properties of a biological system, the properties, roughly, that have accounted for the proliferation and survival of the creature's ancestors. These properties figure in an explanation of how it happened that some critical proportion of historical embodiments of the system under study managed to avoid destruction and ultimately to reproduce themselves. What a biological system does *as a biological system*, and not merely as a pile of atoms, is what its ancestors have historically done that enabled them to survive and reproduce. *As a biological system*, it *does* only what it is its biological purpose, or "proper function" (see chapters 1 and 2), to do.

The behavioral sciences, considered as life sciences, are engineering sciences in reverse. The engineer begins with certain functions in mind that she wishes to see performed and then figures out how to build a device that will perform these functions. The behavioral scientist begins with a device that has already been designed to perform certain functions and then figures out what these functions are and how the device is constructed to perform them. It is not her job to notice or figure out any other things the device might do, like supplying one a good dinner (hens) or making a good alarm clock (roosters). Nor is it her job to notice any other dispositions it might have, like one's knee jerks and one's skin turning red in the sun. So understood, the life sciences do not include studies of how best to exterminate roaches, of breeding techniques, or of how to grow turkeys with more white meat. Nor do the behavioral sciences as life sciences include studies of animal-training techniques, of how to get chickens to lay more eggs, or of how best to keep pigs from rooting. This is not to hurt anyone's feelings but just to

6. That it is not always obvious what constitutes an animal's true behavior is one reason that the ethologist will note highly conspicuous recurrent outputs of an animal even when these are apparently functionless. The explanations of such behaviors as spandrels or as leftovers from an earlier phase in the animal's evolutionary history are, of course, also of interest. But compare the last two paragraphs of this chapter. Behaviors that are species-typical, and hence aid in distinguishing related species, are also noted in the ethologists notebook, of course.

make what I think is a needed distinction. The heart of the life sciences is to understand life, not what can be done with or to life.

Yet if the behavioral scientist studies not chunks of matter but functional systems, how does it happen that the behavioral experimentalist puts out one eye of *Armadillidium* and then reports in the literature that it proceeds to swim around in circles, or removes large portions of a cat's brain and reports on resulting abnormalities in the cat's paw-placing behavior, or presents a newly hatched chick with a mechanical toy in place of a mother and reports effects of the resulting abnormal imprinting, or attempts to teach an ape sign language? Surely this is legitimate research in behavioral science, but just as surely, it is not investigation of proper behaviors of the animals being studied. The point of experiments such as these is to probe into the mechanisms, the machinery, by which proper behaviors *are* produced. To know what will deflect a mechanism from proper performance of its tasks, how it will perform under abnormal conditions or when altered in certain ways, can yield strong clues about how it is constituted, how it works inside, and hence how it normally manages to produce *proper* behaviors. It goes (or should go) without saying that the experimentalist does not perform *random* experiments on the animal to be studied. Not any old facts about how the animal will behave if mutilated in random ways or subjected to random adverse conditions interests the scientist—only facts that cast light on the mechanisms behind proper functioning.

What distinguishes the core life sciences from the physical sciences is a difference not in the natural kinds being studied but in the point of departure for the study. What is logically first for the core life sciences is the study of proper or normal function. Of course, there is also abnormal physiology, abnormal psychology, and so forth, which are studies of common aberrations, common malfunctions, of biological systems. But these subjects cannot even be defined except by *contrast* with proper operation of these systems. The study of biologically proper behaviors is prior and foundational; the study of abnormal function is a study of departures from this norm. As these departures become more extreme, the study of abnormal function merges slowly into a study of mere chemistry and physics.

8

The Green Grass Growing All Around: A Philosophical Essay on Ethology and Individualism in Psychology, Part 2

In the last chapter, I claimed that behavior is the functional form of an animal's behavior. My job now is to spell out implications of this thesis for understanding mechanisms of behavior control. At the far end of the tunnel, I will emerge with a rough thesis concerning what it would be like to understand the role that intentional states—beliefs, desires, intentions, seeings, hopings, etc.—play in the control of human behaviors.

I can summarize the main points I have made and will make in terms of the currently popular image of the organism as an input-output device taking in stimulations and emitting behaviors. In the last chapter, I argued that each organism emits an uncountable number of outputs, each of which is describable in an uncountable number of ways. But the only output forms of interest for the study of the organism as a living system are those that have biological functions. The animals' outputs must be described according to their functional forms. Only these are forms that it is the business of life science to explain.

The rest of the argument is roughly as follows. The functions of behaviors are, by definition, functions performed through mediation of the environment. Indeed, the functions that define behaviors often reach very far out into the environment, both in time and in space. So behavioral-output forms must be described in relation to the organism's environment, both its proximate environment and sometimes its very remote environment.

Special thanks to Colin Beer and Peter Brown for very helpful comments on an earlier draft of this essay.

Similarly, the only inputs of interest among the possible stimulation patterns that might impinge on the organism are those that the organism is designed to use. Not only must these not break or jam the organism's system; they must also be described not arbitrarily but in accordance with their *own* functional forms, those forms that accord with the properly functioning organism's way of using its inputs. But the uses of these inputs are to help mold the forms of the organism's behaviors so as to have appropriate impacts on the environment, and to help determine proper placement of these behaviors in the environment so that their functions will be fulfilled. To understand what relevance the inputs have to success of the organism's behaviors, we must understand their normal environmental causes and accompaniments, both proximate and sometimes very remote.

Last, understanding how and why the mechanisms that mediate between perceptual input and behavioral output manage to contribute to the production of well-functioning behaviors involves understanding how these mechanisms themselves are normally related to the environment. For these mechanisms can adapt the organism's output to its environment only by varying their forms of activity as a function of the environment, both proximate and sometimes very remote.

1   Explaining the Functional Form of the Output

The first point that we need to grasp firmly is the difference between explaining the operations of a system in terms that refer to the functional forms of its inputs, outputs, and mediating innards and explaining its activities in other ways. Let me begin by exploiting the familiar analogy of an organism to a calculator or computer, the analogy responsible for the contemporary input-output view of organisms mentioned above.

First consider the analogy as it likens the animal to a computer. Dennett has persuasively argued that "an animal—in fact any fairly complicated object—can be a number of different Turing machines at once, depending on our choice of input, state descriptions, and so forth" (1978a, 261) and that "as a complicated chunk of the world [a man] will surely qualify for any number of Turing machine characterizations" (p. 262). "No one of these," he says, "can be singled out on purely structural or mechanical grounds as *the* Turing machine interpretation of the animal. If we want to give some sense to that task, we must raise considerations of purpose and design" (p. 261). But to consider purpose and design, "first we have to decide which of the impingements on the animal count as input and which as interference" (p. 260) and "which features of the animal's physical constitution are working as they are designed to, as they were supposed to, and which are malfunctioning, misdesigned or merely fortuitous" (p. 261). These latter points are analogous to those I made in chapter 7 concerning what counts as what an animal is doing for purposes of behavioral science.

Dennett's claim that any complicated object can be a number of Turing machines at once suggests a further important point. If, as Dennett (above) and I (chapters 1 and 2) have argued, the structure and dispositions of a chunk of matter do not alone determine its biological function, then, of course, biological function does not supervene in any simple way on physical structure. Whether the paleontologist has found a tooth or a horn does not supervene just on the physical form of the object found. So whatever one thinks biological function does depend on (and Dennett and I are not always in agreement here), the following point will be valid. If, as I now propose to argue, valid explanations of behavior must explain behaviors by reference to their functional forms, and if, at least in principle, functional forms can differ while physical structures remain identical, then the behaviors of identical physical structures might sometimes need to be given quite different explanations. To put this in a familiar contemporary light, it is a mistake to think that because minutely physically identical "twins" would produce the same physical outputs under the same conditions, the explanations of their behaviors would have to be the same. Notice that this point is supported without making any reference to intentional states. The very behaviors of such twins could, in principle, be different, and this could be so, in fact might more easily be so, if they were organisms too simple to have intentional states.

Now let me turn the animal-computer analogy around. A calculator can be likened to an organism in that (as Dennett also points out) it does both things that it is *not* designed to do and, if one is lucky, things that it is designed to do. I am remembering an enormous, ancient Marchant desk calculator that chattered away in my father's study when I was small. It was powered by an electric motor and consisted otherwise mainly of rods, levers, gears, and cams. It was designed to add, subtract, multiply, and divide, carrying twelve figures. When in use, it often rattled the dishes in the kitchen and always scared the cat. These things it was not designed to do. Nor was it designed to take chewing gum dropped into its works as input, or such was my father's forceful opinion. One could do something like studying its physiological psychology; indeed, I used to do so. One could try to figure out how the levers and gears were hooked up inside so as to effect its proper functions of addition, subtraction, etc.

Now imagine a hugely mechanically gifted child not yet introduced to even the rudiments of arithmetic (recall Meno's slave boy) confronting such a calculator. After studying the mechanism for long enough, it might be that such a child could tell you, for any input to its keyboard that you described, what the corresponding output on its dial would be. He would probably also be able to tell you what would happen if you lodged some chewing gum just *there* in the mechanism, what would happen if you filed off tooth 9 of gear 129, and just which inputs would create large enough and continuous enough vibrations to shake some of the dishes onto the floor or to keep the cat under the bed for an hour. But would such a child command an understanding of the Marchant's psychology? Surely not if he does not understand which are its legitimate inputs and outputs or that the outputs represent arithmetic functions of the inputs. Surely not if he cannot explain how the workings of its insides manage to add up, say, to its adding. Surely not, for example, if he does not realize that what gear 129 just did when it nudged gear 130 was to effect the operation of carrying one. Though he can predict, under some description, every relevant motion that it makes, he understands neither what the calculator is really doing nor, of course, how it does it. He knows, as it were, its function in extension, for he knows (among many other things) the value of its function for each argument, for each input. But he does not grasp, as it were, its function in intension, the function that its raison d'etre is to exemplify, and hence he does not understand its psychology.

But I need to be careful to make the point I intend here. In 1969 Dennett, using precisely the same analogy and nearly the same words, argues an importantly similar yet also importantly different point. It will be best to quote him at some length:

> If we . . . proceed on the assumption that human and animal behavioural control systems are only very complicated denizens of the physical universe, it follows that the events within them, characterized extensionally in the terms of physics or physiology, should be susceptible to explanation and prediction without any recourse to content, meaning, or Intentionality. . . . If we had such a story we would have in one sense an extensional theory of behavior, for all the *motions* (extensionally characterized) of the animal . . . would be explicable and predictable in these extensional terms, but one thing such a story would say nothing about was *what the animal was doing.* This latter story can only be told in Intentional terms, but it is not a story about features of the world *in addition to* the features of the extensional story; it just describes what happens in a different way. Supposing one could have complete knowledge of the mechanics of a computer without the slightest inkling of the rationale of its construction, one would be in a similar situation. . . . One would have nothing to say in this account about the logic of the operations. (1969, 78–79)[1]

When I said above "as it were, its function in extension" and "as it were, its function in intension," I did not mean to speak literally, nor did I intend to make any point here about intentionality, which is quite another (though certainly not unrelated) matter. Certainly I do not wish to suggest that to "understand the psychology" of the calculator, the boy would have to speak in "intentional terms" or to take a different "stance" toward his subject matter (compare Dennett 1978c, 1987). What he must understand is not of a different character from what he already does understand. It is just that he must focus on the physical patterns that show how a particular relation between input and output is achieved, the one the machine is designed to bring about, from among all the other relations there also are between the machine's various "inputs" and "outputs" when described in other ways. This will not require that he move to some further "interpretation" of the machine or to another level than the mechanical. But he must see how the patterns in the gears, cams, and shafts, given certain inputs, are running isomorphically to patterns in mathematics.

---

1. I was astonished when I belatedly discovered this passage of Dennett's some years after writing the first draft of this essay. The comparison between the uses that Dennett and I here make of the same analogy is the clearest and sharpest embodiment imaginable of the similarity and contrast between our views of intentionality. The compression is nearly to a geometrical point.

2   Why Computers Do Not Exhibit Behaviors

Indeed, the analogy between calculator psychology and human psychology is importantly flawed in a way that may precisely prohibit giving an explanation of the calculator's workings by reference to intentional states. Notice that the calculator does not exhibit "behavior" in the sense I have defined (chapter 7). The calculator's outputs do not have functions that are fulfilled via mediation of the environment. Its environment is quite irrelevant to its proper functioning, so long as the environment doesn't destroy it. Mechanisms that calculate *real* behaviors, by contrast, are mechanisms that must take account of the environment every step of the way so that these behaviors will fit with the environment and be strategically placed within it. *Intentional* states are behavior-controlling states that must map onto the world for all to proceed biologically properly and normally (see below and chapters 4–6 above). This is no time for a digression into the philosophy of mathematics, but it is not at all clear that there is some portion of reality external to the calculator (in the realm of Forms, perhaps) that the calculator's states must map onto, one by one, in order for it to be doing its job.

But there is a far more important point that emerges from the fact that computers do not exhibit behaviors. Because it is not part of the proper functioning of a computer to effect environmental changes, we obviously cannot use the computer analogy to help us understand how reference to the environment is needed to explain the mechanisms of behavior control. Employment of the computer analogy is bound to blind us precisely to the role of environment. It is time now to begin removing these blinders.

3   The Environment as an Ingredient in Behavior

Let us begin with walking, a very fundamental and ancient yet rather complex sort of behavior that must to be executed and correctly placed in the walking organism's environment. Compare to the uncomprehending child calculator whiz above an ethologist studying centipedes who has progressed to the point that she can predict and "explain" the exact movement of each of the centipede's legs, given relevant input to its perceptual systems. Given certain input conditions, she knows that leg 16 will move at 10:27:06.23 and that leg 17 will move at 10:27:06.25 and so forth, and exactly *how* each will move. But although this is implied by what she knows, it has not occurred to her to notice that leg 17 will move *just after* leg 16 has moved and leg 16 just after leg 15. More generally, it has never occurred to her to notice how, or wonder why, the individual motions of the legs are related to one another or coordinated as they are, or to wonder what function relates the leg movements and the coordination among these to the location and properties of surfaces contiguous to the centipede. She has not noticed, for example, under what surface-contact conditions these coordinations sometimes result in movement of the whole centipede in a uniform direction. Though she may, after many calculations, notice the remarkable coincidence that the centipede's *whole body* is soon going to move *all at once* in a forward direction, or toward the kitchen clock, or that the legs are about to tap out Yankee Doodle, she clearly has not done her job as an ethologist.

Just the ability to predict movements, even an understanding of why these movements occur, is not what causal explanation in ethology is about. The behavioral scientist must understand movements under descriptions that reveal their *functional* forms. That and how the behavioral forms are functional can only be understood in relation to the environment through which they function. You cannot explain the walking behavior of the centipede without taking into account that its function is to move the whole centipede forward, or without taking into account not just stimulations to its afferent nerves but also relevant properties of the surface on which it walks. Not that one *can't* study the centipede just as an input-output device. Anything with a definite location and boundaries *can*, in principle, be studied as a mere input-output device. The heart or the kidney can, in principle, be studied in this way, and so can half a heart or half a kidney or the right-hand side of a computer. One can study the wheel of a bicycle in this way too, ignoring both the axle it is attached to and the surfaces it moves over, but no explanation of the role of the wheel on the bicycle will come out of such a study.

4 The Inadequacy of the Organism/Environment Distinction

So aspects of the proximal environment of the organism must certainly be taken into account to explain its behavior. Before arguing that aspects of its distal environment, even aspects of its very remote environment, may also have to be taken into account, I would like to loosen the iron grip of the organism-environment dichotomy, which is quite generally and unreflectively assumed to be sharp and theoretically fast. It is a very serious error to think of the subject of the study of psychology and ethology as a system spatially contained within the shell or skin of an organism. What is inside the shell or skin of the organism is only *half* of a system; the rest, if the organism is lucky, is in the environment. The organismic system, especially (indeed, by definition) the behavioral systems, reach into the environment and are defined by what constitute proper, or normal, relations and interactions between structures in the organism and in the environment.

The line between organism and environment, as it is customarily drawn, is useless so far as the study of the organismic system is concerned. Consider some examples. Most crabs molt when about to grow out of their shells, secreting a substance that hardens to become a new and bigger shell. Birds, however, build their nests out of materials that they find in the environment, although some complete these nests by lining them with their own breast feathers. The crab's shell is considered to be part of the crab. Why is the bird's nest not considered part of the bird? Surely, it is no less a part of the organismic system than the shell of the crab. That the bird uses its muscles rather than its glands in constructing its home is clearly not a relevant consideration. Is there a difference because the bird can leave its nest behind whereas the crab must remain with its shell? The nestling, however, cannot leave the nest behind. True, the nestling might happen into some substitute for a nest. But one can also imagine giving the crab a shell transplant. Is there a difference between nest and shell because the bird uses construction materials that it finds lying about rather than materials that it makes for its nest? But we don't claim that the rest of the bird's body is not part of the bird on the grounds that this body has been constructed out of materials the bird found lying around: seeds, berries, etc. Besides, the bird does make the feathers that line the nest.

If the distinction between nest and shell still seems sharp to you, are you clear where to draw the organism-environment line in these intermediate cases? Some moth larvae secrete substances out of which they spin their cocoons. Other moth larvae use leaves, cementing these together with substances that they secrete. All will die if removed too soon from their cocoon shells. Hermit crabs find their shells ready made, conveniently left behind by dead snails, so that, with luck, the only thing they have to do to acquire a shell is to search. Yet they are as defenseless without their shells as is any ordinary crab. There are small marine invertebrates that take over holes in rock originally made by digger clams, growing into and conforming themselves to these homes in such a way that they cannot survive removal. Is it clear in these cases where common sense draws the line between organism and environment? And if it is, is it also clear that the distinction between organism and environment so drawn is of principled biological significance?

The bird needs its nest to function properly in exactly the same way that it needs, on the one hand, its skin and feathers and, on the other, its seeds. The nest, the feathers, and the seeds are all part of the same organismic system. Conversely, the immune systems of the bird are designed to deal precisely with things spatially inside its body but that are not part of the biological system. The distinction between what is spatially "inside" and what is spatially "outside" the bird, as such, has no significance for the study of the avian biological *system*. The only interesting principled distinction that can be drawn between that portion of the organismic system that is the organism proper and that portion of it that is normal environment is not determined by a spatial boundary. It is a matter of degree—the degree of control that the system as a whole has over the production and maintenance of normal structure and normal states for its various portions. Let me clarify this.

Each of the various parts and subsystems within an organismic system has a normal environment, normal surroundings, in the absence of which it cannot perform all of its functions in a normal way. The lungs, for example, cannot perform their function of helping to supply the tissues with oxygen in a normal way unless encased in the airtight chest cavity above the diaphragm displaced periodically by certain muscles, unless the organism is surrounded by an atmosphere under a certain pressure and containing oxygen, unless next to a heart pumping blood through the pulmonary vessels, unless this blood contains sufficient hemoglobin, unless this whole complex is within a certain narrow range of temperature, and so forth. An organismic system involves a coordination among parts or subsystems, each of which requires that the other parts or subsystems have normal structure and are functioning normally. Call those conditions without which a part or subsystem cannot function properly in accordance with a normal explanation "normal conditions for proper functioning" of the part or subsystem.

Normal conditions for proper functioning of a part or subsystem must not be confused with just conditions that the part or subsystem is usually in. Normal conditions are conditions that have historically figured in an explanation of how the part or subsystem has functioned properly *when* it has functioned properly. There are many parts or subsystems that are supposed to function only under quite special conditions. Thus the immune systems, the systems responsible for repair of damaged tissues, the vomiting reflex (designed, presumably, to rid the body of toxins) are only supposed to operate under certain conditions. Similarly, of course, many behavior patterns of simple animals are supposed to be triggered only under quite specific conditions. None of these conditions is a condition that the animal or the functional part or subsystem is usually in.

Also, it is of paramount importance that not all parts and subsystems usually function properly. The function of the countershading on a caterpillar is to prevent it from being seen, and hence from being eaten. But it may well be that the average caterpillar ends up being eaten anyway, the precise conditions needed for its disguise to work properly not being sufficiently prevalent.[2] Similarly, most baby fish get eaten by bigger fish, despite many precautions taken by nature. And, of course, the immune systems do not necessarily manage to perform their proper functions most of the time. Before the advent of modern medicine, the average human died before reproducing, in civilized times most commonly from some kind of infection. This is because the immune systems depend on certain accidental relations holding between antigens intro-

2. Matthew Kramer is concerned that I not leave a wrong impression about the ingenuity of caterpillar predators. Many predators use olfactory cues, and there are also caterpillar parasites. But the general point should be plain enough.

duced and antibodies in the system. By "accidental" I mean that the organismic system has no control over whether these relations hold. Yet that they hold is a normal condition for performance of the proper function of the immune systems. Similarly, to rehearse again my favorite example, the function of a sperm's tail is to propel it to an ovum, but very few sperm find themselves under normal conditions for proper performance of the tail. For most, no ovum chances to lie directly in the path of their random swim. Thus normal conditions for proper performance of an item are often not average conditions but, rather, ideal conditions. Sometimes they are very lucky conditions.[3]

As we move closer to the spatial center of any organism, however, we find a greater proportion of parts and systems whose normal conditions for proper functioning is maintained by some *other* part or parts of the system, or by the whole system. For example, most parts well inside of a mammal must be at a certain normal temperature for proper operation, and it is a proper function of other parts of the system—certain little cells in the hypothalamus, the sweat glands, etc.—to see that this normal condition is maintained. Similarly, presence of a normal heart is one normal condition for proper performance of the lungs, and there are numerous organs and systems within the body that help maintain a normal heart as part of their jobs. Toward the periphery of the body, however, normal conditions for proper functioning tend to be less under the system's control. For example, the countershading on a caterpillar performs its proper function in accordance with a normal explanation only if the caterpillar orients itself correctly in relation to the light, but also only if the lighting conditions are favorable and the predator's perceptual systems are not set to make sufficiently fine discriminations. Over the latter two conditions the caterpillar has no control. Similarly, the sweat glands can perform their proper function of cooling the body only if the humidity outside is not too high. True, if it is too high, other systems of the body may seek a less humid or cooler spot or construct one. But as we move out from the spatial center of an organism, the tendency is for the method of maintaining normal conditions to become less a making and more a seeking or a fitting in. At the outer limit, normal conditions, normal surroundings for portions of the orga-

3. The importance of this point will be discussed at more length in chapter 9.

nismic system, are simply there or not there, maintenance of these conditions being completely beyond the system's control.

But even what is entirely beyond the system's control is not as such *outside the system*. Why should the fact that a part of a system is neither made nor maintained by the rest of the system disqualify it *as* part of the system? On the contrary, destruction of the ocean of air that the bird flies in and breathes oxygen from, of the seeds and berries that it eats, of the twigs and grasses from which it builds its nest, as well as of the nest itself or of the bird's skin and feathers, would not merely cause but *constitute* destruction of part of the avian system. To say that a part or subsystem is in its "normal conditions" is just another way of saying that it is part of a wider *intact* system, that the *rest* of the system to which it belongs is in place.

It is the ethologist's job to study the behavioral dispositions of chunks of avian matter *as* part of this system. This study is continuous with study of the *development* of the bird's behavioral systems and with the study of embryology. Ethology is just one more aspect of the study of how the various parts of the avian system develop or are put in place. To study a bird's bodily behavior apart from its normal environment would be exactly like trying to study the embryological development of its wings without taking account of the wings' normal connections to other body parts or without taking account of properties of the egg white and shell within which it develops.

The ethologist must study the mechanisms of organism-environment interaction that hold when the whole system operates properly, that is, when conditions for avian survival and proliferation are normal. Coordinately, unless she is interested in pathology, she need have no direct concern for what the bird does when conditions for its survival and proliferation are not normal, when the wider avian system is not intact, not whole. Accordingly, the ethologist must produce a theory about what conditions *are* normal for proper operation of the organism, about what relations normally, ideally, hold between organism and environment, or between various states of the organism and states of its environment. That is, she must produce a theory about the constitution of those parts of the system that lie beyond the organism's body and about what relations hold between the parts and states within and the parts and states without when the whole system is operating properly.

5   The Study of Behavior as a Study of the Organism-Environment System

With this perspective in mind, let us return once more to the question of what behavior is. In the last chapter I said that behavior is the functional form of external change or activity on the part of an organism, the functions in question being mediated by the environment. I also drew, or at least tolerated the drawing, of a distinction between bodily motions and the functional effects of these. But from our present perspective there is no principled distinction between organism and normal aspects of the environment, unless it is the graded distinction between parts of the normal organismic system that are controlled or put in place by the rest of the system and those that are not. Under this light, behavior emerges as the functional form of the wider organismic process; functional changes usually considered to be in nonbodily parts of the system have exactly the same status as changes in bodily parts. All are equally just functional changes within the system. What the organism maintains, modifies, or puts in place through the activity of its body is just part of the developing wider organismic system. Behavior, then, is just the functional form of the widest organismic processes. Physiology now becomes the study of behaviors occurring within the body; behavioral science becomes the study of the forms of functional processes occurring outside the body. Traditionally, behavioral science includes also the study of those parts inside the body that control functional processes occurring outside; it includes physiological psychology, for example. For these inner parts are parts of the same systems whose outsides are studied by behavioral scientists—"same systems" in the sense that the lungs and diaphragm are parts of one system, while the stomach and intestines are parts of another.

To turn from birds to beavers, the entire process of building a beaver dam and of using the fruits of having built it are thus, strictly speaking, part of beaver behavior. What the beaver does is not just to move its muscles or put sticks down where water trickles but also to build a dam and create a pond. To understand beaver behavior is to understand how this entire process is accomplished, not just how the muscles happen to become contracted. The ethologist is, of course, interested in the fact that the beaver reacts to the sound of trickling water by dumping any available materials on top of it. But the interest lies in seeing how this reaction, combined with various other instinctive and/or learned beaver responses, contributes, when all goes normally (ideally), to creating a beaver pond. That certain sounds cause a certain reaction in the beaver is of interest because in the beaver's normal (ideal) environment, such sounds are caused by running water, and the beaver's reaction to these sounds helps to cause beaver dams, which in turn cause beaver ponds to form. What the ethologist is studying here is beaver-system development, wider beaver embryology. Similarly, ethologists would love to know, but don't yet, exactly what stimulations cause what responses in mound-building termites so as to produce the typical shape, size, and structure of the mound.

Ethologists are interested in the reaction of ants to oleic acid, but not in their reaction to ammonia or citric acid. This is because the ants respond to oleic acid, a substance secreted by dead ants, by dragging the acid-tainted item out of the nest, thus contributing to sanitation. But ammonia and citric acid are not (to my knowledge) normal in the ants' environment. The ethologist is also interested in what causes bees to dance, but not just in what all *can or might* cause this. Of interest is what triggers and controls the dances so that, in normal conditions for proper operation of the dance-making systems, the dance correctly maps a location of nectar by Beemese semantic rules. The ethologist is interested in how the dance gets correctly placed in the bees' environment so as to constitute, along with the nectar, a normally formed part of the wider organismic system of the bee. She is interested in wider bee embryology.

These principles are pretty obvious when articulated for nonhuman ethology. They should be equally obvious when applied to human ethology. Put (an analogue of) the bee dance inside the body so that it mediates between two parts of the same organism and you have, I have argued (chapters 3–6), an inner representation. Mechanisms that control complex and flexible behaviors are, in general, guided by inner representations (chapter 5). The ethology of humans, insofar as it deals with these systems, is called "cognitive psychology." The job of cognitive psychology is to find out how the systems regulating complex flexible human behaviors are guided by perception so that, in a normal (ideal) environment, they effect formation and placement of behaviors beneficial in the environment.

The physiological part of this task must involve a description of the relations that inner representations normally (ideally) bear to the environment so as to make this formation and placement possible. The behaviors to be explained are wide behaviors, like making dams and ponds, or making symphonies, friends, revolutions, and money. What must be explained is the whole *ideal* process of perception, concept formation, belief and intention formation, how the intentions become imbued with (biological) reasonableness, and how they get themselves fulfilled. What must be explained, that is, is what the various inner cognitive mechanisms do when all goes ideally well so as to account for their continued proliferation in the species. Also, just as the physiologist studies methods of recovery from disease and injury, the cognitive psychologist studies methods of recovery from false beliefs and harmful desires, methods of detecting and jettisoning confused concepts (chapter 14; Millikan, forthcoming). That completes the big picture. Let me now sketch some details.

6   Inner Mechanisms of Behavior: Desires and Beliefs

In chapters 4 to 6, I sketched some details for a theory of "indicative" inner representations, those inner representations that are designed to mirror an organism's world. Here I must say more about "imperative" inner representations, for it is the functions of these representations that connect most directly with behavior. Indicative representations are maps of what is, while imperative representations are blueprints for what is to be done. The simplest representations are undifferentiated between these two moods, as are bee dances, which tell the bees both where the nectar is and where to go. Perhaps we understand the idiom "This is just what one does" in this undifferentiated fashion. Also, perhaps formed intentions, as distinct from mere desires, are undifferentiated between these two moods, serving both as blueprints for action and as maps of how things will be in the future. It seems likely that the development of organisms having the capacity sometimes to separate indicative from imperative representations was a major breakthrough in the evolutionary history of cognition.

Imperative representations are blueprints or plans for what is to be done. Their job is to guide the organism toward achievement of the ends they represent. As in the case of indicative representations, imperative representations are supposed to vary in parallel with how the world varies, but they are supposed to *cause* the world to vary as they vary, rather than be caused to reflect the world's variations.

I have suggested that desires are such blueprints. That is, one proper function of a desire is to help cause its own fulfillment. Jerry Fodor is distressed by this suggestion. He does not see how there could possibly be any sense of "normally" in which desires are normally fulfilled (Fodor 1990, 85). Although "desires are normally fulfilled" isn't exactly how I would prefer to use the term "normally" (see chapter 6), I still think Fodor is rather too fainthearted. Desires can be said to be normally fulfilled, and sperm normally to reach ova, in a sense of normal very close to the one I have been employing, where the normal is what conforms to a biological norm or ideal. Here is the argument.

Presumably, the biological point of the capacity to *represent* goals to oneself is to make it possible to vary them, evaluate them, arrive at them rationally, and arrive at rational means of fulfilling them. It is not, then, that one first has a goal and then represents it; representing it must be a way of having it. But the function of a goal, obviously, is to be fulfilled. Representations of goals are supposed to help guide the organism toward their own fulfillment. Desires, on the other hand, might be thought of as competing with one another for allocation of resources, which, once allocated, turn them into goals, then perhaps later, when belief in their impending fulfillment is warranted, into intentions. The capacity to have desires is maintained in the species, then, only insofar as some desires become goals, then become intentions, and finally are fulfilled. Hence one of the functions of desires too is to guide the organism toward their own fulfillment. Indeed, their function is to get themselves fulfilled even when they are contradictory or when their fulfillment would be devastating to the organism that harbors them. Let me explain.

To see this, let us concentrate on relational rather than categorial descriptions of the functional aspects of representations, as follows. Think of indicative representations, or indicative intentional icons (see chapter 5, section 2), not as corresponding one by one, each to a separate normal condition for proper performance of its (inner) users. Rather, think of each as requiring the same normal condition as every other indicative representation occurring in the same inner representational system. This condition is described relationally. It is the condition that there be an aspect of the environment bearing a specified projection relation to the icon. The imperative representation or icon should be thought of in the same way. Compare the following: The function of a blueprint showing a building with structure A is best thought of not as that of guiding the builder so that he builds a building with structure A. Its function, described relationally, is to guide the builder in building a building that accords with the blueprint by certain standard rules of projection, that bears a specified relation to the blueprint. Similarly for the desire, goal, or intention to build A. This latter way of thinking makes it less mystifying how each new desire or intention apparently manages to have a brand new biological function. The function isn't really new, it is just relational (*LTOBC*, chaps. 1 and 2).

Imagine now a builder with a blueprint in hand that, due to some mistake, shows a building in an impossible space (in the style, say, of M. Escher). The builder tries to follow the blueprint, and, of course, it is the function of blueprints generally, and hence of this blueprint, to be followed. A person can thus intend to square the circle, to trisect an angle, or to find the last prime number. A person can desire not only what is impossible but also what he knows quite well to be impossible or to be completely beyond his control. That a desire cannot succeed, or cannot succeed in a normal way, no more cancels that succeeding is its function than the fact that one is tied down under water cancels the function one's breathing has. To think otherwise is to confuse having a function with actually serving or being able to serve that function (see chapter 1). Of course, one might suppose that if humans were better designed, they would cease desiring what they know they can't achieve. Most of us are designed pretty much that way, in fact. But if what the desire purposes is something extremely important, perhaps it is well if the desire does not retreat as soon as its fulfillment is judged impossible. For such judgments can be wrong.

That desires can be for things that are biologically harmful or useless is no mystery either. Surely it is a function of the bee dance to lead the watching bees to the indicated nectar, even if it is poisoned. Prior to that, it is a function of the dance to lead them to a certain location, even if someone has taken the nectar away or replaced it with a trap. Suppose that a bee makes a mistake and dances a dance that's just wrong, either because the bee is not normal or because environmental conditions are not as required for its accurate functioning. In either case, a function of the dance is still to lead the watching bees to where the dance says the nectar is. (If I pick up an awl mistaking it for a screwdriver, its function remains that of an awl.) Similar points apply to desires and intentions. The fact that if I go on the plane to Chicago, I will be poisoned there or the plane will, in fact, never reach Chicago does not cancel that the biological function of my intention to take the plane to Chicago is to get me to Chicago. Nor do misconceived or unhealthy desires cease to have fulfillment as their function just because they are misconceived or unhealthy.

A similar point about belief is that believing truths can sometimes be fatal, while believing falsehoods may sometimes save lives. But it is not, of course, *because* of their truth or falsity that these beliefs have these properties but for entirely incidental reasons. It certainly doesn't follow that it is not a proper function of the belief-fixing mechanisms to fix true beliefs. Jerry Fodor (1987, 106–107) has suggested that we may be equipped with mechanisms designed to *keep* us from believing truths when these would be unbearable. It would be odd indeed, however, if these mechanisms were designed so as to condone unbearable *false* beliefs. Better to call them overriding mechanisms that prohibit the formation just of unbearable beliefs, truth and falsity having nothing to do with the matter.

7 Intentional Psychology as an Ecological Science

All this has been to make plain how a person's goals and plans can be understood to coincide with the biological functions of her activities. Thus it is that a person's behaviors are largely defined by the person's goals and intentions insofar as these are realized. "Jane pointed to the red block," "Jane said that she was ill," and even "Jane got herself an A.B. degree," when these describe intentional actions, are pure descriptions of behavior in exactly the same sense that "The eye closed," said of a reflex eyeblink, is a pure description of behavior. By contrast, "Jane held her index finger out at a 57 degree angle to the floor," "Jane [by speaking] caused the wine glass to vibrate" and "Jane increased textbook company profits," said of the same activities, fail to be descriptions of behaviors for exactly the same reason that "The upper eyelashes pointed toward the toes" fails to be a description of the proper structure of the eye-blink reflex.

To turn this around, the essence of intentional action is the fulfillment of a certain kind of biological function, the function of an imperative or goal representation. More carefully, it is the fulfillment of this kind of biological function in accordance with a biologically normal explanation, rather than by some accidental means.[4] But while all of a person's intentional actions are behaviors, not all of a person's behaviors are intentional actions, of course. Eye blinks and ducking reflexes, for example, as well as once learned but now automatic patterns and responses, are not intentional actions, these not or no longer being guided, we can speculate, by goal representations.

To explain behaviors requires explaining how functional coordinations between body movements and features of the environment are achieved. The centipede walks on the floor, the chameleon turns the same color as what it sits on, Amos runs from the cat, and Rattus presses the bar down in response to the bell. The behavioral scientist must explain, for example, how Amos' movements coordinate with those of the cat (though not those of the clock) so that a distance is maintained between them. She must explain the principles in accordance with which the bell comes to produce not just a movement of Rattus's paws away from the nose but just that response that will effect the arrival of food. Especially in the case of those behaviors that are intentional actions, reference to mechanisms of inner representation will play a large role in this kind of explanation. The purpose of this reference will be to explain how intentional behaviors are formed and appropriately placed in the environment. An examination of normal (ideal) relations between the environment and coordinated cognitive structures in the organism, and of how these relations are put in place in normal (ideal) conditions (wider developmental psychology), is a central part of the explanatory task. How are adequate concepts de-

4. For a mirror-image interpretation of what knowledge is, see chapter 12.

veloped and true beliefs formed? How do healthy desires arise out of experience and become realized?

Individualists in the philosophy of psychology have expressed incredulity that true and false beliefs might be treated differently for purposes of psychological explanation. They suppose that the truth or falsity of a belief has no effect on the operations of cognitive systems. Their error is to suppose that cognitive systems are located inside people's heads. Rather, cognitive systems are largely in the world. I no more carry my complete cognitive systems around with me as I walk from place to place than I carry the U.S. currency system about with me when I walk with a dime in my pocket. If I don't know that Alice is *wrong* that the bus leaves her corner at 7:37, how will I explain why she breaks her promise to meet me at 8:00?

In sum, predictions of the motions of individual heaps of human cells under random conditions is obviously not what human psychology is about. It is about the (wider) proper development and operation of human behavioral systems under conditions normal for carrying out their biological functions.

9

Explanation in Biopsychology

I would like to explore implications for the science of psychology of the thesis that the categories of intentional psychology are function categories in the biologist's sense of "function," taking this to be a sense in which function is determined by evolutionary history rather than by current dispositions. I would like to explore first the general shape of the discipline that is psychology under this interpretation. What is its subject matter? What kinds of explanations does it seek, for what kinds of phenomena? Second, I would like to bring these reflections to bear on the classic question concerning in what way, if any, giving an individual's reasons for action tells of the causes of that action. I will not attempt to defend the thesis that the categories of intentional psychology are biological function categories, nor the thesis that biological function categories are carved out by reference to evolutionary history, but some clarifications of these theses will, of course, be in order.[1]

1 Teleofunctions

To describe the biological function of an item is not to describe its dispositional capacities. It is to describe the role that its ancestors played in a particular historical process, a concrete cyclical process of birth, development, and reproduction extended over a large number of previous generations. It is to tell how earlier items involved in this historical process that are homologous to this functional item characteristically contributed to continuation of the cycle (thus helping, of course, to account

1. These theses are defended in *LTOBC*, in chapters 1–4, 6, 11, herein, and in Millikan 1991a, 1993.

for this item's existence). To say this is not to *define* the phenomenon of biological function. That can only be done, probably, by reference also to natural selection (see *LTOBC* and chapters 1 and 2 herein). But I wish to call attention to the fact that the focus of the biological notion of function is on only very restricted aspects of the functional item's capacities, namely those that have contributed over and over in the same sort of way to the historical cycle or chain of life.

Not every biological function of every biological item (type) is realized in every historical instance, say in every generation. Some biological functions are very seldom performed. Still, they must occasionally have been performed and performed in such circumstances as to weld an essential link in the historical chain of life, or they are not true functions. Consider, for example, the ability human babies are rumored to have of instant hibernation when submerged in very cold water. Surely it is a rare baby whose life has been saved by this capacity. But there have been enough, apparently, to fix the relevant genes in the gene pool, hence to confer a biological function on this disposition. Alternatively, if the disposition should, as a matter of fact, have no such felicitous history, but arose only as a concommitant of other functions, as a "spandrel" (see Gould and Lewontin 1979), then it has no biological function. We should also note that not every functional item actually has the dispositional capacities to perform its biological functions. Homology is not identity; members of biological-function categories can be malformed, diseased, or injured (see *LTOBC*, chap. 1). We can sum these points up by saying that biological functions are "teleofunctions" rather that "mechanofunctions." They are biological purposes rather than activities or dispositions.[2]

2   Psychological Classification as Functional Classification: Categorial versus Relational Functions

The position is that psychological classification is biological classification, hence proceeds by reference to teleofunction. This means that categories such as belief, desire, memory, percept, and purposive behavior

---

2. What I am here calling "teleofunctions" I called "proper functions" in *LTOBC* and in most earlier papers.

are biological-function categories—very broad and general ones, of course. Compare the categories limb, hormone, circulatory system, eye, visual system, etc. More contentious, the claim includes that such categories or types as belief-that-it-is-raining, desire-to-visit-Paris, percept-of-a-cat, and purposeful-shooting-of-a-rabbit are carved out with reference to biological functions (though in the case of beliefs, not directly according to function; see section 9 below). This more contentious claim presupposes two points that are not wholly familiar from a layman's understanding of biology.

The first point is that heredity does not directly dictate traits but rather patterns of interaction with the environment, thus controlling development. These interaction patterns control development not only before birth but also throughout life, so that how and what one learns is as much (and as little) dictated by heredity as is one's height and hair color. The second point is that the homologies among items that have historically played the same biological role in a species, and the homologies among the biological roles or functions that these homologous items have performed, are often highly relational. Homologous items may differ greatly from one another, as nonrelationally or categorially described, both in structure and in function, their biologically significant similarities being captured only by multiply relational characterizations. To have biological functions an item need neither have the same categorial *properties*, e.g., the same absolute structure, as items that participated in the life cycles of ancestors, nor need its *functions*, when categorially described, be functions performed by any of its ancestors. Let me try to explain this clearly, for it is crucial.

Consider the neurological mechanism responsible for imprinting in ducklings. It has the relational function of imprinting on the duckling the visual character of something related to the duckling in a certain way, namely, as that which bears the relation *mother of* to the duckling. This relational function translates into a different categorial function for the individual imprinting system of each individual duckling, since the visual character of each duckling's mother is different.[3] Taking a still simpler example, this time from the domain of artifacts, consider the

3. In *LTOBC*, I called such categorial functions "adapted" proper functions.

function of a copying machine.[4] Its relational function is to produce something that matches whatever pattern is put into its feeder. But given something particular put into its feeder, it then has the categorial function of producing a particular pattern. Notice that it is possible that this precise categorial function is one that neither it nor any other copying machine in history has ever happened to have before.

Similarly, humans are born with the capacity to develop concepts in accordance with certain general principles that operate upon the matter of the individual's particular experiences, and we are born with the capacity, in accordance with further general principles operating upon experience, to proceed to form desires and beliefs employing these concepts. These capacities are, in the first instance, relationally described capacities, but given the particular experiences of a particular individual, the biological functions of that individual's concept-forming systems and belief and desire-forming systems translate into categorials. Likewise, the modifications of the nervous system that result, the instantiations of particular concepts, beliefs, and desires, have functional descriptions that are categorial. Further, these may, in many cases, be unique in history. Recall the individual mother memory of the individual duckling, the function of which is to enable the duckling to recognize its individual mother, say Sabatha. If the duckling has no elder siblings, then perhaps no biological device has ever had just that biological function before. This is the manner in which we speculate that belief-that-it-is-raining and desire-to-visit-Paris are distinct types carved out, in the end, by teleofunctional analysis.[5]

3 Biopsychology as a Study of Norms: The Ubiquity of Cognitive Failure

If the central categories of intentional psychology are indeed teleofunctional categories, this suggests that the core of the science of psychology should be a study of teleofunction. This core of psychology concerns the

---

4. In *LTOBC*, I argued that all teleology can be analyzed as belonging to the causal order in accordance with patterns analogous to those that establish biological teleology in the causal order. Therefore, I use examples freely from the domain of artifacts, as well as biology.
5. For fuller discussion of these issues, see *LTOBC* and chapter 11 herein.

functions of the mechanisms that regulate those life processes, those links in the life chain from generation to generation, that are completed through the mediation of behaviors. We can call this discipline "biopsychology." The central concern of biopsychology is not to discover laws, neither universal laws nor statistical laws. Indeed, with a few rather special exceptions, the biological sciences do not typically traffic in laws. They seek to understand mechanisms that contribute to the cyclical processes that constitute development, maintenance, and reproduction for the various species. But the rate of failure for many of these mechanisms is exceedingly high, especially when heavy interaction with the environment is involved. These mechanisms unfold in anything but a lawlike manner. Biological functions are not, in general, reliable functions. They quite standardly go awry. Were this not the case, the world would be a marvelously populous place. The central job of the biological sciences is to describe biological norms, normative norms, not necessities or statistical averages. Indeed, these norms might better be called "ideals."[6] Let me detail this point as it applies in particular to the study of cognitive functions.

Some biological devices are such that a failure to perform their functions is immediately disastrous for the organism itself, or disastrous to its reproductive prospects. That is how it is, for example, if the heart or the kidneys fail. Equally often, however, functional failure is neither fatal nor the least bit dangerous. This may be for any of a variety of reasons. Some devices routinely get second chances, even multitudinous further chances, to perform their functions. Consider devices that regulate the performance of mating displays. Their teleofunction is to produce a display that will attract a mate, but if they fail on one occasion, they often have a chance to succeed on the next. Similarly for predatory animals, the mechanisms that issue in food-procuring behaviors characteristically fail numerous times for every success. Many devices have functions that are redundant. They coexist with other devices that serve exactly the same functions in other ways. Thus the human system has several mechanisms redundantly devoted to cooling. These produce sweating, dilation of the capillaries, lethargy, motivate cooling-off be-

---

6. In *LTOBC*, I capitalized the "N" in "Normal" to remind that these norms are ideals rather than averages.

haviors, motivate the seeking of cooler spots, etc. Similarly, many animals have alternative means of procuring food, so that if one fails, another may succeed. Alternative ways of doing the same often take the form of mechanisms that back one another up. For example, most animals possess reflex mechanisms designed to lessen the likelihood of physical harm (ducking reflexes, fall-checking reflexes), as well as exhibiting more sophisticated behaviors with the same purpose, but they also have mechanisms for repairing physical harm should it occur. They have mechanisms for preventing the entry of noxious bacteria, viruses, etc., into the tissues, but they also have mechanisms for destroying those noxious elements that do enter—mechanisms that themselves operate on a number of levels and with considerable redundancy. The multiplicity of devices aimed at the same end attests, in these cases, to the likelihood for each that it may fail.

We should be especially ready to expect failures in the case of mechanisms, such as the cognitive systems, that help to produce behaviors. This is because in order for behaviors to serve their biological functions, hence to complete the functions of the mechanisms that regulate them, mediation by the environment is required. Biological processes, portions of the biological cycle, that behaviors initiate are processes that loop through the world outside the organism. And it is obviously a great deal more difficult for the organism to stabilize its outer environment so as to provide the necessary conditions for completion of such loops than to stabilize its inner environment so as to complete, say, its physiological functions. So there is good reason to speculate that the cognitive systems might be abundantly unreliable in the performance at least of one portion of their functions—that portion which, unlike, say, inference and memory retrieval (though these are surely fallible enough), is accomplished through the mediation of structures and conditions in the world outside. Common examples of such failures result, we may suppose, in the acquisition of empty or confused concepts; in acts of misidentification of objects, kinds, stuffs or properties; in the fixation of false beliefs; in the acquisition of harmful desires; and in the failure of healthy desires to become realized. For each of these mishaps may be occasioned by failure of the environment to provide the ideal conditions which are necessary for proper functioning of the cognitive systems. (Frequently it is the world that fails us, rather than our inner systems.)

It follows that a description of the biological functions of the cognitive systems will in no way resemble a catalogue of psychological laws. It is certainly no psychological law, for example, that our beliefs are true, though it is a (teleo)function of our belief-fixing systems to fix true beliefs.

Of course, there *are* many biological functions that do get performed with pretty lawlike regularity, such as blood circulation and eye-blink reflexes, but it is not because of their lawlike properties that these functions are of interest to the biopsychologist. Turning the coin over, the frequency and, for the most part, the harmlessness of the occurrence of false beliefs, mistaken identifications, and so forth, should not cause us to suppose that these occurrences are biologically normal. Such failures may be frequent, conceivably they are even average, but they are not biologically normal. They do not exemplify patterns that have helped to forge links in the historical life chain. Compare the fact that being eaten by a bigger fish is the average thing that happens to little fish, but it is not on that account a biologically normal happening relative to the little fish, nor is how little fish get eaten, as opposed to how they avoid getting eaten, a part of the ethology of little fish.

4   The Subject Matter of Biopsychology Is a Process

The biopsychologist is not like a physicist or, say, a mineralogist. The object of biopsychological study is not a chunk of matter, warm or cold, lying on the lab table waiting for its structure to be examined, for its input-output dispositions to be tabulated, or waiting to see what causes applied will produce what effects, what "special science" laws may hold for it. Nor is the point of biopsychology to examine or speculate on details of the complex structures inside the black box, to check on the dispositions of the components, nor to examine how the little dispositions inside add up to the complex dispositions of the whole. Biopsychology is not, then, all of what has traditionally been labeled "psychology." There are many industrial psychologists, for example, and many psychologists who work for the advertising industry, and even the education industry, and so forth, who have reason to study certain average behavioral dispositions of people quite apart from reference to the teleofunctional aspects of these behaviors. Also, but less happily, there have been animal studies done under the flag of behaviorism that involved extreme deprivations and other abuses to experimental animals with no thought given to whether the results obtained flowed from normally functioning mechanisms or instead from grievous damage to the animals' insides. Similarly, the Nazis are supposed to have used Jewish prisoners to study aspects of "physiology" with no concern about whether the effects they were observing were the the result of mutilating the physiological systems or whether they were effects of normal, that is, adaptive, functioning under stress. But to study organisms in that sort of way, even for praiseworthy purposes such as the promotion of effective and efficient education, or the fostering of effective psychotherapy, is surely not the core job of the biological sciences. For example, physiologists and ethologists are usually concerned to study healthy animals rather than diseased or mutilated ones, and not because the healthy animal is the average animal. The point is not, in general, a quest for laws holding on the statistical average. Rather, the healthy animal is, indeed, is by definition, the animal that is so constructed that its parts can perform each of their teleofunctions adequately, if given appropriate environmental contingencies. The healthy animal is the animal that does or could function normally, in the normative sense of "normal."

The biopsychologist's study has little to do with averages over chunks of living matter. The subject of the biopsychologist's study is the stages of an ongoing cyclical historical process, an ongoing event in history. As such, it is not, strictly speaking, even the study of a secondary substance or of a natural kind. The chunk of matter, the exemplar of a natural kind, that is the current specimen on the table represents, if it is lucky, a partial cross-section of the target event. It represents a stage in the historical cyclical process. It is an embryo stage, an infant stage, an immature or a mature stage, on its way to the ensuing stage.

Being more precise, it represents cross sections from a numerous set of loosely coordinated intertwined parallel processes, each having strands of its own, each developing through its own inner logic and at its own pace in rough harmony and interchange with the others. In the case of human cognition, for example, the various strands of the processes of perceptual learning, concept formation, the development of beliefs and desires, and of progressively more effective use of beliefs and desires through action, are roughly integrated with stages in the development of various motor skills, with many aspects of physical growth and development, and so forth. It is inevitable that certain strands of these processes should fail in the case of individual animals, and if failure is central and massive enough and redundancy in the system not sufficient to overcome it, the individual dies. The historical species, and to a lesser degree each individual animal, is like a rope with a small central core of overlapping strands running from one end to the other, the majority of strands, indeed the vast majority, being peripheral and very short where they have broken off. The biopsychologist's study concerns only the central unbroken strands of this fabric, and each fiber in these only so far as it has spun itself out in a principled historically precedented way. Such a study is not a study of substances or kinds, and not a study of averages.

5   The Organismic System Penetrates into the Environment

Because psychology is the study of processes resulting in and through external behavior, it focuses where the organism and the environment interlock, or better, merge. For there is no clear line but only the most arbitrary demarcation between the organism considered as a process and its environment. The organismic process has no skin. It is constantly sucking in matter from its surroundings and spewing it out again. Every breath is a refusal of separation from the environment. Nor are those aspects of the biological process that are cyclical in the sense of being reproduced confined within the skin. Spider webs and moth cocoons, bird nests and beaver dams, are reproduced by the genes out of environmental materials exactly as are bones, wings, and eyes. Richard Dawkins (1983) discusses the phenomenon of "the extended phenotype," through which boundaries between biological individuals or species become blurred, the biological projects of (the genes of) one individual or species being carried out through opportunistic manipulation of the bodies or behaviors of others. And he discusses also the more obvious way in which phenotypes are extended into the environment through incorporation into the organismic system of inanimate nonbody parts such as animal artifacts, and of other adaptive effects of an animal's behavior. The extended phenotype may thus reach yards or even miles beyond the animal's body. The unity of the organismic process might better be compared, then, to that of a wave or, say, a whirlpool than to that of an ordinary physical object. Yet it is not as close even as a whirlpool to being encompassed within a unit space-time worm. For example, the beaver and his dam are aspects of the same organismic system, yet they are separable both in space and in time. And the beaver's dam is also part of the systems that comprise each of his kin.

Through its behavior, the biological system that is an animal merges into and incorporates portions of its environment. Inner mechanisms initiate processes completed by outer mechanisms, through outer structures and conditions that are either given in the environment or that have been put in place through prior behaviors of the individual or its kin. It is not just that the teleofunctions of an animal's behavioral systems are, as such, "long-armed" functions. The animal itself, considered as a system of events, extends far out into the extrabodily environment. To study an animal's behavioral systems without at the same time studying the normal integration of these into the environment, without studying the loops through the environment it is the function of these systems to initiate, would be exactly like studying the digestive system without considering what normally passes through it. Digestion without food is an exact analogue of behavior without environment. Turning to another analogue, to study behavior abstracted from the environment would be no less absurd, and for exactly the same reason, as if one were to study the structure and function of the heart's ventricles while ignoring the existence of the auricles and of the blood that passes through. The other half of the system containing the behavior-producing mechanisms lies in the environment in exactly the same sense that the other half of the system containing the ventricles lies in the atrium and in the blood running through.

Imagine attempting to study the inner mechanisms that produce migration in birds, or nest building, or mating displays and female reactions to them, or imprinting in birds, without making reference to the way these mechanisms have historically meshed with the birds' environments so as to perform the functions for which they are named. More vivid, imagine attempting to study the origins of the coordinated motions made by the eyes and the head and the hand that effect eye-hand coordination while leaving completely out of account that there is, normally, a seen and felt object in the environment that mediates this coordination. It is equally ludicrous to suggest studying the deeper systems that produce human behaviors, for example, the systems that process beliefs and desires and intentions, etc., without considering how the environment has historically mediated performance of their functions. To understand what the ventricles do, one must understand also what the auricles and the blood do and understand the relation that the ventricles ideally bear to the blood and the auricles. To understand what beliefs and desires do one must understand what the environment is doing and what relations beliefs and desires ideally bear both to one another and to the environment.

It is always possible to describe any motion that an organism makes categorially. It is possible, anyway, to describe it relative only to the organism itself rather than relative to environmental structures.[7] And to describe sufficient causes of an organism's categorially described motions, one can always begin merely with categorial descriptions of the organism itself plus categorial descriptions of the environmental input to the organism. From this perspective, the organism's relation to its distal environment appears causally impotent in the production of its motions. But its motions are not its behaviors. The changes in categorial structure thus traced are significant biologically, are aspects of behaviors, only insofar as changing certain categorial properties of the organism effects significant changes in the organism's relation to its environment. Good comparisons are not easy to find here, but we can try this one. The dentist has no particular interest in the exact shapes and sizes of individual persons' lower jaws. That is, he has no particular interest in them other than in their relations to the shapes and sizes of the teeth that fit into them and of the upper jaws they must match. Clearly, the details of absolute structure are not significant here, but only the details of relation. The same must surely be true both for the physiological structures supporting cognitive functions and for the behaviors these

---

7. For a discussion of biologically relevant versus biologically irrelevant ways of describing the same behaviors, see chapters 7 and 8.

help to produce. Their relations to one another and their relations to the environment are what is biologically significant and what is, for the normal case, uniformly describable within biological theory, not their categorial properties.

From the perspective of biopsychology it should be evident both that the personal history of the organism is relevant to understanding its psychological nature and that its way of interlocking with the environment is relevant. Whether a person remembers or merely seems to remember, whether a person knows or merely believes truly, are matters of personal history, but equally are matters of whether the biological cycle is proceeding normally or whether some of its links have been forged only by luck.[8] Whether a belief corresponds to the outer world as it should or is false instead is a matter of the interlocking of the organism with its environment, but equally a matter of whether the wider organismic system, which system *includes* part of that environment, is normally, that is, ideally, constituted or whether it is biologically abnormal. If it is biologically abnormal, this shows, in turn, that abnormalities must have occurred in the development of the system, for insofar as the organism-environment system cycled entirely normally (which, of course, it never does), beliefs would all come out true.

6 Biopsychology Is a Predictive Science, If at All, Then Only Accidentally

These reflections on the nature of intentional psychology entail that, as a biological science, it does not aspire to be predictive. Biopsychology studies what happens when biological processes proceed normally, but the normal is neither the necessary nor always the statistically average. Prediction and control do, of course, play an important role under parts of the wide umbrella called psychology—I have mentioned psychological testing, human engineering, psychotherapy, etc.—but prediction and control are not required biproducts of intentional psychology. Indeed, intentional-attitude psychology is a rather unlikely candidate to aspire to the detailed prediction of individual human behaviors.

8. For a compatible discussion of the nature of knowledge, see chapter 12.

This is true for at least two reasons. The first is diversity among individual constitutions. For psychology to predict individual behaviors, just as a starter babies would have to be born cognitively and affectively, indeed, also physically, alike. But it is abundantly clear that different newborns inserted into identical environments would not behave at all alike, unless under the most general and vacuous of descriptions. People are born with predispositions to different cognitive and affective styles, with different cognitive strengths and weaknesses. Nonpsychological factors such as bodybuild, reaction time, energy level, and health also play a large role in determining behavior. Further, it is likely that many aspects of our cognitive processes are partly stochastic, hence that which among many possible solutions to a given problem an individual discovers and executes often is not governed by well-defined psychological principles at all. Surely nothing short of complete physical and chemical analysis could in fact predict the detailed behaviors of any individual. The individual is not a replica of its ancestors or of its friends. It is a bundle of heavily redundant unfolding subsystems adapted each to the others' concrete peculiarities to form coordinated larger units, this in accordance with principles of coordination and development all of which are as yet subject to merest speculation. We are still trying to find out how an individual's muscles and tendons grow the right length to fit the individual's bones, let alone how the various facets of individual cognitive development and function grow into a coherent unit. But there is no reason to suppose that exactly how an individual thinks is governed by laws quantifying over individuals any more than, say, how he walks or plays tennis—or how he reacts to allergens.

The second reason that intentional psychology cannot be required to predict individual behaviors is that there is no compelling reason to suppose that all or even most of the norms that it describes are usually fulfilled. Most obvious, as has already been noted, is that the environment cannot always be relied upon to do its part in completing the functions of the cognitive systems. Because this is so obvious, it has been equally apparent to all that there could not possibly be any reliable laws of organism–distal environment interaction, certainly not for the case of humans. Hence theorists who take it that psychology's main business is to deal in laws have found it necessary to insist that a scientific intentional psychology would have to be "narrow," that it would have to ignore the environment. But it is also likely that those portions of the cognitive functions that are carried out inside the organism are abundantly vulnerable to failure. The cognitive mechanisms seem to be paradigms of functional redundancy and layered backup systems, commanding a variety of means to the accomplishment of the same or functionally equivalent projects. If at first you don't succeed, try another way, is a fundamental heuristic for our cognitive functions. Witness, for example, the well-documented variety of forms of compensation employed by those with brain damage. This redundancy strongly suggests the vulnerability of various cognitive techniques taken separately. It follows that there is little reason to suppose that the exact progression of anyone's inner cognitive systems could be predicted on the basis of even the most exact understanding of all types of human cognitive teleofunction, an understanding of all the biological norms involved.

Suppose, for example, that man is indeed a rational animal, that conformity to certain logical principles is a biological norm for human thought processes. It would not strictly follow that conformity to reason was so much as a common occurrence. Reasoning could be one among other functions of the behavior-controlling systems, one that sometimes worked and was then to the organism's advantage. It could also be one that seldom caused irreparable damage when it failed, due to redundancy and to backing by various cruder behavior-controlling devices such as those found in the lesser animals. Indeed, remembering the way evolution works, it seems that there must at least have been a time when human reason had exactly this tentative status. It is not likely that the ability to reason well or to learn to reason well arrived all at once in a single lucky mutation. And we can raise the question of how well in fact the average modern human reasons. Clearly, from the fact that drawing rational inferences may be a norm for the human cognitive systems, it does not follow that any reliable predictions about inference patterns can be made. Even though man is a rational animal, rational psychology could remain very far from a reliable predictive science.

But a strong contemporary tradition has it that rational psychology must be a predictive science if it is to be a science at all and that its central job is exactly to predict individual humans' behaviors. It is claimed, further, that our layman's way of thinking about intentional mental states constitutes a "folk-psychological theory," the central employment of which is to effect prediction of the behaviors of our fellows, for this is necessary in order to project our own paths through the tangle of other folks' actions.

Do I maintain that it is mere illusion that we thus predict the actions of others? No, it certainly is not an illusion that we do a lot of correct predicting concerning the behaviors of others. Most ordinary forms of social intercourse and social cooperation would be impossible if we could not. But there may be a misunderstanding over the *methods* that we typically employ for prediction. The tool that we most commonly use, I suggest, is not a theory of the inner *mechanisms* that lie behind predicted behaviors. The tool is not, for example, belief-desire theory. Most of our predictions are done with a much blunter tool: the method of brute correlation. In many cases there is, of course, some understanding of the outlines of the psychological mechanisms lying behind predicted behaviors, but our predictions do not usually rest on this understanding, either at all or at least very deeply. They rest mainly on observations of past behavioral regularities for the individual and for the group(s) to which the individual belongs. Within fairly well-defined limits, people, especially people from the same culture, just do behave uniformly in a theater, on the road, at the grocer's, even when recreating in the park. Most people are more likely than not to meet what others consider to be their business and social obligations, to conform to general expectations concerning what is appropriate or seemly and, very important, to do the things they have said they will do. Beyond this, we project ahead patterns observed in the past for particular individuals. Known personality traits, character traits, and habits serve as our guides. Of course, such knowledge merely limits the boundaries of people's likely behavior. It does little or nothing toward actually *determining* behavior in its variety. But seldom do we make an attempt to predict others' behaviors in much more detail than this. How inept we actually are at predicting behaviors, even of our best friends and family members, when these behaviors are not covered by known regularities may be illustrated by friends who become separated in a large crowd, say at a fair, each trying in vain to outguess what the other will do in an attempt at reunion.

7   Reasons and Causes

If we are rational, what that means is that rationality is a biological norm for humans, not that rationality is necessitated by special causal laws of human psychology. Compatibly, it is standard nowadays to claim (though on somewhat different grounds) that thoughts categorized in accordance with their semantics are not the sorts of things that could, even in principle, fall under causal laws. On the account of this essay, the semantic category of a thought is determined relative to its biological functions, which depend in turn upon its history, upon its place relative to certain prior events. But having a certain history is not, of course, an attribute that has "causal powers." Hence reasons cannot be, as such, causes. More generally, that a thing has a teleofunction is a causally impotent fact about it. Especially, it is never directly *because* a thing *has* a certain function that it performs that function or any other function. More nearly the reverse is true. The thing exists and has a certain function because things homologous to it have performed that function (better, had that effect) in the past. Moreover, here the "because" is only partly causal; the other part is constitutive or logical.

But perhaps it will be thought that although things that have functions cannot be supposed to perform these functions either on account of having these functions or in accordance with strict causal laws, still they must perform them in accordance with *ceteris paribus* laws. Roughly, there have to be conditions under which the functional item would perform its functions, since there have to have been conditions under which its ancestors did perform these functions and the same kind of item in the same kind of conditions would do the same kind of thing again. This ignores defective members of function categories: diseased hearts, injured limbs, etc. It also ignores the fact that performance of their functions is, for many items, a relatively rare occurrence. Would we really wish to speak of *ceteris paribus* laws in cases where *ceteris* are not *paribus* most of the time? And it also ignores a third point.

Characteristically, the same function could, at least in principle, be performed by many differently constituted items. But if these items are differently constituted, if they operate in accordance with different principles, then the supporting conditions required for them to effect this function must differ as well. Brain cells performing the division algorithm require oxygen, whereas computer chips require electric currents, and so forth. Similarly, the outer-world conditions that support the bat's mosquito-locating abilities and those that support his mosquito-catching abilities are different from those that support the same abilities in humans. (The bat can perform in the dark on silent mosquitos; humans cannot.) The result is that there are no *ceteris paribus* laws covering all items having a certain function. For *ceteris paribus* conditions are unspecified conditions that must remain the same from case to case for the law to hold, whereas here the necessary conditions would have precisely to vary from case to case. A "law" applying to all such cases could say no more than that the items falling under the law could be made, by adding different circumstances tailored specifically to each case, to perform the function. But surely anything can be made to effect anything if one adds the right intervening media, if one adds enough special enough circumstances. So any such "law" would be empty. There are no causal laws of any kind, then, that directly concern the causal efficacy of reasons as such. The closest we could get would be *ceteris paribus* laws for human reasons, other *ceteris paribus* laws for dolphin reasons, still others for Martian reasons, and so forth.

8   Normalizing Explanations

Our argument suggests that explanation of an agent's behavior by reference to reasons for acting is not best analyzed as explanation by subsumption under causal laws. The question that arises, then is, what kind of explanation the citing of reasons for acting is, and how it can still be causal-order explanation. Intentional-attitude explanations of behaviors proceed, I will argue, by subsumption of behaviors under biological norms rather than laws and/or by noting departures from these norms and perhaps causes of these departures. Following Philip Pettit (1986), to whose views mine run parallel here, I call such explanations "normalizing explanations." The status of explanations of individual behaviors by reference to reasons concerns the relation of normalizing explanations to other forms of causal-order explanation that are, perhaps, better understood.

To explain a phenomenon by subsuming it under norms is to exhibit it as an instance of conformity to or departure from proper operation of some teleological system. A very simple form of normalizing explanation explains the occurrence of a phenomenon by reference merely to something whose function it was to produce that phenomenon. For example, the dishes are clean because they have been put through the dishwasher; the washing machine door is locked because the washer is not finished spinning and the door is designed not to unlock until it is finished spinning; the bear is asleep because it is winter and it is (biologically) normal for bears to sleep through the winter (see note 4 above).

In order to explain a phenomenon this way it is necessary, of course, to classify it appropriately *as* the outcome of a teleofunctional process, and this classifying may itself count as a simple form of explanation. What is happening? What is it doing? It's washing dishes, not making soup or just dirtying the water; it's winding a magnetic coil, not storing wire on a spool; it's resting, cooling its motor between cycles, not playing dead or broken; and so forth.

More complex normalizing explanations tell or implicitly refer to the place an event has in a series or interdependent pattern of functions, or tell where and perhaps why malfunction occurred within such a series or pattern. Thus that cog wheel's turning in the calculator is its carrying one in a certain addition algorithm; the car went through the light because its brakes failed; the outboard stalls because there's dirt in the carburetor that gets into the needle valve. Normalizing explanations often make reference to conditions that must be presupposed for normal operation of a device or system. Thus the outboard won't start because the spark plugs are wet or because there's no gas it the tank, the scuba diver passed out because it was too cold or because his tank ran out of oxygen, and so forth.

Finally, the relation between certain conditions of the functional system itself or of the environment and certain states of the system that normally adapt the system's progress to those conditions may be targeted in a normalizing explanation. Thus the motor is racing because the heavy-load switch is on but the load is not heavy; the washer failed to fill properly because the soap was put into the tub rather than into the dispenser, so that the rising suds tripped the water cutoff before the tub was full; the animal's winter-approaching detectors failed because it was kept indoors, which is why it is attired inappropriately or is behaving inappropriately to the season.

9 The Normal Roles of Beliefs and Desires

Notice how natural it would be to say in the last two of these cases that the washer thought it was full when it wasn't and that the animal's system didn't know it was winter. This is because a belief or a bit of knowledge is likewise a teleofunctional item, one whose function is to adapt the containing system so that it can perform its functions under certain conditions, namely, those conditions which the belief is about. Or, being a little more precise, it is the belief-forming mechanisms that produce the adaptations, the adjustments, of the organism to the environment, the beliefs. Beliefs themselves are functionally classified, are "individuated," not directly by function but according to the special conditions corresponding to them that must be met in the world if it is to be possible for them to contribute to proper functioning of the larger system in a historically normal way. Somewhat similarly, the water switch's being off will promote the washer's tasks normally only if the condition is fulfilled that the washer is full. And the animal's winter detectors' being off will effect appropriate functioning of the animal in accordance with historically normal reasons only if winter is not yet approaching.

Explicit human beliefs, however, are much more than just biological adapters to certain environmental conditions. They are adapters that perform their tasks in a certain sort of way, namely through participation in inference processes. A picture that I advocate but will not try to defend here (see *LTOBC* and chapters 3, 4, and 6 herein) shows beliefs and desires as working for the organism by modeling (in accordance with very abstract mathematical mapping functions) the environment, modeling the organism's goals, and modeling types of environmental transitions that the organism knows how to bring about. Normal practical thinking, then, involves tinkering with these models until solutions are found that will effect transitions from the present state of the environment to various desired states. On this picture, the teleofunctions of desires (which they may not very often perform), like those of blueprints, are to effect what they model, to get themselves realized. When everything goes according to norm, action guided by the models inside is action conformed to the outside world so as to issue in productive loops through the environment. This happens in accordance with explanations that, made fully general, that is, fully spelled out relationally, apply perfectly generally to all successful uses of the (same capacities of the) species' cognitive systems, historical and current. Theoretical inference is then interpreted as a process whereby the internal model of the environment grows or extends itself in accordance with principles that model various logical, geometrical, and causal necessities or regularities or dependencies in the environment.

Be all this as it may, what seems quite certain is that there must exist some sort of systematic teleofunctional organization of the human cognitive systems whereby the making of good practical and theoretical inferences corresponds to normal (but perhaps not average) functioning for beliefs and desires and whereby it is biologically normal (not average) for desires to be fulfilled, at least under certain conditions. (Why else the capacity to have desires?) Accordingly, explanations of behaviors by reference to reasons for action are normalizing explanations.

10   How Normalizing Explanations Circumscribe Causes

Why it is that normalizing explanations explain, how it is that they fall under a general theory of explanation, is too large a question for this essay. Our question here is only how such explanations connect with simpler kinds of causal explanation. One connecting link is that whatever has a teleofunction has a normal way of operating, a normal way of performing its function. For functional artifacts, this may be in part the way the designer proposed that the function be performed; for biological devices, it is the way the function has been performed historically. An exhaustive analysis of the way, given its history, that any functional item operates when operating normally arrives eventually at a description of normal physical structure for such a device and normal physical conditions for its operation such that physical laws generate performance of this function, given this structure and these conditions. By making implicit reference to such causal explanations, normalizing explanations may thus circumscribe quite specific physical explanations without detailing them.

Guided by Cummins (1975, 1983), we notice that the analysis of how a system normally functions may have several parts. First, the larger function or functions of the system may be analyzed into subfunctions that are performed either serially or simultaneously or in some more complicated pattern of interaction. This kind of analysis Cummins calls "functional analysis." Cummins suggests that a functional analysis may generally be represented by a flowchart, but, of course, highly parallel processes, especially those that interact to some degree stochastically, must be represented otherwise. Second, the system may be analyzed into subsystems, which may or may not correspond to discrete physical parts, each of which is responsible for a designated set of subfunctions. This kind of analysis Cummins calls "compositional analysis." Compositional analysis results in a description of the normal (not necessarily actual) constitution of the system by reference to parts described teleofunctionally, that is, normatively rather than dispositionally. (Here I depart from Cummins, who equates functions with dispositions.) Finally, the normal physical constitutions of the elements normally composing the system may be described, along with the surrounding physical conditions required for normal functioning, and it may be shown how these descriptions together account, in accordance with physical law, for cases of normal operation. That is, the system may ultimately be analyzed into a set of physical parts and physical dispositions rather than merely functionally categorized parts and normal functions.[9]

By reference to the possibility of this kind of physical analysis, explanations of behaviors according to reasons for action may circumscribe physical causes. Compare explaining why a man shakes by saying that he suffers from Brown's syndrome, even though the etiology of Brown's syndrome may not be known. Or compare explaining why a

9. This does not imply that, given a certain species, there is a classically understood type-type identity relation between, say, normally constituted and normally functioning beliefs and desires about x on the one hand, and certain physiological structures on the other. Certainly if the physical constitutions of human beliefs are typed categorially, there is no reason at all to suppose that any such identity holds. If there are bridge laws for humans that map the semantics of thoughts onto physiological structures, surely what these laws map are certain semantic relations among beliefs and desires onto physical relations among these, hence principles of logical interaction onto principles of causal interaction, not categorial meanings onto categorial physiological "shapes."

man has brown hair by saying he has genes for brown hair rather than, say, having dyed his hair, though no one knows the constitution of the gene or how it produces brown hair (compare Block 1990).

That this is not the complete answer to how reasons circumscribe causes becomes evident, however, when we remember that devices falling in the same function category can have widely varying constitutions. For example, we do sometimes explain, say, how John managed to get the can open by noting that he finally found a can opener, but given the enormous variety among can openers, the various different principles on which they may work, how could such an explanation possibly do anything toward circumscribing physical causes or types of physical processes lying behind the can's having come open? Similarly, if there really were various other creatures designed quite differently from humans and made of quite different stuffs but who still had beliefs and desires, then explanation of actions by reference to beliefs and desires without mention of the species of creature involved would seem not to circumscribe any particular kind of physical process at all (compare Block 1990).

But looking more closely, whether it circumscribes a kind of process depends on how you type your kinds. Behind every normalizing explanation is a device or system with teleofunctions, and an item acquires a teleofunction only by having a very special sort of causal history. For example, if the cat's purr is explained as produced by a purr box, an organ especially designed, in the smaller cats, to produce purrs, then we know that the purr box itself has resulted ultimately from the operation of prior purr boxes in ancestor cats which produced purrs, these purrs somehow having survival value, contributing an essential link, at least occasionally, to the historical cat chain. Thus a salient cause of the purr is a series of prior purrs. Of course, when the functions referred to by normalizing explanations are described categorially though they are actually derived from relational functions, no such simple analysis applies. Still, to assign to any phenomenon a place in a functional system is to claim that it has emerged from a very special kind of causal-historical process, a kind that defines functionality. It is to distinguish its particular type of causal origin quite sharply from other etiological patterns.

10

Metaphysical Antirealism?

Michael Devitt describes the classical correspondence theory of truth, for sentences of a certain type x, as follows: "Sentences of type x are true or false in virtue of: (1) their objective structure; (2) the objective referential relations between their parts and reality; (3) the objective nature of that reality (1984a, 28). By "objective" Devitt means at least theory-independent.[1] Due partly to the influence of Dummett and Putnam, "realism" or (Putnam) "metaphysical realism" has in some circles recently come to mean, or at least to entail, this sort of theory of truth. Thus, being a "realist" (about this class of sentences or that) has come to be contrasted, for example, with holding a redundancy theory, or a coherence theory, or a Peircean "end of inquiry" theory of the nature of truth, or perhaps with holding that truth is rational assertability. Devitt demurs at this use of "realism," and is surely right in saying that it tends to confound issues that should be kept separate.[2] So the title of this paper should really be "Metaphysical Anticorrespondence Truth." For the most part I will defer to Devitt's remonstrance, but I will occasionally lapse so as to avoid talking with too full a mouth.

Putnam uses "metaphysical" as an epithet to label correspondence theories of the sort Devitt described. It seems to connote nonempirical, verification-transcendent, empty, incoherent, bad. My title hints, and

I am grateful to John Troyer, Crawford Elder, Thomas Kuhn, Michael Devitt, Christopher Peacocke, Christopher Hookway, and Evan Fales for helpful comments on earlier drafts of this essay.
1. Theory independence is not the same thing as mind independence. For example, sense data and thoughts might have objective or theory-independent status without being mind-independent.
2. Devitt's most recent discussion of this issue is in 1984a, chap. 4.

I will argue, that "metaphysical," used this way, snugly fits Putnam's antirealism. It does not fit the traditional correspondence theory.

Two kinds of arguments against correspondence truth dominate the contemporary literature. The first claims that it is incumbent on the correspondence theorist to demonstrate that we "need" a correspondence theory in order to explain at least some phenomena, and that no such need has been demonstrated.[3] The second claims that even if we do need a theory that affirms a correspondence between true sentences and affairs in the world, any such theory can correlate sentences only with theory-relative affairs and hence will not be a correspondence theory of the strong kind Devitt described, and that therefore correspondence of Devitt's strong kind could not *possibly* be the nature of truth. For example, Putnam has claimed that we must draw a distinction between two kinds of correspondence theories, one of which, "internal realism," is an empirical theory and may well be true, the other of which, "metaphysical realism," is the strong kind and incoherent (1978b).[4] Any theory of correspondence between language and the world that is offered to explain certain phenomena in the world is only an "internal realism," not a "metaphysical realism."

Given this situation, the first task of the correspondence theorist is to show that correspondence truth *can* explain some important phenomena not yet explained without it. I will not take up this part of the correspondence theorist's burden here, though I will say a few words about it. The correspondence theorist's second job is to inspect the internal theory/metaphysical theory distinction. The purpose of this paper is to argue that this distinction is illusory, that there can be only one kind of realism and one kind of antirealism. A sound argument that a correspondence theory is needed to explain certain phenomena is all that is required in order to challenge antirealism on the only ground on which it can possibly stand.

The first job of the correspondence theorist—that of showing that his theory can explain some important phenomena—is one that I have undertaken elsewhere and cannot rehearse here (*LTOBC*, pts. 2 and 4). This paper is not, therefore, a full defence of correspondence truth but

---

3. The original statement of this position is in Leeds 1978.
4. The distinction is reiterated in Putnam 1981, 1983.

defends only the claim that correspondence truth requires to be defended on empirical grounds alone. It may nevertheless help orientate the reader if I begin by saying something about the phenomena I believe (and have argued) that a correspondence theory can explain. If I am right that a correspondence theory can explain these phenomena, that constitutes an argument for, at a minimum, *internal* realism. The argument of the body of this paper—that the distinction between internal realism and metaphysical realism is chimerical—then completes the argument for correspondence to a theory-independent world.

First, I think that the correspondence theory of truth may be able to explain how it is possible for us to learn those routines and methods whereby we respond to the world, first with exploratory behavior and then with sentences, in such a way as to come to consistent agreement with ourselves and with others. It is not as though we usually copy either ourselves or others when we think or speak. How, then, does it happen that we can learn to make fresh judgements about the same things as other people, to make observations independently of other people, yet in such a manner that these independent judgements do not contradict? A van Fraassen style of reply is that only those methods of judgment making that produce few contradictions survive, forcing out less effective methods (van Fraassen 1980, 38–40). But one does not explain *how* food digestion is possible by pointing out that any animal that has survived must have been capable of digesting food, nor does one explain *how*, by what mechanisms, mice detect and escape from cats by pointing out that the survival of mice depends on detecting and escaping from cats. Similarly, one does not explain *how* agreement in judgments comes about merely by pointing to the survival value that sentence or belief production methods have *when* they effect agreement. I have argued that the how of agreement in judgements has no trivial explanation and that this agreement is a very striking phenomenon by no means to be taken for granted (*LTOBC*, chaps. 18–19) but that it can be explained on a correspondence-truth hypothesis, granted certain (crucial) assumptions about ontology (*LTOBC*, pt. 4). Rather than copying ourselves or others when we think or speak, we apparently copy the world, which lies between.

Second, I think a correspondence theory of truth may be able to explain why, having learned how to agree with ourselves and others by employing certain concepts, it should happen that the sentences thus generated often have practical use. Most animals, it is reasonable to suppose, have managed to survive without learning how to respond to the world with sentences, either inner or outer, without applying consistency tests to their beliefs and methods of belief production, and indeed, probably without employing beliefs. But that the use of subject-predicate representations and the use of consistency testing has a survival value for man, one that has helped to account for his proliferation, seems highly likely. What needs to be understood is *why* these practices are of value to man, the mechanisms and principles in accordance with which these practices link up with activities more transparently of value. This can be understood, I have argued, by showing how, granted a suitable ontology, adjusting sentence- and/or belief-producing methods until these are producing agreement in judgements tends to effect production of sentences that correspond to the world in accordance with determinate stable rules of projection (*LTOBC*, chap. 18), and by exhibiting principles in accordance with which such sentences can guide behavior so as to make this behavior appropriate to the corresponding structures in the world.

That, in briefest compass, is the strategy I have urged for round one of the realism/antirealism debate. But this paper is primarily concerned with round two, the internal theory/metaphysical theory distinction; its purpose is to spell out the second half of a defence of realism. I am going to discuss the internal theory/metaphysical theory distinction as Putnam articulates it so that it will be clear that I am not merely fighting windmills. The reader may then put the various shoes I fashion on any other antirealist feet they fit.

Metaphysical realism, Putnam claims, is not an empirical theory. He means, I take it, that metaphysical realism is not a theory that we could obtain evidence for or against; it is verification-transcendent.[5] Metaphysical realism differs from internal realism in claiming (1) that the correspondence theory of truth applies to "*all* correct theories at once (so

5. What Putnam actually says is, "Metaphysical realism . . . is less an empirical theory than a model" (1978a, 130). Later he says, "Metaphysical realism was only a *picture*" (1978a 130). I take it that the implicit reference to *Philosophical investigations* here requires us to read "only a picture" as implying lack of empirical content.

that it can only be stated with 'typical ambiguity'" and (2) that the correspondence involved is correspondence to "THE WORLD," i.e., to the world as "independent of any representation we have of it" (Putnam 1978a, 125). Call claim (2) the "t-i-o-correspondence thesis" (correspondence to theory-independent objects). It is, indeed, the thesis that Devitt called merely "the correspondence theory of truth." Putnam thus implies that the t-i-o-correspondence thesis is a verification-transcendent thesis, that no empirical evidence could count for or against it. Putnam further characterizes metaphysical realism as entailing that "the theory that is 'ideal' from the point of view of operational utility, inner beauty and elegance, 'plausibility,' simplicity, 'conservation,' etc., *might be false.* 'Verified' (in any operational sense) does not imply 'true,' on the metaphysical realist picture, even in the ideal limit" (Putnam 1978a, 125). Putnam then proceeds vigorously against the t-i-o-correspondence thesis and, having denied it, concludes that being true is something like being rationally assertable in the ideal limit. An implication seems to be that "the ideal theory" would be necessarily true rather than possibly false.

Before focusing on the main issue here, we would do well to clear some of the mud out of our eyes by examining whether there is substance to Putnam's suggestion that the t-i-o-correspondence theorist, and he alone, is playing with notions that are verification-transcendent in some damaging way.

Putnam describes an ideal theory as one that "can be imagined complete, consistent, to predict correctly all observation sentences (as far as we can tell), to meet whatever 'operational constraints' there are," and so on. Now, notice that it is not only the laws of nature that a complete theory of the world would have to describe but also the disposition in the world of its particulars. It would have to contain or imply something like a state description of the world. For no law can be evidenced without assuming knowledge of the disposition of relevant particulars falling under the law, yet if the shape of our current theories is roughly right, there are no universal laws that determine the disposition of any particulars in the world merely as a function of human experience. Every method of making particular judgments (perceptual judgments, for example) is in principle fallible, its success depending on the circumstance that surrounding conditions, including conditions in the body of the observer, are "normal," that is, upon the disposition of surrounding particulars not currently being observed. Roughly, it is not laws for which experience yields evidence but complexes of laws-plus-state-descriptions. A *complete* theory of the world would have to include an inventory of the world.

But note that on a correspondence view, no theory of the world that was actually in the world, actually held by a person or group of people, could ever contain an inventory of the world, for no portion of the world could be mapped one-to-one onto the whole world including itself. Yet on any correspondence view that claims to be evidenced by its capacity to explain some empirical phenomena, there must be natural-world relations between theories and what they are about. Theories must therefore be *in* the world. It follows that Putnam's description of "an ideal theory" is not coherent on a t-i-o-correspondence view.[6] On the other hand, if the notion "ideal theory of the world" is pared down to reasonable proportions to mean, for example, any theory that was based on as much evidence (and based on as much intelligence) as could, in accordance with physical laws (and in accordance with principles that actually govern the human mind), be evidenced to a human (and exercised by a human), then that an ideal theory might not be true is both evident and unproblematic. Certainly it would beg the question to restrict the notion "ideal theory" to theories (partial theories, of course) based on evidence sets (partial evidence sets, of course) that would necessarily yield *true* (partial) theories. So Putnam is right this far: t-i-o-correspondence truth implies fallibilism. What would the alternative be? The real possibility of a self-warranting theory of the world?

Putnam's brand of antirealism also implies fallibilism. For how, from the standpoint of an ideal theory, would one know that it was an ideal theory? What evidence taken account of by the ideal theory could certify the conclusion that all of the evidence was in and that all of the elegant hypotheses had been examined? (Notice Putnam's fudging inside the parentheses: "to predict correctly all observation sentences (so far as

6. For a list of some of the ambiguities inherent in the notion of an ideal theory, see Devitt 1984a, 31–32, 187, and Hacking 1983, 93–94.

we can tell).") But if the ideal theory would not be self-warranting, it would presumably think of itself that it might not be true, and it would be right. If the ideal theory is necessarily true, it is so only under the description "the ideal theory," which notion is itself at least *strong-verification-transcendent*.

Next consider Putnam's claim that the t-i-o-correspondence theory is not an empirical theory at all, that it is weak-verification-transcendent, that no empirical evidence at all can be gathered either for or against it. Whether this claim is true or not is precisely the central question at issue. Assuming that he has managed to win round one of the correspondence/anticorrespondence debate, the correspondence theorist's claim will be that an empirically based theory of truth is the only kind of theory of truth that is possible and that correspondence truth *is* t-i-o-correspondence truth: empirical evidence for correspondence is empirical evidence for t-i-o correspondence. (It is true that this means his theory can only be stated with "typical ambiguity." But no reason has been given to suppose that this ambiguity leads to any greater paradox than does the typical ambiguity of the sentence "Every English sentence contains a verb.") Soon I will argue that the correspondence theorist is right in his claims. But at the moment I wish only to point out that if Putnam were right that a t-i-o-correspondence theory is necessarily a weak-verification-transcendent thesis, then it would follow that his own antirealism is a weak-verification-transcendent thesis too. If no empirical evidence can be gathered for or against a thesis, presumably no empirical evidence can be gathered for or against its negation. I do not imply that Putnam would duck this conclusion. But notice a corollary: if a t-i-o-correspondence theory is instead an empirical theory, then so is its denial. Antirealism is then also an empirical theory. Hence the full thesis of this paper: the correspondence/anticorrespondence issue is *one* issue, not two, and the winner will have to be determined on empirical grounds alone.

Suppose that the notion that there might be a Putnamesque "ideal theory" of the world is a coherent one. And suppose that according to the ideal theory, the *reason* it is possible to construct coherent theories at all—possible, that is, to learn to react to the world with sentences such that, for the most part, one neither contradicts oneself or others—

is that it is possible to acquire an ability to map the world systematical-ly with sentences in conformity with (though not, of course, by making reference to) definite and predetermined mapping functions. That is, the ideal theory says that *that* truth is correspondence is a universally ap-plicable explanatory theory, not, of course, directly observed to be true, but arrived at by inference to the best explanation of what *is* observed, namely the *coherence* of our theories, including our agreements on observation sentences. Suppose further that if this portion of the ideal theory were dropped, no explanation could be given of why it had been possible to construct any *consistent* theories of the world at all. Apparently, all this would have no effect upon Putnam's antirealism. Even if the ideal theory said truth was correspondence, it wouldn't *really* be—not t-i-o correspondence.

Similarly,

Suppose there is a possible naturalistic or physicalistic *definition* of reference, as Field contends. Suppose

(1)   *x refers to y* if and only if *x bears R to y*

is true, where *R* is a relation definable in natural science vocabulary without using any semantical notions. . . . If (1) is true and empirically verifiable. . . , (1) is a sentence which would be part of our. . . "ideal limit" theory of the world.
   If [i.e., since] reference is only determined by operational and theoretical con straints, however, then the reference of "*x bears R to y*" is *itself* indeterminate, and so knowing that (1) is true will not help. (Putnam 1981, 45–46)[7]

Even if the ideal theory said that reference was *R* and that refer-ence was determinate, it wouldn't really be determinate, not theory-independently.

This is transcendentalism indeed. Reference and correspondence truth may be empirically real, but they are transcendentally ideal, and this is known a priori. And what of the thesis that truth is rational assertabil-ity in the ideal limit? Obviously it too is known a priori. But it may not correspond to any empirical reality; correspondence truth could ulti-mately win out in the phenomenal world. Putnam has derived the rational-assertability thesis from a denial of t-i-o correspondence, which he has equated with transcendentally real correspondence, that is, with a thesis about the relation of language to the noumenal world. So the

7. The reference is to Field 1972.

rational-assertability thesis must express the transcendentally real status of language and truth as opposed to their status merely within the phenomenal world (where truth may turn out to be correspondence).[8] Putnam's antirealism is a metaphysical antirealism.

Now the direct counter to transcendentalism, and to its Cartesian and Lockean roots, is naturalism. Naturalism denies the possibility of constructing an epistemology prior to the rest of one's theory of the world. According to naturalists, thinkers are squarely in the only world there is. Philosophy in the first person cannot be primary, for the first person is as much in the empirical world as anything else and can be accessed at all only by understanding its relation to the rest of the world it is in. Any attempt at a prior epistemology can only be question-begging, relying implicitly on concepts of self, thought, and reason (or of languages and theories), concepts that have been lifted illicitly from a prior understanding of the empirically known world as a whole. To defend naturalism, then, is to attack transcendentalism, and with it the internal theory/metaphysical theory distinction. That is what I now propose to do.

First, let me illustrate the naturalist's point that our empirically based theories about the world insistently intrude upon attempts at a prior epistemology. Consider the thesis that truth must be rational assertability in the ideal limit. What is the argument for this thesis? Putnam does not spell it out. (Taking only the premise that truth is *not* t-i-o correspondence, it certainly does not follow that it *is* rational assertability.) I suggest that the argument goes as follows.

Suppose that someone holds that truth is correspondence. We ask him "How do you know?" and he explains what rational motivations he has for holding this view. Now, we say, consider what you have just been doing. You have been engaging in a purposeful activity. You have been drawing certain inferences which you intend should meet certain standards of rationality, applying, or attempting to apply, rigid standards of consistency, trying to meet certain standards for elegance, simplicity, and so on. The result is that you affirm the *truth* of your theory of truth. You cannot deny that what you have been aiming for all along

8. Is the rational-assertability thesis a thesis about the status of phenomenal language or about the status of language-in-itself? About phenomenal language, one would think, but more of this below.

is the truth about truth. But you did not do this by aiming at making your thoughts correspond to anything; for example, at no point did you compare your thoughts with anything. Rather you aimed at consistency, elegance, and at keeping your inferences rational. It follows that truth, what you were aiming at, simply *is* where you end if you stay consistent, seek elegance, and keep to your standards of rationality. After all, that is all you could have *known* you were doing before you arrived at your theory of truth, and it would make no sense to say that you were really trying all along to do something that you did not know about. Now put that in your hopper, apply your standards of consistency, elegance, rationality, and so on, and see if you do not end up somewhere different.

The assumption behind this argument, one sneaked in from a certain prior vision of one's mind and one's knowledge of one's mind, is that there can be no such thing as a mind that is doing something purposeful but that does not immediately know, at least on reflection, what this something is. The vision is the Cartesian vision of mind as that which is transparent to itself. Suppose, for example, that we ask Putnam how he *knows* that theories evolve by the application of standards of consistency, elegance, and rationality, and that abiding by these standards is the aim of theory construction. He cannot answer that he knows this by having gathered empirical evidence for a theory of theories (theories seem to take the place of minds in contemporary antirealist philosophy), for then his ideas about what theories are and what they are up to when they evolve seeking truth would be merely part of his empirical theory of the world and could be directly countered by someone else's empirical theory on this matter. Rather, Putnam must claim that his theory of theories is prior to his theory of the rest of the world, that our concepts of our theories and of our aims in theory construction are prior to our concepts of natural-world items, invulnerable to attack from empirical evidence. But then Putnam owes us an explantion of how this is possible without adopting the Cartesian position that our theories are transparent to themselves. For example, if our theories of theories are not empirical theories, does this mean that our theories as items that we think *of* are not phenomenal items, that we can have knowledge of the doings of our theories-in-themselves?

But in fact our theories about our minds and our knowledge of our minds, about our motivations and our knowledge of our motivations, about our theory constructions and our knowledge of our theory constructions, and so on, have been quite sensitive recently to empirical input. Freud introduced the theory of unconscious motivation on evidence. There has recently been a rash of experimental work attempting to gather evidence that we are sometimes quite wrong about the contents of our own inference processes.[9] After Wilfrid Sellars's "Empiricism and the philosophy of mind" (1956) there emerged a generation willing to take seriously the proposal that our concepts of belief, desire, and inference, among others, are theoretical concepts, part of a "folk theory" of the mind. Now there is even a movement afoot that suspects this folk theory of being false—*because* of the difficulty of fitting it in with other empirically based theories about the nature of the world and the human mind. Our ordinary notions, "the belief that p," "the desire that q," and so on, are suspected of being either empty or at least enormously vague.[10] Indeed, there is no clearer case of the "revisability" of a once apparently analytic sentence than the revisions of "I am directly aware of the nature of all my own purposes and mental activities"that have been going on in this century.

Elsewhere I have argued that our engagement in the activity of belief and theory construction is indeed motivated by purposes of which we are not aware by Cartesian reflection; the "end" of thought is not simply wherever careful thought ends (*LTOBC*, 1986, and chapters 3 and 12 herein). But my purpose at the moment is not to argue that point but to illustrate that theories of the empirical world, of the activity and ends of theory construction and of the relation of consciousness to it, for example, do intrude into what was trying to be a separate and prior epistemology. The lesson to be learned is clear. There is no inner keep in which theories of language, reference, truth, minds and theories, and so on, can be constructed safe from interaction with the rest of our theories of the world. We have no special evidence or special grasp of

9. A brief discussion of the literature on cognitive dissonance may be found in Stich 1983, 231ff.
10. See, for example, P. M. Churchland 1979; P. S. Churchland 1980, 185–207; Stich 1983. I am not advocating this position. For quite a different view that is still faithful to Sellars's claim, see chapter 3.

self-evident truths in this area, no privileged access to this area that differs in any way from access to other areas of theory construction. No distinction can be drawn, then, between plain empirically supported realism or antirealism and some more recondite, privileged, and prior "metaphysical" perspective on these matters.

On the other hand, if that is so and if the t-i-o-correspondence theory is not actually incoherent or empty, then we should be able to say *how* evidence might be gathered for it, *how* evidence might be gathered for correspondence to theory-independent objects. In a moment I will bring this question to the floor. But Putnam's best-known argument for anti-realism, his "model-theoretic argument," *does* question not only the sensitivity of the t-i-o-correspondence theory to evidence but also the very meaningfulness or coherence of the t-i-o-correspondence theory. So we must deal with that first. Happily, Putnam's argument is well known, and most of its details are irrelevant to what needs to be said.[11]

Put roughly, the argument is that any "theory of the world" (which Putnam takes to be composed of something like a set of sentences, outer and/or inner), no matter how large and complex this theory is, can be mapped onto the world in an indefinite number of ways. Hence simply mapping onto the world cannot be what the truth of a theory consists in. Moreover, we cannot pick out unique mapping rules for the sentences in a theory by appealing to the fact that one and only one set of mapping rules is the one "intended" by the theory user. For any intention that the theory user has about what his terms shall represent is merely *another* representation (a sentence in his head, for example) and the question how that representation could map on to the world in an unique way is the same question all over again. Concerning Field's proposal that there might be a natural-world relation that corresponds to reference, defined by a schema

(1)   *x refers to y* if and only if *x bears R to y,*

Putnam writes,

What Field is claiming is that (a) there is a determinate unique relation between words and things or sets of things; and (b) this relation is the one to be used as

11. The argument may be found in Putnam 1978a, 125ff.; 1981, 22ff.; and 1980, 464–482.

the reference relation in assigning a truth value to (1) itself. But this is not necessarily expressed by just *saying* (1), as we have just seen; and it is a puzzle how we could *learn to express* what Field wants to say.

Putting this last puzzle aside, let us consider the view that (1), understood as Field wants us to understand it..., is true. If (1) is true..., what *makes* it true? Given that there are many correspondences..., what *singles out* one particular correspondence R? Not the empirical correctness of (1); for that is a matter of our operational and theoretical constraints. Not...our intentions (rather R enters into determining what our intentions signify). It seems as if the fact that R *is* reference must be a *metaphysically unexplainable* fact. (1981, 46)

To Putnam's last question, the reply is that the assignment of R is determined by at least these considerations: (1) R is a relation that obtains between "refers" and R itself, between the sign "'reference'" and the word "reference," between the sign "'"reference"'" and the sign "'reference,'" and so on, and between the sign "'cat'" and the word "cat," and so forth, as well, of course, as between "cat" and cats. Moreover, there must be a *causal-order explanation* of the systematic recurrence of R between each of these pairs that is rooted on the one hand in the dynamics of our psychology as speakers of English and on the other in the causal order of the world in which we live. (2) More importantly, R is a relation which has to be cited in giving a causal-order explanation of whatever empirical phenomena they are that the t-i-o-correspondence theory explains, of why we can learn how not to contradict ourselves and others and of why true sentences are useful to us, for example.[12]

Though it is the less important of the two constraints, (1) is worth dwelling on for a moment. Natural languages are in general higher-order languages, that is, languages that contain a metalanguage or a hierarchy of metalanguages that take lower-order parts of the whole language as objects. We refer to higher-order languages in the singular: "a second-order language," "a third-order language," and so on. An antirealist is obliged to give an account of this practice. Does a metalanguage *in use* refer only to a theory-relative object language and not to the object-language-in-itself? If so, it refers equally to the object-language-in-itself and to cats and mats and apples and trees, and the *whole* higher-order language *in use* certainly cannot be treated as *one* language, as the vehicle of *one* theory. For from the standpoint of the

12. I have offered an account of R and of what it explains in *LTOBC*. (This account, incidentally, is not "causal.")

metalanguage part, the *whole* is a mix of phenomenal and noumenal parts, while from the standpoint of the object language, the theory-relative objects to which the metalanguage refers do not exist. If, instead, the metalanguage in use refers unambiguously to its object-language-in-itself, then the metalanguage in use must constitute an unexplained exception to the rule that reference is never to things-in-themselves. To take this tack is, of course, merely to vary the Cartesian theme that mind is transparent to itself: language is transparent to itself; theories are transparent to themselves. The naturalist realist will not put up with this. Whatever natural relation R there is between parts of a first-order language and their referents in the world, this relation must be the same R that binds a metalanguage so that it refers to its object language.[13]

The puzzle about how we could "learn to express what Field wants to say," put more generally, is the question how we could learn to use any term whose referent was connected to that term only by a mind-independent or external-to-mind relation. The answer is that we do not of course consciously aim at mapping cats with "cat," and so on. We do not *consciously* aim at not contradicting ourselves either—certainly not usually. However, that usually we non-consciously aim at consistency is certainly a good *theory*. That is, we purposefully react to the presence of contradiction in our thought by attempting to make adjustments in our ways of applying concepts, the purpose being to develop perceptual and conceptual skills or strategies that will not lead us into contradiction. And (as I have argued elsewhere) the purpose toward which that purpose is a *means* is to learn to map the world with thoughts in a systematic way, such that these thoughts can be useful guides to action.[14] This last purpose is not, of course, a conscious purpose either. (I have

---

13. Consider the following from Putnam on internal realism: "Since the objects *and* the signs are alike *internal* to the scheme of description, it is possible to say what matches what" (1981, 52). But is the sign that gets *used* the same sign that is internal to the scheme of description? Or did that sign get lost among the cats and the apples as soon as we tried to think of it? How can Putnam think about the scheme of description so as to write about it without losing it among the mats and trees? Only by drawing only *one* distinction: external/internal. Once you are inside, all is safe; there is no problem about using a scheme of description to refer to itself or to other parts of itself.
14. The explanation of *why* aiming at noncontradiction can serve that purpose spans *LTOBC*, chaps. 14 and 16–18. It is brought to a focus in chap. 18.

argued that it is a biological purpose, and that conscious purposes also are a species of biological purpose.[15])

So I have argued that t-i-o-correspondence is not, as Putnam supposes, an incoherent theory. But could it be evidenced in experience? Turning this around, might the empirical world be the only world there is, so that our theories, if they manage to be about anything at all, are necessarily about THE WORLD?

The question turns on the nature of experience and of evidence, on what it *is* for something to be evidenced in experience. Let me begin by reminding the reader of a thesis that I take to be central to the Wilfrid Sellars corpus.[16] I will not put it quite in Sellars's way (that would take a long time), but in a way that reflects my own belief that perception may well be cognitive *prior* to the application of concepts and sentential inference.

The thesis is negative: having evidence from experience does not equal there appearing before the mind or consciousness some real object (an object from some realm of real being, say a sense datum or a piece of a phenomenal world or an "experience') the reality of which and the character of which is infallibly and immediately revealed in a bare act of awareness. That is, of course, there is no "given." Put it a second way: there is no kind *K* of thing of which it is true that "It is as though I were aware of a *K*" entails "There is a *K* of which I am aware." Or put it a third way: experiencing is not as such any kind of knowing. It is not knowing what is experienced; it is not knowing the nature of one's experience. Consciousness is radically nonepistemic. Ofness, intentionality, *always* lies partly outside of consciousness, as does every object that is intended or known. For me to be aware of something or to know something, there must be something there for me to be aware of or to know. But *that* there is something there for me to be aware of or to know and *what* this thing is is not something that is simply *in* con-

15. Ibid. and chapter 11 herein. For a full discussion of the problems that must be faced by a t-i-o-correspondence theorist who wishes to know what understanding a language consists in and how one learns to use a language, see Millikan 1986. Solutions to these problems are offered in *LTOBC*, especially chaps. 9 and 15 (as well as chaps. 18 and 19).
16. Sellars is not, I think, invariably true to his thesis. Like all great philosophers, he has taken a huge leap and occasionally trails some of his equipment behind him. See, for example, Dennett 1981b.

sciousness. Consciousness does not *contain* either intentionality or knowledge.

Now if that thesis should be true, then it does not follow from the fact that it is as though I see a cat that there is anything at all that I see—neither an idea, nor a sense datum, nor an intentional object, nor a phenomenal object, nor (of course) a theory-dependent object. Whether or not I see a cat, there certainly is not some *other* object that I am staring at that has got itself lodged between. If there is no cat there, then either I am staring at something else out there that I have (perceptually) mistaken for a cat, or else I am staring at nothing at all.[17]

Similarly, from the fact that it is as though I were thinking of or intending something, it does not follow that there is anything at all that I am thinking of or intending—neither an idea (Locke, Hume), nor a bit of objective reality (Descartes), nor a phenomenal object (Kant), nor an intentional object (Brentano), nor a concept (Moore 1899), nor a noema (Husserl), nor (of course) a theory-dependent object. (If they are going to change the name of that alley every few years they really should put up a permanent sign saying "blind.") My thought may in fact be entirely empty. (Putnam explicitly grants this at the start of *Realism, truth, and history* when he tells of a man who has sentences running through his mind that he does not understand but that he thinks he *does* understand [1981, 4–5]. But Putnam's sketch shows a man mentally staring at or listening to these mental sentences, the possibility remaining that the man's awareness makes the existence at least of the sentences secure or that he has a sure knowledge at least of the nature of his experience.)

But if one rejects the given unforgivingly (and I am sure that Putnam really wants to do this), it also follows that there is no problem about evidence for theory-independent objects. *Theory-independent objects are the only objects there are, anywhere.* When I do manage to see or to think of or to know about an object—any object whatsoever, even an experience or a thought—this cannot be my mind's or my conscious-

---

17. Of course, there are also secondary uses of "see," as when, during an eye examination, the reply to "What do you see now?" is "Green spots that keep fading and returning again." Here "It is as if I saw green spots fading" is rendered simply "I see green spots fading." The description is, however, not of an object seen but of an experience. In addition, the experience is not a knowing about itself, and the describing of it is not infallible.

ness's or my brain's rubbing up against that object, or containing that object, but must be a much less immediate relation. So perhaps I can see CATS, not just phenomenal cats (there are no such things) but theory-independent cats. I see them not only without rubbing my mind or brain up against them but without seeing any of the various things in between, like light waves, retinal images, and optic-nerve firings. And, of course, I can think of cats without rubbing my mind or brain against them.[18] In order to do so, I must certainly do some sort of constructing or reconstructing with my mind or in my head. But it is not the results of this constructing that I think of when I think of cats. The construction is not something that has insinuated itself *between* my mind and cats; it is a *mechanism* for thinking of cats, that is, of CATS.

Now if you insist (and again I am sure that Putnam does not really wish to) that empirical evidence must be the kind of thing that arrives as the real object of a bare, unmediated, and infallible act of awareness, then it follows that there can be no empirical evidence for the t-i-o-correspondence theory. Then, of course, it also follows that you *may* have to go all your life without ever encountering any evidence for anything. For consciousness just *may* not be constituted that way; it just may not be intrinsically epistemic. (Indeed, if a Sellarsian denial of givenness is so much as *coherent*, that is proof that there is no given that is given, anyway, with apodictic certainty.) On the other hand, if you will grant that acts of awareness routinely offer evidence without being infallible on any level or about any kind of thing, then you have granted my thesis. It follows that *that one has evidence* is no more a given than is anything else but that when one has evidence, it is *always* evidence precisely concerning theory-independent objects, concerning objects not simply *constituted* by, or as a correlate of, one's thought or awareness of them. So you can think of, and have evidence for, what is not in your mind; you can think of what was around before your thoughts and theories came along. Being no longer trapped behind the veil of your present ideas, perhaps you can even think of Putnam's yesterday's thoughts. (Can Putnam?[19])

18. To see this one must, of course, also be careful not to fall into Berkeley's "I can not think of an unthought-of thing" fallacy.
19. A question that I have not pressed, but that would be worth pressing, is whether Putnam's antirealism leads inevitably to (meaning-)solipsism of the moment. Can Putnam refer to his yesterday's thoughts-in-themselves or only to phenomenal yesterday's thoughts?

I have argued that the t-i-o-correspondence theory is not, as Putnam claims, incoherent or empty and that it is not verification-transcendent in any damaging sense. I have argued that Putnam's distinction between metaphysical realism and internal realism rests upon the untenable assumption that we have concepts and/or data available to us with which to think and talk about the nature and status of (noumenal? phenomenal?) theories, truth, inferences, language, and so on, concepts that are somehow prior to and independent of our concepts and theories of the rest of the world. Granted that the only theories we can have of language, of thought, of our theory constructions, and so on, are empirical theories and granted a Sellarsian view of what empirical evidence is, then *if truth is correspondence at all* (round one of the realism/anti-realism debate), it is precisely correspondence to "THE WORLD," i.e., to the world as "independent of any representation we have of it."

11

Truth Rules, Hoverflies, and the Kripke-Wittgenstein Paradox

"The sceptical argument that Kripke attributes to Wittgenstein, and even the 'sceptical solution,' are of considerable importance regardless of whether they are clearly Wittgenstein's. The naturalistically inclined philosopher, who rejects Brentano's irreducibility and yet holds intentionality to be an objective feature of our thoughts, owes a solution to the Kripke-Wittgenstein paradox" (Loar 1985, 280).

The challenge is a welcome one. Although I will argue that the Kripke-Wittgenstein paradox is not a problem for naturalists only, I will propose a naturalist solution to it. (Should the Kripke-Wittgenstein paradox prove to be soluble from a naturalist standpoint but intractable from other standpoints, that would, I suppose, constitute an argument for naturalism.) Then I will show that the paradox and its solution have an important consequence for the theories of meaning and truth. The Kripke-Wittgenstein arguments which pose the paradox also put in question Dummett's and Putnam's view of language understanding. From this view it follows that truth rules must be "verificationist rules" that assign assertability conditions to sentences, rather than "realist rules" that assign correspondence truth conditions. The proposed solution to the paradox suggests another view of language understanding, according to which a speaker can express, through his language practice, a grasp of correspondence truth rules. This will block one route of Putnam's famous retreat from realism:

Earlier versions of this paper were read at the University of Wisconsin at Madison, Western Michigan University, the University of Maryland, Trinity University, the University of New England (Australia), Australian National University, Monash University, and Vanderbilt University. I am grateful to the members of these departments, to Margaret Gilbert and John Troyer, and to unknown referees for the *Philosophical Review* for helpful comments and suggestions.

The point is that Dummett and I *agree* that you can't treat understanding a sentence (in general) as knowing its truth conditions; because it then becomes unintelligible what *that* knowledge *in turn* consists in. We both *agree* that the theory of understanding has to be done in a verificationist way . . . , conceding that *some* sort of verificationist semantics must be given as our account of understanding. . . . I have given Dummett all he needs to demolish metaphysical realism . . . , a picture I was wedded to! (Putnam 1978b, 129).[1]

(By "metaphysical realism" Putnam means roughly the traditional correspondence theory of truth.) In chapter 10, I argued that the distinction Putnam draws between "metaphysical realism" and "internal realism" is illusory, that naturalist arguments for correspondence truth are inevitably arguments for truth as correspondence to theory-independent objects, and that there is nothing incoherent in this notion of correspondence. So in giving a naturalist argument to show that grasping correspondence truth rules is no more problematic than grasping verificationist ones, I take myself to be defending the strongest possible kind of correspondence theory of truth and the most flat-footed interpretation possible of the truth-conditions approach to semantics.

1 The Kripke-Wittgenstein Paradox

The Kripke-Wittgenstein paradox, as Kripke explains it, is an apparent dead end we encounter when trying to explain what it is that constitutes a person's meaning something by a word. Kripke takes addition as his central example: what constitutes my meaning addition by "plus" or "+"? "Although I myself have computed only finitely many sums in the past, the rule for addition determines my answer for indefinitely many new sums that I have never previously considered. This is the whole point of the notion that in learning to add I grasp a rule: my past intentions regarding addition determine a unique answer for indefinitely many cases in the future" (Kripke 1982, 7). What is it to "grasp" such a rule? What is it for me to have grasped a rule that determines that $68 + 57$ yields the answer 125, in the case that I have never happened to add 68 to 57? No such rule is determined merely by extrapolation from previous cases in which I have applied "+" to pairs of numbers; there are always infinitely many functions that accord with a

1. Michael Dummett's statement is in Dummett 1975, 1976.

given finite list of such argument, argument, value trios. For example, the "quus" rule might accord,

x quus $y = x + y$, if $x, y < 57$
$$= 5 \text{ otherwise (Kripke 1982, 9).}$$

Nor (and this is more obviously a Wittgensteinian theme) can we suppose that my meaning addition by "+" consists in my having given myself general directions for what to do when encountering "+". To give myself general directions would be to lay down a rule of procedure for myself. What, then, constitutes my meaning by this set of instructions, by this laid-down rule, one procedure rather than another? Certainly this set of instructions does not include a thought of each of the infinitely many sums there are. And my past performances when having this set of instructions in mind do not exemplify a unique general procedure but many such possible procedures. Supplementing the instructions with another set of instructions explaining how to follow the first set leads only to a regress. How, then, *is* the correct interpretation of the instructions in my mind determined?

Changing the example, Kripke writes,

It has been supposed that all I need to do to determine my use of the word "green" is to have an image, a sample, of green that I bring to mind whenever I apply the word in the future. When I use this to justify my application of "green" to a new object, should not the sceptical problem be obvious to any reader of Goodman? Perhaps by "green," in the past I meant *grue*, and the color image, which indeed was grue, was meant to direct me to apply the word "green" to *grue* objects always. If the *blue* object before me now is grue, then it falls in the extension of "green," as I meant it in the past. It is no help to suppose that in the past I stipulated that "green" was to apply to all and only those things "of the same color as" the sample. The sceptic can reinterpret "same color" as same *schmolor*, where things have the same schmolor if. . . . (1982, 20)[2]

Now it is true that arguments of this sort take hold only if we reject the possibility that intentionality is a *sui generis* feature given to consciousness.[3] We must assume that what comes before the mind, whatever it is that enters or informs consciousness when one means

2. Kripke's ellipsis points at the end; Kripke's footnotes omitted.
3. Loar claims that Kripke has not demonstrated that intentionality is not this. Kripke's text does, however, contain several footnotes commenting on the relevant arguments in Wittgenstein's text. I mention these arguments below.

something, does not *itself* determine a use for itself, a purpose for itself, a particular kind of connection that it is to have with one's activities. Rather, whatever comes before the mind is, in this respect, not different from any other item standing alone: "And can't it be clearly seen here that it is absolutely inessential for the picture to exist in his imagination rather than as a drawing or model in front of him?" (Wittgenstein 1953, par. 141). Wittgenstein argues against the possibility that intentionality is a *sui generis* feature by showing, for each of a series of cases, that the results of introspection, when one means, understands, or is guided in accordance with rules, are not the only or the final criteria that we use to determine what we mean or when we understand or are being so guided. What lies before consciousness does not determine its own significance; knowing what one means is not a matter merely of apprehending the contents of one's mind. In short, meaning is neither a state of awareness nor an epistemic given. It does not occur encapsulated within consciousness; it is not a state that simply *shows* its content or its significance. If there *is* such a thing as meaning something, say meaning addition, its nature must lie in part in what is *not* simply given to consciousness.

Nor is it merely because the object thought of or meant is external to mind that meaning has an ingredient not given to consciousness. Meaning to perform a mental activity like adding in the head, that is, having intentions about one's own thoughts, is fully infected with this nongiven ingredient. Thus the problem posed is no different for the purest idealist than for the metaphysical realist. Nor is it only "naturalistically inclined philosophers" who need a solution to the Kripke-Wittgenstein paradox. It is anyone who has been convinced by Wittgenstein to doubt Brentano or, say, convinced after Sellars to reject epistemological "givenness" in *all* of its multifarious forms.

Could it be that the nongiven ingredient that pins down what rule I intend to follow for "+" is the *disposition* I have to proceed in a certain way when encountering "+"? Setting aside the problem of what Wittgenstein may have intended as an answer to this question, surely Kripke is right to answer no. Kripke gives two main reasons for his answer. First, people are in fact disposed to make mistakes in arithmetic. Second, the addition function applies to numbers of any magnitude, but "some pairs of numbers are simply too large for my mind—or my brain—to grasp" (Kripke 1982, 26–27). Nor will it help to take into account dispositions I may have to correct myself or to accept correction from others. Some of my dispositions are dispositions to miscorrect myself. (I often do this when trying to add long columns of figures.) And there are surely conditions under which I would be disposed to accept miscorrection from others.

Kripke concludes, or he claims that Wittgenstein concludes, that there is indeed *no fact to the matter of what I mean by "+"*. This conclusion is what I am calling the "Kripke-Wittgenstein paradox."[4] Wittgenstein, Kripke claims, offers only a "sceptical solution" to this paradox, a solution that "begins . . . by conceding that the sceptic's negative assertions are unanswerable" (Kripke 1982, 66). I propose to offer a "straight solution" to this paradox, one that "shows that on closer examination the scepticism proves to be unwarranted" (Kripke 1982, 66).

4. Kripke places a great deal of emphasis on the failure to find anything that "justifies" my proceeding as I do when I follow a rule, and he seems to think of a "justification" as something that must be, by its very nature, open to or within consciousness. Similarly, "Even now as I write, I feel confident that there is something *in my mind* [italics mine]—the meaning I attach to the 'plus' sign— that *instructs* me [italics Kripke's] what I ought to do in all future cases" (Kripke 1982, 21–22). And "The idea that we lack 'direct' access to the facts whether we mean plus or quus is bizarre in any case. Do I not know, directly, and with a fair degree of certainty, that I mean plus?" (Kripke 1982, 40). Indeed, many passages in Kripke's essay suggest that what bothers him the most is not that nothing seems to determine what rule I am following but that nothing *before my mind* determines it. The feeling is conveyed that Kripke finds the real blow to be that the intentionality involved in rule following does not reside *within* consciousness. If *that* is what Kripke takes to be the root "Wittgenstein paradox," then all will agree that Wittgenstein made no attempt to give a "straight solution" to it. Nor will I. On the other hand, if that were the main paradox, no one would ever have supposed that a dispositional account would be a "straight solution" to it, and Kripke's discussion of dispositional accounts should have been placed not with his account of "Wittgenstein's paradox" but with his discussion of "Wittgenstein's sceptical solution," that is, as an account of what Kripke believed this skeptical solution was not.

Margaret Gilbert suggests (in conversation) that one paradox may be that meaning strikes one as being something that can be fully constituted at a given time *t*, whether or not meaning is something that happens within consciousness. And to be sure, dispositions are usually taken to exist at given times, so that a dispositional account might be viewed as an attempt at a straight solution to Gilbert's paradox. Gilbert's paradox, if one finds it paradoxical, is another that I will not attempt to solve. I will merely try to show how there is a fact to the matter of what I mean by "+".

Kripke distills the essence of the failure of dispositional accounts to capture the nature of rule following thus:

A candidate for what constitutes the state of my meaning one function, rather than another, by a given function sign, ought to be such that, whatever in fact I (am disposed to) do, there is a unique thing that I *should* do. Is not the dispositional view simply an equation of performance and correctness? Assuming determinism, even if I mean to denote *no* number theoretic function in particular by the sign "*", then to the same extent as it is true for "+", it is true here that for any two arguments *m* and *n*, there is a uniquely determined answer *p* that I would give. (I choose one at random, as we would normally say, but causally the answer is determined.) The difference between this case and the case of the "+" function is that in the former case, but not in the latter, my uniquely determined answer can properly be called "right" or "wrong." (Kripke 1982, 24; notes omitted)

The fundamental problem...is...whether my actual dispositions are 'right' or not, is there anything that mandates what they *ought* to be? (Kripke 1982, 57)

The problem is to account for the *normative* element that is involved when one means to follow a rule, to account for there being a *standard* from which the facts, or one's dispositions, can diverge.

2   General Form of the Solution

In the case of meaning, the normative element seems to be the same as the purposive element: to mean to follow a certain rule is to have as a purpose to follow it. Whether my actual dispositions are "right" or "wrong" depends on whether they accord with what I have purposed. The possible divergence of fact from a standard is, in this case, simply the failure to achieve a purpose.

Now, having as one's purpose to follow a rule might involve having a representation of that purpose in mind, for example, in one's language of thought. But as Wittgenstein observed, any such representation would itself stand in need of interpretation. It would stand in need of a prior rule governing how it was to be taken, that is, how it was to guide one. And that one was to follow this prior rule could not *also* be a represented purpose, not without inviting a regress. To understand what it is to have an explicit purpose that one represents to oneself, we must first understand what it is to have a purpose the content of which is *not* represented. Basic or root purposes must be *unexpressed* purposes.

"Intend" strongly suggests an explicitly represented purpose, that is, a purpose that is thought about. So let me use the verb "to purpose" (yes, it *is* in the dictionary) to include this more basic way of having a purpose. We can then put matters this way: root purposing is unexpressed purposing; our job is to discover in what this purposing consists. Let us also distinguish among three ways of conforming to a rule: (1) merely coinciding with a rule (this is the way in which we conform to "quus" rules and to rules to which we have mere dispositions to conform), (2) purposefully following an explicit or expressed rule, and (3) purposefully conforming to an implicit or unexpressed rule. Way 3 involves having an unexpressed purpose to follow a rule and *succeeding* in this purpose. It is the same as displaying a *competence* in conforming to the unexpressed rule or displaying an *ability* to conform to it. Another way to explain our task, then, is to say that we need to learn what a competence in conforming to an unexpressed rule consists in and how it differs from a mere disposition to coincide with the rule.

My thesis will be that the unexpressed purposes that lie behind acts of explicit purposing are biological purposes; a competence to conform to an unexpressed rule is a biological competence. By a biological purpose I mean the sort of purpose the heart has, or those of the eyeblink reflex and the human brain. The purposes of these are functions that they have historically performed which have accounted for their continued proliferation. Biological purposes are, roughly, functions fulfilled in accordance with evolutionary design. It does not follow that capacities to perform biological functions are in general innate. For example, it is surely in accordance with evolutionary design that the newly hatched chick follows its mother about, but the chick is not born with that disposition. It is not born knowing which *is* its mother but must imprint on her first. Yet the imprinting, and hence the following, both take place in accordance with evolutionary design. (Later in this chapter I will devote considerable space to clarifying how even quite novel biological purposes can emerge as a result of experience and learning.[5])

Suppose that explicit intending involves something like representing, imaging, or saying something to oneself and then using, or reacting to,

5. Full details of the notion of biological function that I rely on in this paper are given under the label "proper functions" in *LTOBC*, chaps. 1–2. See also chapters 1 and 2 herein.

or being guided by, this representation in a purposeful way, that is, in a way that expresses a competence. My thesis, then, is that the purpose that informs this reacting, that makes it into a competence, is a biological purpose. Similarly, if knowing a language involves having a competence in following certain rules for construction and interpretation of sentences, the purpose that informs this competence, I will argue, is a biological purpose.

3   Purposive Rule Following, Competence to Follow a Rule

Let me begin with a very simple example of an organism that displays a competence in conforming to a rule. According to the biologists Collett and Land,

Males of many species of hoverfly spend much of the day hovering in one spot, thus keeping their flight muscles warm and primed so that they are ready to dart instantly after any passing female that they sight. This chasing behavior is on such a hair-trigger that all manner of inappropriate targets elicit pursuit (pebbles, distant birds, and midges so small as to be scarcely visible to a human observer) as well as a very occasional female. Although selective pressures have favored a speedy response above careful evaluation of the suitability of the target. . . , the response itself is precisely tailored to optimize the capture of objects which are roughly the same size and speed as a conspecific. (1978)

Rather than turning toward the target in order to track it, the hoverfly turns away from the target and accelerates in a straight line so as to intercept it. Given that (1) female hoverflies are of uniform size, hence are first detected at a roughly uniform distance (about .7 m), (2) females cruise at a standard velocity (about 8 m/sec), and (3) males accelerate at a constant rate (about 30–35 m/sec^2), the geometry of motion dictates that to intercept the female, the male must make a turn that is 180 degrees away from the target minus about 1/10 of the vector angular velocity (measured in degrees per second) of the target's image across his retina. The turn that his *body* must make, given as a function of the angle off center of the target's image on his retina, equals the (signed) angle of the image minus 1/10 its vector angular velocity, plus or minus 180 degrees. According to Collett and Land, whether it is dried peas, male hoverflies, female hoverflies, or flying blocks of wood that he spots, that is exactly the rule to which the hoverfly conforms. Taking note that this rule is not about how the hoverfly should behave in relation to distal objects but rather about how he should react to a proximal stimulus, to a moving spot on his retina, let us call this rule "the proximal hoverfly rule."

I have chosen the proximal hoverfly rule as my first example of rule following because it seems so unlikely that the hoverfly calculates over any inner representation of this rule in order to follow it. Rather, the hoverfly has an unexpressed biological purpose to conform to this rule. That is, the hoverfly has within him a genetically determined mechanism of a kind that historically proliferated in part *because* it was responsible for producing conformity to the proximal hoverfly rule, hence for getting male and female hoverflies together. This mechanism may account for various other dispositions of the hoverfly, for example, causing him to attract predators by his conspicuous darting movements or causing characteristic, uniform, mathematically describable patterns to play on his retina as he turns after the female. But mentioning these latter dispositions does not help to explain why the mechanism has survived, why it has proliferated in the species. Conformity to the proximal hoverfly rule, on the other hand, has helped to explain the reproductive success of (virtually) every ancestor hoverfly, hence to explain the continued presence of the mechanism in the species. Conformity to the proximal hoverfly rule, then—not attracting predators or producing certain patterns on the retina—is a biological purpose of this mechanism, hence of the hoverfly. For similar reasons, a biological function of the heart is to pump blood but not also, say, to make a jazzy sound, and a biological function of the eyeblink reflex is to cover the eyes momentarily but not also to swing the eyelashes in a graceful arc away from entanglement with the eyebrows, nor to point with them at the navel.

The hoverfly displays a *competence* in conforming to the proximal hoverfly rule when his coinciding with it has a "normal explanation," that is, an explanation that accords with the historical norm. That his behavior coincides with the rule must be explained in the same way, or must fit the same explanation schema, that accounted in the bulk of cases for the historical successes of his ancestors in conforming to the rule. Presumably, this normal explanation makes reference to the way the hoverfly's nervous system is put together, how it works, how it is hooked to his retina and muscles, etc. If the hoverfly ends up coinciding with the rule not because his nerves and muscles work in a normal way but only because the wind serendipitously blows him around to face the right direction, he fails to express a competence.[6]

Not just anything a human effects is a human action. Effects that are actions must be intended, or at least foreseen, and must be generated from intentions in a normal way. Effects of human bodily movements that are not actions are called "accidental." Similarly, not just any process that originates in an animal's organs or behavioral systems is a biological activity. Biological activities are only those that express competencies. They correspond to normally fulfilled biological purposes, that is, to what the animal does in accordance with evolutionary design. Conversely, behavior that fails to express a competence corresponds to what an animal effects, biologically, only by accident. Thus the heart's saying pit-a-pat, the eyelashes' moving away from the eyebrows in a graceful arc, and the hoverfly's coinciding, but due only to the wind, with the proximal hoverfly rule are not biological activities but biological accidents.

To say that a given male hoverfly has a biological purpose to conform to the proximal hoverfly rule is very different from saying either that he himself has a history of having conformed to it (perhaps he has just reached adolescence) or that he has a disposition to conform to it. The normal hoverfly has a disposition to dart off when it sees a flying bird, and also a disposition to squash when stepped on, but these dispositions do not correspond to biological purposes or to competences. Conversely, male hoverflies that are crippled or blind have no disposition to conform to the proximal-hoverfly rule, but still it is one of their biological purposes to do so. As male members of the hoverfly species, conforming is the biological norm, the standard, for them.[7]

To say that the hoverfly has as a biological purpose to follow the proximal hoverfly rule is also quite different from saying that this rule is the only rule that fits all past instances of hoverfly turns, say, that resulted in hoverfly procreation. Suppose it were so that never in history had a male hoverfly spotted a female that happened to approach him at such an angle as to produce an image on his retina with a clockwise

---

6. For a full discussion of normal ("Normal") explanations for performance of proper functions, see *LTOBC*, chaps. 1 and 2, and chapter 4 herein.
7. On the proper functions of imperfect members of a biological category, see *LTOBC*, chaps. 1 and 2.

angular velocity between 500 and 510 degrees per second. Then the proximal *quoverfly* rule "If the vector angular velocity of the target's image is *not* counterclockwise and between 500 and 510 degrees per second, make a turn that equals the (signed) angle of the image minus 1/10 its vector angular velocity, plus or minus 180 degrees; at ease otherwise" fits all past actual cases of successful female encounters. But it is not a rule the hoverfly has as a biological purpose to follow. For it is not because their behavior coincided with *that* rule that the hoverfly's ancestors managed to catch females, and hence to proliferate. In saying that, I don't have any particular theory of the nature of explanation up my sleeve. But surely, on any reasonable account, a complexity that can simply be dropped from the explanans without affecting the tightness of the relation of explanans to explanandum is not a *functioning* part of the explanation. For example, my coat does not keep me warm because it is fur-lined *and red*, nor because it is fur-lined *in the winter*, but just because it is fur-lined. (True, I am making the assumption that the qualifications and additions that convert the proximal hoverfly rule into the proximal quoverfly rule are objectively qualifications and additions rather than simplifications. This assumption rests on a metaphysical distinction between natural properties and kinds and artificially synthesized gruelike properties and kinds or, what is perhaps the same, depends on there being a difference between natural law and mere de facto regularity. But my project is to solve the Kripke-Wittgenstein paradox, not to defend commonsense ontology. Nor should either of these projects be confused with solving Goodman's paradox.[8])

To say that the hoverfly has as a biological purpose to follow the proximal hoverfly rule is also quite different from saying that this rule is the only rule that fits the actual dispositions of normal hoverflies or of past hoverflies that managed to procreate. Suppose that, given the principles in accordance with which the hoverfly's turn-angle-determining devices work, engineering constraints necessitated a mechanism normal

---

8. Goodman's paradox is a paradox in epistemology. Kripke, on the other hand, is concerned not about how we could know or discover what someone means by "plus" but about what this determinate meaning *consists* in. Note too that assuming commonsense ontology does nothing by itself toward solving Goodman's paradox, which concerns how we can *know* or reasonably guess which entities are the basic ontological ones, *supposing* there to be such.

for hoverflies with a blind spot for clockwise angular velocities between 500 and 510 degrees per second. These particular velocities produce no reaction at all on the part of the male. Then the same proximal quoverfly rule mentioned above fits the actual dispositions of all normal hoverflies, but it still would not be a rule that the hoverfly has as a biological purpose to follow. The hoverfly's biological purposes include the expression only of dispositions that have helped to account for the proliferation of his ancestors. By hypothesis, the disposition to rest at ease when the target's image is counterclockwise and between 500 and 510 degrees per second did not help the hoverfly's ancestors to propagate. It was only the times that the proximal hoverfly rule was obeyed that the ancestors procreated. So the hoverfly resting at ease behind his blind spot is not displaying a competence. It is conformity to the proximal hoverfly rule, not the quoverfly rule, that he biologically purposes, even if normal hoverflies are not especially accurate in fulfilling this natural purpose, in conforming to this ideal.

4   Proximal versus Distal Rules

My plan, as I have indicated, is slowly to make plausible the claim that the normative element that is involved when one means to follow a rule is biological purposiveness. Meaning to follow a rule differs from having a disposition to coincide with a rule, in the same way that the hoverfly's biologically purposing to follow the proximal hoverfly rule differs from having a disposition to coincide with it. That is how I aim to solve the Kripke-Wittgenstein paradox concerning what *constitutes* rule following. At the same time, however, I wish to build a case that language understanding or language competency is competency in the biological sense. And I wish to argue that it is possible to have a biological competence to follow correspondence truth rules, and hence that a "realist" theory of language understanding is possible on the biological model. To gain this latter end, we need to discuss distal as well as proximal rules.

Conforming to the proximal hoverfly rule is a means, for the hoverfly, of following a less proximal or more distal rule: "If you see a female, catch it." Call this "the distal hoverfly rule." To say that conformity to the proximal hoverfly rule is a means to conformity to the distal rule is the same as to say that the mechanism that has historically accounted for the overwhelming majority of ancestor hoverflies' successes at conformity to the distal hoverfly rule begins with conformity to the proximal rule. That is, the normal explanation for conformity to the distal rule contains the specification that the hoverfly first conform to the proximal rule.

Now whether the hoverfly succeeds in following the proximal hoverfly rule depends, for the most part, only on whether his insides are working right, that is, on whether he is a normal healthy member of his species. But whether or how often he manages to conform to the distal hoverfly rule depends on more. It depends on conditions that are outside his body and over which he has no control, such as how hard the wind is blowing, whether the females that pass by are in fact of normal size, traveling at the normal speed, and perhaps whether they are willing. Without doubt, then, hoverflies are worse at conforming to the distal than to the proximal hoverfly rule. That is, their competence or ability to conform to the distal rule is less reliable than their competence or ability to conform to the proximal rule. But that the hoverfly may not be very reliable in his conformity to the distal hoverfly rule bears not at all on whether it is one of his biological purposes to conform. Compare: It is a biological purpose of the sperm to swim until it reaches an ovum. That is what it has a tail for. But very few sperm actually achieve this biological end, because ova are in such short supply. Reaching an ovum is a purpose of the sperm, since it is only because ancestor sperm reached ova that they reproduced, and thus proliferated the tail. Similarly, it was only when ancestor hoverflies conformed to the distal hoverfly rule that they *became* ancestors.

Turning the coin over, the hoverfly is very reliable in his coincidence with this "overkill rule": "Dart off after everything that flies by you subtending about .5 degree on your retina, whether it's male or female; animate or inanimate; bird, plane, or Superman." But this overkill rule does not correspond to any biological purpose of the hoverfly. True, conforming to the proximal hoverfly rule is one of the hoverfly's biological purposes, and conforming to this rule will *result* in his coinciding with the overkill rule if there are objects other than female hoverflies flying about it (even if there are not). But it is not coinciding with the overkill rule that has helped to account for hoverfly proliferation. Only the times when the distal hoverfly rule was obeyed did hoverfly ancestors procreate.[9] It is conformity to the distal hoverfly rule that explains the ancestor hoverflies' *successes*. As the hoverfly chases after a distant bird, he expresses no competence except, of course, competence to conform to the proximal hoverfly rule. Conformity to the distal hoverfly rule, not to the overkill rule, is what he biologically purposes, though at the moment he is accidentally, that is, nonbiologically, doing something else.

That is how purposes inform the rule-following behavior of the hoverfly, how norms, standards, or ideals apply to his behaviors, hence how the hoverfly comes to display competences or abilities to conform to rules rather than mere dispositions to coincide with them.[10] But the unexpressed rules that humans purposively conform to, at least most of those that they purposively conform to when using inner or outer language, are not rules that they are genetically hard-wired to follow but rules that they have learned. How, then, can humans biologically purpose to follow such rules? Before turning directly to the problem of human rule following, let us examine a simpler case of learned biological purposes, of learned competence, the case of a simpler animal that learns to follow rules.

5   Learned or Derived Rules and Competences

If a rat becomes ill within a few hours after eating a specific food, it will later shun all foods that taste the same. For example, if the rat eats soap and soon becomes ill, thereafter it will refuse to eat soap. Although the rat may have dragged certain nesting materials home or explored new territory just before becoming ill, it will not on that account shun that kind of nesting material or that territory. Nor will it shun foods that merely look the same or that are found in the same place as the food

9. More precisely, only the distal hoverfly rule would be mentioned in giving a "most proximate normal explanation" of the function of the hoverfly's turning mechanism. See *LTOBC* and the discussion of "normal explanations" in chapter 4 herein.
10. Notice that the reference to evolutionary *history* has been doing all of the work in explaining how norms come to apply to the activities of an animal, in explaining how there can be a standard from which the facts of individual behavior diverge. I defend the position that function always derives from history in chapters 1 and 2.

eaten prior to illness.[11] It thus appears that a quite specific mechanism is harbored in the rat, a proper function of which is to produce conformity to the specialized rule "If ingestion of a substance is followed by illness, do not ingest any substance with that taste again." Call this rule the "proximal rat rule." Clearly, following the proximal rat rule is a biological means to following a more distal rat rule, say, "Do not eat poisonous substances"; helping to produce conformity to this rule is a further proper function of the relevant inborn mechanisms in the rat.

Now the proximal rat rule, like the proximal hoverfly rule, tells the animal what to do given certain experiential contingencies. There is a difference, however, in the normal manner of executing these two rules. When the hoverfly conforms to his rule, nothing in his body undergoes a permanent change, but this is not so in the case of the rat. Suppose, for example, that the rat has just become ill after eating soap. In order to conform to the proximal rat rule, in order to avoid henceforth what tastes like soap, the rat's nervous system must first conform to certain preliminary "rules," rules that dictate that a certain sort of permanent change take place in it. The rat, we say, must "learn" in order to conform to his rule. But the fact that the rat's evolutionary history dictates that it is normal for him to undergo learning in order to follow his rule rather than following it directly does not affect the biological status of the rule. That he should follow his rule is one of his biological purposes for exactly the same reason that the hoverfly's rule following is biologically purposed. Conformity to the rat rule is what ancestor rats had in common in those cases in which possession of the relevant inborn mechanisms aided them to flourish and proliferate, so it is what the mechanism, hence the rat, biologically purposes.

Now the rat that conforms to the proximal rat rule, if he ever becomes ill after eating, ends by conforming to a *derived* proximal rat rule, say the rule "Do not eat what tastes like soap." Indeed, if a rat becomes ill after eating soap, it immediately becomes one of his biological purposes to follow the rule "Do not eat what tastes like soap." That he is to follow this derived rule is logically entailed by the proximal rat rule plus the premise that he has in fact become ill after eating soap. Similarly,

---

11. The reference is to studies by John Garcia. A bibliography of his papers may be found in the *American Psychologist* 35 (1980): 41–43.

the hoverfly that currently has an image of appropriate size traversing his retina at a 60 degree angle with an angular velocity of 100 degrees per second currently has as a biological purpose to make a turn of 130 degrees. Notice that the hoverfly has this biological purpose quite independently of whether or not any hoverfly has ever been in exactly this experiential position before. It is theoretically possible, even if unlikely, that no hoverfly has ever had exactly *this* biological purpose before. This is similar to our rat who is sick after eating soap. It is now one of his biological purposes to follow the derived proximal rat rule "Do not eat what tastes like soap," even if it should be true that no other rat in history has ever become sick after eating soap, and hence true that no rat in history has ever had this particular biological purpose before.

In this manner, animals that learn can acquire biological purposes that are peculiar to them as individuals, tailored to their own peculiar circumstances or peculiar histories.[12] Although biological purposes are functions fulfilled in accordance with evolutionary design, they need not be innately given purposes. Similarly, biological competences need not be innate. A proper biological activity of an animal can be something that experience has prompted or "taught" the animal to do, experience coupled with an innate mechanism for being guided to learn by experience.

Nor is there need for such mechanisms to be as specialized as the mechanism that conforms the rat to the proximal rat rule. Not long ago many learning theorists believed that all animal learning took place in accordance with principles that were not species-specific but universal. Suppose that this were true. Suppose that every species learned in accordance with the principles of one person's favorite general theory of operant conditioning, so that no reference to the particular evolutionary niche of a species was ever needed to explain how its learning mechanisms had historically enhanced its fitness. Then there would have to be some rarefied hypergeneral explanation of how and why these learning principles worked. Such an explanation might make reference, for example, to specific principles of generalization and discrimination used in differentiating stimuli and in projecting what is to count as "the same"

---

12. A much more detailed discussion of "derived proper functions" may be found in *LTOBC*, chap. 2, and in chapter 3 herein.

behavior again, that is, reference to universal proximal rules followed during learning. It would have to tell how and why these particular ways of generalizing and discriminating effected, often enough, isolation or zeroing in on sufficiently reliable causes of reinforcement, and in what universal manner (!) reinforcers are connected with the well-being of animals. Thus it would tell *how* possession of the universal mechanism had normally, that is, historically, enhanced fitness in animals generally. Specific applications of this general explanation schema to individual animals in individual circumstances would then determine which among the various effects of their motions were the proximal and distal biological activities of these individuals as they learned and applied their learning. Such applications would determine, for example, what specific reliable causes of reinforcement were purposefully being zeroed in on by particular animals at particular times, that is, what these animals were "trying" to learn and, after they learned it, what the specific goals of their learned behaviors were.

Now it is important to note that to fulfill a biological purpose is not always to take a step toward flourishing or propagating; it is not always good for an animal to fulfill its biologically determined goals. For example, a rat might come to have as a biological purpose to follow the derived rule "Do not eat what *t*astes like soap" even if it were true (I suspect it is true) that soap does not *make* rats sick, does not poison them. Suppose, rather, that the rat eats soap and then becomes ill due to a bout with rattus enteritis. Still, in order to conform to the proximal rat rule, he must now conform to the derived proximal rule "Do not eat what tastes like soap," for this derived rule is entailed by the proximal rat rule, given his situation and experience. Yet following this derived rule may, in fact, have no tendency to bring him into conformity with the more distal rat rule "Do not eat poisonous substances." So it can happen that the rat acquires a biological purpose and acquires a competence to conform to a derived rule which does not further the end that is this rule's own raison d'être. Indeed, the rat *could* acquire a derived purpose and a competence to behave in a manner that was actually detrimental to him, say a purpose to follow the rule "Do not eat what tastes like corn" when, in fact, unless he eats corn, given his circumstances, he will starve. Compare: the hoverfly, dutifully conforming to the proximal hoverfly rule (the rule that tells how he is to react to a moving image on his retina) may thereby dart off after a bird, who would not otherwise have spotted the hoverfly, hence would not have *eaten* him. Thus it is that an individual may have a biological purpose and a competence to follow a derived rule that has no tendency to further the interests either of the individual or of his species and, more specifically, no tendency to produce conformity to more distal rules toward which following it was biologically supposed to be a means.[13]

What an animal is doing in accordance with evolutionary design need not be anything that any member of its species has ever done before. And it need not be anything that is good for the animal to do. So surely it need not be anything that common sense would call "natural" for it to do. Consider a circus poodle riding a bicycle. It is performing what common sense would call a most "unnatural" act. Yet it is one of the dog's biological purposes to perform that act. Biologically, the (typical circus) dog's distal action is procurement of his dinner. The dog harbors within him an intricate mechanism, operating in accordance with certain largely unknown but surely quite definite and detailed principles, in accordance with which dogs have been designed to develop perceptual, cognitive, and motor skills and to integrate them so as to effect procurement of dinner in their individual environments. Living in an unusual environment, the circus dog acquires unusual purposes and competences when he applies his "dog rules" to his environment. But although he may be making the audience laugh by accident, he is certainly not balancing on that bicycle by accident. He is balancing purposefully, or in accordance with evolutionary design—in accordance with another application of the same general principles that procured his ancesters' dinners during evolutionary history.

6 Human Rule Following

Humans are very sophisticated creatures, so we tell ourselves. We not only learn but learn new ways to learn, develop new concepts, and so forth. Further, much of our behavior results not just from learning but

---

13. For further details on conflicting proper functions, see *LTOBC*, chap. 2, and chapter 3 herein.

from theoretical and practical inference. But there must still be a finite number of inborn mechanisms, operating in accordance with a finite number of natural principles, having a finite number of biologically proper functions, that account for our dispositions to do these things. Coordinately, there must be a finite number of proximal and distal "*Homo sapiens* rules" that we have as biological purposes to follow, and there must be mechanisms to implement these rules built into the basic body and brain of normal persons.

Consider, then, any bit of human behavior produced by biologically well-functioning behavior-regulating systems, by systems that are not broken or jammed. (Behavior that results from malfunction is, of course, overwhelmingly unlikely to bear fruit of any interesting kind.) There will be a way of describing this behavior that captures its aspect as a *biological* activity, a description that tells what proximal and distal biological purposes, and what biological competences if any, the behavior expresses. This will be so even if the behavior is totally unique or systematically self-destructive or not "natural" by any commonsense standards. But, of course, there will also be numerous ways of describing the behavior that fail to express its biological purposiveness, many "quuslike" descriptions, as "pointing toward the navel with the eyelashes" quus-describes the eye-blink reflex. So the questions arise, What is the relation of *ordinary* human purposes, of human intentions and meanings, to biological purposes? Are descriptions of human intentional actions quus descriptions from the standpoint of evolutionary design? Do ordinary human intentions merely accidentally *cohabit* with biological purposes?

Surely a naturalist must answer no. Ordinary human purposes, ordinary intentions, can only be a *species* of biological purpose. To suppose otherwise would be to suppose that the whole mechanism of human belief, desire, inference, concept formation, etc., the function of which culminates in the formation and execution of human intentions, is, as functioning in this capacity, an epiphenomenon of biology, an accidental by-product of systems that nature designed for other purposes. And what would these other purposes be?[14]

14. For a more detailed defense of this claim, see chapters 2 and 3.

This accords with conclusions we reached earlier on the nature of explicit intentions. Explicitly meaning or intending, if this requires representing what one intends, presupposes a prior purposing: purposing to let the representation guide one in a certain way. This is true whether we are talking about representation in an inner medium, say in a "language of thought," or representation in a public medium—talking, say, about the use of "plus." But this prior purposing cannot be analyzed as the original explicit purposing was analyzed without regress. Rather, a prior unexpressed purposing must be assumed. The reasonable conclusion seems to be that ordinary explicit intending rests on biological purposing—biologically purposing to be guided by, to react this way rather than that to, one's representations. Whether this biological purposing is innate (compare Fodor's version of the "language of thought") or whether it is derived via learning, mechanisms of concept formation, etc., it must *ultimately* derive its content from the details of our evolutionary history.

So unless doing arithmetic results from a total breakdown of the cognitive systems (in which case there may be nothing you purpose when you encounter "plus": how you react to it is accidental under every description) then *whatever* you mean to do when you encounter "plus," that content has been determined by your experience coupled with evolutionary design. But, reasonably, whatever you mean by "plus" is the same as what other people mean who are endowed with the same general sort of cognitive equipment and have been exposed to the same sort of training in arithmetic. This meaning has been determined by the application of *Homo sapiens* rules of some kind to experience. It is likely that these are extremely abstract, general-purpose *Homo sapiens* rules, in accordance with which human concept formation takes place, and it is likely that the explanation of the efficacy of these rules makes reference to very deep and general principles of ontology. But it is not my task to speculate about the precise form these *Homo sapiens* rules take or about how the experience of standard training in arithmetic elicits from them the capacity to mean plus. Speculation about the specific forms that our most fundamental cognitive capacities take is the psychologist's job.[15]

15. But, people still persist in asking, How do you know that we really *do* end

I believe that these considerations constitute, albeit in very rough and broad outline, the solution to the Kripke-Wittgenstein paradox.

7   Truth Rules: Verificationist or Correspondence?

I have sketched a theory about meaning in the sense of purposing, both expressed and unexpressed purposing. It remains to connect this theory with the theory of semantic meaning.

Truth rules are rules that project, from the parts and structure of sentences in a language, the conditions under which these sentences would be true. Such rules express, of course, an aspect of the meaning of the sentences. The question is whether the conditions referred to by truth rules are to be understood in a "realist" way as correspondence truth conditions or in a "verificationist" way as assertability conditions. Dummett's concern about truth rules is this: Whatever connection there is between sentences and that which determines their truth has to be a connection that is established via the actual employment of the language. Whatever form truth rules take, realist or verificationist, the *practical* abilities of speakers who understand a language must reflect these rules, indeed, must determine their content. Hence an analysis of the structure of the abilities required for language use and understanding should reveal the kind of rules truth rules are. But, Dummett argues, the only truth rules we could possibly exhibit a practical grasp of are verificationist truth rules.

In section 8 below, I will claim that Dummett's argument hangs on treating language abilities or competencies, hence the following of language rules, as mere dispositions, or alternatively (perhaps), as taking place wholly within consciousness, and I will add to the arguments already piled up by Wittgenstein and Kripke against the adequacy of this sort of treatment. In the present section, however, I wish to propose a positive thesis. My claim will be that if we interpret rule following and, in general, purposes and competencies, in the biological way, then

---

up meaning *plus* by "plus"? How do you know we don't mean *quus*? Because if we meant quus, then "plus" would mean quus, and the way to *say* that we all meant quus would be "We all mean plus," which is what I said. Compare Davidson 1987 and Burge 1988.

we can see how, on the contrary, reference to correspondence truth rules might *easily* fall out of an analysis of language competence.

Begin by observing that whatever the content of truth rules may be, realist or verificationist, the intent or purpose of anyone engaged in making sincere assertions in a language must be to conform their sentences to these rules. The sincere speaker purposes to make assertions that are true. It follows that the *way* that the actual practice of a language embodies truth rules is that these are the rules in accordance with which the competent speaker (or thinker), when sincere, purposes to make (or think) assertions. These are rules that he is, as it were, *trying to follow insofar as he is sincerely speaking (or thinking) *that* language. On the bottom layer at least (perhaps the layer that governs the language of thought) these rules must, of course, be unexpressed rules. But precisely because truth rules are at bottom unexpressed rules, introspection can give us no handle on what kind of rules they are. Rather, it is necessary to develop a *theory* about truth rules, an explanatory hypothesis about what rules we are purposing to follow when we make sincere assertions.

Assuming a biological standpoint, the question whether truth rules are realist or verificationist can be expressed by asking how "proximal" versus "distal" truth rules are. The proximal hoverfly rule was a rule about how the hoverfly was to respond to a moving image on his retina, that is, roughly, to sensory stimulations. The distal hoverfly rule was a rule about how the hoverfly was to end up interacting with his more removed environment, namely, with females that entered his life at a distance. "Verificationist" truth rules, as Putnam and Dummett envision these, would be rules that governed responses to prior thoughts and, as Dummett has put it, "bare sense experiences," hence would be proximal rules (Dummett 1976, 111). "Realist" or correspondence rules, on the other hand, would for the most part be distal rules, rules that governed the manner in which assertions were to correspond to affairs that lie, very often, well beyond the interface of body and world. Convinced by Wittgenstein and Kripke that purposing to follow a rule is not something encapsulated *within* consciousness, we are not compelled to suppose that truth rules have to be rules about what is to happen either in the mind or at the interface between mind (or body) and world. So let us ask what it would be like if truth rules were distal correspondence rules.

The first thing to note is that if truth rules were distal rules, they would surely have to be *backed* by proximal rules, rules about how to respond to our thoughts (inference) and to the immediate fruits of our perceptual explorations (perceptual judgment). They would have to be *backed* by rules that determine assertability conditions, the innermost of these conditions being within the mind or brain or at the interface of mind or brain and world. Call these backup rules "proximal assertability rules." Proximal assertability rules would concern the most proximal conditions under which we should say or think certain things. Conformity to these rules would have, as a biological purpose, to effect conformity to distal rules, that is, to correspondence truth rules. These truth rules would concern distal conditions under which we should say or think certain things. The truth rules might imply directives with this sort of form: if you have reason to speak (think) about the weather in Atlanta, say (think) "It is snowing in Atlanta" when and only when it is snowing in Atlanta; if you have reason to speak (think) about the color of snow, say (think) "Snow is white" if and only if snow is white. For a simple biological model here, compare worker honeybees. They (biologically) purpose to follow rules of this kind: when dancing, angle the axis of your dance 10 degrees off the vertical if and only if there is a good supply of nectar 10 degrees off a direct line from hive to sun. (Proposals concerning how humans might *learn* how to [purpose to] conform to distal correspondence truth rules are detailed in *LTOBC*, chaps. 9, 17, and 18.)

Conforming to the proximal hoverfly rule and the proximal rat rule often fails to bring hoverflies and rats into conformity to the distal hoverfly and rat rules. Similarly, conforming to proximal assertability rules might often fail to bring humans into conformity to truth rules. One can unknowingly say what is false even though one has good evidence for what one says. And one frequently fails to say what is true, indeed, to say anything at all, because one lacks any evidence at all, either for or against. Also, whether conformity to the proximal hoverfly and rat rules helps to produce conformity to the distal hoverfly and rat rules on this or that occasion often depends upon factors in the hoverfly's or rat's external environment over which it has no control. Similarly, whether conformity to proximal assertability rules would bring us into conformity to truth rules in this case or that might depend upon factors over which we had no control. For example, circumstances responsible for most perceptual illusions are circumstances outside the observer which, normally, he neither controls nor needs to control. Nor is not having enough evidence either to affirm or to deny a proposition typically something that it is within one's control to remedy. The principles in accordance with which biological devices perform functions that are proper to them always refer, in the end, to conditions external to these devices. These are conditions that have *historically* been present often enough to enable a critical proportion of ancestors of those devices to perform these functions, or to perform them a critical proportion of the time, but that cannot be counted on always to be present. All biological devices are fallible devices, even when normal and healthy.[16]

It follows that the proximal assertability rules for a sentence would not *define* its semantics, for they would not determine what its truth conditions were. Rather, following proximal assertability rules would be means that were merely approximations to the end that was following correspondence truth rules—more or less helpful and more or less reliable means to that end. Let us reflect for a moment upon certain consequences of this model.

If proximal assertability rules were rules that we followed only as a more or less reliable means to following distal truth rules, then it would not, at least, be obvious that those who shared a language in the sense of having competences to abide by the same truth rules would have any need to share proximal assertability rules as well. The male hoverfly follows the distal rule "If you see a female, catch it" by following the proximal hoverfly rule. The male housefly follows the same distal rule by tracking the female rather than by plotting an interception path, employing different proximal means to the same distal end. Now consider how many different ways there are to make a map of a city, for example, by walking about with a yardstick, paper, and pencil; by working from aerial photographs; by using surveyors' instruments; etc. Might there not also be various ways to make sentences that map onto the world in accordance with the same truth rules? Is there really any

16. For amplification of this very crucial theme, see chapters 3, 4, and 9.

reason to suppose that only one set of proximal assertability rules could effect a reasonably reliable competence to conform to a given set of distal correspondence rules? Consider, for example, how many ways there are to tell whether a solution is acid or whether it has iodine in it. Consider how many alternative visual and tactile clues we use, on one occasion or another, to perceive depth. And consider: Were the proximal assertability rules that Helen Keller used when she spoke English the same as those that you use? If not, does it follow that she did not really speak English after all?

Indeed, there is a sense, there is a way of individuating rules, in which it is impossible for people to share proximal assertability rules. Proximal assertability rules that I conform to correlate happenings at the periphery of my nervous system or body with sentences. Proximal assertability rules that you conform to correlate happenings at the periphery of your nervous system or body with sentences. For us to "share a set of proximal assertability rules" could not, of course, be for me to purpose to correlate happenings at the periphery of *your* body with *my* sentences. If I purposed to do that, I would be purposing to conform to a distal rule, not a proximal rule. We could "share proximal assertability rules" only in the sense that our rules ran parallel. But it is not immediately obvious what the point of running parallel to one another with language might be. Why would you take any interest in the sentences I uttered if these correlated only with what was happening at the ends of my afferent nerves? Only if the proximal assertability rules that you and I used effected relatively reliable conformity to the same *distal* correspondence rules would there be any point in talking to one another. But if agreement is effected on the distal level, what need would there be for agreement on the proximal level? Hence, what reason is there to assume, say with Quine, that comparison of only proximal rules *ought* to yield determinate translation between idiolects?[17]

---

17. For further discussion of the relation of proximal assertability rules to truth rules, see Millikan 1986 and also *LTOBC*, esp. chaps. 8 and 9. Proximal assertability rules are close relatives of what I there called "intensions." (In this essay I am not emphasizing that perception characteristically is an activity involving overt exploration, a fact that was in the foreground when I spoke of intensions in *LTOBC*. Thus the notion "proximal assertability rules" is a somewhat duller tool than I intended "intensions" to be in *LTOBC*.)

8   Causes of Verificationist Myopia

Given a biological approach, then, there are reasons to think that truth rules may be distal correspondence rules, hence that classical truth conditions may do work for semantics. But Putnam and Dummett claim that any such view is unintelligible. Why?

Although there are passages in both Dummett and Putnam that could be given a less sympathetic reading, the reason is not (or at least is not simply) that these philosophers take understanding to be something that must transpire before consciousness. A more explicit theme is that understanding a language is a practical ability, constituted by a set of *dispositions*, in the case of language, learned responses: "Now when someone learns a language, what he learns is a practice; he learns to respond, verbally and nonverbally, to utterances and to make utterances of his own" (Dummett 1976, 82); "language understanding [is]...an activity involving 'language entry rules' (procedures for subjecting some sentences to stimulus control), procedures for deductive and inductive inference and 'language exit rules'" (Putnam 1978b, 110). It follows, Putnam and Dummett now agree, that if a language is characterized by certain truth rules, this fact must be one that shows up in the speech dispositions of the language users. And it follows that if there are no *dispositions* to recognize correspondence truth conditions, sentences can not have correspondence truth conditions.

Putnam's phrase "language entry rules" is a reference to Sellars, but, of course, many other central figures have also held that understanding a language must yield to a dispositional analysis, among them Quine, Davidson, many would say Wittgenstein, and, in the philosophy of mind (re: inner language), the functionalists. Despite this distinguished advocacy, surely Kripke's remark about illegitimate "equation of performance with correctness" is applicable here. To be competent in a language involves that one have a practical grasp of its truth rules. About that everyone agrees. But "true" is clearly a *normative* notion. "True" is how my sincerely uttered sentences are *when they come out right*, when they are, to use Kripke's expression, as they "ought to be," when I achieve what I purpose in sincerely uttering them. And no mere set of dispositions, no mere performance, determines a measuring "ought," a standard or norm. No set of dispositions, then, could determine truth rules.

Nor is the normative ingredient in truth provided by the fact that the dispositions that constitute competence in a language must agree with a public norm. Compare games. Consider first a case in which I intend to play the same game as the others do, say the one they call "chess," but I mistakenly play by different rules than the others. This is a case of playing wrongly in the sense that I have not played the game I intended or, perhaps, the one others expected me to. Similarly, if I intend to use the same language as the others but in fact adopt different truth rules, then I speak wrongly, for I have not spoken the language I intended or that others expected me to. This is called "not knowing the language" or "making mistakes in the language." Second, consider a case in which I have no intention to play with the chess pieces as the others do, nor do the others expect me to. Then playing by different rules is just playing a different game. It is neither playing chess wrongly nor doing anything else wrongly. The linguistic parallel to this is called "speaking a *different* language." But speaking wrongly in the sense of speaking *falsely* is still a *third* possibility. Speaking falsely is not just a way of being out of step, nor is it just marching to the beat of a different drummer. Suppose we call it a "rule" of chess that you are supposed to checkmate your opponent. Then speaking falsely is like failing to checkmate the opponent. Better, it is like failing to pick up one straw without moving the others when playing jackstraws. Just as learning the rules better is not the cure for losing at chess or jackstraws, learning the community's language better is not the cure for bad judgment. And just as whether one succeeds at jackstraws, that is, at not moving the other sticks, does not depend on any agreement with the community, neither does whether one succeeds in speaking truth in one's language. To purpose to follow certain truth rules is to set a standard for *oneself*, a standard that one may fail to meet.

It is because purposes set standards that "true" is a normative notion and that no set of dispositions could determine truth rules. Similarly, although Dummett and Putnam are right that semantic meaning must be resident somehow in language competence, no set of dispositions equals a competence. First, a disposition does not express a competence unless it is a disposition informed by a purpose. My disposition to fall if left unsupported is no competence, nor is the hoverfly's disposition to chase birds. Conversely, having a competence does not, in general, imply that one has any particular dispositions. If I know how to *A*, say to sharpen a drill bit, it doesn't follow that I have a disposition to succeed in *A*-ing if I try. Perhaps my hands are too cold, or the only grindstone available is not the kind I am practiced at using, or you insist on joggling my elbow. Though I know how to walk, sometimes I trip when I try. Recall the hoverfly, who exhibits a competence whenever he conforms to the distal hoverfly rule in a normal way, yet, due to the inconstancy of conditions outside him, often does not manage to conform to it at all. Nor are there specified conditions under which a person must succeed in order to know how. If I can only sharpen the bit using one sharpening tool whereas you know how to use another, then normal conditions for exercise of my ability to sharpen a drill bit will be different from normal conditions for exercise of yours; each may fail where the other succeeds. Knowing how to do *A* entails, at best, only that there are *some* normal conditions under which one succeeds in doing *A*.

Now there is an evident reason why knowing how to *A* does not, in general, entail having any simple disposition to succeed in *A*-ing. The reason is that most know-how involves *distal* action, and there is no such thing as a simple *disposition* to involvement with anything distal. How one interacts with things at a distance always depends upon what lies in between, on surrounding conditions. Simple dispositions can concern only reactions to and actions upon that which *touches* one or, perhaps, what is inside one. It follows that to assimilate language competence to a set of dispositions directly begs the question against distal truth rules. There is no need for tortuous arguments to demonstrate that truth rules must then be verificationist. On a dispositional account, to "grasp" correspondence truth rules for each sentence in one's language would be to have a "capacity. . . to evince recognition of the truth of the sentence when and only when the relevant condition is fulfilled" (Dummett 1976, 80–81). But if a "recognitional capacity" is a disposition, it must be a disposition to respond to a proximal stimulus, there being no such thing as a disposition to respond to something distal. And dispositions to respond to proximal stimuli with sentences could correspond, at best, to assertability conditions, certainly not to distal correspondence truth conditions. Q.E.D.

Compare the hoverfly. Assuming that his insides are working right, what he has a *disposition* to do is, at best, to conform to the proximal hoverfly rule. Does it follow that he has no ability to catch females?

It is significant, I think, how close the dispositional view of language understanding is to the more classical view that understanding takes place wholly within consciousness. On the classical view, understanding must ultimately involve relations only to things that touch the mind. On the dispositional view, understanding still involves only what touches the mind or, say, the nervous system. It is easy, then, to slip back and forth between two ways of interpreting the Dummett-Putnam attack upon realist truth.[18] Yet what Kripke has shown is that *neither* view of language understanding is a tenable view. Hence, whatever may be said for or against the positive theory of rule following that I have offered, the verificationist vision is surely unnecessarily nearsighted. If Kripke (and Kripke's Wittgenstein) are right, then *whatever* the status of rule following, we have no reason to think that the following of correspondence truth rules is any more *problematic* than is the following of verificationist truth rules.

On the other hand, perhaps what is most puzzling about the following of any kind of language rules is how one could "know" these rules without having a prior language, a prior way of "meaning" or thinking about these rules. Yet surely even the medium of thought, even whatever is currently before the mind or in the head, stands in need of interpretation. Knowing the rules is not a disposition, nor can it be explained in the end by reference to prior representations of the rules. The biological account agrees with both of these considerations.

18. I will not attempt to prove that Dummett and Putnam themselves do some sliding, but on Putnam, see *LTOBC*, Epilogue.

12

Naturalist Reflections on Knowledge

What *more* is needed in order to have knowledge besides having a belief that happens to be true? For many years the traditional answer to this question was that the belief must also be justified. Edmund Gettier (1963) challenged this answer twenty years ago by giving the first of a great variety of examples of true beliefs that many would call "justified" yet would not be happy about calling "knowledge." Since then a voluminous literature has accumulated on what has come to be called "the Gettier problem."

The tradition that has dealt with this problem has understood itself to be attempting to analyze something, to be taking something or other apart so as to show its structure. Robert Shope says that "lack of clarity in talking about concepts, and widespread contemporary suspicion of the analytic/synthetic distinction have led most authors to avoid committing themselves" to the view that what is being analyzed is "the content of the concept knowledge" (1983, 34). Most have simply been silent on the question of what it was they were analyzing. I have recently argued (*LTOBC*, chap. 9, and 1986)—though on grounds quite different from those that led Quine to reject the analytic/synthetic distinction—that in most cases there is no such thing as "*the* intension" of a public-language term, hence, presumably, no such thing as "an analysis of *the* concept" expressed by a public-language term. But surely many simple public terms (e.g., "water," "acidity," "tuberculosis") do denote natural (not nominal) kinds of various categorical sorts, and characteristics and peculiarities of these kinds are always a proper subject for study, study grounded ultimately in experience rather than a priori reflection (*LTOBC*, chaps. 16–19).

In this chapter, I propose to describe knowledge in the same sort of spirit in which science has described, say, tuberculosis or acidity or genes. Whatever else it is, knowledge surely is a *phenomenon in the world* that we need to understand. Or perhaps it is several phenomena that have got mixed together under one term "knowledge"—as there are two quite different kinds of acidity and several ways of counting genes, discovered by scientific inquiry, not just by a priori reflection. The setting within which I will explore the phenomenon of knowledge is that of evolutionary theory. Thus I make an immediate and obvious departure from conceptual analysis. Indeed, should the phenomena I discuss turn out to have no connection with the term "knowledge," that would surprise but not unduly pain me. They would still be phenomena deserving of philosophical reflection, interesting in their own right.

1   Proper Functions and Normal Explanations

In order to make my points succinctly, I will need to introduce two technical terms: "proper function" and "Normal explanation." These terms have been defined with considerable care in *LTOBC*, chaps. 1–2, but a feel for their use is all that should be necessary here.

Very roughly, the proper functions of any body organ or system are those functions which helped account during evolutionary history for survival or proliferation of the species containing the organ or system. *That an organ or system has certain proper functions is determined by its* HISTORY. It is *not* determined by its present properties, present structure, actual dispositions, or actual functions. For example, although it is a proper function of every heart to pump blood—indeed, it is because pumping blood is one of its proper functions that a thing is called a "heart"—some hearts are diseased or malformed or excised from the body that once contained them, hence unable to pump blood. These hearts are *hearts*, first, because originally produced by mechanisms (genetic materials operating in a specific environment) that proliferated during their evolutionary history in part because they were producing items that managed to circulate blood efficiently. They are hearts, second, because produced by such mechanisms in accordance with explanations that approximated, in some undefined degree, to Normal explanations for production of hearts in the relevant species and bear, as a result, a resemblance to Normal hearts of that species. By a "Normal heart" I mean a heart that matches, in relevant respects, the majority of hearts that, during the history of the species, managed to pump blood efficiently enough to aid survival and reproduction.

Associated with each of the proper functions that an organ or system has is a Normal explanation for performance of this function, which tells how that organ or system that species historically managed to perform that function. For example, there are a number of proper functions that *can* be performed by certain systems of the human body, given the presence of appropriate lithium compounds in the bloodstream, but that historically have been performed using calcium. The Normal explanations for how these functions are performed make reference to the presence of calcium in the blood rather than lithium. Similarly, the heart of a person who wears a pacemaker to assure that the electrical signals sent to the heart muscles are properly timed does not pump blood in accordance with a fully Normal explanation.

2   Normally Acquired True Belief

A distinctive kind of phenomenon occurs—of a kind central in the world of living things—whenever a thing performs one of its proper functions in accordance with a Normal explanation. Consider, then, the phenomenon that is a person's belief-making systems producing a true belief in accordance with a Normal explanation.

Our belief-making mechanisms or systems are capable not only of forming beliefs but of learning how to form beliefs (e.g., perceptual learning, acquiring new inference patterns), of learning how to form new types of beliefs (concept formation), and possibly even of learning how to learn how to form new types of beliefs (developing methods of concept formation). Assuming that the capacity to form and to use beliefs has survival value mainly in so far as the beliefs formed are true (or close enough), and assuming that humans currently have this capacity in part because, historically, having it had survival value, the mechanisms in us that produce beliefs, learn new concept, etc.—mechanisms, perhaps, that program other mechanisms that program still other mechanisms, etc.—all have in common at least one proper function: helping to produce true beliefs.[1]

And there will be Normal explanations of how each of these mechanisms contributes to this end—explanations that tell about the Normal constitution and proper operation of the mechanism, about the general kinds of environmental conditions it has historically relied upon, about the performances of other cooperating devices within the body it has historically relied upon, etc., *when* it has managed to perform the function of helping in the production of true beliefs or in the learning of new ways to produce true beliefs. A true belief that is true in accordance with a Normal explanation has been derived from the application, under historically Normal conditions, of methods of belief formation that have either been programmed via evolution into the human at birth or learned in accordance with a Normal explanation for proper performance of prior learning mechanisms that were built via evolution into the human at birth.

Now my first suggestion is that it is characteristic of those true beliefs that we call "knowledge" at least that they are true in accordance with a Normal explanation. Let me illustrate this by showing, for several kinds of traditional Gettier examples (examples of true justified beliefs that do not constitute knowledge), that these describe beliefs which, though true have not acquired their truth Normally. Later I will examine the question of what else may be needed before one has knowledge.

Suppose that a set of mirrors is arranged so as to project a virtual image of a candle at the exact place the candle in fact is, given a special placement of the observer.[2] A man placed in the right spot and unaware that there are reflecting surfaces present might justifiably believe there to be a candle right where the candle in fact is. Yet such a man seems to be lucky in having true belief or seems to have been manipulated into having it rather than being a possessor of knowledge. Notice that such a man would not have acquired a true belief in accordance with any Nor-

---

1. It does not necessarily follow that the beliefs produced by these mechanisms are usually true. Compare: it is a proper function of the swimming mechanism of a sperm to propel the sperm to an ovum, but very few sperm in fact reach ova. For many more details here, see *LTOBC* and chapter 3 herein.
2. This example is Gilbert Harman's as modified by Marshall Swain.

mal explanation. The man's perceptual systems were not designed via evolution to operate under the conditions described. Nor had the perceptual know-how *that* he *used* been developed or trained by higher systems for use under those conditions (compare learning how to see what one is doing in a mirror). Nor did the man have beliefs about the special situation he was in that led to taking acount of the abnormal perceptual situation he was in in accordance with some proper and Normally explained interaction of his perceptual and cognitive systems. In short, his belief matched the world for reasons that completely bypassed evolutionary design.

Here is another Gettier example. Roger has thrown a certain switch by one door of the laboratory on ten occasions and each time the overhead light has come on. The light has come on because the switch was operating correctly and was connected to the overhead light. Today Roger's switch is broken. He throws it for the eleventh time, believing that the light will come on, and he is right. The light comes on because a friend happens simultaneously to throw a working switch at the other end of the laboratory. Roger is right, but not in accordance with any Normal explanation. For presumably the mechanisms that produced Roger's true belief have historically worked to produce true beliefs *when* they have worked to produce true beliefs (as they evolved or as they were being programmed or trained) because lying behind past uniform sequences were uniform causal connections and because the situations in which new expectations arose were like the situations in which the past uniform sequences had occurred in that they supported the *same* causal connections.

One kind of Gettier example, a kind that Gettier himself suggested, describes a person who believes a false proposition p yet believes it on good evidence. He then correctly deduces a weaker conclusion from p, say the conclusion p or q, and this weaker conclusion happens to be true. Now any inference that moves to a true conclusion by relying on (as opposed to merely considering) a false premise or that relies on any false intermediate step cannot be an inference that produces a true conclusion Normally. To see this, I first define an "inference" as a movement in thought that is produced by "inference mechanisms" (contrast, say, mechanisms responsible for free associations) and then define "inference mechanisms" as those that (1) have as a proper function to produce true beliefs from prior beliefs and (2) that do this Normally by conforming to *logical* principles. Logical principles are principles that move us to true beliefs *reliably*, or relatively reliably (inductive inference), from other *truths*, not just from any beliefs at all.[3] Given this definition of what an inference mechanism is, if true beliefs are ever properly produced in accordance with a Normal explanation via reliance on false beliefs, that could only be because some methodological principle was at work here *other* than a logical principle, hence the mechanisms producing these true beliefs would not be mere inference mechanisms but some other kind of mechanisms instead or as well.

Now consider a contrasting case. Long before the Copernican revolution there were astronomers who, by using, for example, the theory of epicycles, were able to make remarkably accurate predictions about where and when the planets would make future appearances. In order to make these predictions, they used premises or reasoned through intermediate steps that were false. Yet it cannot be denied that they often *knew* where Mars or the Morning Star would appear next day and even five years from the next Tuesday.[4] Were their true beliefs about future planetary positions true in accordance with Normal explanations?

Granted the definition I have given of "inference mechanisms," certainly their inference mechanisms were not producing true beliefs in accordance with detailed explanations Normal for them qua inference mechanisms. But perhaps there were more general mechanisms or mechanisms that were not *just* inference mechanisms at work here that were functioning Normally. Consider those very general mechanisms in us that produce repetitions of behaviors, mental processes and the like that have consistently led to successful outcomes, to getting what one wanted, in the past. Presumably, outcomes that result from the opera-

---

3. Or in some case move us to true beliefs from the mere entertainment of propositions. For example, in the case of reasoning by *reductio*, not only false hypotheses but false beliefs may occur along the way to true conclusions they finally induce. But in such cases the Normal explanation that tells why a final conclusion that is *true* was reached does not pass through belief in the false propositions entertained and later denied. It passes only through the fact that these propositions were entertained and their implications investigated. That they were at one time also *believed* is not part of why the inference process resulted in a true final conclusion.

4. Gilbert Harman constructs a fictitious example of this type in *Thought* (1973).

tions of these mechanisms are successful in accordance with a Normal explanation so long as there were consistent reasons why the behaviors or mental processes, etc., uniformly produced the outcomes they did in the past and so long as the repetitions of these behaviors or processes produce the same results again for the same reasons. Imagine a child who has accidentally discovered the trick of adding the digits of a number to see if they sum to 0 or 9 in order to tell whether the number is divisible by 9. Though the child may not understand why this works— indeed, he may entertain wild hypotheses about why it works—still, if he's tried it numerous times and found that it does work, any true beliefs that he gains by using this method are true in accordance with a Normal explanation. For similar reasons, the pre-Copernican astronomers had true beliefs about where the planets would show up that were true in accordance with a Normal explanation, even though what I have narrowly defined as their "inference mechanisms" were not themselves working correctly in accordance with a detailed Normal explanation.

We should test the thesis that knowledge characteristically involves Normally derived true belief by trying to think of examples of knowledge that do not meet this requirement. For instance, is a person who must wear strong lenses in order to see clearly or who must wear a powerful hearing aid in order to hear capable of acquiring true beliefs by the use of his eyes or ears in accordance with a Normal explanation? If not, we are in trouble, for no one would suggest that such a person could not gain knowledge by the use of vision or hearing. So as to move the argument along at a fast enough pace that its outlines will not become obscured, I will discuss only common cases of this sort in this section, reserving discussion of more bizarre cases for an appendix.

In the usual sorts of cases in which a handicapped person has been fitted with a prosthetic device that aids perception, this has been done with her knowledge, consent, and trust, and/or she has had time to adjust to the device, undergoing any perceptual learning that may have been necessary and gathering evidence along the way of the veracity of her perceptual judgments when employing the device. In all such cases there is a Normal explanation for the truth of beliefs formed by the use of such devices. Although the eyes and the ears are not operating in ways that are Normal for them, the belief-making mechanisms *are* operating in ways or in accordance with principles that are Normal for *them.* Trusting in the doctors that, after they have fixed you up, you will not seem clearly to see or hear things that aren't there can certainly be well placed trust acquired in accordance with a Normal explanation, hence one's resulting true beliefs about what one sees and hears can certainly have been acquired Normally. When perceptual learning has taken place and/or when one's past experience with use of a perceptual aid has produced one's confidence in the reality of what one seems to see and hear, it is even more evident that true beliefs are acquired Normally despite perceptual aids. Similarly, one gains true beliefs Normally by the use of microscopes, telescopes, volt meters, CAT scans, oscilloscopes, or any other devices devised to aid perception if one has learned to use them properly and trusts them for good reason.

Let us tentatively conclude, then, that knowledge does characteristically involve true belief that has been acquired in accordance with a Normal explanation. In order to understand what more knowledge involves, it will be helpful first to examine the phenomenon of degrees of strength in belief.

3   Degrees of Strength in Dispositional Belief

Kent Bach has recently described what he calls "the dynamic roles of beliefs" thus:

To believe something is to be prepared, when the thought of it occurs, to assume it and reason from it without reconsidering it (unless, of course, some new consideration occurs to you). Thus if you believe that *p* and the thought of it occurs, you will take it that *p* without further ado. Because you already believe it, the question of whether or not *p* does not arise when the thought of *p* occurs; the question is answered already. (1984, 48)

On the other hand,

Believing that *p* does not mean being unwilling to reconsider it when the thought occurs. Unless your belief that *p* is not just strong but downright dogmatic, new considerations relevant to the question of whether or not *p* can lead you to reconsider the question, even if you end up retaining your belief. (1984, 49)

Clearly, Bach's description here is a description of *dispositional* belief. To have the dispositional belief that *p*, he claims, is to have a disposition to take it that *p* in the context of theoretical or practical reasoning "without further ado." But, of course, dispositions can change. New considerations can lead one to change one's dispositional beliefs. Concerning such changes, Bach says,

Beliefs come in a variety of strengths ranging from hesitance to conviction, and a rough measure of a belief's strength is its resistance to being given up in the face of other beliefs. (1984, 49)

But what could it mean to say of a particular dispositional belief that it was more versus less "resistant to being given up in the face of other beliefs"? Presumably, a Normal person's beliefs at any given time form a consistent set, or close enough. Hence, presumably, if one gives up one belief "in the face of" another, this will usually be because this other is a new belief that has just entered the belief set and that threatens the consistency of the whole. So on Bach's account, the strength of a belief would have to be measured not relative to other beliefs that one actually has but relative to beliefs that one might possibly acquire. Belief strength cannot be measured as desire strength is measured, by pitting actual desires against one another, because one's actual beliefs do not compete in the Normal case. But whether one would or would not give up a belief that one now actually has in the face of these or those merely *possible* beliefs would surely depend upon the strength assigned to those possible beliefs. And for every belief that one actually has, exactly the same can be said: if one acquired new beliefs that conflicted with it and were stronger than it, then one would give it up; if one acquired new beliefs that conflicted with it but were weaker than it, then one would give up some or all of the new beliefs. To describe a measure of resistance to change in dispositional belief is not, it seems, an entirely straightforward matter.

Let me suggest another way to put a rough measure on dispositional-belief strength, a measure not of resistance to *change* of disposition but a measure of the strength of the disposition itself. There are some beliefs that one would rely on—one would "take it that *p* without further ado"—in the context of an activity even though heaven and earth depended on the outcome of that activity. But there are other beliefs that one would rely on in the context of an activity only if very little depended upon the outcome. For example, no matter what were at stake, I would rely without further ado on my belief that a rock will fall if left unsupported. But if very much were at stake, I would not rely without further ado (as I usually do rely) on my belief that the electrical outlet in our living room that has never worked for us still doesn't work. Certainly I would not allow any baby to poke a metal object into that outlet. This shows that my belief in the law of gravity is stronger than my belief that that outlet won't suddenly start working again. To look at this another way, compare the following cases. I always take it without further ado that my automobile will operate in the usual manner unless, as Bach has said, some new consideration occurs to me. (Such a consideration might be that my engine has lately been making a new and distressing noise.) But the commercial airline pilot does not ever take it without further ado that his plane will operate in the usual manner. He always goes through an elaborate series of checks to make sure before taking off. It does not follow that my daily belief that my car will run properly is *stronger* than the airline pilot's daily belief that his plane will run properly. For if as much depended on the proper operation of my car as depends on the proper operation of his plane, I too would see that elaborate checks were made before I would take it without (still) further ado that my car would run properly.

Besides the kind of ado that is checking again, either in one's mind or by external tests, whether *p*, there is taking it that *p* in the context of an activity but with a lack of confidence that *p*, and hence a lack of confidence that the activity will succeed. This kind of ado may consist in making backup plans for the event of failure or in casting about for some way of performing the activity that would not depend upon *p*'s truth before going ahead on the assumption that *p*. But whether or not this kind of ado takes place will likewise vary with the perceived importance of avoiding failure in the task at hand. So the fact that I make this kind of ado over whether *p* on one occasion but not over whether *q* *on another occasion* does not necessarily show that my dispositional belief that *p* is stronger than my dispositional belief that *q*. Rather, strength of dispositional belief in *p* is measured by the importance that the success of an activity proceeding on the assumption that *p* must have for me before I will make an ado over whether *p*.

If this is a measure of the strength that dispositional belief has, then Bach's description of the dispositional belief that *p* as a simple preparedness—one that one either does or doesn't have—to take it that *p* without any ado is too simple. Of course, in the case of any *occurrent* belief that *p*—any particular episode of assuming and reasoning from *p*—either one does or one does not make an ado before taking it that *p*. But if having a dispositional belief that *p* is having a disposition to believe-without-any-ado that *p occurrently*, then dispositional belief is not in general something that one either does or doesn't have. Rather, one will very commonly have a disposition occurrently to believe-that-*p*-without-any-ado only up to a certain threshold of anxiety about the consequences of failing the task that one uses the belief that *p* to implement. (This task might, of course, be a purely intellectual task. One may be very anxious about the possibility of getting the wrong results on an intellectual task, especially if the results are to be made public.) Thus for each proposition that one dispositionally believes, a certain *strength* of disposition must be assigned.

Now it would seem to be no accident but a wise choice of evolutionary design that our dispositional beliefs come in varying strengths. To waste time checking over and over whether *p* when it doesn't really matter that much whether *p* would be an inefficient design. But to fail to check whether *p* when it really matters a lot whether *p* would be disastrous design, *unless* the methods by which one had already come to have the dispositional belief that *p* were extremely *reliable* methods. Sensible design, then, would make us sensitive to the relative reliability of the methods by which we acquired and perhaps later reinforced our various dispositional beliefs, and would allocate strength of dispositional belief accordingly. It would equip us not only with mechanisms for forming true beliefs and for learning to form new kinds of true beliefs but with further mechanisms for evaluating the relative reliabilities of our various belief-forming methods and for translating these evaluations into relative strengths of dispositional belief. (Compatibly, the question "Are you sure?" or "Are you really certain?" is often followed or replaced by the question "How do you know?" or the question "What makes you think so?") Similarly, sensible design would make us resistant or, on the other hand, ready to *change* the strength of a dispositional belief in the wake of relevant new beliefs entering the belief system in a manner consonant with the relative reliabilities of the methods by which these various interacting beliefs had been formed. For example, beliefs formed by and/or subsequently reinforced by less reliable methods would defer to conflicting beliefs formed by more reliable methods. Thus the strength of the dispositional belief that p as measured by how high the stakes must be before one makes an ado over it should accord with a readiness to give it up in the face of conflicting beliefs that are stronger by this same measure.

If we have equipments in us that are designed to evaluate the reliability of our various methods of belief formation, these equipments must have Normal explanations for proper performance. They perform *properly* when they produce appropriate strength in dispositional belief. They perform Normally when the explanation telling how it has come about that this strength is appropriate is the same explanation that routinely accounted for proper operation of the relevant strength-of-belief-regulating devices during evolutionary history or for proper operation of mechanisms that were responsible for training or programming our strength-of-belief-regulating devices.

4   Occurrent Knowledge

I have argued that knowledge is connected with belief that is true in accordance with a Normal explanation for proper performance of one's belief-making systems. But is it occurrent belief or dispositional belief or both with which knowledge is connected?

An obvious hypothesis is that it is dispositional belief that corresponds in the first instance to knowledge, for (1) only dispositional belief admits of degrees of strength, (2) the highest degree of strength is surely subjective certainty, and (3) it is clear that the notions "knowledge" and "certain" have a strong tendency to be linked both in ordinary and in philosophical contexts. Knowledge, on this hypothesis, might be dispositional belief that is true in accordance with a Normal explanation *and* that exhibits a high, perhaps an ultimate, degree of appropriate strength (e.g., exhibits subjective certainty and appropriately so) in accordance with a Normal explanation. Secondarily, knowledge might be occurrent belief that makes manifest this kind of dispositional belief.

This hypothesis is obvious enough, but it has two shortcomings. The first is that it represents the "high degree of appropriate strength in accordance with a Normal explanation" requirement and the "true in accordance with a Normal explanation" requirement as being separate requirements on knowing, as though the notion "knowledge" were like the term "bachelor," which corresponds to being, it just so happens, *both* a man *and* unmarried. Surely it would be more elegant to suppose that knowledge corresponds to some naturally unified phenomenon, if we could make this out.

The second failing is that the hypothesis does not fit the facts. When the stakes are not high, the term "knowledge" is routinely applied to cases of true occurrent beliefs that manifest dispositional beliefs that are *not* particularly strong, let alone appropriately strong. For example, "How did you know that *p*?" (e.g., "How did you know where I was?") is very often answered to everyone's satisfaction *just* with "So-and-so told me," even though all realize that believing what people tell one is not a superbly reliable source of information. Unless the stakes *are* high, we do not require of the person who "knows that *p*" because he has been told by so-and-so that he be ready to place extremely high stakes on the truth of *p*, let alone that he have spent time checking on so-and-so's sources or on so-and-so's general reliability on matters like that *p* or on so-and-so's record for truthfulness. The challenge "So you didn't *really* know that *p*, did you, for you never questioned either so-and-so's sources or his honesty" is appropriate only when an occurrent belief that is under scrutiny occurred without any ado in a context that mattered enough to *require* an ado, a context that required stronger belief, more subjective confidence or certainty, than was in fact warranted. For example, if I swear sincerely under oath that Xavier was in Billy's Bar at 8:00 P.M. on Tuesday the 27th, but my occurrent belief-without-any-ado, as I swear, though true, has no more basis than that Xavier's best friend, whom I have no special reason to believe is always truthful, told me so, I *can* be accused of having sworn to something that I did not really *know* was true. But the problem here is not that my *dispositional* belief lacks sufficient appropriate strength for knowledge. Had I arrived at Billy's Bar at 8:00 P.M. that Tuesday and, on finding Xavier, said, "I knew you were here because your friend told me," I would have said something quite true. Rather, the problem is that my *occurrent* belief-without-ado, as I swear under oath, is inappropriate, given the stakes in *that* context.

A better hypothesis, one that will allow us to understand both the unity and the tensions within the notion "knowledge," is that the primary instances of knowledge are instances of Normally derived true *occurrent* beliefs-without-any-ado. We then extend the notion "knowledge" to certain kinds of dispositional belief.

Notice that if knowledge corresponds in the first instance to Normally derived true *occurrent* belief-without-any-ado, Normal and correct operation of the mechanisms that produce degrees of strength in dispositional belief must be *part* of the phenomenon that is first-instance knowledge. For one takes it that *p* without any ado in accordance with proper functioning of one's cognitive systems only if the reliability of the methods used in forming the belief that *p* was enough to *warrant* taking it that *p* without any ado, given what is at stake in the context, enough to make this strength of dispositional belief appropriate. And that this strength should be appropriate in accordance with a Normal explanation requires that one's mechanisms for producing varying strengths in dispositional belief be operating properly in accordance with a Normal explanation. For example, in the case of my swearing that Xavier was in Billy's Bar at 8:00 P.M., I am accused of having sworn to what I did not know was true, despite the fact that I may have acquired the true dispositional belief that Xavier was in Billy's Bar in accordance with a perfectly Normal explanation. What went wrong was that the strength of my dispositional belief was not appropriate. My belief was stronger than it should have been, given its origin. (Or perhaps I did not understand the gravity of the situation; I should have believed more strongly before swearing under oath.)

That first-instance knowledge is just Normally acquired, true occurrent belief-without-any-ado explains the casualness with which we sometimes apply the notion "knowledge" and the strictness with which we apply it other times. When little or nothing is at stake, a person may be said to know a thing even though he is acutely aware that his dispositional belief is very weak. For example, when playing Trivial Pursuit, the question "Who took over Soviet leadership after Stalin's death?" may be answered with a very hesitant "Malenkov?" and the answerer is given credit for having known the answer so long as he hesitantly remembered that rather than merely having guessed from among plausible possibilities. Similarly, subjects of experiments on subliminal perception are said to know what they have seen or heard subliminally if they can answer questions correctly on the basis of this perception even though they answer with no assurance and have no notion why they are able to answer at all. But if a doctor were to prescribe a drug for a patient on the basis of a memory as hesitant as that of the person playing Trivial Pursuit or on the basis of a hunch as obscure as that on which the subject of the subliminal-perception experiment depends, no matter how correct the prescription and no matter how Normal the explanation for this correctness, she would be prescribing irresponsibly, prescribing without *knowing* that the drug is the right one.

That first-instance knowledge is just Normally acquired, true occurrent belief-without-any-ado also explains why true occurrent belief that results from still remembering what one once knew is often regarded as knowledge even though one may have forgotten how one came to know, hence can no longer give reasons for or "justify" one's belief. So long as the strength of the belief as it emerges from memory still correctly reflects the reliability of the method by which the belief was originally acquired and reflects this in accordance with a Normal explanation (one correctly remembers how confident one should be) and so long as the strength fits the occasion of use-without-any-ado of the belief, such an occurrent belief does constitute knowledge.

5 Dispositional Knowledge

Over and over again during John Armada's life he is asked, "What is your name?" Each time he answers, he expresses a different occurrent belief-without-any-ado that his name is John Armada, which belief constitutes an occurrent knowing that his name is John Armada. It is reasonable to call this general disposition that John has a "knowing" too. Compare: if I have a disposition, realized on numerous occasions, to swim, then I am said to swim, period. Similarly, John knows his name, period.

Now since dispositional beliefs come in various strengths, one would expect that the dispositional notion of knowledge would have looser and stricter applications, the strictest requiring the strongest possible dispositional belief, i.e., requiring that no project could be so important that one would make an ado before using the belief that p in trying to implement it. An example of laxness in speaking of dispositional knowledge is our willingness to say of the man playing Trivial Pursuit who occurrently (but very hesitantly) knew that Malenkov took over after Stalin that he may have known this for a long time, perhaps since Stalin's death. Knowings that take place over a long period of time clearly are dispositional knowings. Similarly, I have known since shortly after we moved into this house that that outlet in the living room doesn't work. But to speak more strictly, it may be said that I haven't *really* known (all that time) that that outlet wasn't working, because never was I confident enough that I would have let a baby poke a metal object into it. "*Really*" knowing, dispositional knowing in the very strictest sense, seems to require absolute subjective certainty.

Indeed, if my analysis is correct, dispositional knowing in the strictest sense should require not just subjective certainty, but subjective certainty that is appropriate and appropriate in accordance with a Normal explanation. What would such certainty be like?

To be absolutely certain that p is to be so confident that no matter what was at stake, one would unhesitatingly use the belief that p without any ado. For such a certainty to be appropriate, the method by which the belief that p was derived would have to be a very reliable method indeed. But it would not have to be an infallible method. (Probably there are no infallible methods of arriving at beliefs. Or if there are infallible methods, surely there are no methods of determining infallibly whether one has applied such a method.) It would only have to be reliable enough that wasting time and energy making ados over beliefs derived by its use would not pay off on the average no matter how important the contexts were in which these beliefs were used. In order for a belief to be subjectively certain and appropriately so in accordance with a Normal explanation, the mechanisms in the believer that produced the certainty must have produced certainty when it was appropriate not by accident but by design—by a method, that is, that accords with evolutionary design. But again, there is no reason why this method would have to be an infallible method. It is enough if it works often enough that deriving subjective certainty by its use is more likely to be beneficial than harmful in the long run, due to the time saved by not having to make ados before action.

6 Skepticism

Now if that is what dispositional knowing in the strictest sense is, I submit that we do quite a bit of strict-sense dispositional knowing. For example, it is likely that, speaking perfectly strictly, I know my own name, that massive unsupported objects always fall, that my eldest was born in the summertime, and that I will never observe an object that is only 500 years old but that has a carbon 14 ratio of .01. Yet according to a long philosophical tradition, I do not know, in the strictest sense, any of these things. According to this tradition, if strict-sense knowing ever occurs or could occur, it certainly is not an everyday phenomenon, natural and normal. On what footing does this tradition rest?

Recall Kent Bach's description of belief: "To believe something is to be prepared, when the thought of it occurs, to assume it and reason from it without reconsidering it (unless, of course, some new consideration occurs to you)." A new consideration that occurs to you might be something you have known all along but that suddenly occurs to you, for the first time, as being relevant (or that is brought to your attention by someone else who claims that it is relevant). Or it might be something *new* that you have learned that occurs to you to be relevant. In either case, it may be that the result of reconsidering a belief is that the strength of one's dispositional belief is altered. Now it is part of what it is for your strength-of-belief-determining mechanisms to operate correctly, to perform their proper function, that certain kinds of things that you already believe or that you newly come to believe *do* occur to you as relevant and *do* enter appropriately into the process that determines the strength of your dispositional belief. For example, suppose that after swearing under oath that Xavier was in Billy's Bar at 8:00 P.M., I candidly admit that I did so because it really never occurred to me to wonder whether Xavier's friend was reliable or whether he might be covering up for Xavier. That is, it didn't occur to me to bring my knowledge that people sometimes do lie and that they often cover up for friends to bear here. It *didn't* occur to me, but it certainly *should* have! That is, my strength-of-belief-determining mechanisms were not operating properly or it *would* have occurred to me. It is for *that* reason that it is true that I have sworn under oath without really knowing that what I said was true. Similarly, suppose that John strongly believes something that his truthful friend Bill has candidly said but believes this strongly only because—out of blind loyalty to Bill, nothing more—he has stubbornly ignored rampant false rumors impugning Bill's honesty.[5] John *should* have considered what was being said about Bill and weighed it appropriately before settling into this or that strength of dispositional belief. Hence he does not really know that what Bill said is true.

In order for a person to have dispositional knowledge in the strictest sense, then, it will be necessary that everything that he knows and that *should* have occurred to him as relevant *will* have occurred to him and that each of these considerations shall have been given appropriate weight in the process that led to his being subjectively certain. This is the vulnerable place through which philosophical skepticism enters.

It enters with the introduction of a theory about what sorts of things ideally should occur to a person as relevant to consider in determining his strength of dispositional belief and/or about the weight that ideally should be put upon these considerations. For example, the most usual route to philosophical doubt is to claim, explicitly or implicitly, that no belief *p* attains subjective certainty with propriety unless one knows it to have been derived by an infallible method. It follows that before one is subjectively certain that *p*, one should be appropriately subjectively certain of the infallibility of the method by which one arrived at *p* and also appropriately certain of the infallibility of the method by which one came to believe that this method was infallible, etc. Clearly, on this view, strict-sense knowledge will only be possible if there are some beliefs that not only are derived by infallible methods but by methods that somehow bear their infallibility on their very faces (candidates: methods used in grasping self-evident truths or truths about current sense data). If there are no such methods (and surely there are none), then there is and can be no strict-sense knowledge.

But why "should" skeptical questions or considerations of this sort occur to a person and be dispelled before he can be appropriately subjectively certain? What kind of a "should" is this? The "should" of reasonableness? Surely not. It is *Nature* that has been reasonable in so constructing us that we do not make an ado when doing so would be a

5. A similar example is discussed in Swain 1981, sec. 1.4.

pure waste of valuable time or when the ado, once started, could never be brought to a close.[6] Surely, being reasonable is following Nature's plan in this regard. And as numerous writers have noted, for the most part Nature has her way. Philosophical doubt becomes real doubt only in rare pathological cases.

7   Knowledge That Is Later Defeated

But there is a more homey tradition than that of the skeptic that needs to be examined too. A variety of Gettier example standard in the philosophical literature concerns a person who has acquired a true belief that p in accordance with a Normal explanation, who believes relatively strongly that p, and who has, moreover, acquired this strength of belief in accordance with a Normal explanation. That is, the method that he used to arrive at the belief that p is *usually* a highly reliable method, and it is due to this that he is quite confident that p. But it just so happens that he is in a very special situation, one in which, it is claimed, the method he used to arrive at p is not reliable. For example, he acquires the true belief that there is a barn over there by looking and seeing clearly that there is. What he doesn't know is that he is where a movie was recently made and that most of the things that plainly look like barns from there are false fronts.[7] Or perhaps he correctly and confidently judges that the road to Boston turns to the right here because a prominent road sign at the intersection says so, but in fact, no matter from which direction that intersection is approached, there is a road sign showing Boston to one's right.[8] So far as I know, no one writing on the Gettier problem has taken examples such as these to be examples of knowledge. Yet two of three teenage youngsters that I recently questioned do take them to be examples of knowledge. (The third was not ready to admit that road signs ever give anyone knowledge.) Although the responses of these two youngsters were philosophically unorthodox, I think they are defensible.

A crucial question is whether the man, say, who took the right road to Boston had a belief that was *appropriately* strong enough to support

6. Compare *LTOBC*, chap. 3, and Bach 1984.
7. The example is from Goldman 1976.
8. A. J. Holland (1977) gives a similar example.

his proceeding without any ado to trust the sign he saw. That is, the crucial question is whether the method he used to determine which road went to Boston was reliable enough to support a belief strong enough that he could appropriately have an occurrent belief-without-any-ado about the way to Boston, *given the practical context in which he used the belief.* Presumably, the reliability of a method corresponds to the statistical probability of the method's yielding a correct result. Statistical probabilities are determined relative to a reference class—in this case, a class of possible applications of the method. But which class of possible applications of the method is the right one to refer to here? The class that includes only readings of the four signs saying "Boston" at this one intersection? The class that includes readings of all signs posted at this intersection (including the one that says "Kentucky Fried Chicken")? The class of all signs posted on this road? In this town? In this state? In this country? The class of all things written in English?

Clearly, the relevant reference class is the reference class the man actually *used*, the class he implicitly referred to as he confidently turned right on the Boston road. Whatever it was about that sign—say its placement relative to the intersection; that it looked like such and such other signs that he believed to have been placed by the proper Massachusetts authorities, the part of the country it was in; that it was new and not bent; whatever—those things that in fact combined to produce a certain strength of belief in what the sign said were what determined this reference class. Without question, this reference class included many more than the four signs at that intersection that said "Boston." Indeed, it is very plausible that this reference class was such that the probability that the method he used would yield a true belief *was* high enough to warrant his occurrent belief-without-any-ado that this was the road to Boston, given the context in which he used this belief. Hence, it is plausible that he arrived at his true occurrent belief-without-any-ado in accordance with a perfectly Normal explanation. Why, then, have philosophers dealing with this sort of case univocally insisted that such a man could not have known that he was taking the right road to Boston?[9]

9. Why, that is, besides the fact that many have not addressed the problem of a relevant reference class but have uncritically fallen for the class of road signs

First, these philosophers are thinking of *dispositional* knowing as first-instance knowing—the first target of analysis—and thinking of occurrent knowing as merely an exercise of dispositional knowing. Now if my analysis is right, the notion of dispositional knowing derives from that of occurrent knowing as the notion of dispositional swimming (he swims) derives from that of occurrent swimming (he is swimming). Most dispositional applications of verbs of human doing correspond to *abilities*. For example, if he swims, he has the ability to swim; if he plays the violin, he has the ability to play the violin; etc. It will be very tempting, then, to assimilate the notion of dispositional knowledge to that of an ability, tempting not only to philosophers but to laymen. But abilities are things that once one has, one always has, unless something goes wrong, unless something in one ceases to perform properly. For example, if I once could swim but no longer can, that could only be because some part of me has been damaged or has decayed. Perhaps I have been injured or forgotten how. To think of dispostional knowledge as an ability will thus result in supposing that dispositional knowledge is the sort of thing that can't be lost unless something goes wrong, like being brainwashed or hit on the head or fed a lot of lies or just forgetting. Knowledge couldn't possibly be lost as result of mere Normal and proper functioning of one's cognitive systems. Especially, it could not be lost as a result, just of gaining more knowledge (unless, of course, this knowledge was so shocking that it caused one's cognitive systems to malfunction). It is because the man on his way to Boston would lose his knowledge of the way to Boston should he happen to discover those other three signs pointing in other diections that he is thought not to have knowledge at all.

But if my analysis is correct, this is simply a confusion, though an understandable one. Dispositional knowledge is something that can sometimes be lost in a perfectly healthy way. Especially evident is the fact the *inductive* knowledge is subject to loss. If I believe that x is B because I know that x is an A and that nearly all As are B, I can lose this belief upon discovering that x is also a C and that very few

---

nearby. Apparently, philosophers' intuitions about knowledge can be as bad as unsophisticated gamblers' intuitions about when the luck should strike.

Cs are *B*. Still, my original dispositional belief that *x* is *B* may have been true and may have constituted dispositional knowledge (though not, perhaps, in the very strictest sense of knowledge; recall the third teenager who said that no one ever gains knowledge by reading a sign, and recall the the sense in which I have not really known all along that that electrical outlet doesn't work).

I have described knowledge as a unified phenomenon deserving an important place in a naturalist description of man. It is easy to understand why we have a word for such a central phenomenon. And it is also easy to see why we have a tendency to become confused about what is and what is not knowledge, for the *phenomenon* of knowledge (contrast this with the "concept of" or "criteria for" knowledge) is complex.

Appendix

There is another kind of case, of a bizarre kind familiar only in the philosophical literature, in which a person might use a prosthetic device as a perceptual aid. Suppose that that you are knocked unconscious and your eyes are mutilated in an accident. While you are unconscious, the doctors hastily replace your ruined eyes with devices that are quite unlike eyes but that serve the same purpose as far as correlating ambient light patterns with optic nerve patterns is concerned. When you wake up and before you discover that your eyes have been replaced, you make various true judgments about your surroundings on the basis of visual data. Are your judgments true in accordance with a Normal explanation?

Certainly not in accordance with a fully expanded Normal explanation of how *your* belief-making systems produce true beliefs. To cover this case, one would have to be satisfied with a certain gappiness in this explanation: light reflects off the surfaces of objects in the vicinity, which objects structure the light in accordance with such and such (specified) principles; some of this structured light reaches devices (constitution *unspecified*) in the front of your head, which devices translate (in accordance with *unspecified* causal principles) the structured properties of the light into sequences of optic neuron firings, the translations conforming to such and such (specified) formulas, and these neuron firings in turn, etc. On the other hand, presumably your judgments based on visual data *are* true in accordance with Normal explanations for proper performance of the *doctors'* cognitive and conative and motor systems, plus those of the designers and makers of the devices that replace your eyes so satisfactorily. (That all human purposes correspond to proper functions of a certain sort is argued in *LTOBC*, chap. 2.) So your beliefs are true in accordance with *a* fully expanded Normal explanation, though not in accordance with one that fits *your* native equipment.

Now let me ask you a question. Does the patient, in the case in which the surrogate eyes have been installed without her knowledge, possess *knowledge* of her surroundings based on visual data? (I ask *you* because *I* haven't the slightest idea.) If you say no, she does not have knowledge, your response fits with the hypothesis that knowledge must be belief that is true in accordance with a fully Normal explanation for proper performance of the believer's native perceptual/cognitive systems. If you say yes, she does have knowledge (this is what my teenage informants say), let me try to make plausible that underlying your response is the fact that truth is still produced here in accordance with *a* Normal explanation. To see this, subtract the doctors and the designers and makers of the surrogate eyes from the story. Let the molecules that are to compose the patient's surrogate eyes be ones that were formerly in random motion but that suddenly coalesce by awesome cosmic coincidence in the front of her head at just the right moment. Were that to happen, would you still say that her beliefs derived by the use of these devices—before these devices had been tried and found true, of course—constituted knowledge? If not, I suggest that this is because there is no Normal explanation at all for the truth of her beliefs or, putting things intuitively, because her beliefs turned out true by accident rather than by design.[10]

But, it may be asked, why then is no one (not even my teenage informants) tempted to say of the man who unknowingly saw only the virtual image of a candle that he had knowledge of the candle's location? Surely he acquired true belief by design, in accordance with a Normal

10. If you *would* say that her belief constituted knowledge, let me recommend S. Kripke's devastating critique of R. Nozick's *Philosophical Explanations* (1981). Lecture delivered at the University of Connecticut, 17 December 1984.

explanation for operation of the cognitive, conative, and motor systems of the person who designed the placement of the mirrors and lured him into the right spot in the room?[11] The answer, I suggest, is that in this case not only can no Normal explanation be given but no *general* explanation can be given for how his *own* belief-forming systems produced a true belief. Normal explanations for how people acquire true beliefs via vision make reference to principles that apply to wide ranges of object-perceiver positionings, not just one special positioning. Or they make reference to a person's "taking account" of the specialness of his positioning in accordance with some general Normal explanation of how people manage to "take account" of and/or how they learn to "take account" of special situations. The temptation to say that knowledge might be acquired by use of the doctor-made surrogate eyes rests on the fact that there is merely a gap to be filled in an otherwise Normal explanation for how the patient's own visual systems work, that this gap is filled by an explanation that is just as general as a Normal explanation would be and, indeed, *is* a Normal explanation for proper performance of certain systems (e.g., the doctors' cognitive and conative systems) that had the same proper function, namely production of true beliefs in the patient. The case thus bears a rather extraordinary resemblance to the Normal case of believing truly on the basis of visual perception.

11. Compare Unger 1968 and the critique of Unger's view in Pappas and Swain 1978, Introduction, and Swain 1981, sec. 5.2.

13

The Myth of the Essential Indexical

Thesis So-called "essential indexicals" in thought are indeed essential, but they are not indexical. It is not their semantics that distinguishes them but their function, their psychological role.

A strong contemporary current runs to the effect that the ability of an agent to project knowledge of the world into relevant action in the world depends on the ability to think indexical thoughts. For example, if I wish to get to Boston, it may be helpful to know that the 8:25 train goes there. But I cannot put this knowledge to use unless I also come to know, at some point, that *there* [a place indexed via perception] is the 8:25 train. Similarly, should my life be endangered by an approaching bear, it might help me to know it. But it will not be enough for me to know of this danger to me under some impersonal description of me, such as "the person sitting in Bruno's favorite berry patch" or even under the name "Ruth Millikan," unless I further know that *I* am the person in Bruno's favorite berry patch or that *I* am Ruth Millikan (I might not know, for example, should I be amnesiac). But this kind of thought—*there* is the 8:25; *I* am Ruth Millikan—is, it is supposed, indexical. Thus Dennett, summing up the literature, remarks, "Indexicality of sentences appears to be the linguistic counterpart of that relativity to a subjective point of view that is a hallmark of mental states" (Dennett 1987, 132).[1] He clarifies, using a (ubiquitous) quotation in which Perry remarks, "When you and I have beliefs under the common char-

---

1. Dennett cites Castañeda 1966, 1967, 1968; Perry 1977, 1979; Kaplan 1989; and Lewis 1979. Another clear example is McGinn 1983. There are also clear gestures toward such a thesis, alas, in *LTOBC*.

acter of 'A bear is about to attack me' we behave similarly, . . . [whereas] when you and I both apprehend that I am about to be attacked by a bear we behave differently" (Perry 1977, 494). That is, our behaviors hinge not so much on the *objects* of our thoughts, on their propositional contents, but on what Kaplan calls the "character," in this case the indexical type, of our thoughts. Kaplan too identifies "the context sensitivity of character" with what he calls "the context sensitivity of mental states" and remarks, "Dare I call it ego orientation?" (Kaplan 1989a, 531).

No, he should not dare. For it is not indexical thoughts that serve to orient an agent in his world. A picture that holds us captive portrays the index as a pointing finger, showing the direction of its referent from here, so that we may act from here regarding it. But, I will argue first, it is not true for the general case that the relation an indexical or the interpreter of an indexical bears to the indexical's referent is a relation that needs to be taken account of during action. Conversely, it is not true for the general case that those relations of self to world that one must take into account in order to act in the world are relations of the sort that an indexical or the interpreter of an indexical bears to the indexical's referent. Second, it is no part of the job of an indexical token to *signify* the relation either of itself to its referent or of its interpreter to its referent. Conversely, inner signs that do signify relations between agent and world as needed for action are not as such indexical. Finally, if an agent employs a mental term to represent herself, this in principle cannot be a mental indexical: there can be no *thought* that has the (Kaplan-style) character of "I."

An indexical sign has no constant referent, no referent qua sign type. Tokens of an indexical type have referents when they are situated in appropriate contexts. An appropriate context contains something bearing a designated relation to the indexical token, which something is thereby that token's referent (e.g., a person, an object) or is thereby that variant in world affairs that the token indexes (e.g., a time, a place, a property). This designated relation for a given indexical type I call its "indexical adapting relation."[2] The indexical adapting relation for "I,"

---

2. The reason for this terminology is explained in *LTOBC*, chaps. 2 and 10. Notice also that I am not using "context" quite in Kaplan's recommended way.

for example, is being the producer of the token; for "you" it is being the addressee of the sentence containing the token; for "here," being a position near the origination point of the token; for demonstratives, being suitably related in any of various conventional ways to, say, a gesture accompanying the token, to other words bearing certain relations to the token; and so forth.[3] Thus the meaning of an indexical type can be thought of as expressed by a function from token context to token referent. Kaplan (1989a) calls this function (or close enough) the "character" of the indexical type. It is a thought's "character," in this sense, that is taken by Kaplan and many others to connect directly with action, with behavior."[4] "We use the manner of presentation, the character, to individuate psychological states, in explaining and predicting action" (Kaplan 1989a, 532).

Our first question concerns the relation of the referent of an indexical token to the token's interpreter: is this relation relevant to action? In the case of a mental indexical, the indexical token would be *inside* the interpreter. Let us begin instead with the easier case of public-language indexicals, where the full structure of the relation of interpreter to indexed referent is out in the open. For public-language indexicals, it is evident that there are actually two relations to be considered. First, there is the relation the indexical token bears to its referent as dictated by the character of the sign: this is the indexical's adapting relation for the sign. Second, there is the relation the interpreter bears to the indexical token. Different interpreters may, of course, bear quite different relations to the same indexical token, hence to its referent. Should a public indexical serve to alert or accommodate its interpreter to the relation of its refer-

---

3. For a discussion of the various kinds of indexicals and their adapting relations, see *LTOBC*, chap. 10.

4. Castañeda (1989) is an exception. He argues from his well-known internalist view of mental content that the thoughts conventionally expressed through public-language indexicals are neither possessors of Kaplan-style character nor are they thoughts of Kaplan-style character-functions. He concludes that Kaplan's equation of the character of a public-language indexical with its grammatical meaning must be wrong. My argument will not presuppose content internalism; indeed, my general position on thought, though there will be no need for it to emerge below, is radically externalist. Further, I have argued in *LTOBC* that public-language meaning should be defined independently of mention of conventionally underlying speaker or hearer thoughts, and I submitted a detailed proposal on how to do that. I will return to these themes at the end of this essay.

ent to the interpreter, it is clear that the interpreter would have to *sum* two prior relations to find this relation: the interpreter's relation to the token plus the token's relation to the referent. The same structure is there, though less evidently, when the relation of interpreter to sign is constant, the sign being inside the interpreter.

The first thing to notice is that this pair of relations does not as such or necessarily yield a sum relevant to action. I'll give two examples of failure to sum in a relevant way. These should be enough to make the general point. The first occurs when the indexical adapting relation is *being a* (certain sort of) *cause of* the indexical token. The second occurs when the referent or variant indexed by the indexical token is a type or kind rather than a particular.

Suppose that you receive an undated postcard from Barcelona signed by Alvin that says, "I am leaving for a few days in Rome." You know what the referent's, Alvin's, relation to the indexical token "I" is: the referent wrote it, he was its cause; that's what makes him the referent. And you know what *your* relation to that token of "I" is: you have it in your hand. But this yields no clue concerning your relation to the referent, to Alvin. At least, it yields no clue concerning any salient relation, any relation you are likely to need to take account of in order to act regarding Alvin. The given relation of you to the token plus the given relation of the token to its referent has, as it were, no vector sum.

Nor does it help to move the sign that indexes its cause to the inside of the interpreter. Suppose that it were true that your thought-tokens "Iris Murdoch" were indexical tokens, referring (as do tokens of public language "I") to their salient cause, which was in this case the cause, Murdoch herself, of the first ancestor token of "Iris Murdoch" produced at Murdoch's baptismal ceremony. (I am not recommending this theory of thoughts of Murdoch.) Thinking this indexical thought, even if it involved knowing quite exactly about this adapting relation between thought and referent, would not reveal to you any salient relation you presently bear to Murdoch.

To take a more plausible case, consider the popular theory that percepts are mental indexicals referring to their salient causes. The fact that the perceiver contains the percept plus the fact that the percept was caused by the perceived, by the referent, does not sum to a determinate usable relation between perceiver and perceived. Think of seeing an object via a set of trick mirrors. You perceive the object alright, but you perceive it as in a different spatial relation to you than it in fact bears. The bare fact that the object perceived equals what causes your percept does not entail that you can locate it, that you grasp its relation to you as needed for action.

Of course, there generally is a usable relation between perceiver and perceived, one that *shows* in the veridical percept: there are (mathematical-style) transformations of the percept that correspond systematically to transformations of the spatial relation of perceiver to perceived. For example, one *sees how far* one is from objects. But this relation is not determined merely by adding the fact that the percept is within the perceiver to the fact that the perceived is a salient and circumscribed sort of cause of the percept; it is not a resultant of those facts. Rather, the spatial relation is *independently* shown in the percept. Because percepts often do show certain relations of the objects I perceive to me and because I often need to know about these relations to me in order to act, I often need to perceive something in order to act. But this has nothing to do with the *indexicality* of perception. Although the percept that shows relations may also be indexical, it is not indexical because it shows relations, nor does it show relations because it is indexical. (Relations shown in perception are, of course, relations *to me*. Soon I will raise the question whether, in order to show a relation *to me*, the percept must index me or my place, but that is a separate question. I will also discuss *what it is* that makes a percept indexical.)

A second illustration of the irrelevance to action of an indexical adapting relation is when the indexed is a type or kind: *that* color, *that* word type, *that* species, *that* metal, and so forth. Similarly, if quotation marks are indexicals (Davidson 1979, *LTOBC*) or if intentional contexts ("believes that," "wishes to," etc.) are indexicals (Davidson 1968, *LTOBC*, Boër and Lycan 1986), these must index types rather than tokens. Conceivably, in these cases the indexical token brings the interpreter into some sort of non-vector-sum relation with the type that is indexed. But how would a grasp of this relation help the interpreter to *act* in relation to the indexed type?

There does not seem to be anything about indexical adapting relations per se, then, that makes them especially relevant to action. That an indexical thought token was inside one and bore its adapting relation to its referent would not, by the bare nature of indexicality anyway, sum to a purpose. Conversely, there are many relations between self and world that an agent must take into account when acting that do not appear as any indexical's adapting relation, which are actively taken account of without the introduction into thought of any special indexicals. To act, I must, of course, take account of the nature and disposition of things in my world relative to my powers of action. The example we all think of first is that I must take account of the places of things I would act upon relative to my place, since I must act on them *from* my place. (Notice that this is contingent: if I had the power of telekinesis, I might not need to take account of my spatial position among objects in order to act.) And the characteristic way of knowing their places relative to me is through perception. But it is perfectly clear that my grasp of *most* action-relevant relations is not via indexical thoughts. Consider, for example, my grasp of the size of things I would act upon relative to my size, of various forces relative to my strength, of various distances relative to my reaching powers, climbing powers, leaping, throwing, walking, running, and shouting powers, etc. Further, though it may be that perception usually or always displays indexicality, it is not true that all action is based on perception. I do not need to perceive my arm in order intentionally to raise it, or to perceive my eyelid in order intentionally to blink it. Similarly, should I come to know that the trigger that releases the catch to the door of my jail cell is directly under my left index finger (say, the kindly guard tells me), then I don't need to perceive anything at all in order to act so as to free myself. I need only know *how* to depress my left index finger. Indexicality certainly is not "the linguistic counterpart of that relativity to a subjective point of view that is a hallmark of mental states," then—not if the subjective point of view is the point of view needed for action.

But a worse trouble with the view that it is indexicals that orient me in my world for action lies here: Even if the relation that an indexical bears to its referent *should* turn out to be relevant to action, it is not the job of an indexical to display this relation between itself and its referent. Instead, to interpret an indexical, one must have prior knowledge of, one must already know independently and ahead of time, what item bears the indexical's adapting relation to the indexical token. One must already know both that this referent exists and how it is related to the token, hence to the interpreter. One does not find this out by interpreting the indexical; one needs already to know it in order to interpret the indexical. For example, a token of "I" does not tell me who the originator of that token is, that it is, say, Alvin. Rather, if I am to understand a token of "I," I must *already know* who the speaker is. That is why Alvin had to sign his postcard. Similarly, a token of "here" does not tell me where it is. To understand "here," I must independently know what place the token is in, or was in when originated. A "here" shouted in the dark is of no use to a person with one deaf ear, a person who cannot localize sounds. Similarly, turning an example of Perry's to a different purpose, suppose that a postcard arrives with illegible postmark, return address, and signature; it says "I am having a good time now." Perry says that the "truth conditions" of this inscription are, merely, that "the person who wrote the postcard was having a good time at the time he or she wrote it" (1988, 9). But the "truth conditions," understood this way, reveal the character but not the propositional content of the inscription. The content concerns its actual writer and time and place of writing. Clearly, in order to get to that content from the "truth conditions," it would be necessary to *know* who wrote it, when, and where. If the interpreter lacks the knowledge, the intended message does not get through. Nor does the message *contain* that information.

Exactly the same principle applies to the most paradigmatic of indexicals: "that" accompanied by a pointing finger. The pointing finger is understood only if what it points *at* is visible or otherwise independently identifiable. Or suppose it is the job of "that" to point out a direction, "that way." The interpreter must have a clear view of the surroundings so as to see in *what* direction the finger points. The interpreter must be able independently to *identify* that direction, not necessarily with a name ("east," "west") but, say, via an ability to track it, to know what it would be to continue following that selfsame direction, as opposed to turning away from it. To know what an indexical indexes, to identify the indexed, requires that one have a *second* route to thinking of it, a route other than via the indexical token, and that one grasp this second route *as* one arriving at the same referent. Indexicals do not in this sense *tell* what they point at, what it is that they bear their adapting relations to. It is their interpreters that do the telling. Indexicals do not tell *about* their contexts. The context of an indexical is not what its content is about but what *determines* its content.

Nor should we allow ourselves to be confused by the fact that it is often possible to *use* a sign to obtain information that it is not the function of the sign to convey. For example, you can use any public-language sign as evidence that there existed a person, who spoke a cer-language, at its point of origin—like footprints in the sand. Similarly, you could use Perry's partly illegible postcard as evidence that there existed a person who wrote the postcard and who was having a good time at that time. You could reach this conclusion, as Perry has suggested, by making the assumption that the sentence on the postcard is true. If the postcard had said, "I will meet . . . in Rome," the blank filled in with an illegible name, on the same assumption you could infer that *someone* had at some time planned to meet *someone* else in Rome, and so forth. But it was not the purpose of the postcard to convey this general proposition. Its purpose was to tell about, say, Alvin. Similarly, from a pointing finger accompanied by the sentence "This is a carpenter ant," you may gather that close to the end of the finger is a carpenter ant, even though you cannot see it from there. But that is not what it is the speaker aims to impart. The speaker intends you to see *what* is a carpenter ant.

And we should not allow ourselves to be confused by the fact that sentences whose public meanings are indexical can also *intentionally* be turned to nonindexical purposes by individual users. Consider an anonymous threat over the telephone, "I'll see that you die," or the child who says, "This is what you are getting for Christmas," while coyly holding it behind her back. These are indexical sentence types, but they are not serving indexical purposes. They are not functioning in a normal way.[5]

All of these uses of language are possible. But what *defines* the indexical use of a sign is that its context is used by the interpreter to *determine* the content, to determine the referent, not talked about in the content. A representation that told of its own relation to something else would not be indexical but self-referential, and it would be its con-

---

5. That is, they are not serving their stabilizing functions. See *LTOBC*, chaps. 3 and 4.

tent, not its character, that told of the relation.[6] Similarly, an *inner* representation that told or showed the relation of itself to the world would not on that account be indexical.

But what of an inner representation that told of the relation of its *thinker* to something in the world, that relation being crucial for action? Wouldn't such a representation have to be at root indexical? Colin McGinn says, "All the [essential] indexicals are linked with *I*, and the *I* mode of presentation is subjective in character because it comprises the special perspective a person has on himself. Very roughly, we can say that to think of something indexically is to think of it in relation to *me*, as I am presented to myself in self-consciousness" (1983, 17). It will not be enough, a substantial literature agrees, that an agent entertain representations the *content* of which concerns the relation of herself to the world. That might be done by the use of relation terms along with an inner Millian name that the agent has for herself, or along with any description that happens to catch her uniquely.[7] What is required is that the agent recognize any such name or description as a name for *herself*, that she identify its content with that of her inner term "I." Only when she grasps that the person so positioned in the world is "I" can she act from a knowledge of that position. And this grasp requires thinking an indexical thought.

Now it is trivial that if I am to react in a special and different way to the knowledge that I, RM, am positioned *so* in the world, a way quite unlike how I would react knowing anyone else was positioned so in the world, then my inner term for RM must bear a very special and unique relation to my dispositions to act. *But what does that have to do with indexicality?* My inner name "RM" obviously is not like other names in my mental vocabulary. It is a name that hooks up with my know-hows, with my abilities and dispositions to act, in a rather special way. Conceivably, I might also have other mental names for RM that didn't hook up with these know-hows, because I didn't recognize them, didn't iden-

6. I accept Kaplan's remarks on Reichenbach's confusion of indexicality with self-reference, a confusion embodied in Reichenbach's term "token reflexive," as definitive. See Kaplan 1989, 519–520.
7. By a "Millian name" I mean one about the semantics of which nothing can be said beyond that it is a name with such and such a referent. The semantics of mental names of this sort, their psychological possibility, and how they get their referents are discussed in *LTOBC*. Or, for a very brief indication of the general position, see chapter 4 herein.

tify them, *as* having the same content as "RM"—as I might think "Cicero" and then "Tully" without knowing these thoughts to be of the same person. My inner "RM" is indeed special. Let us call it @"RM," or RM's "active self name." It names a person whom I know, under that name, *how* to manipulate directly; I *know how* to effect her behavior. But in order to know how to manipulate this person, why would I need to think indexical thoughts? What has know-how to do with indexicality?[8]

An indexical term is one whose referent varies with context, this referent being identified, for each of the term's tokens, via its bearing the indexical's adapting relation to the token. To apply this principle to indexicals in thought, a thought will be indexical if its context determines its content, its referent, and if there are normal procedures for *identifying* this referent for any token, which procedures depend upon the fact that the referent bears the adapting relation to the token. That is, these procedures *work* only *because* the referent bears the adapting relation to the token. By a "procedure for identifying the referent of a thought token" I mean just a manner of determining what other *thought tokens* it coincides with in content or in reference, for example, determining when it can be paired with another term token such that these two may serve as a middle term during inference. To illustrate, in the case of a mental Millian-name token, surely one procedure for identifying the referent is to pair the token with other tokens of the same type. The procedure for pairing a mental *indexical* token with other tokens having the same referent would have to be routed via the relevant *context* of the token, which means, via the referent itself. Otherwise, the term would not be functioning *indexically*. How might that work? Let me give an example; indeed, let me give *the* example, the only one I have confidence might actually be an example of indexicality in thought.

The example is perception. It is plausible that in perception the percept is about, refers to, its cause, that is, to the cause of the percept *token*. What the (veridical) percept token *shows* is certain properties of

8. I give an account of abilities or "know-hows," calling them "competences," in chapter 11, an account based on *LTOBC*. According to this account, abilities express purposes, biological purposes. Abilities are very different from simple causal dispositions.

this cause plus, often, the spatial relation of that cause to the perceiving subject. But the percept is not about the generality that there exists a something of a certain character so related to the perceiver; it does not, as it were, translate with an existential quantifier. Rather, it is about, it is a percept of, its *particular* cause. This particular aboutness is expressed through the ability that the normal perceiver has to *track* the particular referent with eyes, head, and, if necessary, feet in order to accumulate more information about it. This process involves *identifying* or, what is the same, *reidentifying* the tracked object, for it involves using a series of percepts of it, of the same thing, conjointly (compare the function of a middle term) so as to extract information presumed to be about just *one* thing, about *one* particular individual.[9] And the method of determining that these various percepts belong together as percepts of the same—the method of tracking—is routed through the fact that the perceived was the *cause* of the percept. It was the cause of the percept in accordance with a certain way of causing normal for that kind of perception, and it will accordingly cause later percepts in a traceable pattern, other percepts with the same referent.

Is that the sort of way that my mental term @"RM," the term that bears that quite unique and special relation to my dispositions to act, hooks up with its referent, hooks up with me? Do I succeed in identifying the content of various tokens of my mental @"RM," that is, do I succeed in reidentifying myself, only because *each token* of @"RM" independently bears an appropriate adapting relation to the same thing, namely me? Or is my mental @"RM" simply a mental proper name: I take different tokens of @"RM" to refer to the same *not* because of their individual contexts, not as a result of some relation each of these tokens independently bears to me, but simply because they are tokens of the same type?

If the thought @"RM" were indexical in my system of mental representation, then its referent would have to be identified via its context. Correlatively, its referent would have to *shift* in accordance with context. And what sort of context would that be?

Perhaps we are supposing the relevant context to be the *mind* @"RM" appears in. (Devitt: "The reference of 'I' is determined by the

9. For a full discussion, see *LTOBC*, chap. 15, and Millikan 1993, forthcoming.

head it is in" [1984b, 400].) Are we supposing, then, that in *my* language of thought, in *my* inner system of representation, tokens of @"RM" might appear in *your* head so that I must check whose head @"RM" appears in before identifying its content? Or are we supposing, perhaps, that my mental language is some sort of universal language, one selfsame language that all people speak in their heads, so that rather than @"RM," I must think "I," the self-name in universal Mentalese? But even if this were the case (maybe Jerry Fodor thinks that it is), in what sense would the self name be *indexical*? Certainly there would be no interpreter for *whom* it would be indexical. Or is the claim that it would be indexical for God, or for an intrusive mind or brain reader?

But the language of thought, if there is such, is not God's language, nor brain-reader language, but the thinker's language. God might read tokens of the universal self name, tokens of mental "I," indexically, determining the reference of each by first noting whose head it was in. Similarly, I might "read a chameleon's back" descriptively, as a *natural* sign telling what color the chameleon has been sitting on, although the chameleon's color has no descriptive meaning for the chameleon. The universal self name would not be an indexical for the selves who named themselves with it, and when read by someone else, it could function only as a natural sign, not as a sign in the language of thought.

So my mental "I," my @"RM," is not an indexical. More reasonably, it is a (Millian) *name* for me; your "I," which may well have quite a different mental shape, is a (Millian) name for you. There is a special connection between @"RM" and my use of the public-language indexical "I" not because @"RM" is indexical but because in knowing how to effect the action of the referent of @"RM," I know, among other things, how to effect her public self reference. In making RM's public self references, in purposefully[10] and competently using "I," I *manifest* the activity of my active self name, the name of the person I know how to act.

Similarly, although it is true that in order to act in the world, I must take account of, hence may find it necessary to represent, certain of my relations to things upon which I would act, it is not mental *indexicals*

10. See note 7 above.

that represent relations-to-me. For example, the aspects of my percepts that show how far the perceived is from me represent relations-to-me, that is, (impure) relational properties, and my thoughts "near" and "here" are thoughts of positions-relative-to-me. But a relational property is not as such something indexed. My percepts of distance from me and my thoughts "near" and "here" are about relations to RM. But they do not shift their contents with context. What makes them special is not their semantics but their *functions*, their psychological roles, their impacts on my behavior.[11]

If these claims are correct, two further theses follow. First, the semantics of a public-language expression does not necessarily reflect, in a direct way, the semantics of the thought it customarily expresses. That is, Frege was wrong that a proper analysis of public-language meanings necessarily proceeds via an examination of the thought contents customarily expressed. This is a point that Howard Wettstein has also made recently (1988). Consonant with this point, in *LTOBC*, I proposed that neither is language meaning a function of speaker (or hearer) meanings, nor is speaker meaning a function of language meaning, and I gave independent analyses of these.

The second thesis that follows is that the semantics of thought is not sufficient to determine the psychology of a rational person. What is the same thought as another semantically may be a very different thought psychologically. This second thesis is defended with considerably more care in chapter 14, where I claim that there is, *in general* no reason to suppose that a person must always recognize the same thought content as the same, even under the same mode of semantic presentation. The assumption that a person must always recognize the semantically same thought as the semantically same is, of course, the very heart of Meaning Rationalism, the font of the last Myth of the Given.

11. More precisely, what make them special are their *proper* functions. See *LTOBC*.

14

White Queen Psychology; or, The Last Myth of the Given

Special thanks to Bill Lycan, Christopher Peacocke, John Heil, and Justin Broakes for helpful comments on an earlier version of this essay.

Thesis   An intact thinker need not recognize that the semantic contents of two of her own thoughts is the same, even when this content is presented through an identical semantic mode of presentation. One result is that there can be no such thing as logical possibility known a priori. Rationality too depends upon the ability to reidentify thought content. Rationality too is not a priori, is not contained just in the head, but requires an appropriate environment. Nor can rationality be defined over "narrow contents." A seeming implication is that no science of psychology based on intentional-attitude ascriptions is possible. This follows, however, only if intentional psychology is falsely assimilated to the physical sciences, rather than to the biological and ecological sciences. Rationality is not a lawful occurrence but a biological norm effected in an integrated head-world system under biologically ideal conditions.

1 Introduction

The White Queen, you recall, exercises her mind by believing impossible things for half an hour each day, while Alice declares herself quite unable to believe any impossible things at all. True, Alice is being unnecessarily prim. Physically impossible things, like perpetual motion, are not hard to believe, assuming, that is, that you don't already know they are impossible. And one *needn't* know that such things are impossible, because we don't have a priori knowledge of natural law—a well bred Victorian child knows that. Moreover, complicated logical impossibilities, like claims to have squared the circle or long but wrong mathematical equations, are not always hard to believe. This, Alice has been taught, is because our minds, though rational, are not very powerful. But complicated logical impossibilities, like complicated logical truths, can in general be unpacked into a series of simple steps, each of which no rational person could fail to see, until the original impossibility is reduced to a very simple one. And concerning very simple logical impossibilities, like that one and the same city both is and is not pretty or that one and the same man is and is not a spy, Alice draws the line quite firmly. What is and what is not logically possible is, for a traditional well-bred child, an a priori matter. No sane child could fail to reason far enough to know the very simplest of these impossibilities for what they are, and a rational person will not believe what she knows to be impossible.

Alice's incapacity thus derives from a capacity, an aptitude, for immediately recognizing simple logical impossibility as such, a ready a priori knowledge of simple logical truth. Being a traditional child, Alice is a rationalist about knowledge of logical possibility. This suggests that if the White Queen really can do better, say if she really can believe in simple contradictions, perhaps this is not because she irrationally insists on believing what she knows to be impossible but because she can't always tell a priori that a simple logical impossibility *is* impossible. Perhaps her secret is that for *her*, not even knowledge of the simplest logical possibilities is a priori.

If that were the case, the White Queen would be quite contemporary, indeed, advanced, in her ways of thinking. For it is implicit in contemporary "externalist" accounts of the contents of thought that what is consistent versus inconsistent, indeed, I will argue, what is rational versus irrational, is not epistemically given to the intact mind. If the externalists are right, then human psychology must be White Queen psychology. Let me first make a quick cut to the core of the White Queen's argument. Later we will dwell on the details.

Alice's view that knowledge of logical possibility is a priori knowledge is traditional, and it is still very much in style. For example, in the same breath in which Kripke denies that the metaphysical modalities are known a priori, he affirms that analytic truths, of which logically necessary truths are traditionally a variety, *are* known a priori. Indeed, he suggests that the fact they are so known is "stipulative." So Alice's position might better be expressed simply as the view that logical possibilities and necessities *exist*, that there are such things. Kripke says, "An analytic statement is in some sense true by virtue of its meaning and true in all possible worlds by virtue of its meaning. Then something that is analytically true will be both necessary and a priori. (That's sort of stipulative)" (Kripke 1980, 29). On this view, presumably, logical contradictions and logical incompatibilities among statements will also be recognized a priori by understanding the meanings of the statements involved. And prior to that, that two statements have the same meaning is surely a truth "in virtue of meaning," and hence will be recognized a priori by understanding the meanings of the statements involved. Compare Dummett: "Meaning is *transparent* in the sense that, if someone attaches a meaning to each of two words, he must know whether these meanings are the same" (1978, 131).

Not so, the White Queen claims. Alice has made an illicit assumption. She has assumed that the only thing that could be in question here is whether one understands each of the two statements to be compared. But, the White Queen argues, one might understand each of the two perfectly well and yet fail to know that these *understandings* were the same, that they were understandings of the same meaning, or of the same proposition. For example, suppose that without knowing it, one had two different ways of thinking what was in fact the very same proposition. Then one might think the negation of the proposition and simultaneously think its affirmation without knowing it. In general, one might not then have an a priori grasp of logical possibility. Or perhaps it would be better to say that then there would *be* no logical possibilities or necessities for one.

To illustrate, suppose that Alice understands the statement "Snow is white" and also the statement "Schnee ist weiss." To each she attaches a thought with identical content. But suppose that the vehicles of these two thoughts are different, that they produce somewhat different alterations of consciousness for Alice or that they are in different mental languages. If Alice can speak in two languages, might she not also think in two systems of thought? Logical truth is traditionally supposed to be readable off the surface form of a language, but, of course, only granted that the language is a perfect one, that its interpretation is consistent, complete, and nonredundant. Doesn't Alice have to make precisely the same assumption to read logical truths off her thoughts? And why does she think such an assumption is justified? Why does she think that her thoughts form a system with a consistent, complete, and nonredundant semantic interpretation? How can she know this a priori?

To start with familiar examples, the White Queen continues, there are a number of popular contemporary views that would argue that, at least for certain kinds of thoughts, the determination of their semantic content depends not only on what is within the thinking head or immediately accessible to the thinking subject but also on the thought's present external context, or on its external or normal causes, or perhaps on its historical or social-linguistic context. Call such views "externalist" views of the way thought content is determined. If any of these externalist views are correct, isn't it reasonable to suppose that two different thought vehicles might have, say, the same cause, and hence content, without the thinker's grasping that? The same thought content might then play more than one psychological role. For example, it might be both affirmed and denied. Similarly, isn't it reasonable that different tokens of the same thought vehicle might have different causes, and hence contents, without the thinker's grasping that? Then different thought contents might end up playing the same psychological role.

Turning to less familiar territory, the White Queen urges that the introduction of "modes of presentation" of content will not help Alice either. The illusion that it will help results from a false assimilation of psychological modes to cognitive/semantic modes, a confusion that results from what the White Queen calls "meaning rationalism." This is the traditional but unargued assumption that there *must* be a level on which psychological differences and samenesses automatically track semantic/cognitive differences and samenesses, an assumption the queen claims is false. The illusion that modes of presentation will help Alice save logical possibility also rests on a failure to see that rationality pivots essentially on *referential* content, or *Bedeutung*, and not at all on mode of presentation, that rationality cannot simply be lifted up and attached to mode of presentation. The capacity to reidentify content but only under a mode is a *restriction* on rationality, a lessening of rationality, not a removal of rationality into an inner and safer sphere.

With regard at least to her points about mode of presentation, the queen is not entirely on familiar ground. To evaluate her entire position, I will have to talk at some length about different conceptions of the content of thoughts, about modes of presentation, and about psychological roles, especially about the relation of various externalist theses to verification-influenced claims that psychological roles *determine* thought content, and hence, ipso facto, *are* modes of presentation of thought content. Anticipating that the queen may win her argument, however, let me say a word to avert panic. From the queen's thesis it does *not* follow, Kripke's (1979) Pierre to the contrary, that there is something incoherent in our ordinary ways of attributing beliefs to persons nor, Schiffer (1986) to the contrary, that reference to the propositional contents of beliefs is incoherent, and so forth.[1] What follows is merely that belief attributions are rather like eye and nose attributions. Let me explain.

Compare these questions and answers:

Q: Are Alice's eyes blue?
A: Well, one of them is, but the other is brown.

Q: Does Alice have freckles on her nose?
A: Well, it depends which you have in mind; one is freckled, but the other is not.

Q: Does Alice believe that London is pretty?
A: Well, she has two thoughts about London being pretty, one affirmative and one negative.

If there is anything puzzling here, I will argue, it is not how Alice could have differently colored eyes, two noses, or two thoughts disagreeing about whether London is pretty. It is, rather, why people don't more *often* have differently colored eyes, two noses, or two different thoughts with regard to London's prettiness, etc. In each of these cases it is nor-

---

1. Contrast Marcus (1981, 1983), who faces the White Queen's challenge squarely.

mal physical or psychological development, rather than logic or physical necessity, that precludes mismatch or redundancy. And in each case, though such aberrations may be comparatively rare, the mechanisms preventing them are not at all obvious, not at all to be taken for granted.

No problems arise, the White Queen claims, about the ascription of intentional attitudes. But there does arise an apparent problem for intentional-attitude psychology, should it aspire to become an exact science. For the laws of an intentional psychology—whether rationalist, associationist, gestaltist, Freudian, or whatever—are supposed to govern patterns of thoughts described in accordance with semantic mode and content. That is what defines a psychology as an intentional psychology. But if the White Queen is right, semantic thought mode and content do not govern psychology. Thoughts having exactly the same mode and content might simultaneously behave in quite different ways in the same individual. And thoughts having different mode and content might behave in exactly the same way in the same individual. If the White Queen is right, then that Alice has a coherent system of thought, that she possesses, for example, only one thought of each semantic kind, and hence that she thinks in accordance with laws, say, of rational psychology, depends on a felicitous *coordination* between Alice-the-organism and Alice's environment. It depends, in fact, on much the same kind of felicitous coordination that constitutes Alice's thinkings of *true* thoughts; rationality fails to be in the head in the same sort of way as does truth. How, then, might laws of reason play a role in a science of psychology?

I will argue that psychology is no more hindered by the real possibility that persons can believe in contradictions, have conflicting attitudes toward the same proposition, hold the same belief in two psychological ways, etc., than anatomy or physiology is hindered by the real possibility that a person can have differently colored eyes, two noses, six fingers on a hand, or a damaged heart. Genetic defects aside, abnormal anatomy or physiology results when the development of the fetus takes place in an abnormal uterine environment and/or when the child is born into an external environment that is not biologically ideal, not favorable to normal biological development or to effective utilization of the normal means the organism has of avoiding harm. Similarly, genetic defect and prenatal damage aside, abnormal cognitive development results when the development of a person's concepts or the genesis of a person's intentional attitudes takes place in an unfavorable environment.

A difference between normal physiology and normal cognitive psychology, however, is that whereas normal physiology concerns, for the most part, only the inner structure of the organism, normal psychology concerns the adaptedness of the individual organism to its individual environment, that is, organism-environment *relations*. What is cognitively normal versus abnormal shows in a *comparison* of the organism's structure with that of its environment. Psychology, both developmental and nondevelopmental, is more obviously an ecological science than is physiology (compare chapter 8). A resulting difference is that cognitive development is a great deal more likely than physiological development not to proceed entirely normally. It is statistically more likely not to accord with the biological norm, that is, the biological ideal. Doubled up beliefs, empty beliefs, confused and ambiguous beliefs, and hence irrational thought on the part of intact, undamaged, nondiseased (sane), intelligent persons, are not statistically rare. And, of course, *false* beliefs, which are also biologically abnormal (chapters 3–6), are ubiquitous, though, to give another contrast, surely beliefs are true more frequently than, say, the frequency with which baby mice manage to grow up and complete the life cycle (completing the life cycle being, of course, a biological norm for every species). Because the biological sciences deal with biological norms, not universal laws or statistical norms (chapter 9), the White Queen's claims pose no problems for psychology. The job of psychology is to describe the biological norms and to explain their mechanisms. It is irrelevant how often or how seldom these norms, these ideals, are actually attained in nature.

2   Meaning Rationalism Defined

Belief that there is such a thing as logical possibility rests on rationalism concerning meaning. Meaning rationalism comes in several varieties, corresponding to various ways in which semantic meanings are understood to be individuated. Meanings correspond to terms (in the logician's sense) and propositions. I will first state the doctrine of meaning rationalism using the traditional but ambiguous notions *term* and *prop-*

osition. Later I will discuss various conceptions of proposition and term identity, and hence the various different forms of meaning rationalism. I will argue that none of these forms withstands content externalism. But the alternative to externalism is to hold that all objects of thoughts lie within or directly before the mind. I conclude that meaning rationalism is untenable, that there are no (a priori known) logical possibilities.

Meaning rationalism divides into three entwined epistemological theses are that deserve to be stated separately.

1. The epistemic givenness of meaning identity and difference   A rational person has the capacity to discern a priori whether or not any two of her thoughts comprehend the same term or proposition, the same meaning.

2. The epistemic givenness of univocity   A rational person has the capacity to discern a priori when she is entertaining a thought with double or ambiguous meaning (if ambiguous thoughts are possible at all). (This thesis would follow from (1) on the assumption that ambiguity in thought could occur only if there sometimes were difficulty in telling whether two thoughts meant the same, which would result in the merging of thoughts comprehending different propositions or terms into one thought.)

3. The epistemic givenness of meaningfulness   A rational person has the ability to discern a priori whether she is meaning a term or proposition or whether her thought is empty of meaning.

Without these three givens, one might fail to know when one was thinking contradictory propositions, confused propositions, or nonpropositions, and hence fail to distinguish logical possibilities from impossibilities and nonpossibilities.[2]

Of these three epistemological claims, the givenness of meaning identity is the most central. It implies that thinking a proposition or term entails being able to *identify* and *reidentify* that proposition or term and knowing exactly *which* proposition or term that is. A strong

---

2. On one interpretation (Marcus 1981, 1983), thoughts corresponding to contradictory propositions are not really thoughts, say beliefs, at all, nor are thoughts corresponding to propositions containing terms with empty content really thoughts. On this view, what the meaning rationalist holds is more simply put: knowledge of when one is thinking a term or proposition and of what one is thinking is a priori knowledge.

form of this claim entails what Evans called "Russell's Principle": "In order to be thinking about an object... one must *know which* object is in question—one must *know which* object it is that one is thinking about" (Evans 1982, 65).[3] A weaker form would entail that one must know "which object" it is, but only when it appears under the same mode of presentation again.

3   Meaning Rationalism and Rational Psychology

Projected onto the psychological plane, the epistemic givenness of meaning identity and difference implies that a person could be disposed to be psychologically lawfully moved always in the same way by thoughts that comprehend the same propositions or terms, in different ways by thoughts that comprehend different propositions or terms, and hence that the *meanings* of thoughts might govern their roles in a rational person's psychology. With the doctrine of the givenness of meaningfulness, which suggests that a person need never countenance, and hence need never be cognitively moved by, meaningless thoughts, the way is apparently cleared for a lawful intentional psychology. Intentional psychologies can take various forms. Earlier I suggested associationism, gestalt psychology, and Freudianism, as well as rational psychology, but it is rational psychology that has figured in the contemporary philosophical literature on intentional attributions. The doctrines of meaning rationalism apparently open the way for a hopeful science of rational psychology to introduce various laws of reason in the guise of psychological laws. The following are obvious examples.

Psychological law of identity   If the term or proposition comprehended by two thoughts is the same, a rational person identifies these thoughts, does not differentiate between them for cognitive purposes.

Such a person believes *p* if she believes *p*; she will not believe *p* in one thought context but not another. Also if such a person "fails to believe

---

3. For a partial *defense* of Russell's principle, however, see Millikan, forthcoming. Denial of Russell's principle should be carefully distinguished from denial that we have privileged access to our own thoughts. Nothing in this essay is intended to cast doubt on the truth of Davisdon's "Knowing one's own mind" (1987) and Burge's "Individualism and self-knowledge" (1988).

that *A* is *B*," then "*A*" and "*B*" must correspond to thoughts of hers that comprehend different terms (in the logicians' sense).

Psychological law of noncontradiction   A rational person cannot be brought to believe a simple contradiction or simultaneously to believe and disbelieve the same proposition.

Psychological laws of simplest logic   A rational person cannot fail to make the very simplest of inferences, such as modus ponens or the simplest inferences that turn on transitive relations, at least not when she occurrently believes the premises and also considers the conclusion.

Psychological laws of rational motivation   A rational person obeys a series of simple laws defining rational motivation, such as that wanting *p* and believing that only *q* will procure *p* leads, if one has nothing independently against *q*, to wanting *q*, to acting so as to procure *q*, etc.

These psychological laws all require the givenness of meaning identity and difference, because without this givenness, the repeated or "middle" terms or propositions upon which these inferences turn might not be recognized as the *same* terms or propositions again on second occurrence or might be mistaken for the same when they were not the same.

Projecting also the givenness of univocity and meaningfulness onto the psychological plane, we get the following:

Psychological law of univocity   Careful rational persons do not cognitively process equivocal thoughts (though they may, of course, make false *judgments* of identity).

Psychological law of meaningfulness   Rational persons do not cognitively process meaningless thoughts.

4   What Is a "Rational Person"?

How are we to read the notion "rational person" as it appears in the meaning rationalist's claims and in the derivative laws of rational psychology? Like the god Janus, the notion of a rational person traditionally faces two ways. In one way, a rational person is one whose head is intact, in good mechanical order, not diseased, not broken; a person who is not deranged, whose psyche is in no way at fault, who is normally intelligent and cognitively mentally healthy. Call such a person "psychologically" or "mechanically rational." In the other way, a rational person is one whose thoughts follow logical patterns, whose thought processes are governed in logical ways by the meanings, the significance, of thoughts. Call such a person "semantically rational." Facing both ways, as it invariably has done in the tradition, the notion "rational person" embodies the assumption that the intact mind is, as such, semantically rational. It thus begs exactly the questions that need to be at issue: whether semantic rationality is "in the head" or whether to be semantically rational one must also be ensconced in a fitting environment; whether semantic rationality is or is not an a priori matter.

The meaning rationalist cannot, then, have gratis the traditional two-faced notion "rational person" but must choose between its faces. Nor can the meaning rationalist claim only that semantically rational persons conform to the rationalist psychological principles, for that claim is trivial. To be uniformly *semantically* rational, *of course* a person would have to exhibit the rationalist's epistemic capacities. To deal with the questions that need to be discussed, then, the only option is always to give the term "rational" its psychological reading. The only substantial question is whether a *psychologically* or *mechanically* intact person (or possibly an ideally cognitively healthy and intelligent one) must fit the meaning rationalist's claims, and hence must be capable of conforming to the laws of rational psychology. We must read the term "rational" to mean merely intact, nondiseased, nonperverse, etc.

Let me try firmly to fix this last point with an example, for it is of the utmost importance that we keep it ever in mind. In "A puzzle about belief" (1979), Kripke tells us a fable about Pierre. Pierre was raised in Paris speaking only French, and there he learned that "Londres est jolie." Later he learned English and now lives in the East End of London and, not realizing that this is the same city, expresses the belief "London is not pretty." So it looks as though Pierre has two beliefs, one that London is pretty, the other that it is not, which are straight-out contradictory. However, there surely is, as Brian Loar expresses it, a "respect in which Pierre is indisputably consistent" (1987a, 175). Why *indisputably*? It is indisputable because Kripke has described Pierre as a healthy fellow having nothing mentally wrong with him. From the *inside* of Pierre there is no way of detecting anything amiss. Pierre has an intact mind. He is mechanically rational, psychologically rational.

What, then, is puzzling? What is puzzling is that despite this, Pierre's thoughts appear, on the surface at least, to be *semantically* inconsistent, *semantically* irrational. But notice that this is puzzling and requires a solution only if one has merged in one's mind the two faces of "rational," and thus has adopted meaning rationalism. Then the project must be to find a way to describe Pierre's two beliefs that will show them *really* to be, despite appearances, semantically consistent, to be beliefs about London, say, under different semantic modes of presentation. But an alternative is simply to drop the meaning-rationalist assumption and settle for the possibility that the intact healthy mind may sometimes believe things that are contradictory. An alternative is to embrace White Queen psychology.

5   Inverted Meaning Rationalism

Meaning rationalism was originally an accompaniment to the view that meanings or propositions are abstract entities or forms grasped directly by the mind or literally informing the mind. Then the meaning rationalist's thesis was perfectly straightforward. Meanings that inform the mind can also *move* the rational—the unclouded, well-oiled—mind in accordance with their intentional natures. On this view, the meaning of a person's thought is taken to have a source or nature that is entirely independent of its effectiveness in *actually* moving the mind. Hence a clear distinction could be drawn between the norms of logic, which tell how the mind should ideally move, and the facts of empirical psychology. The claim of intentional rational psychology that the nature of the human mind is such that the healthy mind *actually* follows logic or approximates to following it (rather than following, say, certain laws of association) could thus be understood as a straightforward contingent claim. In particular, there would be no *incoherence* in attributing radical irrationality to a human. Having beliefs and desires is one thing; processing them in a rational way is quite another.

Contemporary externalist theories concerning the source of the semantic contents of thought divide over the question of whether this content is determined independently of a thought's psychological role or whether, on the contrary, psychological role is itself a determinant of the semantics of thought. The division makes the difference between introducing meaning rationalism as an empirical claim about the patterns of human thought and *inverting* meaning rationalism into a theory of what *constitutes* a thought's having a certain content. According to inverted meaning rationalism, part of what constitutes a thought's having a certain content is its actually following (or approximately following) the logical patterns that would be appropriate *to* that content. Then the distinction between logical norms for thought and empirical psychological laws that parallel these norms threatens to collapse. Thoughts follow the relevant norms for the same reason that squares insist on being four-sided. That they follow these patterns is what *makes* them the thoughts they are; if they followed different patterns, they would be different thoughts, or no thoughts at all. On this conception of thought content, radical irrationality is ruled out as philosophically incoherent. If there is an empirical question left, it is not whether the intact mind is necessarily rational but whether the intact mind necessarily has any thoughts at all.

An analogy may help to make this clearer. Contrast two kinds of theories concerning what constitutes the "of" relation when a picture is a picture of something. These two theories differ in the role that they assign to the likeness of the picture to the subject pictured. According to one theory, the "of" relation is entirely independent of the likeness relation. It is grounded, say, in the fact that the pictured has caused the picture in a certain way or in the fact that it is the purpose or function of the picture to be a likeness of the pictured. That the picture should be a likeness of the subject pictured is then interpreted as a norm or standard for pictures, not as what constitutes their picturehood. On this theory, it is possible for a picture to bear no resemblance whatever to the pictured (for example, a child's drawing).

The second theory of pictures claims that the "of" relation between picture and pictured is constituted through some sort of likeness relation. What makes the picture a picture of this subject rather than that is in part that it is a better likeness of this subject than of that. For this kind of theory, the defining likeness between picture and subject pictured is not a norm, for this likeness cannot fail to exist. If any subject at all is pictured, necessarily the picture is like it. But what is sufficiently unlike every subject will, of course, fail to be a picture at all. Notice, however, that on this kind of theory, granted that *perfect* faithfulness is not required for a picture to be a picture at all, it is hard to motivate the drawing of a boundary, even a very broad and fuzzy boundary, between pictures and nonpictures. Just how much like the pictured must the picture be in order to be a picture at all? And why just *that* much? Moreover, if likeness is a major determiner of what the picture pictures, the more unlike the pictured the picture is allowed to be, the more chance there is that the picture will be sufficiently like many things, and hence the more room there is for indeterminacy concerning what the picture is of, for equivocation in the reference of a picture.

Analogous to the first theory of pictures, on some externalist theories, semantic contents of thoughts are determined quite independently of whether or not these thoughts exhibit psychological roles suitable to these contents. This is true of pure causal and/or historical theories of content, it is true of informational theories, and it is true of the "biosemantic" theory of content (chapters 3–6). These theories make it possible to ask the question, in a straightforward manner, whether or not our psychology is governed by the rationalist's laws. On other externalist theories of mental content, that the psychological processing, the psychological roles, should be suitable to the semantic content of one's thoughts is part of what *determines* what those contents are. On these inverted-meaning-rationalist theories, that one's psychology obeys the rationalist's psychological laws is not an empirical theory but rather is constitutive of what it is to have the thoughts one has or to have thoughts at all. For example, that one thought or thought type is insistently incompatible under all psychologically normal conditions with another thought *constitutes* that one is the negation of the other.

Inverted-meaning-rationalist theories make it possible to ask not whether our cognitive psychology is lawfully governed by reason but only whether it is a law that we must, as intact humans, *have* a cognitive psychology at all, that we must possess *some* set of beliefs and desires if we are not broken and not ill. Could a human head innocently be hooked onto the outside world in a way that some or all of its would-be beliefs and desires were totally devoid, in fact, of meaning, of a semantics? Similarly, inverted-meaning-rationalist theories are characteristically vague on the question of *how* reasonable a person must be to be a thinker at all. And they often admit the theoretical possibility of a very large degree of indeterminacy concerning the facts of what thought means what, thus sanctioning the theoretical possibility of radical ambiguity in thought.

When discussing upright meaning rationalisms, I will be arguing that content externalism undermines the epistemic givenness of meaning identity and difference as well as the givenness of univocity and meaningfulness. But when discussing inverted meaning rationalisms, my argument will characteristically be that externalisms undermine the epistemic givenness primarily of univocity and meaningfulness in thought.

6   Varieties of Propositions and of Meaning Rationalism

According to how the notions "term" and "proposition" are understood, the meaning rationalist's claims bear different interpretations. Three broad positions on term and proposition identity are traditional. They can be distinguished, using a rough heuristic principle, as follows:

1. Terms or propositions are the same when they can be represented by the same functions in extension from possible worlds to extensions. Call such terms or propositions "Kaplan-style contents" or, for short, "kontents" or, for reasons to be given immediately, "unstructured kontents." (I will discuss Kaplan's views shortly.)
2. Terms or propositions are the same when, besides (1), they can be represented, roughly in a Fregean manner, as the result of taking exactly the same arguments to exactly the same functions in exactly the same order. For example, by criterion (1), the following sentences express the same proposition, whereas by criterion (2), they do not: "Alice has 10 fingers," "Alice has 3 + 7 fingers." Call terms and propositions of the second kind, those individuated in this second way, "structured kontents" of expressions and thoughts.
3. Terms or propositions are the same when, besides (2), all the arguments and functions involved are "presented in the same manner" or through terms "having the same sense." Call these terms and propositions "kontents under modes of presentation."

Especially the third kind of meaning rationalism, the kind that concerns "propositions" and "terms" taken in the third of these senses, will require considerable discussion. Kaplan-style characters—for short, call them "karacters"—will be treated as "modes of presentation" under (3) above. In fact, I will ultimately argue that karacters of one kind or another are the *only* things legitimately treated as *semantic*, and hence as term-distinguishing and proposition-distinguishing, modes of presentation. Various other phenomena in the neighborhood of Frege's own *Sinne*, or termed "senses" by others, either are not semantic but merely psychological or correspond to differences merely in structured kontent. The contemporary notion "narrow content" will also be treated under (3). Differences in "narrow content" have explicitly been assimilated by the inventors of that notion to something at least very like differences in karacter (Loar 1986, 1987b; Fodor 1987).

The unstructured kontent of a proposition can be represented by a function from worlds to truth values, that of a one-place predicate by a function from worlds to sets of individuals, that of a singular term by a constant function from worlds to a designated individual, and so forth. Or we can be realists about properties and represent the unstructured kontents of predicate terms by constant functions from worlds to simple or complex properties. More radical, we might substitute a modified *Tractarian* Wittgenstein understanding, or an early Russell understanding, of how language maps for a Fregean one. The details do not matter. What does matter with regard to interpretation (1) is that logically equivalent propositions always have the same unstructured kontent as one another. For example, all logically necessary truths have the same unstructured kontent. So a meaning rationalist of type (1), an "unstructured-kontent rationalist," claims that any person who believes one truth believes all logically equivalent truths, anyone who believes one logical truth believes them all. This has not been a popular position.[4]

I will argue against unstructured-kontent rationalism indirectly, by arguing against meaning rationalism of type (2), against "structured-kontent rationalism." Presumably, if not even propositions and terms with identical structures are necessarily recognized as the same when encountered again in thought, equivalent terms and propositions with different structures haven't a chance. The arguments against structured-kontent rationalism will also cover the possibility that propositional

4. Stalnaker (1984) does hold a related position: that "acceptance" of any proposition entails "acceptance" of all its entailments. On the other hand, Stalnaker allows incompatible beliefs, so long as these are "displayed in different kinds of situations" (p. 83).

thoughts may have no compositional nature, no structure at all, in which case the distinction between structured and unstructured kontent would be moot. Moreover, these arguments will focus in other cases on terms that do not have structured kontent, on kontent primitives. Hence the arguments against the two kinds of kontent rationalism are really the same. It will not hurt, then, pretty much to ignore the distinction between structured and unstructured kontent, to speak simply of "kontent" and of "kontent rationalism." So that is what I propose to do. The primary kinds of meaning rationalism, then, are "kontent rationalism," covering (1) and (2) above, and "mode-of-presentation rationalism" or, for short, "mode rationalism," covering (3) above.

7   "Kontent" and "Karacter"

I am going to make heavy use of Kaplan's (1989a) notions of content and character and of his notion "direct reference," so let me pause to explain these notions to the uninitiated and dress them appropriately for the work at hand.[5]

Kaplan's contents (kontents), I have said, can be thought of as functions from possible worlds to extensions: to truth values for propositions, to sets of individuals for predicate terms, etc. On the other hand, in the case of some expressions, those that Kaplan calls "directly referential," this way of thinking can be misleading. Consider what we may call "simple names"—terms about which nothing can be said within the theory of *kontent* except that they possess, as types, a certain individual as referent. Simple names are represented in the possible-worlds story by constant functions *from worlds* to a particular referent. But in fact, what the referent of a simple name is depends in no way on the possible world it is used to talk about. Thus, using the idiom "circumstances of evaluation" rather than "possible worlds," Kaplan tells us, "In actual fact, the referent, in a circumstance [possible world], of a

5. Kaplan's notions "content" and "character" run parallel in important ways to the notions "adapted sense" and "relational sense" in *LTOBC*, used there especially in the analysis of indexicals and descriptions. Unlike my treatment, Kaplan's is purely semantic and not entangled with idiosyncratic ideas about biological norms and functions. I adopt his terms here gratefully, but I put some of my own gloss on them.

directly referential term is simply *independent* of the circumstances [possible world] and is no more a function (constant or otherwise) of circumstances [possible worlds] than my action is a function of your desires when I decide to do it whether you like it or not" (1989a, 497). Simple names refer to what they refer to because the semantics of the language of which they are parts *says* that is what they refer to, and that language is determined to have that semantics by affairs in *this* world, not any other. In other worlds people speak other languages, but if I, here in this world, am to talk about another world, I have no option but to bring my own language of this world with me to perform that task.

Although this is not Kaplan's way, a similar point might be made about simple predicates, predicates about which nothing can be said within the theory of kontent beyond that as types they may stand (according to your ontology) for Fregean concepts (real, though incomplete, entities) or for properties or functions from worlds to sets of individuals. *Which* concept, *which* property, or *which* function is settled independently of the circumstances of evaluation by the facts of language use at home. If one is squeamish about using the term "reference" here, these predicates might be said to have "direct *Bedeutung*," but I will not be squeamish. I will say they are "directly referential."

According to Kaplan, all directly referential expressions are like that. They are the primitives for the theory of kontent, as applied in all circumstances of evaluation alike, and what they mean is determined at home. Their meanings do not vary with the possible worlds they are used to talk about. In fact, I think we can grasp what direct reference is without resorting to any reflections on possible worlds at all, without considering modal semantics. Suppose that one thinks of structured propositions more as Wittgenstein did in the *Tractatus*, rather than in Frege's way. Then propositions appear as representation types or as thought structures that, when true, are isomorphic with the world in accordance with designated projection rules. Directly referential terms are then those that have no structure *relative to the isomorphisms defined by the projection rules*. If they have significant structure of any kind, that structure is used only to determine *what the projection rules shall be*, to determine what is to correspond to the structured term as a whole. It is not structure that is itself *projected* onto the world. It is not structure claimed by the proposition to match the world.

Besides simple names, there are, according to Kaplan, other simple terms that are directly referential, namely the indexicals. For ease of exposition, I include demonstratives among the indexicals. Indexicals differ from simple names in that their contribution to kontent is not fixed for the type but varies with the context of the token. The token being in this world, of course its context too is in this world. The indexical's variation in kontent can thus be represented as a function from home context to kontent. Kaplan speaks of these functions as expressing "character" (karacter). Simple names, which, as types, have stable or fixed kontent, are then represented by constant functions from context to kontent. They have "fixed character"; indexicals have "variable character."[6] Thus the home context of an indexical token determines its meaning, and that meaning, its kontent, is, of course, carried over when one talks with it about other possible worlds, as it is also when one uses it in constructing semantic maps of portions of this world.

Kaplan roughly equates karacter with linguistic meaning. For example, the linguistic rule, the meaning rule, that determines the referent of "I" to be, in each context, the speaker of "I" gives the karacter of "I." In Kaplan's terminology, the karacter is not part of the "proposition" expressed by a sentence token containing "I." If I say "I am tired" while you say to me "You are tired," we express the same proposition, though our sentences differ in karacter. If you add "I am tired," you add a sentence with the same karacter as mine but that expresses a different proposition. Kaplan's usage accords with the first sense of "proposition" discussed in section 6; his propositions are "unstructured kontents."

Besides simple names and indexicals, Kaplan suggests that there may be, or theoretically could be, descriptions that are directly referential. He calls these "dthat" descriptions and designates them in this manner: "dthat [the inventor of bifocals]."[7] The kontent of a "dthat" description

6. I find Kaplan's terminology somewhat confusing here. Better names for fixed versus variable character might be "fixed content" versus "variable content."
7. That "dthat" descriptions really were intended to be directly referential, despite some vacillation on this in his formal semantics, is affirmed by Kaplan (1989b, 578–582).

is fixed by the context that is the actual world so that whatever fits the description in the actual world is its fixed referent, no matter which possible world it may be used to speak about.[8] To revert to the *Tractarian* picturing image, the description that goes with "dthat" is not used to picture the world but to determine what the projection rules shall be for the token of "dthat" it accompanies. The structure within the "dthat" description makes no contribution to the proposition, the kontent, expressed by the sentence containing that structure. Here, for example, are three sentences all of which express exactly the same proposition in the sense of kontent:

Jupiter is inhabited.

Dthat [the fifth planet out from the sun] is inhabited.

Dthat [the largest of the sun's planets] is inhabited.

These three sentences differ only in karacter.

It will be well to keep in mind that definite descriptions are often used in constructing predicate terms, as well as subject terms. Presumably, there could be "dthat" descriptions entering into predicate terms, such as "dthat [the color of cherries]," "dthat [the way Heifitz played Bach]," and "dthat [what David did to Goliath]." Such "dthat" descriptions, I will say, also have "direct reference."

8 Fregean Senses and Definite Descriptions, Fregean Senses and Millian Terms

"Dthat" descriptions may differ in karacter while having exactly the same kontent.[9] In the case of "dthat" descriptions, then, it would make

---

8. I don't know whether Kaplan remarks on this, but if a dthat description is read as uniquely specifying an object, rather than merely as a demonstrative with clothes ("dthat striped cat"), then *in this world* its kontent really does not vary with context. No matter where you put it, it has always the same kontent. And the dthat description is a strictly this-world creature. To say what it might have meant in other possible worlds *should* be as irrelevant as to talk about what "slithy toves" might have meant in other worlds. It seems to follow that dthat descriptions should really be said to have a "fixed character." Their contents are not determined as functions of *context*, unless as constant functions of context. But I am ignoring this complexity.

9. Perhaps this use of "karacter" should be considered an extended usage of the notion "character" (see note 7).

sense to think, as Frege did, of there being two radically different semantic dimensions connected with a description, one of which (for Frege, *Sinn*) determines the other (for Frege, *Bedeutung*) with a many-one correspondence. Notice also that one might easily grasp the karacters of two "dthat" descriptions without knowing whether their kontents were the same. This might tempt us mistakenly to compare *Sinn* to karacter and *Bedeutung* to kontent. Indeed, the temptation is momentarily strengthened when we contrast "dthat" descriptions with Russellian descriptions. So long as Russellian descriptions are not logically equivalent, they always have different kontents, both structured and unstructured. For although different Russellian descriptions may denote the same entity in *this* world, they represent different functions from *possible* worlds to extensions. And Russell, of course, explicitly denied that there was any distinction of the kind Frege attempted to draw between *Sinn* and *Bedeutung*. Unfortunately, however, things are not this neat. For Frege's *own* way of handling definite descriptions puts them on the same side of the kontent-karacter divide as Russell's descriptions. The peculiarity of the Fregean description is not that its kontent is fixed, not that it is directly referential, but that it is represented by a *partial* function from worlds to extensions. For a Fregean description, there usually are worlds that, when taken as arguments, yield no extension at all. But different Fregean descriptions that happen to have the same *Bedeutung* in this world differ, just as the corresponding Russellian descriptions do, in *kontent*. Frege's distinction between *Sinn* and *Bedeutung*, as he applied it to definite descriptions, corresponds to the distinction between two levels of structured kontent. It is a distinction within the theory of (structured) kontent.

What this means for us is that the kontent rationalist who believes in Fregean descriptions need not claim epistemic givenness for the identity of referents thought of under different Fregean descriptions, for these thoughts have different structured kontents. Differences in Fregean descriptions are not merely differences in "mode of presentation," as I am using that notion, namely, to mean mode of presentation of the simples of *kontent* (section 6).[10] But we must be very cautious here. Other uses

10. Carving out a clear and also accurate terminology here is very difficult. I realize that "mode of presentation" is a Fregean notion and that Frege con-

that Frege made of his notion "*Sinn*" require separate analyses. That in the case of Fregean descriptions, difference in *Sinn* corresponds to difference in structured kontent does not mean that difference in *Sinn* corresponds to difference in structured kontent in the case of indexicals or names. The *Sinne* of names and indexicals will have to be discussed separately. And it is well to reiterate here that if there do exist Kaplan-style "dthat" descriptions, these do differ in what I am calling "mode of presentation."

That out of the way, I propose now to introduce the locution "Millian term," after Mill's theory of names as mere tags, to denote *structureless* terms with *fixed* karacter. Both simple names and simple predicates, then, are "Millian terms."[11] And if there should happen to be any totally unstructured, noncompositional, propositional thoughts, these too are "Millian," Millian thoughts of propositions. In introducing this terminology, I am not prejudicing the issue whether Millian terms have modes of presentation, for short, "senses." If sense is identical with karacter, then Millian terms have sense, for they have a fixed karacter. If sense is something more subtle, such as the method of (nondescriptively) identifying the referent of the term (an Oxford neo-Fregean move) or such as aspects of the functional role of the term, we have left open the possibility that Millian terms can have that kind of sense too, so long as they remain unstructured *internally* and have fixed rather than variable karacter. Only if Frege's distinction between *Sinn* and *Bedeutung* can be shown to collapse in every case either into a distinction within the theory of structured kontent (as it does in the case of Fregean descriptions) or into a merely psychological, rather than semantical, distinction (section 17) will there be a conflict between being a Millian term and having a sense or mode of presentation. These possibilities concerning Millian terms I will discuss later (section 20).

---

sidered different descriptions of the same thing to be a paradigm case of difference in mode of presentation. But Frege collapsed crucial distinctions in his notion of mode of presentation that need to be separated out.
11. The notion that proper names are "mere tags" was originally revived by Ruth Marcus (1961).

9   The Transition from Language to Thought

I have been discussing language. And I am about to use the results in an argument about thought. Am I assuming, then, that there is a language of thought?

Not, I think, unless you stretch the notion "language" past the breaking point. I *will* be assuming that the mind or head, or what is before the mind or in the head, needs to be structured for thought to take place, structured with regard to its states, its state transitions, or both. And I will assume that this structure corresponds in some methodical way, and for some methodical reason, to kontent, structured and/or unstructured, to a mapping of true thoughts onto the world. But I certainly am not assuming, say, that thoughts are like sentences. Perhaps some or all are more like maps or pictures, which have structured kontent but no propositional kontent. (Maps don't have negations, nor subject terms or predicate terms—see *LTOBC* and chapter 5 herein.) Or perhaps they have no internal structure at all, all their relevant structure being in the organization of state transitions. I will try my best not to prejudice any issues, to cover all the angles.

But, of course, I cannot possibly cover all the angles, certainly not explicitly. For the most part I will talk about thought as though it breaks up into languagelike parts, thoughts of objects, thoughts of properties, etc. The fact is that the principles that lie behind the White Queen's arguments are extremely general. A few specific applications of her arguments should make it evident how to generalize it so as to include any theory of the structure of thought that pleases, so long as the theory allows thought to have kontent, to correspond, somehow, to states of the world.

10   Kontent-Rationalist Prohibitions against "Dthats," Indexicals, and Fregean Descriptions

The White Queen is to argue, then, against two kinds rationalism: "kontent rationalism" and "mode rationalism" (section 6). Many of the arguments against kontent rationalism are already well understood. For those familiar with the literature in this area, what I will be adding is mainly a bit more systematicity and thoroughness than has perhaps been offered before and some details intended to suggest the degree to which the tradition of philosophical analysis of this century has been a product of kontent rationalism.[12] I am driven by a naive but fanatical desire to make it utterly clear not only to Alice but to Every Reader that, and why, meaning rationalism is a Very Bad Idea and a Hopeless Dead End. Readers who are convinced already (or who become satiated) may wish to skim, or to skip altogether, from here through section 14 below. The more novel part of the White Queen's argument picks up again in section 15.

The argument against kontent rationalism focuses at the level of what, broadening Kaplan's notion, I have called "direct reference." The central argument is that the primitives for constructing thought kontent, the simples of the theory of kontent for thought, cannot have kontents that are epistemically given in the way required by the kontent rationalist. More precisely, these kontents cannot be epistemically given unless we resort to direct-apprehension theories for thought kontent, and that, I take it, should settle the matter. But if the simple terms of thought kontent do not conform to the kontent rationalist's requirements, clearly the complexes cannot either. For example, if the simple terms out of which thought descriptions are built cannot necessarily be correctly reidentified by the thinker, clearly the descriptions themselves cannot, nor can any propositions built on these descriptions.

I have distinguished three broad categories of kontent primitives: Millian terms, "dthat" descriptions, and indexicals. The first step in the White Queen's argument is to show Alice why, should she aspire to be a *kontent* rationalist, she must eliminate all kontent primitives other than Millian terms from her mental vocabulary. Later the White Queen will worry Alice about her Millian terms.

Alice may think of items by Russellian descriptions if she likes, but she must be careful not to employ any "dthat" descriptions of things not directly before her mind—call such descriptions "external 'dthat'

<hr/>

12. Much of the literature in this area (e.g., Owens 1989, 1990) mixes together questions concerning what *thoughts* are possible, compatible, and incompatible and questions about the ways we *describe* thoughts using "that" clauses. These are completely different questions, and I will not discuss the second at all. My position on the semantics of "says that" and "believes that" is stated in *LTOBC*, chap. 13.

descriptions." This is because none of the rationalist's epistemic requirements hold for external "dthat" descriptions. Whether different external
"dthat" descriptions do or do not have the same kontent obviously is
not an epistemic given, is not given a priori, so the givenness of kontent
identity and difference fails for external "dthat" descriptions. Nor is the
existence of an item corresponding to an external "dthat" description an
epistemic given, so the givenness of meaningfulness, of kontentfulness,
fails for "dthat" descriptions. Further, uniqueness of an item corresponding to an external "dthat" description is not generally an epistemic
given, so the givenness of kontent univocity fails for "dthat" descriptions. Alice must entertain no mental "dthat" descriptions that reach
beyond items of direct awareness. Nor may Alice employ any external
Fregean descriptions in thought. Fregean descriptions that differ in unstructured kontent (compare "*Bedeutung*") must, of course, also differ
in structured kontent (compare "*Sinn*"). So the problem here does not
concern the givenness of identity and difference in kontent. But external
Fregean descriptions can lack kontent (can be empty), and hence the
would-be propositions of which they are parts can lack truth values,
without the thinker knowing this. Moreover, external Fregean descriptions can have equivocal kontent (nonunique reference) without the
thinker knowing this. So external Fregean descriptions fail the given-
ness-of-kontentfulness and givenness-of-univocity requirements.

Russellian descriptions, on the other hand, are perfectly all right for
Alice. She can denote whatever she likes with Russellian descriptions,
as long as the terms used in these descriptions are themselves allowed.
This is because difference and sameness in Russellian descriptions *is*
difference and sameness in kontent, nothing more or less, so if one
can tell which description is which, one can tell which kontent is
which. It is also because Russellian descriptions assert the existence and
uniqueness of their denotations, rather than presupposing it in order to
have kontent. Russell was the champion kontent rationalist, and his
analysis of descriptions was the cornerstone of his kontent-rationalist
program.

Along with "dthat" descriptions and Fregean descriptions, Alice must
forswear all indexical thoughts referring to things external to mind.
Suppose, for example, that Alice picks up a spoon from the set in her
mother's silver drawer on Monday, thinking to herself, *This was once*

my grandmother's. On Tuesday she does this again. Then depending on whether it happened to be the same spoon or a different spoon that she picked up, either she did or she didn't think the same kontent on Monday and Tuesday. But, of course, she may not have any way of telling which. So the givenness of kontent identity and difference fails for external indexical thoughts. It is also possible mistakenly to pick up two things, say two pieces of paper, while saying or thinking *this*, or to hallucinate and pick up none. So the givenness of kontent univocity and the givenness of kontentfulness fail for external indexicals. Quite generally, if Alice has any thoughts with variable karacter, thoughts with karacter depending on context, and if the relevant contexts are external to the head or mind, Alice can never be certain a priori whether or not two such thoughts have the same kontent, whether they have kontent at all, and whether that kontent is unambiguous. As Russell saw, only when the relevant context is totally internal, and hence only when the indexed object is wholly within experience in such a way that it cannot fail to be correctly identified, that is, only when it is an object of "direct acquaintance" in Russell's very special sense, can the kontent rationalist admit context-sensitive thoughts. Other indexicals Russell turned into Russellian descriptions, to illustrate roughly, "There exists one and only one spoon I am holding in my hand" or better, "There exists one and only one spoon causing (or consisting in part of) this spoonish sense datum."[13]

11 Trades among Indexicals, Presemantics, and Analysis

The remaining step in the White Queen's argument against kontent rationalism is to show that there can be no Millian thoughts that fit the rationalist's requirments of givenness unless their objects are directly apprehended by the mind. (Remember, Millian thoughts are structureless thoughts with constant rather than variable kontent.) This step ought to be perfectly straightforward, for, to review section 5 above, there are only two possible basic kinds of Millian thoughts with external kontent to consider. First are Millian thoughts whose kontents are determined externally but holistically, determined along with the kon-

13. For a contemporary position along these lines, see Searle 1983.

tents of other thoughts with which they were dispositionally connected. Second are Millian thoughts whose kontents are determined externally but separately rather than holistically, determined, say, in accordance with a causal or biosemantic theory. Millian thoughts with holistically determined kontents are championed by inverted meaning rationalisms; those with separately determined kontents by upright meaning rationalisms. But there is a complication. Millian thoughts have a way of metamorphosing when they are accused of failures of givenness. It will be best to examine the mechanism of this metamorphosis before trying to pin Millian thoughts down.

A number of writers have noted that there is a difficulty about which variations of kontent with context to attribute to variable karacter and which merely to "presemantic" (Almog 1984; Kaplan 1989a, n. 78) or "metasemantic" (Kaplan 1989b) factors. Take, for example, Marcus's and Kripke's suggestion that the referent of a proper name corresponds to whatever person happens to be at the origin of a historical chain of the name's tokens leading backward from the current token. Kripke's theory might be taken as a partial description of what *creates* the semantics of ordinary Millian names, for example, of what makes the Millian name "Aristotle" a semantic entity referring to Aristotle. That would be to interpret Kripke's theory as a presemantic theory, a theory not *within* semantics but a theory about where these Millian names *get* their semantics. Alternatively, Kripke's theory might be taken as a claim that ordinary proper names are like indexicals: they have variable karacter; their *historical* contexts, their being situated at the end of such and such historical chains (compare, for example, a context including a pointing finger and something pointed at) determine their referents. On the first, the Millian-name, interpretation, "Aristotle" is a homonym, for there have, of course, been many people named "Aristotle." On the second, the indexical, interpretation, all tokens of "Aristotle," no matter which person they refer to, are tokens of the same indexical word, which has a univocal karacter but whose referent varies with (historical-chain) context. More startling, and I don't know whether this has been noticed, on the indexical interpretation it appears that all proper names are synonyms. The assembly of proper names is like Russell's strange choir of "genuine proper names": "this," "that," "thot," "thut," "thet," etc., which are synonyms with identical variable karacter.

This last consideration may make indexical theories of proper names look intuitively silly, but that is not an argument. The question that needs to be answered is, By what *principles* does one distinguish between variable karacter and various presemantic contextual externals that may go into creating the meanings of Millian terms? More generally, how do we distinguish between truth conditions that are *determined by a sentence's semantics* to vary with context or external conditions, and conditions that *determine the semantics* of the language or determine that it *has* a certain semantics? The language has to be meaningful, has to have a semantics, before anything said in it can be true. Hence the meaning conditions or meaningfulness conditions for a sentence are also conditions for the sentence's truth: it can't be true unless it's meaningful. How do we separate off its semantically determined truth conditions from its presemantic meaning conditions? To answer this kind of question, we would have to agree on a theory of what semantic meaning *is*. Then we might agree about when meaning is being created anew, as opposed merely to being used or applied.

Now what makes a Millian term Millian is precisely that nothing involved in fixing its reference is a semantic factor; everything involved is a *presemantic* factor. A Millian name is a simple invariant for purposes of semantic analysis. Some traditions have supposed that many of our unstructured *public*-language terms are in fact abbreviations for highly structured thoughts and hence are not truly Millian in character. But regarding thoughts, of course, no such move can be made. Assuming that not all simple thoughts are indexical, then at some level we *must* have Millian thoughts, whether, to go to one extreme, they are Millian terms for whole propositions about middle-sized objects or whether, to go to another extreme, they are Millian terms for sense data and their properties. The difficulty is that what one person interprets as a presemantic factor helping to fix the semantics of a Millian term in thought, the next person may always attempt to pull inside the semantics of thought, seeing it as context that provides an argument for a function defining a thought with variable karacter. There is no agreement on why or where to blow the whistle on such attempts.

Consider another variety of attempted trade between presemantics and variable character. On the theory that the kontent of a thought is sometimes derived from the kontent of the public term through which one acquires the thought, followers of Putnam (1975b) on the semantics of natural-kind terms may think of public *terms* for kinds as handing us Millian *thoughts* of kinds. Then the Putnam apparatus operates on the presemantic level to fix the semantics of one's language-derived kind thoughts. Alternatively, the Putnam apparatus may be thought of as operating on the semantic level to fix the kontents of mental-kind terms indexically. Putnam himself may have leaned toward this latter interpretation. Notice, however, that in this case the rules that fix the referents of kind terms in thought fix them for all tokens of a specific kind-term *type* at once. If there is "indexicality" involved, then it is not the same as ordinary "indexicality," which goes token by token. We can call such proposed semi-indexical mental terms "variable names" to distinguish them from ordinary indexicals.

A trade of presemantics for indexicals can be attempted even in the case of holistic presemantic theories of mental-kontent determination for Millian thoughts. A recent interpretation of the notion "narrow thought content" represents it by a function from possible outer-world contexts for (narrow) thoughts (for what is in the head) to the kontents of these (Loar 1986, Fodor 1987). Thus interpreted, "narrow content" appears as a sort of karacter that determines the kontents of the variable names in an individual's thought, given that person's position in a world. There is no reason in principle why such a view might not be coupled with holism. Indeed, in section 22 I will argue, contra Fodor, that "narrow content," in order to do the rationalist's job it is introduced to do, would have to be holistically determined.

So one can, in general, attempt to trade presemantic treatments of the origin of the kontent of unstructured thoughts, that is, attempt to trade treating these thoughts as Millian, for indexical treatments of these thoughts. And there is a second kind of trade that may also be attempted. One can always attempt to convert presemantics into definite description, either into Russellian description or into "dthat" description. That is, one can attempt to substitute explicit conceptual analysis for presemantics. For example, the Kripkean line on names can be projected onto the level of thought as the view that thinking of the referent of a public-language name is thinking a description such as "the person at the origin of the historical name chain that culminates in this name token."[14] (To make this compatible with Kripke's claims about how names operate in modal contexts, one would have to make this description a "dthat" description. But a Russellian description is another theoretical possibility.) Similarly, Putnam's natural-kind terms might correspond to thoughts that are descriptions such as "the kind the experts designate by the term ____" or "the kind exemplified by the samples with which the term ____ was introduced" (see Block 1986).

To turn to holistic theories of mental-kontent determination, consider the classical thesis that the kontents of theoretical Millian terms are determined by their place in a theory. The description version of this presemantic holistic theory is the Ramsified theory (F. P. Ramsey): theoretical terms correspond to complicated Russellian descriptions, expressed through simultaneous existential quantification over all theoretical entities and properties in the relevant theoretical domain. The Russellian description that is the Ramsified theory might be replaced, of course, by a "dthat" description. Or the description version might be replaced by an indexical thesis, like the narrow-content thesis mentioned above, where the description is taken to describe a complicated indexical-like relation between the theoretical-term type and its referent, a relation that must be mentioned within the semantics of thought.

12   The White Queen's Strategy for Capturing Millian Thoughts

These sorts of trades can be attempted in every case for any externalist theory of content determination for any kind of Millian thought. This makes the possible moves in the dialogue between the kontent rationalist and the White Queen very numerous, yet they are relatively easy to summarize. Take any externalist presemantic theory of the origin of kontent for a Millian thought. By an externalist theory, I mean one that rests the origin of the connection between thought and kontent on facts not internal to mind, characteristically, on some kind of contingent relation between the thought and its referent. The White Queen begins her argument by pointing out that, given this externalist theory, the kontent

14. Salmon (1981) and Wettstein (1986) discuss the various possibilities for a semantic interpretation of Kripke's and Putnam's theories. Felicia Ackerman proposed a fourth option in (1989). But this option has the same consequences for the kontent rationalist as do the other three.

rationalist's requirements of epistemic givenness are not met. The rationalist may then try to substitute an indexical analysis for the presemantics of the Millian thought. But the White Queen has already shown that an indexical analysis will not help the rationalist if the original analysis is an external one, one that placed the factors conditioning the determination of kontent outside the mind (section 10). Nor will substituting a "dthat" description for the indexical analysis help, for the queen has already made the parallel point about "dthat" descriptions (section 10). What is still left to the kontent rationalist, however, is to make the classical *Russellian* move. Analyze via Russellian descriptions, for example, turn proper names into unique descriptions, Ramsify theories, etc. But to make this move is, of course, to introduce a new level of Millian thoughts, the level of the simplest terms in the postulated descriptions. If the presemantics determining the kontents of any of these simple thoughts is assumed to be externalist, then we go round again.

Clearly, the only way out for the kontent rationalist is to claim that there is a level of thought on which an *internalist* presemantics is possible. Ockham thought we could directly apprehend ordinary individuals, both actual ones and possible ones (McGrade 1985). He thought that ordinary individuals were, in the necessary sense, internally related to mind. Russell thought that sense data and their properties had this status. As a loyal student of Wilfrid Sellars and weaned on *Philosophical Investigations*, I believe that nothing has this status. I also believe that the historical motivation for supposing that something has this status, though always merely implicit, was in fact univocal. The only argument there ever was for the possibility of direct apprehensions of kontents by minds was that this is what would be needed to make kontent rationalism true.

But we have not yet presented the White Queen's arguments against kontent rationalism for externally determined Millian thoughts. The simplest kind of argument is that it is perfectly plain that people *do* occasionally have two thoughts of the same thing (Hesperus, Phosphorus) without knowing it, that they *do* occasionally get two items mixed in their minds so that their thought has ambiguous kontent, and that they *do* occasionally think of nothing at all (phlogiston, Santa Claus) without knowing it. If the impulse to conceptual analysis is inhibited—

as it should be as soon as its motivation has been exposed and one has seen to what dead end it is destined to lead—the facts stand perfectly plain. That kontent rationalism is mistaken is a matter of empirical fact. Yet this remains a comparatively subtle argument. For such mishaps of human thought are comparatively infrequent. This is because, in the everyday world, humans are ensconced in the sort of environment they were designed by evolution to be in. Contrast brains in vats or worlds where other laws of nature hold or where nature's category structure or the structure of time and space are radically different. To the degree that we are well adapted to do our thinking in this, our normal, environment, any dependency that the rationality of the subject has on the structure of the environment remains nearly invisible. To allow us to observe how radical the dependency really is, the White Queen would have to take us on adventures underground and far beyond. In my exposition of the White Queen's arguments I will for the most part stay above ground, but keeping in mind also such possibilities as brains in vats hooked up to computers giving random inputs or inputs designed to deceive or perhaps no inputs at all may help to bring home her points.

Let us proceed, then, with instructions to Alice concerning how to be a kontent rationalist. We will examine a small handful of contemporary externalist views, taking these as presemantic theories of kontent determination for Millian thoughts. We will show Alice how each fails the requirements of kontent givenness, and hence why each must be forbidden to her. We will assume that Alice can generalize from these examples.

13   How to Be a Kontent Rationalist: Separately Determined Kontents

According to the accounts of contemporary externalists, which individual one is thinking of via a Millian name in thought depends upon which individual actually bears some specified causal or historical relation to one's thought. However, if the historical or causal mechanisms, the appropriate causal or historical facts, that determine these mental names to have the referents they do are facts external to the mind, on any such theory, no a priori guarantee can be given to Alice that any such historical mechanisms are in fact in place. The bare possession of an apparent thought vehicle cannot by itself guarantee that there is an appropriate history in place to make it the vehicle of genuine thought. How will Alice know, for instance, that her thoughts of Homer and Moses are indeed backed by appropriate histories giving them referents? On any such externalist theory, clearly the givenness of kontentfulness fails. Similarly, there can be no guarantee to Alice that any such mental name is not duplicated in her mental vocabulary, that she does not have, without knowing it, a mental synonym for that name in her mind. She might have a mental *Phosphorus*, say, as well as a mental *Hesperus* but without knowing *Phosphorus is Hesperus*, because she had no way of knowing that the actual causes of these names are the same. So on any such theory, the givenness of kontent identity and difference fails. Last, Alice can have no guarantee that any such name is not ambiguous in her mental vocabulary. She cannot know a priori that there are not two or more items equally well historically or causally positioned to count as the referent for a given mental name of hers. Suppose, for example, that she has acquired a certain mental name from a public-language name used by a community that has confused together two people. I have heard that Saint Patrick is such a double personality: there were actually two of him. Or suppose that Alice herself has mixed several people together in her mind.[15] On any such theory, clearly the givenness of kontent univocity fails as well. If Alice is to be a kontent rationalist, then she will have to think of ordinary individuals not on an externalist model, but directly, as Ockham did, or if that seems too strenuous for a Victorian child, then by Russellian definite descriptions.

Putnam proposed that natural-kind terms function rather as Marcus and Kripke said proper names do. They refer to whatever kind is exemplified in certain samples, which samples are related in specified external ways to the term's original tokens. Suppose that thoughts of natural kinds are structured in some similar way. Thoughts of kinds will then have kontent only if appropriate external relations to some natural kind are in fact in place. But this is not something that Alice can know a priori. The thought of phlogiston, for example, seems to have been a thought that lacked the appropriate relation to a natural kind, and

---

15. Compare Stich's example of Mr. Binh, who wishes to learn more about "Jefferson, the black patriot and statesman who made significant contributions to logic while building a dry-cleaning empire" (Stich 1983, 146).

hence, on this view, had no kontent, but that was not discovered *a priori*. Putnam's view also suggests that Alice might think, say, *sulfuric acid*, then *muriatic acid*, these being simple synonyms in her mental vocabulary, without knowing that they are synonyms.[16] And it suggests that Alice might have ambiguous thoughts of natural kinds without knowing it. She might, for example, think of jade without knowing that she was really thinking of two kinds jumbled together, nephrite and jadite (from Putnam 1975b). Or should she be "stealthily switched" (Burge 1988) at intervals between Earth and Twin Earth (where the "water" has the formula XYZ), she might end up having an equivocal thought of the two water stuffs merged.[17] Alice must be more cautious. She must adopt a more classical method, thinking of natural kinds as sets of properties necessary and sufficient to determine membership in the kind. Or perhaps she could forgo thinking *of* kinds altogether and merely denote them with Russellian descriptions.

An externalist concerning thoughts of properties claims that the relation between the thought of a property and the property itself is a relation in the causal-historical order rather than the logical order. That is, this relation requires that the instantiated property and the thought of it should interact or potentially interact or be externally related to one another in some other way in space-time. The internalist, by contrast, does her thinking of properties without benefit of causal-historical

---

16. Schiffer (1986) gives some sophisticated examples of this sort of thing.
17. The hold of kontent rationalism even on explicit content externalists is strikingly illustrated in Burge 1988 and Bach 1986. Burge discusses cases in which one is "stealthily shifted back and forth" between twin environments. He assumes that there would have to be a point, though likely a vague point, at which the contents of one's thoughts too would shift after, though perhaps with a delay, each shift in context. Burge doesn't consider that the result of such context shifts might not be shifts in thought but a merging of thought contents, which would result in equivocal thoughts. Bach assumes that although you can have two persons confused in your mind so that there is no difference between what you believe about one and what you believe about the other, this could not be to have a single set of ambiguous beliefs. It would be to have a *duplicate* set of beliefs, each set about one person, each person corresponding to his own separate mode of presentation. A false *judgment* of identity would then constitute the confusion. Surely this blindness has its roots in the rationalist tradition—in fact the *only* tradition on this matter—that ambiguity or confusion in thought content cannot possibly exist without being manifest subjectively. For extended discussion of equivocation in thought, see Millikan 1993, part 2, and Millikan, forthcoming.

mediation. Her mind directly grasps noninstantiated forms, or her mind is informed in a way that it somehow matches or pictures or contains a "mode" of the properties she thinks of, or perhaps it grasps Fregean senses or intensions that determine these properties. Anyone who takes thoughts of properties to constitutively rest on dispositions to interact with propertied objects under specified conditions or on a history involving the thinker's or anyone else's interaction with the property or with its component properties or, minimally, with other properties in the same determinable family, etc., departs from internalism—from Platonism, some might say. Alice must not attempt any such departure.

The reason she must not should by now be familiar. If what makes a thought of a property to be of that property is a causal-historical relation to that property, then unless this relation, and hence also the property itself, is internal to the mind, Alice cannot have an a priori grasp of the reality, of the identity, or of the singularity of that property. For example, if Alice tries thinking of red via the external causal-historical order, how can she be sure a priori that her thought *red* is not an ambiguous thought? Perhaps there is more than one property out there that (to take one sort of externalist view) typically causes or has historically caused red appearances in her under the relevant conditions. Indeed, on an externalist view, weren't mass and weight, and many other properties now recognized by scientists to be importantly different, incorrectly identified with one another, confused together in thought, throughout most of history? And how will Alice be sure that she has no hidden synonym for *red* in her mental vocabulary? Perhaps under certain conditions she can hear when something is red but then calls red by another name. (Does Alice still remember when she first discovered that "acid" from science class was "sour" in her daily vocabulary?) Indeed, if Alice insists upon thinking of properties via the causal-historical order, how will she know that her thought *red* is of anything at all? Perhaps it is really like thoughts of the property *laudable* as in "laudable pus" or like thoughts of the property *choleric*, properties now thought to have been simply chimerical. Indeed, if Alice's brain had been brought up in Putnam's fabled vat, on an externalist view it is likely that none of her "*color*" thoughts, perhaps none of her property thoughts, would have had any kontent at all. Clearly, Alice must avoid all forms of externalism when thinking of properties. She could respond by thinking Platonist thoughts of properties. For example, she might try directly apprehending the form redness. Or Alice could use Russellian descriptions for property thoughts, descriptions that depend on prior thoughts of properties only of sense data, to illustrate, *the property that usually causes red sense data in me.* Or Alice could go straight over to phenomenalism.

Suppose it were claimed that there exist unstructured thoughts of *propositions*, mental Millian names for propositions, the kontents of which were determined externally, but separately rather than holistically. Such Millian names of propositions would be vulnerable to failures of givenness in all the same ways as externally anchored thoughts of individuals, kinds, or properties. Consider, for variety, a causal theory according to which the kontent of a Millian propositional name equals whatever world affair or condition would be its cause under "normal conditions."[18] How is Alice to know that there *is* some proposition whose truth would cause a given thought under "normal conditions," or that there is only one such proposition? And unless she makes the impossible assumption that "normal conditions" for the formation of all of her thoughts on all subjects are the *same* conditions and further that she somehow knows when these conditions are met, how can Alice know whether any two of her Millian propositional names are names of the same or of different propositions?

14 How to Be a Kontent Rationalist: Holistically Determined Kontents

According to one tradition, we have "theoretical terms" in our public and mental vocabularies. These terms derive their meaning from inferential connections to other theoretical terms, as in a logical system, and from inferential bridging connections to nontheoretical terms. Whether such theoretical terms have kontent, that is, whether, when all goes well, they determine extensions, is a matter of dispute. For the kontent rationalist, however, the matter is settled. Theoretical terms are notorious for the fact that they are not known a priori to determine extensions. Nor can it be known by reflection alone whether two theoret-

18. Stalnaker (1984) seems to hold some such view.

ical terms have the same kontent, say, whether two known kinds of physical forces are or are not really the same or whether two kontents may have got mixed together under a single theoretical term. So if Alice is to be a kontent rationalist and wishes also to admit theoretical terms into her mental vocabulary, she cannot be a realist about them. She might adopt an instrumentalist attitude toward them, declaring that such terms do not contribute to the thinking of real propositions, that they have no kontent. Then there would be no such thing as either correctly or incorrectly reidentifying their kontents again, and no such thing as these kontents being empty or ambiguous. Or, of course, she might adopt Ramsey's attitude toward theoretical terms, turning them into Russellian descriptions.

The view held by some functionalists that the psychological role of a thought (its "narrow functional role") plus the external environment of the thinker (together these equal its "wide functional role") determines the thought's kontent is one more externalist trap against which we must warn Alice. Suppose, as a coverall, that we think of the psychological role of a thought as described by a listing of the thinker's current beliefs states containing the thought (for noncompositional theories of thought, by a listing of just the thoughts), by a listing also of the thinker's dispositions to arrive at or abandon belief states containing the thought on the basis of sensory input or inference, and by noting which beliefs and inference dispositions would be insistently maintained regardless of sensory input and other beliefs held. There is, of course, a nonaccidental similarity between this sort of description of a term's psychological role and the classical description of a theoretical term's role. But the psychological role may also include dispositions of beliefs to interact with desires and other propositional attitudes, such as hopes and fears, and dispositions to produce motor "output," described in some suitable way. Also, classical discussions of the meanings of theoretical terms tended to obscure or mystify the distinction between inference connections as norms and inference connections as psychological facts, whereas contemporary holistic functionalist accounts of kontent determination are more likely to be clear that roles are psychological dispositions.[19]

19. On the other hand, some theorists, following Wittgenstein and Wilfrid Sel-

Contemporary externalist theories that would fit kontents of thoughts onto psychological roles diverge in various ways, but they all agree that the most important condition for such a fit is that the thinker emerge as rational as possible under the construction. That is, they agree in being *inverted*-meaning-rationalist theories (section 5). But all inverted rationalisms agree that there have to be *other* constraints as well as maximal rationality on the fitting of roles to kontents. For example, the constraint may be added that as many of the thinker's current beliefs as possible should turn out true under the interpretation or that, given the uniformities that characterize the thinker's actual world, she should have as high a proportion of dispositions to *come* to believe true things as is possible ("reliability theories") or that the right sorts of causal relations or historical relations should *fill out* this basic picture of holistically determined kontent ("dual aspect" theories), etc.

The result is that all such theories have the same drawback for Alice. The tighter the constraints on kontent determination for such a theory—the more tightly rational the thinker must be, the higher the proportion of her beliefs that must be true, the more reliable her disposition must be to form true beliefs, etc.—the more possible-world environments there will be (recall *Wonderland* and brains in vats) in which not all or not any of the thinker's thoughts could be *made* to fit those constraints, and hence in which the thinker would have some or all kontentless thoughts, thus failing the third of the rationalist's givenness requirements. But if the constraints are made looser, so that there are more possible-world environments in which all of a given thinker's thoughts would have kontent, then there inevitably emerge *alternative* ways of fitting thoughts to kontents for some or all possible-world contexts. There inevitably emerge contexts in which kontent would be *indeterminate* among various options, and hence ambiguous (section 5). Simultaneously, looser requirements allow lesser *degrees* of rationality; that is, they explicitly allow breaking of kontent-rationalist psychological laws (section 3), and hence *failures* of the givenness of kontent identity and difference. (Indeterminacy might, of course, be treated not as

---

lars, explicitly take roles to be normative, the norms being derived from public-language roles.

ambiguity but as forcing abandonment of a realist semantics. Giving up kontents altogether is the most direct way of giving up kontent rationalism.) If kontent is determined in part by holistic psychological role, then it looks as though Alice will have to Ramsify *all* of her thoughts, using names of sense data and of their properties as her base, so that narrow role alone, and nothing external, determines that kontent.[20]

In sum, if Alice is to be a kontent rationalist, then, like Russell, she must not think *of* anything she cannot directly apprehend. If she can follow Ockham, directly apprehending ordinary individuals, or Plato, directly apprehending forms, well and good. If she cannot, then everything but her sense data and their properties must be merely denoted Russell-style, that is, judged to exist under a Russellian description. Alice is advised, of course, to ignore the attacks of Wittgenstein, Sellars, and others on the epistemic givenness of sensory data and their properties, or she may end with nothing to think of at all.

15   Logical Possibilities Cannot Be Kontent Possibilities

The contemporary mood clearly is not favorable to the kontent rationalist, and I hope we have managed to persuade Alice not to be one. What effect will this decision have on her views about logical possibility?

Suppose that, with Kripke, Alice requires logical possibility to depend on meanings and to be known a priori (Kripke: "That's sort of stipulative"; section 1). One classic reading of the notion of logical possibility correlates logical possibilities with either structured or unstructured kontents (section 6). Propositions that have the same truth values as one another in every possible world, or perhaps propositions that determine the same truth values as one another by presenting exactly the same arguments to the same functions in the same order, are thought to articulate the same logical possibility. But if kontent rationalism is false,

---

20. Of course, it will not help Alice to try determining the kontents of her intentional states by mapping them holistically directly from her *external* behavioral dispositions either. The indeterminacy, and hence irresistible pressure against realism, that results from this sort of procedure is not merely acknowledged but touted by its adherents. Kontent rationalism requires both realism for the attitudes and a priori univocity for thoughts.

possibilities of this kind—call them "kontent possibilities"—are not grasped a priori. They are not known simply in virtue of grasping the meanings, in the sense of the *kontents* of the terms through which they are expressed. Nor, of course, can equivalences between kontent possibilities always be unpacked into a series of simpler equivalences, each of which no rational person could fail to see. For—and these are roughly equivalent—none of the rationalist's psychological laws (section 3) hold for terms and propositions that are individuated by kontent. Clearly, kontent possibilities are not logical possibilities, not in the stipulated sense. Let us dwell on this truth for a moment.

It is not an epistemic given for Alice that any thought of hers has kontent. So knowledge that she is thinking of any kontent possibility at all is not a priori knowledge for her. And it is not in general an epistemic given for Alice that one thought of hers does or does not have the same kontent as another. Assuming that she needs to recognize the same thought kontent again to recognize this kontent under negation, and hence to avoid kontent contradiction in thought, knowledge that she is not thinking something kontent-contradictory will not be a priori either. It is instructive to compare these conclusions about the a posteriori nature of knowledge of kontent possibilities with Kripke's claims about the a posteriori nature of knowledge of metaphysical possibility.

In *Naming and Necessity* Kripke claims that "we have all found out that there are no unicorns," that this is an a posteriori discovery, and yet that it is false that "there *might* have been unicorns," false that "under certain circumstances there would have been unicorns" (1980, 24). To project this onto the plane of thought, note that although someone might harbor a Millian thought *unicorn* (or if you don't think *unicorn* could be Millian, choose your own example, but don't forget that thoughts of properties too are in the frying pan here) and might have no way of knowing a priori that this thought is kontentless, yet this thought still does lack kontent. This means that there are no kontent *possibilities* corresponding to (attempted) propositional thoughts about unicorns, no possible worlds in which these propositional thoughts are true. Now the thought *unicorns do not exist* will be true, however, "*in virtue of its kontent.*" That is, the impulse to delete *unicorn* from one's working, world-grappling mental vocabulary is a *correct* impulse and is correct in virtue of the kontent(lessness) of the thought *unicorn*.[21] But what is true—better, "correct"—in virtue of kontent alone is not a priori known.

Similarly, Kripke, also Marcus (1961), tells us that although we had to find out that Hesperus was Phosphorus empirically, still it is not true that it might have been the case that Hesperus was not Phosphorus. To project again onto the plane of thought, we might have had two Millian thoughts *Hesperus* and *Phosphorus* (or choose your own Millian examples) without grasping that the kontents of these are the same. But because their kontents are the same, to think something true of *Hesperus* but false of *Phosphorus* would be to think a kontent impossibility, to contradict oneself in kontent. Still, the thought *Hesperus is Phosphorus* is correct in virtue of kontent. That is, the impulse to merge these two thoughts into one, to use them interchangeably in one's mental vocabulary, would be a correct impulse and would be so in virtue of the kontents of the thoughts alone.[22] But what is correct in virtue of kontent alone is not known a priori.[23]

If we follow Kripke, then, we can only conclude that what is true in virtue of kontent alone is not the same as what is true in virtue of "meaning"—not in Kripke's idiom or, we are supposing, in Alice's. What is true in virtue of "meaning," Kripke has said, must be known a priori. It seems, then, that we must seek "logical possibilities" somewhere other than in the realm of kontent possibilities. And to correspond to them, it seems that we must seek another kind of meaning than kontent.

16 Logical Possibilities Cannot Be Kontents under Modes

Call this other kind of meaning "mode of presentation" of kontent. Suppose that there are such things as modes of presentation of kontents

---

21. For details on the function of the notion "exists," see *LTOBC*, chap. 12.
22. For discussion of the function of identity statements, see *LTOBC*, chap. 12; Millikan, forthcoming; and section 26 below.
23. It is telling that the one example that Kripke gives in which epistemic givenness and knowledge of the metaphysical modalities do not come apart lies exactly where I have argued that givenness and kontent *would* not come apart, namely a case in which kontent is directly before the mind. They do not come apart, Kripke claims, for the case of pain. It is clear that Kripke holds a Russellian rather than, say, a Sellarsian view of how one thinks of pain.

as well as kontents. Is there any way in which this might help us with the notion of logical possibility?

At first glance it appears that modes of presentation might help with the problems that result from the fact that sameness and difference of kontent is not a given. Perhaps sameness and difference of kontent is a given when these kontents are presented *under the same mode of presentation*. Frege's claim, for example, was that a rational person will not affirm and deny the same propositional kontent under the same mode of presentation. If this is a coherent claim, then the logical modalities might apply to kontents under modes of presentation. What can be known a priori is then not what is kontent-possible, versus kontent-impossible, *tout court*. But, given certain things under the right modes of presentation, one can tell that they are kontent-impossible, and hence that their opposites are kontent-necessary. The rest, the merely logically *possible*, then corresponds to whatever thoughts one cannot know a priori either to be kontent contradictions or to be negations of kontent contradictions.

Notice, however, that on this interpretation of "logical possibility," many "logical possibilities" will correspond as a matter of fact to kontent contradictions. The incoherence of this position is suggested when we press questions concerning the ontological status of the logical modalities under this interpretation. On this view, logical necessities and logical impossibilities lie on the plane of possible worlds. They are things that fit either all possible worlds or no possible worlds. But mere logical *possibilities* lie on another plane, the plane of thought. They bear no correspondence to possible worlds. A logical possibility may be something that all possible worlds fit or that no possible worlds fit or that some possible worlds fit. Logical possibilities correspond not to sets of possible worlds but to *thoughts* that cannot be rejected without further evidence. But what things can perfectly well be and what thoughts can perfectly well be thought by a healthy mind are things on two quite different ontological planes. Logical possibilities, on this view, would merely be thinkable thoughts, whereas logical impossibilities and necessities would reach through to the plane of possible worlds.

The incoherence of this view will become more evident as I discuss modes of presentation (sections 19–23). For I will argue that in fact there are no semantic modes of presentation under which sameness and difference of kontent is an epistemic given. There is no level on which the thinkable versus the unthinkable, merely as such, reaches through to the plane of possible worlds. If this is right, it follows that logical possibilities (assuming always that these would have to be grasped a priori) can be nothing whatever over and above psychological possibilities. I say "grasped a priori" because by definition they are what governs the psyche. Merely as such, psychological possibilities make no contact at all with the semantic, with the genuinely *cognitive*. But this argument will have to wait for its completion. On the other hand, if we turn to examine the effects of the failure of the givenness of kontentfulness, we run into fatal problems for this view of logical possibility immediately.

How will adding that kontents are presented to minds under modes of presentation help with the problem that we can't tell a priori whether our thoughts have kontent? One might say, well, at least maybe Alice can tell a priori that her thoughts have semantic modes, senses, and hence that they *might* have kontent. So Alice can think to herself, *The slithy toves did gyre and gimble* (or pick your own example, but on the assumption that each of the simple terms in the thought seems meaningful to Alice). What she has thought is a logical possibility, on this view, because all of the parts of her thought seem kontentful or possibly kontentful. They have modes of presentation, and under these modes no contradiction can be discerned. Moreover, of course Alice knows for sure that all the slithy toves are slithy and that it is impossible that any are slithy and not slithy. But surely it is transparent that *this* kind of possibility and impossibility takes hold only at the psychological level, that the only thing involved here is whether Alice's healthy mind can or cannot think certain would-be thoughts. No light at all is cast from here onto the level of possible worlds.

Of course, perhaps it is true that there are possible worlds in which these very thoughts of Alice's about toves and slithyness would have kontents, or worlds in which thoughts with the same modes of presentation as these thoughts of Alice's would have kontents. But it is important not to suppose that because it is possible that her thoughts might have been about something there is a something, a supposed possibility, that her thoughts are about. That would be to confuse semantics with presemantics. It may be that the internal aspect of a kontentless thought, for example, its conceptual role, might always have been supplemented, in some possible world, with an external context or with a history that would have created for it a kontent. Perhaps it is true for every (seemingly) kontentless thought that under certain conditions it would have had a kontent. But this is very different from having a kontent that, under certain conditions, would have been real or true. That an item has truth conditions, that there are possible conditions under which it would have been kontentful and true, does not entail that it is about these conditions. There is no possibility that Alice's thought of slithy toves is about. But, of course, she doesn't know this a priori.

The situation is similar to that of an empty indexical that Alice may carelessly think. Suppose that she thinks, *That spoon was my grandmother's,* but in fact there is no spoon there. Has she thought something logically possible? Again, it is true that this thought of Alice's has truth conditions, expressible by a Russellian description: *there exists a spoon. . . .* But the Russellian description does not express a possibility that her indexical thought comprehends. It corresponds only to the possibility that her thought might have comprehended something.

I conclude that there is no way to save Alice's (Kripke's) traditional notion "logical possibility." What are possible thoughts, things psychologically possible to think, things that might have had kontent, are not the same as thoughts of possibilities. But which thoughts are of possibilities, rather than impossibilities (contradictions) or nonpossibilities (vacuous thoughts), is not knowable a priori.

17   The Two Faces of Modes of Presentation

We have, I hope, convinced Alice not to be a kontent rationalist. But the White Queen rejects all meaning rationalisms. She rejects the rationalist's epistemic givens for all modes of presentation of kontent: for senses, for karacters, for narrow contents. Her thoughts do not obey laws that rest on meanings of any kind.

The doctrine of mode rationalism is difficult to state clearly, for every established term designating a proposed mode of presentation faces two ways, exactly as does the notion "rational person" (section 4), which conflates ideas that must be kept separate if the mode rationalist's position is not to seem analytically true. Each term has, as it were, ingested mode rationalism, so that to use any of these terms tends to beg just the questions that should be at issue.

Consider first "mode of presentation." It suggests the way something is presented to the mind, the way it *appears* to the mind. Now clearly the mind will differentiate among things that appear different to it and assimilate things that appear the same to it. So it looks as if it should be a truism that the same mode of presentation will automatically be recognized as the same.[24] Similar remarks apply to Frege's notion "*Sinn*," which, he tells us, is the "manner of presentation" of the meant and is what is "grasped by the mind," that is, presumably, the mind recognizes it. Indeed, invariably treated as a *criterion* for two thoughts of the same thing to have different senses is that it is possible for an intact person to take opposing cognitive attitudes toward these thoughts, for the psyche to treat them differently.

As for the notion "narrow content," it has been introduced by philosophers especially for the purpose of being what feeds into the laws of intentional rational psychology in order to predict behavior. So, clearly, the psyche must react the same to thoughts having the same narrow content, differently to thoughts with different narrow content. Pierre's two thoughts of London's being pretty (Kripke 1979, sec. 4), for example, are thought to have different narrow contents because one is accepted, the other rejected. But mode of presentation, sense, and narrow content are also supposed to be *cognitive* categories, intentional or semantic categories. They are to be categories carved out ultimately by reference to how the thoughts exemplifying them determine truth conditions, references, or extensions. Senses are supposed to be what determines extension, modes of presentation are modes of presentation of *kontent*. Loar (1986, 1987b) and Fodor (1987) suggest that narrow contents are semantically represented by functions from possible external contexts for heads, or possible worlds that heads might have been in, to kontents the thoughts in these heads would have had in these contexts. The problem is that whether these two sides, psychological sameness versus sameness in semantics, are two sides of the same coin is

---

24. In fact, in Millikan 1991, 1993 (part 2), forthcoming, I argue that even if modes are individuated by thought vehicle, or by how they appear to the mind, it does not follow that the mind always *grasps* this sameness as indicating sameness of kontent.

exactly the question that should be at issue. For example, do Pierre's two thoughts of London correspond to genuinely different *semantic* functions from world-contexts to kontents? To put things crudely, if narrow content, sense, or mode of presentation corresponds to the form of whatever mechanical leverage moves the mind, they cannot also be assumed to correspond to the semantic significance of what moves the mind. Not, at least, without an argument. Semantic significance is not a mechanical force, nor vice versa. Semantic manner of presentation is not analytically the same thing as mechanical efficacy of presentation.

Kaplan's notion "character" is a little different. It originates as a semantic notion. Character (karacter) is first introduced as that semantic feature that can be represented by a function from the context of an indexical token to its kontent. But Kaplan also says, "Character may be likened to a manner of presentation of the content" (1989a, 532) and that character is "the way the content is presented to us" (p. 533). He speaks of character as "'meaning' in the sense of what is known to the competent language user" and then muses ruefully that "this suggests (even if it does not imply) that if two proper names have the same character, the competent speaker knows that. But he doesn't" (pp. 562–563). Kaplan is puzzled by the results of his mode rationalism, with which he has superfluously burdened his originally purely semantic term "character."

The umbrella notion "cognitive significance," which covers all the proposed modes of presentation, tends also to be Janus-faced. Surely what is "cognitive" should be individuated with reference to what is thought or meant, in accordance with how this is determined *from* the thought, that is, by the thought's semantics. But "significance" is universally read as significance *to the thinking subject*. Subjectively different thoughts, thoughts with different psychological mechanics, are assumed always to have different cognitive significance. The meaning-rationalist current runs deep. For this reason I use my own umbrella term in place of "cognitive significance." I will speak of various modes of presentation that have been proposed, insofar as the criterion of identity for these can be taken to be semantic, as "*semantic* modes of kontent presentation." I will contrast semantic modes of kontent presentation with "psychological modes of kontent presentation" or, for vividness, "mechanical modes." My purpose, of course, is to distinguish clearly between semantics and psychology so that we can examine the relation between them.

18   Mode Rationalism Defined

Reviewing the rationalist's givenness requirements and applying them specifically to semantic modes of presentation of kontent, we obtain the following as the theses of mode rationalism:

1. Givenness of identity and difference in mode   An intact person has the capacity to discern a priori whether two of her thoughts exemplify the same or different semantic modes of kontent presentation.

2. Givenness of univocity in mode   An intact person has the capacity to discern a priori whether or not a semantic mode of kontent presentation for her thought is ambiguous (if ambiguity in thought is possible at all).

3. Givenness of meaningfulness   An intact person has the capacity to discern a priori whether she is entertaining a thought or instead a meaningless form having no semantics, a mental impression that exemplifies no semantic mode of kontent presentation at all.

Projected onto the psychological plane, these claims are associated with psychological laws. For example, there is the following:

Mode rationalist's psychological law of identity   If two thoughts exemplify exactly the same semantic mode of kontent presentation, a cognitively intact person identifies these thoughts, does not differentiate between them, and has the same cognitive attitudes toward them.

From this it follows that if a person can "fail to believe that A is B" when A is B, then "A" and "B" must express, for her, thoughts with different semantic modes of kontent presentation.

Mode rationalist's psychological law of noncontradiction   A cognitively intact person cannot be brought to believe both a proposition and its negation when these are presented through the same semantic mode of kontent presentation.

Similarly, the mode rationalist may embrace psychological laws of simplest logic and of rational motivation for cases in which kontent is presented via identical semantic modes. And she may embrace psychological laws of univocity and of meaningfulness: cognitively intact persons may think ambiguities in kontent but never in mode of presentation or sense; they may think kontentless thoughts but never senseless ones.

There is, however, an important ambiguity in these various mode-rationalist theses that needs to be discussed. Gareth Evans (1981, 1982) has alerted us to this ambiguity in the case of Frege's notion *Sinn*. Frege says that *Sinn* corresponds to a particular manner of presentation of the *Bedeutung*, a phrasing that leaves unclear whether or not *Sinn* includes kontent. Specifically, can there be a manner of presentation of a *Bedeutung* that does not in fact present any *Bedeutung*? For example, does an empty description have a *Sinn*? Evans thinks that Frege was not always clear on this point and further claims that he *should* have required a *Bedeutung* for a thought to have *Sinn*. Let us call modes counted up or individuated in these different ways "bare modes" and "kontent-including modes." Which of these kinds of modes do the mode rationalist's claims concern?

The question is important not only with regard to kontentless thoughts but also with regard to indexicals. For if "semantic mode" is interpreted as "kontent-including mode," if it is interpreted as individuated in part by the kontent presented, then of course no single semantic mode can present one kontent on one occasion, another kontent on another. If we suppose that the semantic mode of presentation of an indexical involves its karacter, then not the karacter alone but rather the karacter *plus the kontent* would have to individuate the content-including semantic mode. Thus one would have to know the kontent already in order to differentiate the mode. Alternatively, one might argue that for mental indexicals, the bare semantic mode includes, besides just karacter, some sort of completing component, for example, a percept, so arranged that the entire bare mode behaves like a "dthat" description, uniquely fixing a content. Then individuation by bare semantic mode would automatically effect individuation by kontent as a byproduct; to know the bare semantic mode would be the same as to know the kontent-including mode. Compare Kaplan's (1989a) analysis of demonstratives, according to which a demonstration plays this completing role. But that either percepts or demonstrations in fact provide the sort of completions needed to uniquely determine indexical kontents cannot be taken for granted (as we will soon see).

Externalism entails that neither kontentfulness nor kontent univocity is an epistemic given. Hence the mode rationalist's claims about the givenness of univocity and the givenness of meaningfulness, along with the corresponding psychological laws, can reasonably pertain only to *bare* semantic modes. If one cannot know a priori that one has a univocal kontent in mind, or indeed any kontent at all, one surely cannot know this about one's kontent-including modes either. On the other hand, if one wishes to use mode rationalism as a base for constructing an intentional rational psychology, if one wishes to move on to embrace the psychological laws of identity, noncontradiction, simplest logic, or rational motivation (section 3), it is crucial to see that none of these claims are sensible claims unless kontent-including modes are the ones intended. Roughly put, this is because these psychological laws concern logical coherence, *but logic turns on identity of kontent.* For example, it is *the same propositional kontent* under the same mode of presentation that I must not both affirm and deny.

To illustrate, suppose that the same bare indexical mode *could* present one kontent in one context or on one occasion, another kontent in another context or on another occasion. Then if the psychological laws were to range directly over indexical bare modes, they would prove blind to differences in kontent. The psyche would treat different kontents as though they were the same whenever they were presented in the same bare indexical mode. To parody, it would treat everything thought of as *this* just like every other thing thought of as *this*, merging all *this* thoughts as though they had identical kontents. Such laws obviously would not be laws of *rational* psychology. The psychological laws of identity, noncontradiction, simplest logic, and rational motivation must operate on kontent-including semantic modes, if they operate on any semantic modes at all. This means that for the rationalist thesis to support laws of intentional psychology, the mode rationalist's principle of the givenness of meaning identity must allow one to reidentify the same kontent-including mode, not just the same bare mode. (Could the psychological laws be reformulated relative to the context of the thinker? Perhaps, but the result would be that the thinker's semantic rationality will be contingent upon her happening to be in a suitable external context, something she cannot know a priori to be the case. The rationalist's laws were supposed to concern the intact psyche simply as such.)

On the other hand, suppose that a certain bare mode of presentation necessarily determines one and the same kontent on every occasion. Call such a mode a "single-kontent" mode. For example, "dthat" descriptions, if unique descriptions, would exemplify single-kontent modes. Kaplan apparently thought that his demonstratives with demonstrations exemplified them, and I suggested above that thought indexicals and percepts might do so.[25] If all mental modes of presentation were single-kontent modes, wouldn't it be just the same for a set of psychological laws to range over bare modes as to range over kontent-including modes?

But a single-kontent mode might still be empty of kontent or, unless this counts as just another form of emptiness, might still be ambiguous in kontent. Whether laws ranging over single-kontent modes might correspond to laws of rational psychology would depend on whether you consider inferences turning on kontentless thoughts, thoughts with no referents or truth values at all, to be rational inferences, and whether you consider inferences turning on ambiguous kontents to be rational. I have argued that the possession of an intact mind is no charm against emptiness or ambiguity in the kontent of thought. If it is irrational to reason with thoughts empty of kontent or with radically kontent-ambiguous thoughts, it can be no guarantee against irrationality either. Perhaps, then, I have already demonstrated that rationality cannot be in the head.

Let me postpone further discussion of this last issue to section 24, and pursue instead the question of whether it is possible that the modes of presentation of mental kontents might satisfy at least the first of the rationalist requirements, the givenness-of-identity requirement. Given what has been said, there are actually two requirements that would have to be met. First, all mental modes of presentation would have to satisfy givenness of identity when taken bare. Second, all bare modes

---

25. Of course, Frege thought of his *Sinne* as each determining a unique *Bedeutung* in this manner, but I have shown that as he went on to analyze definite descriptions, at least, this determination turned out to be merely the determination of one *Bedeutung* by prior *Bedeutungen*.

would have to be single-kontent modes; otherwise, recognizing the same mode again would not entail recognizing the same kontent again.

19   Dependent Semantic Modes

Semantic modes of presentation can be divided into basic modes and dependent modes. The dependent modes presuppose prior thoughts in basic modes. "Dthat" descriptions and terms whose references are fixed by "dthat" descriptions would exemplify dependent semantic modes, for the terms in descriptions cannot all rest on prior descriptions without regress.[26] On a traditional view of thoughts of theoretical entities, if these exemplify special modes of presentation, theoretical modes, these would also be dependent modes, for they would rest on thoughts of nontheoretical entities. If a thought in a dependent mode were to rest on a prior thought or thoughts for which the bare-mode identity or the single-kontent requirements were not met, clearly the dependent-mode thought could not meet these requirements either. For example, suppose that the bare semantic mode of one term in a thought description was not recognized when it was encountered again in a mechanically different mode. Then the bare semantic mode of the entire description might not be recognized when encountered again. Similarly, if this term failed the single-kontent requirement, then the kontent of the term, and hence also of the description, might fail to be recognized. That "dthat" descriptions were single-kontent modes would help not at all unless all the basic terms in "dthat" descriptions could be shown to meet the rationalist's standards as well.

So it is basic semantic modes of kontent presentation that we must examine. Starting with upright meaning rationalisms, I propose to examine possible modes of presentation for Millian thoughts, simple indexical thoughts, and variable names in thought. I will argue that unless we invert our rationalism, taking semantic modes of presentation to involve psychological roles, there are no such modes that fit both the requirement of the givenness of bare-mode identity and also the single-kontent requirement; every candidate for a mode of presentation fails

26. Russellian and Fregean descriptions do not correspond to semantic modes. They are part of structured kontent (section 8).

one or the other or both. Then I will argue that the idea of "narrow modes of content" makes sense only if we invert our rationalism (section 22), but the result of inverting one's rationalism is, in the end, to produce a parody of the idea of rationality rather than the foundation for a rational psychology (section 24).

20 Modes of Presentation for Millian Thoughts

My first job then is to show that there is nothing sensible that might be meant by "sense" or "mode of presentation" for a Millian (structureless, kontent-invariant) thought that would meet the upright mode rationalist's requirements.

Perry (1977, 1979) and Kaplan (1989a) have suggested that karacter may be a kind of sense. Millian thoughts do, of course, have karacter, *fixed* karacter. The karacter of a Millian thought is represented by a constant function from any context to the same predesignated kontent. But it follows that the karacter of any two Millian thoughts is the same if and only if the kontent is the same, so that to identify the karacter is exactly the same thing as to identify the kontent. If the mode of presentation of a Millian thought is individuated by its karacter, then the identity of the mode cannot be an epistemic given if the identity of the kontent is not. Recall Kaplan: "This suggests . . . that if two proper names have the same character, the competent speaker knows that. But he doesn't." On this interpretation of "mode of presentation," modes for Millian thoughts do not meet the givenness-of-identity requirement.

Gareth Evans (1982) tells us that a mode of presentation of an object is "a way of thinking of an object" and not something that "mediates" between a thought and it's object, "render[ing] thought about the object somehow indirect." "The fact that one is thinking about an object in a particular way can no more warrant the conclusion that one is not thinking of the object in the most direct possible fashion, than the fact that one is giving something *in a particular way* warrants the conclusion that one's giving is somehow indirect" (p. 62). The sense of a thought is merely "what makes a subject's thought about its object" (Evans 1985, 301), so, of course, every thought about an object must have a sense. Evans then proceeds to individuate senses on the Fregean model, so that two senses are different if it is possible for a person to take different cognitive attitudes toward kontents thought of in these two manners. Evans equates the way one is thinking about an object with the way in which the object is identified (McDowell's formulation for Evans, Evans 1982, 82) or the way in which the subject knows which object he is thinking about (Evans 1982, chap. 4). Similarly, Dummett takes sense to be a method or procedure for determining a *Bedeutung*, paradigmatically, for determining the presence of the *Bedeutung* (e.g., 1973, 95ff.).[27] Evans and Dummett agree, for example, that grasp of a certain way of recognizing a referent when encountered in perception corresponds to a mode of presentation of the referent. Surely, different Millian thoughts of the same thing could be associated with different ways of recognizing the referent, so certainly Millian thoughts can have, indeed must have, senses.

The question at issue has been begged twice here. First and most obvious, the use of Frege's principle for the individuation of senses presupposes that psychologically different thoughts, thoughts one can (mechanically) take different cognitive attitudes toward, must be semantically different. What needs to be demonstrated is that there are various ways in which one can think of the same thing via a Millian thought that are *semantically* different, not just psychologically different. We need an argument that the capacity to recognize Alice by her voice, say, as opposed to by her looks (or, for dogs, by her smell), or the capacity to recognize her by her footsteps (for blind persons) rather than her face, yield different *semantic* modes for the Millian mental names for Alice that they govern. Second, to assume without argument that these differences produce semantic differences just because they embody different "ways of thinking of" Alice or because they supply different answers to the question "What makes the [Millian] thought about its object?" begs the question concerning the difference between presemantic and semantic analyses. These different recognition capacities may supply different ways for the Millian thoughts they support to get to be about Alice, but what dictates that they produce differences *in* semantics? Modes of presentation are supposed to be on the level of

27. Similarly *enough*, that is. Evans is at pains to distinguish his views from Dummett's, but not in ways that affect the points at issue here.

meanings had by thoughts, not on the level of what gives thoughts meanings.

Turn the matter this way: what kind of thing is it that is supposed to have a semantics? Presumably it is *thoughts* that are meaningful, *thoughts* that have the semantics. How, then, do they get a semantics, where does this having of a semantics come from? Possibly they get it partly from their manners of being applied or the ways in which they are potentially iterated in grounded judgments. That, at least, is what many neo-Fregeans suppose. Does it follow that their manners of being applied or the mechanisms responsible for performing these applications are part of what *has* the semantics? No, the thoughts alone have the semantics. Similarly, it is only dimes and dollars that have monetary value, not also the mechanisms that happen, in the American economy, to give them these monetary values.

But what it is for a thought to have a semantics is for it to be subject to rules (functions) that determine a kontent for it, perhaps given certain contextual features as additional arguments. If the blind man who recognizes Alice by her footsteps has a Millian thought of her that is in a different semantic mode from mine, this can only be because different rules govern our two Millian thoughts. But there seem to be only two possibilities with regard to these rules, granted that they are semantic rules for unstructured *thoughts* rather than for psyches taken whole (compare economies taken whole). The first possibility is that the semantic rules for our two thoughts of Alice are exactly the same: each moves directly from the thought *Alice* to Alice; each says simply, "*Alice* denotes Alice." Then the method of recognition is only a presemantic factor. The second possibility is also that the rules for our two thoughts of Alice are exactly the same: each moves from the thought *Alice* to whatever it is that the mechanisms that iterate *Alice* in grounded judgments apply the thought *Alice* to; each rule says simply, "*Alice* denotes what its iterating mechanisms are applying *Alice* to." According to the first possibility, *Alice* is for each of us a genuine Millian name. According to the second possibility, *Alice* is what I have been calling a "variable name": its kontent is a function of its context, in particular, of what the mechanisms producing it are relating to in the environment. In neither case does the difference in methods of recognizing Alice produce a semantic difference in thoughts of Alice. The conclusion seems to be that the difference in "mode of presentation" involved is a difference only in psychological mode, not in semantic mode.

But perhaps there is another way of thinking about this issue. If the way of recognizing a thing is interpreted as *determining* the semantics of a Millian term rather than following after, meaning rationalism has simply become inverted (see section 5). Contrast a position according to which the semantics of a Millian thought is wholly determined by historical-causal or social factors. Then the way of recognizing follows after as a fallible means of getting one's sentences or thoughts to come out true. For example, then Helen Keller and Alice might have thoughts with identical meanings, identical semantics, but use different means, different input and inference dispositions, for getting these thoughts to accord, by and large, with the facts in the world (compare chapter 11, section 7). But if ways of recognizing, these being aspects of psychological roles, are determinants of meaning, the rationalism has been inverted. Indeed, to turn any part of psychological role into a mode of presentation of kontent requires an inversion of meaning rationalism. Without this, differences in psychological role are just that, just differences in *psychology*, and have nothing to do with meaning or semantics. Certain "dual aspect" theories notwithstanding,[28] if differences in psychology do not accord with differences in semantics, that does not turn differences in psychology *into* differences in semantics, unless one simultaneously performs an inversion. Inverting one's rationalism would, of course, pull psychological role into the semantic field, either as part of presemantics or in some more direct way. I will discuss inversions in section 22. The question presently on the table concerns only upright mode rationalisms.

Where would anyone ever have got the idea that there are such things as semantic modes of presentation for Millian thoughts unless moved precisely by a transcendental argument for the possibility of meaning rationalism? Or unless moved by verificationism, which derives from the same source? The traditional argument is, of course, Frege's argument from the supposed informativeness of identity statements. But

---

28. For a clear discussion of the nature of such theories, see Lepore and Loewer 1989.

Frege's argument assumes exactly what needs to be proved. It assumes that if some sentence "*A* is *B*" is to effect a change in one's cognitive processes, this could only occur because it effects a change in one's bank of information. That is, psychological processing of cognitive materials, for a cognitively intact person, is assumed to be governed solely by information content, by the semantic nature of thought. That is exactly the rationalist thesis. What is ignored is the possibility that sentences of the form "*A* is *B*" might have a purely *psychological* function, the function of producing, in the interpreter, a merging or identifying of thoughts previously expressed with "*A*" and with "*B*." That the thought vehicle associated with "*A*" differs from the thought-vehicle associated with "*B*," even that the method of recognizing associated with "*A*" differs from that associated with "*B*," need not imply that the meanings, the semantics, of these thoughts are different.[29] After all, what information does "Hesperus is Phosphorus" convey? What possibility does it affirm that was before in question? Behold, it is a statement *true in virtue of kontent alone*. So how can it inform? But that it cannot inform does not entail that it cannot jog the psyche to move into new channels.

I conclude that unless modes of presentation should derive from psychological roles, then there are no such things as semantic modes of presentation for Millian thoughts. There are merely different psychological modes of presentation, different mechanical modes. Or if fixed karacters are counted as semantic modes, Millian thoughts at least have no modes of presentation that vary while kontents remain the same or that can be recognized as the same again when kontents might otherwise go unrecognized. Similarly, in that case Millian thoughts have no bare modes of presentation that accord with the givenness-of-univocity and meaningfulness requirements. Their bare modes are the same as their kontent-including modes. Hence Millian thoughts can have identical semantic significance, different semantic significance, ambiguous semantic significance, or no semantic significance at all without any of this being manifest subjectively, without there emerging any hint of this on the level of psychology.

---

29. For a more complete formulation of this position, see *LTOBC*, chap. 12, and Millikan, forthcoming. For compatible remarks about the function of "exists," see *LTOBC*, chap. 12.

The case of Millian thoughts is a particularly disturbing case for aspiring upright mode rationalists. If being the same semantic mode again is not an epistemic given across Millian thoughts, then not only may Millian thoughts exhibiting the same mode fail to be identified as such, Millian thoughts exhibiting different modes, and hence different kontents, may be mistakenly identified. But if two Millian thoughts are identified as having the same kontent, this must be the same as merging these thoughts into one, or replacing them by one, Millian thought. Compare: the difference between mere orthographic differences and differences that amount to word differences is only that the latter are conventionally *taken* as determining different words. For every Millian thought, then, the question can arise, How many different Millian thoughts with different origins was this Millian thought originally, and how many mistakes have been made during its amalgamation process? There are rich possibilities here both for redundancies in the determination of thought and for ambiguities in thought (Millikan 1993, part 2).

Further, recall that Millian thoughts with external kontent cannot be known a priori to have any kontent at all. If, for them, exemplifying a specific semantic mode is the same as having a specific kontent, then whether they exemplify a semantic mode, that is, whether they have any meaning at all, cannot be known by rational reflection. Not merely kontentless thoughts but also thoughts that are pure gibberish cannot be distinguished by reflection from genuine thought, for in this case kontentless thought and gibberish are the same.

21   Modes of Presentation for Indexicals and Variable Names

If she assumes an upright rather than an inverted position on mental content, the White Queen would be entirely right to reject all rationalist principles for the case, at least, of Millian thoughts. Is it possible, however, that we have no Millian thoughts, that all of our thoughts are carried in less direct semantic vehicles?

The suggestion that all of our simple referring thoughts might be indexical is not that far from certain contemporary views. Recall that for those who follow Kripke and Putnam, one of the options concerning the semantics of thoughts of individuals and kinds is that these are either indexical or variable names (section 11). This option is also open for simple thoughts of properties. If an indexical or variable name has a characteristic semantic mode of presentation, presumably this will be, or will at least include, its karacter (the latter if a percept is part of the bare mode). Will this kind of mode of presentation be of any help to the meaning rationalist?

Consider first ordinary indexical thoughts, the kontents of which vary token by token with context. If the semantic mode of presentation in these cases is karacter, would being the same bare semantic mode again be an epistemic given in the case of such indexical thoughts? Graphically, could a person harbor two mental words, say for *here* or for *I*, or various subjectively different but semantically identical thoughts *this*, without grasping that the karacter of these was the same? I don't know how to settle this question briefly. For the sake of the argument, let us allow the mode rationalist that having the same indexical karacter again might be an epistemic given for simple indexical thoughts, and hence that the first of the meaning rationalist's two givenness-of-identity requirements, the givenness of identity for modes taken bare (section 18), might be met. What about the second requirement, the single-kontent requirement?

Unless kontent-including indexical modes as well as bare modes meet the givenness-of-identity requirement, the rationalist's psychological laws cannot cover any thoughts containing ordinary indexicals. For these psychological laws must govern kontent under a karacter, not karacter alone. Suppose, for example, that all of Alice's thoughts *here* exemplify the same semantic mode, a variable-karacter mode, and that the referent of each *here* is determined by the spatial context of the token. And suppose that Alice thinks, first, *The Eiffel Tower is close to here* and rather later thinks *The Statue of Liberty is close to here*. The fact that these two thoughts have occurred to her must not, in accordance with apparent laws of simplest logic, have the result that Alice is now disposed to think *The Eiffel Tower is close to the Statue of Liberty*. Nor must the thought *The Eiffel Tower is close to here* produce, by some supposed psychological law of identity, a disposition to have random later occurrences of thoughts in the same bare mode. If it produces a disposition to have later thoughts in the same mode, they had better be later thoughts in the same kontent-including mode, later *close-to-here* thoughts occurring in roughly the same location. To be rational,

Alice must be capable of recognizing not just being the same bare indexical mode again but being the same kontent-including mode.

The argument against Alice's a priori ability to do this seems straightforward. However one recognizes a kontent-including mode as the same one again, clearly this involves recognizing its *kontent* as being the same again. But I have already argued (section 10) that the kontents of indexical thoughts, if these kontents are external to mind, are not necessarily recognized as the same when encountered again. Consider, for example, Alice's Monday thought and her Tuesday thought about her grandmother's spoons (section 10). If these thoughts exemplify the same bare indexical mode, then Alice's inability to tell a priori whether they do or don't have the same kontent entails that they could have the same kontent-including mode without her knowing it. She might judge, for example, that one was her grandmother's, the other not, even though the two spoons were one and the same.

Perhaps, however, the example is flawed. For, it may be said, what the rationalist claims is not that Alice cannot have different cognitive attitudes toward the same kontent under the same mode but that she cannot do this simultaneously. The judgments, in this case, were not simultaneous. True, Alice did not change her mind, not in any ordinary sense. But without pressing that, perhaps we can find a better example. It is also true, and perhaps awkward, that Alice could not "fail to know whether the two spoons were identical" in the sense of openly wondering whether *this* (the spoon as presented on Monday) was the same as *this* (the spoon as presented on Tuesday). Thoughts had on different days cannot participate in the same explicit identity judgment. By the time Alice gets around to wondering on Tuesday whether these are the same spoon or not, she must be thinking of Monday's spoon under a different (though perhaps still indexical) mode of presentation, a mode directed through memory. We definitely need another example.

McCulloch (1989, chap. 6) has provided an excellent one. Suppose that Alice sees two ends of a very long train, the center of which is hidden from view by some barrier, perhaps by a shorter train. Viewing the two ends of the long train, Alice thinks to herself, *I wonder if that train is the same one as that.* The two *that*s that Alice thinks apparently exemplify the same semantic mode, so once again Alice has two thoughts exemplifying exactly the same kontent-including mode without recognizing this.

McCulloch argues that there is a way around this conclusion. For, he suggests, the mode of presentation of the two ends of the train is in fact different. One is presented to Alice on her visual left, the other on her visual right. The move here is parallel, of course, to Kaplan's inclusion of a "demonstration" as part of the semantic entity involved when a demonstrative is used, not just as part of the context. And what of Alice's Monday thought and her Tuesday thought of her Mother's spoons? Perhaps McCulloch will say that they exemplify different modes of presentation because they occur at different times, the times being parts of the modes of presentation, so that we could have dismissed that example too without so much foot shuffling.

McCulloch's move here is highly instructive. It is a paradigm of the unquestioning assimilation of psychological mode to semantic mode, about which I warned in section 17. The question on the floor, we must remember, is whether identical *semantic* modes of presentation, when presenting the same object, are always recognizable *as* presenting the same object. Being visually presented on the left and being visually presented on the right are obviously different psychological modes of presentation. But they cannot be assumed to be semantically different without an argument.

To be semantically different, these modes would have either to fall under different semantic rules or to exemplify the same semantic rules but with a different result due not to context but to properties of the modes themselves. But in the case of the right- and left-hand visual presentations, the rule is exactly the same. The rule takes no account of whether the presentation is on the right or the left. The rule is that the perception, whether right or left, represents its salient cause. Nor is the difference in kontent due to any difference in internal properties of the two presentations. For example, were Alice to be looking through right-left reversing lenses, her perceptually left thought *that train* would refer to the train actually on her right. So the example stands. The left- and the right-hand presentations are no more different in indexical or demonstrative *meaning* than if one was pink and the other blue, or if one made Alice prickly, the other tickly. (Compatibly, I argued in chapter 13 that, despite a great deal of confusion on the matter, aspects of percepts that indicate relations of perceived objects to the subject are not, on that account, indexical.)

Another way to consider the matter is this. The kontent of an indexical varies with its context. So to recognize the same kontent under the same karacter would have to involve the ability to recognize both the karacter and the same determining context again. But if we look carefully, we see that what constitutes sameness of determining context for two tokens of the same indexical type just *is* presence of the same referent, appropriately related in the same way again to each of these tokens. The determining context *contains* the referent of the indexical and contains it essentially. It is because *that item* is in the context and is so-related in that context to the indexical token that *that item* is determined to be the referent of the token. Being able to reidentify the determining context, then, requires a prior act of identification of the kontent, of the referent, itself. But this can be guaranteed a priori only if the referent is in or directly before the mind.

Alice's ability to reidentify the same indexical kontent-including mode again, to the degree that she actually displays such an ability, is an ability to "track" the object thought of (Evans 1981; *LTOBC*, chap. 10; Millikan, forthcoming). Tracking, however, is an activity that takes place in and through the outer world of the tracker. The success of this activity is not guaranteed by having an intact mind. One must be in the right kind of environment as well, a kind suited to one's tracking skills.[30] (I will say more about this in section 26.)

If thoughts of individuals, kinds, or properties are variable names (section 11), they will not serve any better than ordinary indexical thoughts for the mode rationalist's ends. The kontents of mental variable names, I have said, would not vary from token to token but would be determined by context for each psychological name *type*, in one package. Two such names would exemplify the same bare semantic mode (compare having the same karacter) if their kontents were deter-

30. On Gareth Evans's (1981) view two indexical thoughts have the same sense if they are connected by one's ability to track the indexed object through space and/or time. The problem again is that we cannot know a priori when we are in fact manifesting this ability. We can lose track without knowing it. Since Evans holds that to lose track is also to lose the sense, we cannot know a priori whether we are thinking sense, let alone kontent.

mined by the same function from context. For example, two mental variable names would exemplify the same bare semantic mode if the same kind of historical or causal relation between referent and thought-name determines the name-to-referent relation for each. Assuming that there were various *classes* of mental variable names—classes of proper names, of common names, of names of properties, etc.—that acquire referents from context in accordance each with some uniform principle, then all members of each of these classes would exemplify the identical semantic mode. Compare the case of *this, that, thot, thet,* etc., all of which exemplify the same mode. Hence, as in the case of ordinary indexicals, these modes would not be single-kontent modes. So even if the same bare semantic mode again were an epistemic given in these cases, this would be far from sufficient to make the same kontent-including mode a given. Indeed, at least in the case of thoughts of individuals, it is quite certain that we actually can and do sometimes fail to recognize the same kontent again, nor do I see the slightest reason to suppose that the semantic mode, as opposed to the psychological mode, has to vary when this occurs. Similarly for thoughts that may be supported, for an individual, by public names of kinds and properties.

22   What Narrow Contents Cannot Be

Narrow contents are supposed to correspond to whatever semantics for thoughts is determined by what is in the head alone. For the purpose of introducing the notion of narrow content is to provide a semantic level for thoughts, the characterization of which can feed into laws of rational psychology to predict behavior, on the assumption that behavior, in the sense that it needs explaining, is fully determined by the structure of the head and its immediate input.[31] The level of narrow contents is thus a hypothesized level on which healthy brain mechanics and healthy logic, that is, mechanical rationality and semantic rationality, converge. In section 4, I mentioned that Loar, discussing Kripke's character Pierre who believes that *Londres est jolie* but that London is not pretty, refers

31. This is an assumption with which I disagree sharply, for reasons discussed both throughout this chapter and in chapters 7–9 and 11.

to "the respect in which Pierre is indisputably consistent" (Kripke 1979; Loar 1987a, 175). This respect concerns the "narrow content" of Pierre's beliefs. I pointed out that this indisputable respect, as indisputable, is merely Pierre's mechanical rationality, the nondiseased, nonperverse character of his mind. Compatibly, Loar equates this respect with the way or manner in which Pierre thinks the content of his thought. But manners of presentation, as we have seen, are traditionally taken also to be semantic manners. Narrow contents are to match one-one with mechanical modes of presentation, but at the same time these are to be semantic modes of presentation. It is in terms of narrow contents that the laws of intentional rational psychology are to be stated, from which individual behaviors are to be predicted. It is at the level of narrow content that the semantics of the thoughts in a person's mind is to predict behavior. But how is this kind of meaning to be *described* semantically, that is, described as helping to determine kontents or truth conditions? What about narrow contents is to make them, as such, be *semantic* modes?

The suggestion that has been put forth is that narrow contents are semantically represented by functions from possible external contexts for heads, or possible worlds the heads might have been in, to kontents that the thoughts in those heads would have had in those contexts (Loar 1986, 1987b; Fodor 1987; compare Stalnaker 1981, 1990). Such functions are in the same family, of course, as Kaplan's character. In fact, one way of attempting to implement this suggestion would be to treat the individual constants and predicate constants in the language of thought as variable names. For example, that, I take it, is what Fodor proposes to do in *Psychosemantics* (1987), where he combines a defense of narrow content with the view that mental kontent is determined by causal covariance.

But this will not work. Nor will any other *separatist* theory of kontent determination, any theory that determines content for mental terms separately rather than holistically, combine with the theory of narrow content. No separatist theory will yield a semantics for narrow modes of kontent presentation so that these correspond one-one to psychological modes. This is because, on any such view, there are large classes of terms in the language of thought all of whose members exemplify exactly the same bare semantic mode, say the mode of kontent determination by causal covariation. Identifying the semantic mode, the kind of function from context to kontent, of any separately determined thought will place it in a far larger equivalence class than telling either about its kontent or about its mechanical mode of presentation, its psychological type. Nor should it be thought that the different routes through perception and perhaps cognition that kontents would have to take to covary with the different variable names in a person's thought would lend these thoughts different modes of presentation. It should not be thought, for example, that the thoughts *red* and *blue* must have different karacters because of the different visual channels connected with them. If these thoughts are variable names, the differences in these channels are no more determinative of the *semantics* of these names than the differences in the channels that lead to right-hand visual presentations versus left-hand visual presentations (section 21) are determinative of the semantics of percepts. To suppose that these differences enter into semantics is a verificationist's move, not an application of the notion of karacter. In no way, then, can predictions of behavior be based on descriptions of "narrow contents," conceived as thus separately determined. To make semantic modes match one-one to psychological modes of kontent presentation, one would need to determine mental kontents holistically, not separately.

23   Psychological Roles as Narrow Semantic Modes

We have not yet studied the effect of inverting mode rationalism on the givenness of identity. What happens if we posit psychological roles as senses or modes of presentation, allowing the fitness of roles to kontents to help determine what those kontents are?

First, notice that if the roles that are to be senses are individuated coarsely enough that two or more of a single person's thoughts might count as having the very same role, and hence sense, then the resulting modes of presentation will not be single-kontent modes. That is, the same mode again will not automatically present the same kontent again. Instead, roles must be individuated, for the rationalist, so that each sense corresponds to a completely unique role. The mode rationalist who wishes to identify senses with roles must determine kontents from whole roles, that is, holistically. Thus the whole role of a term might be thought of as determining its kontent somewhat as a "dthat" description would: *dthat* [*the item that fits thus and suchly with this role*].

Our understanding of what this sort of holistic interpretation of the notion of a mode of presentation would entail may be sharpened by contrasting it with a standard sort of separatist interpretation, the view that thoughts of individuals are variable names whose kontents are determined by causal-historical factors. Suppose that Alice has separate thoughts of Tweedledum and Tweedledee. Call these thoughts *Dum* and *Dee*. Suppose that the only internal difference between *Dum* and *Dee* is that Alice thinks of the referent of *Dum* as being named "Tweedledum" and thinks of the referent of *Dee* as being named "Tweedledee." Everything else she knows of the referent of *Dum* she believes true of the referent of *Dee* as well, the two men do not look different to her, and so forth. Now on a separatist causal-historical view, supposing *Dum* and *Dee* to be variable mental names, they will have the same variable karacter. Each is determined to be a thought of its particular referent by its having the same sort of causal-historical relation to that referent. Nor is anything *other* than this relation relevant to determining the referent. In particular, if the person at the end of the suitable causal-historical chain that resulted in the establishment of Alice's thought *Dum* is in fact Tweedledee, then Alice's thought *Dum* is in fact a thought of Tweedledee. Suppose that it is because Tweedledee is round and grinning that Alice thinks *Dum is round and grinning*; if Tweedledee had not been round and grinning, she might have thought the referent of *Dee* round and grinning but would not have thought the referent of *Dum* to be. In that case, however Alice got their names mixed, she has nonetheless mixed them, and she is wrong that the one she thinks of via *Dum* is called "Tweedledum." (This situation would be unstable, of course. Soon enough Alice's thought *Dum* would begin to have ambiguous content, as she merged new thoughts and perceptions of the fellow who calls himself "Tweedledum" with her thought, *Dum*, of Tweedledee.) Similarly, should the person at the end of the suitable causal chain that resulted in the establishment of Alice's thought *Dum* be Tweedledum, then *Dum* is a thought of Tweedledum. And, of course, exactly the same semantics applies to Alice's thought *Dee*. Her thoughts *Dum* and *Dee* are defined by exactly the same function from context to content. The mode of presentation of *Dum* and of

Dee is identical. Hence it obviously is not a single-kontent mode. Compatibly, *Dum* and *Dee* might both have the same referent without Alice's knowing it. Then she would be thinking of the same kontent under the same mode of presentation without knowing it.

Not so if the modes of presentation of *Dum* and *Dee* are their psychological roles. According to a role theory of modes, however Alice distinguishes between the thoughts *Dum* and *Dee*, it is the difference that determines these thoughts to exemplify different modes, to be defined by different functions from possible-world contexts to kontents. For example, perhaps, on some favored view of how role determines kontent, *Dum* must refer, in each possible-world context in which it refers at all, to someone in that context who is actually called "Tweedledum," whereas *Dee* must refer to someone who is actually called "Tweedledee." If in fact the same person is called both "Tweedledum" and "Tweedledee," then Alice has failed to reidentify him in thought. However, her two thoughts of him were not, in this case, under the same semantic mode of presentation.

By taking the whole psychological role of a thought to be what determines its kontent, we seem finally to be approaching the mode rationalist's goal. We seem finally to be uncovering the possibility of narrow content, a level on which psychological and semantic modes coincide. But there is an important complication we have not yet considered. Let us reflect for a moment on the question of what constitutes a thinker's taking the kontents of two thoughts to be the same.

Should any two of a thinker's thought types play entirely independent cognitive roles in that thinker's psychology, this will surely be enough to constitute the thinker's not having identified the kontents of the various tokens of these thoughts as being the same. It does not follow that a thinker's identifying the kontents of two thought tokens as being the same *consists* merely in their being of the same type, in their having but a single role, in the psyche's drawing no distinction between these.[32] Suppose that thoughts are taken to be compositional in nature. Tokens of the same thought type can occur configured in various ways within larger encompassing thought types, subject and predicate terms can

32. More extended discussion of this point is in *LTOBC*, chap. 15, and in Millikan 1993, forthcoming.

occur in sentences, sentences can occur in larger sentences, etc. Then
mediate inferences will turn on identifiable middle terms, and acts of
mediate inference will require that the utilized tokens of these middle
terms be identified as having the same kontents in the two premises. But
such an act of identifying is not accomplished by psychological indis-
tinguishability of the two tokens, by their having the same mechanical
efficacy. For example, to reidentify the element common to *A is taller
than B* and *B is taller than C* so as to conclude *A is taller than C* will not
be to react to the two tokens of *B* in the same way. It will be to react
appropriately to the *pair* of tokens of *B*, taken both together, and
together with their contexts, and to react that way *on account* of the
commonness, *on account* of the sameness of these.

Turning whole roles into senses will not, then, automatically solve the
whole of the rationalist's problems. The rest must be done by further inverting the rationalism, forcing kontent interpretations so that the inferences that actually take place, in particular, the acts of identifying
psychologically identical middle terms that actually take place, are the
ones that should take place. For example, the kontent of thought R is a
transitive relation only if xRy and yRz invariably produces xRz for all
psychologically identical thought types x, y, and z: R stands for a transitive relation only if appropriate acts of identifying over psychologically
same middle terms always occur. In a similar way, thoughts of symmet-
rical versus asymmetrical and nonsymmetrical relations, thoughts of
reflexive relations, the logical constants of the mental vocabulary, etc.,
are identified.

All this should be familiar enough. The inverted rationalist who
accepts holism and compositionality believes that there is something
rather like an automated formal logical system unfolding inside the
head.[33] Its individual constants and predicate constants have as their interpretation whatever makes the system as a whole best reflect (on some
preferred interpretation of this phrase) states of the world outside. The
criterion of being best is not, however, generally taken to rule against
redundancy in thought. In some cases, distinct constants may be interpreted as having identical kontents. Then the same is thought of again
without the thinker's knowing this, but that is all right, because it is

33. Millikan 1993, part 2, offers a sustained attack on this view.

thought of under a different mode of presentation. Knowing the complete semantics of a person's thought, including all about the modes of presentation, will now enable prediction of her actions, for the semantics has been tailored to accord exactly with the psychology. Is mode rationalism in this final guise a coherent doctrine? Has the White Queen finally lost to Alice?

Jerry Fodor has complained against "semantic holism" that it leaves us with organisms that don't share any meanings at all, whereas intentional psychology must manage to "quantify over organisms" (Fodor 1987, chap. 3). If semantic holism were correct, Fodor thinks, there would be no *laws* of psychology with application to both you and me, for the psychological roles of our thoughts are none of them holistically the same. But the holist's claim should be that the laws that quantify over narrow-content modes need be no more and no less than the psychological laws of identity, noncontradiction, simplest logic, etc. To predict a person's actions on the basis of laws quantifying over narrow-content modes, we would have to begin, of course, by telling what all her narrow beliefs and desires are. Narrow beliefs correspond to whole psychological roles. But to tell about whole psychological roles, we need not mention the parts of these roles that rested on explicit logical structures. These parts of roles would have been told already in telling of the universal "laws of rational psychology," in telling about the automated formal system built inside. Surely it is not reasonable of Fodor to demand more of an intentional psychology. You obviously cannot legislate a priori that there should be fewer semantic modes than there are just because it would make psychology easier.

24 Modes of Presentation of *What?*

The real problem with the identification of modes of presentation with roles lies elsewhere. It concerns, first, the sense in which the intact human, on the rationalist's account above, would necessarily be *rational*. In no sense at all, I will argue. It concerns, second, whether it is plausible that psychological role alone determines the semantics of thought. I will argue that it is not plausible.

The philosophical tradition has been so insistently rationalistic that it has become nearly impossible for us to think of reasoning except as something fully contained within or before a diaphanous consciousness, or at least within a head. But think: Rationality obviously pivots on *kontent*. It is kontents, for example, that must not be both affirmed and denied by the rational person. To be able to draw logical inferences from kontent to kontent but only when these kontents are presented in a certain *way*, under certain modes, is a *limitation* on rationality. It is not, as the rationalist tradition teaches, a relocation of rationality into some inner, purer, safer realm. To recognize the same kontent as the same so as to reason about it appropriately but to do this only when this kontent is presented again under the same semantic mode is to be capable of *moments* of rationality. The fewer these moments are, the less one will be rational. Multiplying modes, then, cannot possibly increase one's rationality. To be rational, one needs to reencounter kontent in such a way that one recognizes it. Diversifying modes of presentation does not help that.

Suppose that every time I encounter Alice, I think of her in the same variable-character, and hence multiple-kontent, mode: *this girl*. And suppose that I find that I am completely unable to track Alice, stepping through mirrors, growing bigger and smaller, lengthening and shortening her neck as she does. Never once am I able to reidentify her as being the same girl again. In that case I could not exhibit any rationality at all toward Alice. I would be totally *irrational* regarding her, totally unable to apply what I learned about Alice on one occasion to any other or to put two and two together regarding her. But how would it help me to be more rational about Alice if every time I met her I instead thought of her under a new mode of presentation? Clearly, it would not help at all. I would remain just as irrational toward Alice as before. On the other hand, I would be no worse off, no less rational, if I always recognized Alice, always called her by the same mental name, but then failed utterly to abide by the supposed laws of rational psychology wherever that name was involved.[34]

Because rationality pivots on kontent and does not reside in some more inner, safer realm, it is also true that no manipulation of bare

34. In Millikan 1993, part 2, I argue that these apparently different ways of being irrational concerning Alice are, in fact, equivalent, because the criterion for being another token of the same Mentalese type must rest, in the end, on what the thinker *recognizes* as the same type.

modes without regard to whether or not these in fact have kontent, and without regard to whether they have, perhaps, multiply ambiguous kontents, could possibly be a manifestation of rationality. Having an automated formal logical system unfolding inside one is not being a rational creature if the system has no interpretation. Nor is it being a rational creature if each symbol ambiguously means, or is undifferentiated among meaning, several things at the same time, many quite different things. Imagine a head full of definite descriptions that are all empty because all their component terms are empty, or that all rested on other descriptions whose component terms are empty. Imagine a head full of a thousand descriptions and (indexical) names all of the same object but without the head's knowing this. This would be rationality?

What the rationalist would need to show to make her case, then, would be that meaning holism cannot only be fleshed out but fleshed out in such a way as to guarantee that *whatever the world outside the head is like*, still, often enough, the same kontents are presented to the mind under the same modes again, rather than always under new modes. That is, the rationalist must be able to guarantee, first, that for each possible-world context, a person's thought will not be unrecognizably and absurdly redundant. And the rationalist needs to show that meaning holism can, at the same time, guarantee nonempty kontent for thoughts, at least for some reasonable proportion, and guarantee relatively unambiguous kontent, whatever the world outside the head might turn out to be like. It may be that, for humans, the contribution of the environment in the normal case is in fact both consistent and benign, tending to produce true rationality in normal people. But the rationalist has claimed that no contribution by the environment is needed, that the head by itself determines itself to be a rational head.

What are the prospects for developing a holistic theory of meaning determination in accordance with which, no matter what marvels occur in Alice's Wonderland environment, she will remain significantly rational? Or if you prefer Putnam's vat to Alice's Wonderland, what are the prospects for such a theory's yielding kontents for brains in vats no matter to what they are hooked? For example, what is the kontent to be of a brain-in-a-vat's thoughts when *nothing* is hooked to its input and output channels at all? Or (sordid image) when its outputs are hooked directly to its inputs again? Is it possible that this content will really be determinate enough, nonempty enough, and nonredundant enough, to count this brain in as a rational creature?

25   Semanticity Is Not in the Head

The second problem with attempting to save rationalism by inverting it and positing psychological roles as modes of presentation concerns the *origin* of semanticity in thought. Recall the mode rationalist's third epistemological given: an intact person has the capacity to discern a priori whether she is entertaining a thought or instead a meaningless form having no semantics at all. We have seen that what gives thought its kontent would have to be in the head or before the mind for kontentfulness to be an epistemic given. Similarly, whatever it is that lends thought its semanticity, its intentionality, would need to be in the head or before the mind for meaningfulness, semanticity, to be an epistemic given. For the mode rationalist, only the kontents of thoughts must be allowed to vary with context, to depend on the placement of the head in a world, not also their very semanticity. It seems to follow that something about the narrow psychological roles of thoughts would have to be the very source of the intentionality of thought if the mode rationalist is to be right. Similarly, since narrow contents are posited for the purpose of predicting behavior on the basis of what is in the head alone, that a thought *has* a narrow content should be determined by looking only at the head. None of the presemantics of thought must rest on anything external.

Is this plausible? It is important, first, not to fall into the following trap. It must not be supposed that just because one might take what is in the head and, by adding alternative external world contexts, produce alternative kontents for it, what is in the head must have had a semantics all along. Obviously, every piece or aspect of a thought is something that, if you add to it the remainder of whatever makes it a thought, yields a whole thought. It does not follow that every piece or aspect of a thought has a semantics. So it does not follow that whatever piece or aspect of thought happens to reside in the head is something with a semantics. Every arbitrary scratch mark is something that, if you add the right possible-world context to it, namely, if you put it in a suitable language community, will yield a kontent. It does not follow that every arbitrary scratch mark has a semantics.

What, then, about the psychological roles of certain things in the head or before the mind is supposed to determine that these things have a semantic nature—without looking, that is, at how these are disposed to interact with their actual environment, without looking at their actual history or historical connections, etc.? First, there is the problem that there is no such thing as *the* functional organization of a given system, any more than there is such a thing as the physical realization of a functional organization. Every functional characterization has to rest on a settled prior scheme of physical characterization. One cannot describe dispositions to go through state changes without having first settled on criteria of identity for the same state again versus a change of state, nor can one describe input-output dispositions without having settled on criteria for the same input again and the same output again. What determines these criteria for a bodiless, environmentless, historyless brain?

Second, there is the problem of what kind of functional organization yields semanticity or intentionality. What brand of formal logical calculus must be mimicked? And whatever brand that is, couldn't something be found mimicking it in the details of the capillaries or the kidneys, or fitted into the spleen, where, as a side effect, it promotes digestion?

In "Mental representation" Hartry Field proposes

> to divide the problem of giving a materialistically adequate account of the belief relation into two subproblems: *subproblem* (a): the problem of explaining what it is for a person to believe* a sentence . . . ; *subproblem* (b): the problem of explaining what it is for a sentence to mean that *p*.
>
> The rough idea of how to give an account of (a) should be clear enough: I believe* a sentence of my language only if I am disposed to employ that sentence in a certain way in reasoning, deliberating, and so on. This is very vague, of course, but providing that the vagueness can be eliminated and providing that a physical basis can be found for the dispositions invoked, then believing* will not be a relation that poses any problems for the materialist. (1978, 80–81)

Field applies this division of the problem to an analysis of the language of thought. Others, including Ned Block (1986) and Jerry Fodor (1987), have followed Field, also making this division.

Now the disposition to employ mental sentences "in a certain way" is, presumably, a way that conforms to some sort of logical calculus. But it is "sentences," things that have "meanings," that are so employed, and the formal calculus, if it produces "reasoning" and "deliberation," must fit onto these meanings in an appropriate way. What constitutes these "sentences" as sentences with appropriate "meanings"? Not, I should think, the mere fact that these items are processed in a manner isomorphic with some formal calculus. Rather, whatever is the solution to (b) will tell us which are the "sentences" and which of them "mean that p," which "that q," etc., so that we can see that the calculus indeed fits the meanings. Alternatively, perhaps *part* of what it is for something to be a sentence and to mean that p may be that the sentence is also believed* (or desired*, etc.). Either way, the fact of being an item with a semantics, with a meaning, surely depends upon the item's being interpretable as having a *specific* meaning in accordance with the solution to (b). But that the item has a specific meaning, a kontent, will depend on the world the head is in, or perhaps has historically been in. Hence the item's being a "sentence" at all, its having semanticity, will depend on the world it is in. What you cannot do on the basis of such a theory (but I suspect some of trying) is to determine which are the sentences versus mere aberrations in the spleen by seeing which have kontent, *given the context they are actually in*, then turn around and claim narrow content for these items. If these items truly had narrow content, then the presemantic facts that determined them to be semantic items with a certain variable karacter, a certain way of connecting with truth conditions, would be facts determined by what is *merely* in the head.

I conclude that if psychological role could play any part at all in determining mental semantics, it would have to play a presemantic role, not a semantic one, and that it cannot play that role alone, unsupported by the environment. Thoughts cannot have their roles as their senses.

26   Contrast with Stich

I think it is clear that the White Queen wins. Neither rationality nor semanticity is in the head alone. Tweedledum and Tweedledee may be as alike as two peas with regard to the insides of their heads, but if supplied with environments that are sufficiently different, one may be as sane as little Alice, while the other is as mad as the Hatter. A corollary is that intact people need not follow logical patterns of thought. Whatever a person believes, she can simultaneously believe its contradictory without mechanical irrationality, and she can fail to recognize its simplest logical implications. From this it follows immediately that intentional-attitude ascriptions, even if these capture every nuance concerning semantic mode of presentation, cannot be relied on for the prediction of behavior. But it is important clearly to distinguish the White Queen's dissatisfaction with intentional-attitude psychology from the sorts of well-known complaints against "folk psychology" that Stephen Stich (1983) has leveled.

Stich is concerned about whether a psychology based on intentional-attitude ascriptions could (as Fodor would put it) quantify over organisms. This is because he is impressed by the diversity among the belief states of different people that might still be described using the same intentional-attitude description. Implicitly assuming that thought referents are determined, at least sometimes, in accordance with externalist principles, Stich argues that two subjects can refer in thought to the same individual without there being anything in common between the causal roles that their thoughts of this individual play, or in common between their beliefs about this individual. Conversely, two subjects may refer in thought to different individuals, yet the causal roles that their thoughts of these individuals play and their beliefs about these individuals may be exactly alike in every respect. Stich concludes that intentional characterizations of beliefs can, at most, pick up different kinds of similarities among various people's beliefs, for example, similarities among roles, but not identities. Intentional laws that quantify over people can only be very crude, rough and ready generalizations—nothing of any interest to the exact scientist.

Now suppose that we were to challenge Stich as follows. It is well known that the effect that any belief will have on behavior depends on what other beliefs and desires are paired with it. No one thinks that the intentional characterization of a belief taken alone should yield knowledge of its causal effects. And dispositions to make inferences are, after all, themselves beliefs, implicit ones.[35] For example, if one has a reliable

35. On my own theory of intentionality, articulated in *LTOBC*, this is not always the case. Inference dispositions, in order to correspond to beliefs, must exemplify normal functioning, and the states that underlie these dispositions must be subject to transformations placing them within a (biological) representational system or a system of "intentional icons."

disposition to move from *x is a man* to *x is mortal*, the state that accounts for that disposition itself constitutes a belief, at least an implicit one, that all men are mortal. Now surely Stich will have to admit that an intentional characterization of *all* of a person's beliefs, implicit as well as explicit, *would* determine the causal roles of all of those beliefs. It would be the same thing, really, as telling about all the causal roles. Stich's problem seems to be that he wants to run a predictive intentional psychology on too small a base of initial intentional-state descriptions. He expects intentional psychology to be far simpler than anyone has ever supposed it was.

Now such a challenge to Stich on belief would not be adequate on this ground, at least: it does not address the part of causal role that equals input dispositions (for desires, output dispositions). Surely it could be argued (though Stich doesn't in fact do this) that observation beliefs having the same intentional characterizations might differ even in stimulus meaning for different persons. Quine's suggestion that there exist public-language "observation sentences," in the sense of sentences about objective phenomena for which all speakers of a language agree in stimulus meaning, is, in fact, implausible. But my purpose here is to contrast Stich's sort of worry about intentional psychology, to which the above reply is surely a reasonable response, with the White Queen's, which undercuts that response in a way quite unforeseen by Stich.

As the White Queen sees it, the real worry does not concern, in the first instance, quantifying over different persons. It concerns describing the thoughts of a *single* person. Her claim is that there can be no description, no matter how long-winded and complex, given in intentional idiom, in purely semantic idiom, of the causal roles of a single person's thoughts. So, of course, there can be no laws, stated in this idiom, that quantify over all persons. The idea is fundamentally mistaken that a specification in intentional terms of all of a person's beliefs, including all those manifested only in inference dispositions, would necessarily equal a characterization of the internal psychological roles of those beliefs. Only if psychological modes of kontent presentation corresponded one-one to semantic modes of kontent presentation would that assumption be true.

Let me illustrate the difficulty by reviewing once again the simplest possible case, that of Millian thoughts. These, the White Queen has argued, have no senses unless having fixed karacter is having sense. Suppose that Alice thinks partly in Millian thoughts. She might then have two thoughts of Humpty-Dumpty, thought *Humpty* and thought *Dumpty*, without knowing that these two were thoughts of the same. But there is only one way to describe the semantics of a Millian thought: you give the referent. The complete semantic characterization of Alice's thought *Humpty* is that it is a thought of Humpty-Dumpty. The complete semantic characterization of Alice's thought *Dumpty* is also that it is a thought of Humpty-Dumpty. But Alice's thoughts *Humpty* and *Dumpty* differ in psychological role. A list of all of Alice's thoughts about Humpty-Dumpty (including, perhaps, that he is smashed and also that he is not smashed) will not tell us about the causal roles of *Humpty* and of *Dumpty*. Nor can we complete what we need to know with a description of Alice's implicit beliefs, a description of her inference dispositions. The *Humpty* inference dispositions and the *Dumpty* inference dispositions are different dispositions, so we need to speak of them separately. But a semantic characterization draws no distinction between *Humpty* and *Dumpty*, and hence cannot articulate this difference. Similarly, suppose that Alice thinks *Tweedledum* but she is dreaming. In reality, there is no *Tweedledum* at all. No purely semantic characterization of her thought Tweedledum is then possible at all. But, of course, this thought has a psychological role. Stich is right, then, in his conclusions about intentional-attitude ascriptions. They cannot be used to characterize cognitive states for the purpose of building a psychology based on laws, laws to which the intact human mind necessarily conforms. But Stich has proposed the wrong reasons for drawing this conclusion.

To take a more difficult example, consider Stich's Mr. Binh. According to Stich, Mr. Binh has failed to distinguish among three different Jeffersons of whom he has heard. He consequently confesses an interest in "this fascinating fellow Jefferson, the black patriot and statesman who made significant contributions to logic while building a dry-cleaning empire" (1983, 146). Stich claims that there is no correct way of describing Mr. Binh's beliefs involving the thought *Jefferson* with ordinary intentional-attitude ascriptions. Binh's thought bears both similarities and dissimilarities, but certainly nothing approximating identities, to various ordinary persons' thoughts *Jefferson$_1$* and *Jeffer-*

son_2 and *Jefferson*$_3$. But it is not more like any one of these thoughts than any other. I suggest that Mr. Binh's thought *Jefferson* is ambiguous or equivocal in kontent. Just as words can be equivocal, so thoughts can be. But are there really no intentional-attitude descriptions that would correctly describe Mr. Binh's thought?

Certainly no description using merely the name of Jefferson$_1$ or Jefferson$_2$ or Jefferson$_3$ will describe Mr. Binh's thought. To describe Mr. Binh's thought using a single name, we would need to have an ambiguous name in our public language—as "Saint Patrick" may be an ambiguous name. (It is thought, as I've mentioned before, that Saint Patrick may really have been two people.) But couldn't we say of Mr. Binh that he has a certain implicit belief that, once described, will complete our characterization of the causal role of his thought *Jefferson*? We need merely say that Mr. Binh believes that Jefferson$_1$ is Jefferson$_2$ and that Jefferson$_2$ is Jefferson$_3$. We say that Binh thinks these three men are the same. After all, isn't that how Stich got us to understand what was going on in Mr. Binh's head?

The issue here turns on whether the description "Mr. Binh believes that Jefferson$_1$ is Jefferson$_2$" is an "intentional" description in the sense of a properly *semantic* description of Mr. Binh's thought. In section 20, I suggested that the underlying sentence "Jefferson$_1$ is Jefferson$_2$" has no semantics, in the sense of truth conditions. Like "ouch," it has instead a function. Its function is to cause a *merging* of the thoughts that the hearer would express with the public-language names "Jefferson$_1$" and "Jefferson$_2$." Merging these thoughts, we are supposing, would be an incorrect thing to do. But it would not be the making of a false *judgment*. Mr. Binh's problem is not that he believes something false but that his Jefferson$_3$ *concept* is inadequate. That is, his representational *system* is what is inadequate.[36] Compatibly, notice that although Mr. Binh may truly be said to believe that Jefferson$_1$ is Jefferson$_2$, there is no structure in his head articulated to match the clause "Jefferson$_1$ is Jefferson$_2$," for there is only one thought-type *Jefferson* in Binh's head. The effect, then, of saying that Mr. Binh believes that Jefferson$_1$ is Jefferson$_2$ is not to represent the semantics of Binh's thought but to make a metacomment on the representational system he uses. Talking

36. For a fuller treatment of this issue, see *LTOBC*, chaps. 12 and 15; Millikan 1993; and Millikan, forthcoming.

about this representational system is not the same as translating his thoughts. Similarly, to say that Alice has two separate Millian thoughts of Humpty-Dumpty, which thoughts she does not equate, is to talk *about* her representational system, not to translate her thoughts. We can, of course, indulge in such metatalk. But intentional psychology is postulated as dealing in translations, not metathought observations. If we allow metathought comments, we might as well go all the way to straight-out descriptions of mechanical roles, to full documentation of how all Mr. Binh's thought vehicles behave. But such a description would be totally nonsemantic, nonintentional.

27 The White Queen's Results: The Centrality of Kontent Identification

Central to the White Queen's position is that semantic rationality occurs on the level of thought kontent, not on some prior, safer, more inward level. Indeed, her view is that thinking really takes place only on the level of kontent. Any meaning prior to kontent or that occurs without kontent is "meaning" only in that there are semantic rules telling the conditions under which it would yield a kontent and telling what that kontent would be. Thought without kontent is only would-be thought, not, as the rationalist tradition teaches, the essence of thought distilled.[37] Rationality occurs on the level of kontent because genuine thought occurs only on that level.

The core of the White Queen's position, then, concerns reidentification of kontent. She claims that the ability to represent, to think of, a kontent does not entail the ability to reidentify that kontent when one thinks of it again.[38] Thinking of a thing does not entail "knowing what" one is thinking of, if that means always recognizing it when encountered again in thought. This is because the identity versus difference

37. From a biological perspective, to "mean," prior to having kontent, is to be biologically "supposed" to have a kontent. It is to have been derived from mechanisms that were designed to produce kontentful items of a certain semantic kind. Compare *LTOBC*, chaps. 2, 11, and 13.
38. On the other hand, I suggested in *LTOBC* and Millikan 1993 that representations are distinguished from more primitive intentional icons by the fact that they are *supposed* to be identified, that they have as a proper function that their kontents should be identified.

and equivocity versus univocity of thought kontents always depend on how matters stand in the world, not just in the head. It is never dictated by the insides of thought alone. But to be (semantically) rational requires that one reidentify the kontents of one's thoughts correctly. So rationality does not occur on the inside of thought either. The ability to be rational loops through the outside world. To grasp the queen's position fully, we should now examine this loop. We should examine the way that reidentification in thought rests on the structure of the environment.

No one doubts, of course, that whether identification of the kontents of two definite descriptions in thought is correct turns on matters external to mind. But identifications of this kind have traditionally been assimilated to judgments, to propositions affirmed, rather than to conceptual abilities exercised. A better view of the know-how that goes into thinking and of the nature of its dependence on the outside world is gotten by examining how thought arises from perception. Thought meets the world, in the first instance, indexically—not as mediated by descriptions.

When a thought indexes an individual by way of perception—*that girl, this book*—the indexed individual is as such a cause of the perception. An elementary ability to reidentify an individual indexed through perception is the ability to keep track of that individual by tracking it with the eyes, the head, the feet, as one gathers more information about it, about *the same thing*. Another is the ability to integrate perceptual information received through different sensory modalities as being about *the same thing*. These capacities to put information together about the same object over time and over modalities are not judgments, nor do they rest on judgments. For example, the thoughts *that rabbit*$_1$ and later *that rabbit*$_2$, thought ten minutes apart but joined by a tracking procedure, cannot participate in one judgment *that rabbit*$_1$ *is that rabbit*$_2$. The act of reidentifying kontent is not a judgment but an activity, a doing. But the fact that it is an activity does not, of course, preclude that it might be done *wrong*. One can lose track of a rabbit, mistaking another one for it. Equally important, the activity of tracking is done in the world, not in the mind. Similarly, coordination of information gathered concurrently from one's various senses is achieved by virtue of the physical natures of the energy forms affecting the sense organs and the physical interactions of the energy forms with the objects that they reveal. This coordination does not take place inside heads.

Another sort of ability that we have, to reidentify an individual indexed via perception, is exercised without moving our eyes and without footwork. We keep track of objects by knowing how to recognize them on reappearance. For example, we are remarkably good at specifically remembering human faces, presumably because this is a good way to keep track of people and because the ability to keep track of people was important to us during our evolutionary history. Similarly, we are surprisingly good at recognizing places again, regardless of the angle of our approach. This is in part because we are enormously good at recognizing the same three-dimensional shape again, no matter from what angle it is seen. We are good at reidentifying colors under a wide variety of lighting conditions. We are good at recognizing sounds, especially speech sounds, even through quite massive interference and distortion. Again, these (largely innate) abilities to reidentify objects and properties all depend on the structure of our environment as much as on our own structure. Just as Alice's abilities to ride a bicycle and to run would no longer be abilities if the laws of dynamics were different, so her abilities to reidentify people and places and properties will vanish if the structure of Wonderland fails to support them.

Besides innate or largely innate abilities to reidentify, we acquire capacities to reidentify things through both perceptual and conceptual learning. In *LTOBC*, I argued that this kind of learning constitutes concept formation, which is quite different from acquiring factual knowledge, and I discussed mechanisms by which this kind of learning may take place. I also argued that language comprehension is a form of perception, so that identifying via language and acquiring concepts via language is continuous with identifying and acquiring concepts via perception. The result, if this view is correct, is that adults possess very many and very sophisticated learned abilities enabling them to identify *this* individual with *that*, *this* kind with *that*, *this* property with *that*, etc. All of these abilities rest heavily on both the general structure and the particular facts of the adult's world.

From one perspective, the very essence of thought is the ability to identify *this* with *this*, to identify one and the same thing, about which one is acquiring information, over various informational modalities and over time, and then later to identify it with *that*, the same perceived now as a thing to be acted upon. From this viewpoint, Millian thoughts merely mediate among indexical thoughts, between various *this*'s: *this child* on Tuesday is identified with *this child* on Wednesday by each being identified as *Alice*. The ability to identify the kontents of indexical thoughts is thus continuous with the ability to know when the kontents of Millian thoughts are the same. Similarly, recognizing a person by face and recognizing her by description are fundamentally similar acts.

Each of these acts of identifying is right or wrong, depending on the structure of the world and not of the head alone. Thinking takes place through the world. And none of these acts can be described in purely intentional idiom. Intentional idiom assumes that these acts are performed correctly, that thoughts *this* and *that* are merged or kept separate appropriately, that kontents of Millian names are not ambiguous and not redundant. These abilities or disabilities are not themselves intentional attitudes. To describe a person's dispositions with regard to correct and incorrect performances of such acts is to describe mental mechanics, not mental semantics, and mental mechanics comprises both brain mechanics and world mechanics.

28   Implications for Intentional Psychology

Were it the job of intentional psychology to predict individual behaviors on the basis of intentional characterizations, then intentional psychology would fail. For abilities to identify, like physical abilities, cannot be guaranteed. Not just abilities to identify but all abilities depend on conditions in the world being normal or as expected or as assumed by evolution when it designed the relevant systems. For example, one may know very well how to walk but still there are things that can trip one. Other pursuits, such as catching fish or mending broken china or pleasing Grandfather, we may know how to do but less well. If acts of identifying were always done right, perhaps we would always believe truly. For false beliefs generally result from failures to identify objects or properties correctly, either through direct perception, through the speech of others, or through risky identifications in thought (induction). The number of false beliefs that we have suggests that failures to identify correctly not only occur but are frequent. It seems clear, then, that intentional psychology can be no sort of lawful predictive science.

Jerry Fodor mourns for intentional psychology what he terms "the idealization problem": "how to fit actual causal roles onto logical implications" (Fodor 1985). This is a problem that arises for all inverted rationalisms, because people in fact make very few of the inferences logically available to them, given what they believe, and often make wrong ones at that.[39] How can it be that the very trait, rationality, that is supposed to define what it is to have beliefs is a trait that believers don't always have, or have much of? Similarly, how can it be that the very trait, a capacity to reidentify kontents of thought, that defines the essence of human-style thought is a trait human thinkers may be weak on? Granted that triangles are by nature or definition things that have three straight sides, could it happen that most of them turned up with bent sides?

That an item lacks a defining trait is invariably diagnostic, I suspect, that the item falls in a function category (chapter 1). Function categories are defined according to what the items falling under them are supposed to do, have as proper functions to do, rather than according to what they in fact do. It is a properly functioning head that reasons well and makes correct identifications. And it is a properly functioning head that it is the job of normal psychology to study. The rub is that no actual person has a head that functions entirely properly. Let me explain why that should be so and why the study of ideal rather than actual or average cognitive functioning is the core of cognitive psychology.

No one questions that the physiologist must first study normal physiology: normal organs performing their proper biological functions under conditions normal for them. The study of abnormal physiology is possible only by reference to norms that it reports departures from. No one questions this principle for psychology either, but there is confusion over the notion of normalcy to which the principle refers.

---

39. There seems little doubt that people are not *designed* by nature to reason like deductive logical systems (see Cherniak 1986 and Harman 1986). But whatever principles we are designed to use, it is clear that many of us don't use them at all well and that all of us make errors not built into the heuristics.

In the case of physiology, for the most part what is biologically normal is also statistically average. Hence to study the normal appears to be to study the average. But I have argued (chapters 3 and 9) that this is in fact an illusion. The biological sciences, including physiology and psychology, are distinguished from the physical sciences by their interest not in lawful happenings or statistically average happenings but in biologically proper happenings, in mechanisms through which survival and proliferation of life forms is accomplished. Proper biological happenings not only sometimes fail to be average happenings but often are quite rare occurrences. It is a rare human sperm that finds an ovum, and a rare fish that is not eaten before it has a chance to lay eggs. What remains to be assimilated here is that human psychology is less like physiology and more like the fish in its rate of failure than might at first be supposed. Not functioning biologically properly is an everyday aspect of perfectly healthy psychology, an aspect of the average progress of the intact cognitive faculties. It is not average functioning that normal psychology studies.

Biological mechanisms fail to perform properly when they fail to accomplish tasks on which their proliferation in the species has historically depended. Some of these kinds of failures are invariably disastrous to the organism involved, as when the heart fails to pump blood or the protective coloring of the caterpillar fails to make it invisible to a predator. But other failures are of consequence only infrequently, as when the eye-blink reflex fails to keep a grain of sand out of the eye. This may lead to infection, blindness, and death, but more likely, the grain is removed or washes out without harm. Many biologically useful mechanisms make relatively minor contributions, or make major contributions only occasionally or only to the occasional member of the species. Biological systems typically are highly redundant, securing performance of the most important functions by multiple parallel mechanisms or by backup systems sometimes many layers deep. Thus there are mechanisms of injury avoidance and also mechanisms to secure healing in case of injury; there are mechanisms to prevent the entrance of harmful substances into the body and also mechanisms of several kinds for fighting harmful bacteria and eliminating or neutralizing toxins; there are several layers of the immune systems; etc. These particular systems are all defensive, handling, as it were, emergencies. It is more obvious still that systems designed to secure positive effects—food, shelter, etc.—can afford to be fallible, to work only once in a while. It is not surprising, then, that the behavioral systems of higher animals, certainly the cognitive part of the behavioral systems of man, are both prolifically redundant and highly fallible.

It is not often that a confused concept, a mistaken identification, or a false belief leads directly to irreparable injury or death. Unlike many physiological mechanisms, the mechanisms of concept formation, identification, and belief fixation operate directly through the environment, which is unstable and in constant flux. The lucky environmental conditions required for proper performance of these mechanisms simply cannot be relied on. If one belief fails to contribute to well being (which can happen and routinely does happen for any of numerous reasons, only one being falsehood of the belief), the next belief, one hopes, will be more successful. Thus the presence of false beliefs is routine, even though it is biologically improper or abnormal. Incorrect identifications and the introduction of confused or empty concepts into cognitive systems are biological mistakes, failures of proper function, yet they infrequently cause disaster and are entirely commonplace.

Cognitive psychology is a biological science, which means that its job is to study how the cognitive systems *work*. In the first instance, it must simply ignore the multitude of instances in which these systems *don't* work. The job of core psychology is not to predict behavior but to explain the mechanisms, including the contributions of supporting environmental structures, that together account for cases of *proper* cognitive functioning. Thus the White Queen's arguments are no threat at all to intentional rational psychology, so long as it understands itself properly as an ecological and biological science.

References

Ackerman, F. 1979. Proper names, propositional attitudes, and nondescriptive connotations. *Philosophical Studies* 35:55–69.

Ackerman, F. 1989. Content, character, and nondescriptive meaning. In *Themes from Kaplan*, ed. J. Almog, J. Perry, and H. Wettstein, 3–21. Oxford: Oxford University Press.

Almog, J. 1984. Semantical anthropology. In *Causation and casual laws*, Midwest studies in philosophy, vol. 9, ed. P. French, T. Uehling, Jr., and H. Wettstein. Minneapolis: University of Minnesota Press.

Almog, J., J. Perry, and H. Wettstein, eds. 1989. *Themes from Kaplan*. Oxford: Oxford University Press.

Armstrong, D. M. 1968. *A materialist theory of the mind*. London: Routledge and Kegan Paul.

Bach, K. 1984. Default reasoning: Jumping to conclusions and knowing when to think twice. *Pacific Philosophical Quarterly* 65:37–58.

Bach, K. 1986. Thought and object: De re representations and relations. In *The representation of knowledge and belief*, ed. M. Brand and R. M. Harnish, 187–218. Tucson: University of Arizona Press.

Bastock, M. 1967. *Courtship: A zoological study*. London: Heineman.

Bedau, M. 1991. Can biological teleology be naturalized? *Journal of Philosophy* 88:647–655.

Beer, C. G. 1973. A view of birds. *Minnesota Symposia on Child Psychology* 7:43–86.

Beer, C. G. 1975. Multiple functions and gull displays. In *Function and evolution in behavior*, ed. G. Baerends and C. Beer. Oxford: Oxford University Press.

Beer, C. G. 1976. Some complexities in the communication behavior of gulls. *Annals of the New York Academy of Sciences* 1:413–432.

Bennett, J. 1964. *Rationality*. London: Routledge and Kegan Paul.

Bennett, J. 1976. *Linguistic behaviour*. Cambridge: Cambridge University Press.

Bigelow, J., and R. Pargetter. 1987. Functions. *Journal of Philosophy* 84:181–196.

Block, N. 1980. *Readings in the philosophy of psychology*, vol. 1. Cambridge: Harvard University Press.

Block, N. 1986. Advertisement for a semantics for psychology. In *Studies in the philosophy of mind*, Midwest studies in philosophy, vol. 10, ed. P. French, T. Uehling, Jr., and H. Wettstein. Minneapolis: University of Minnesota Press.

Block, N. 1990. Can the mind change the world? In *Meaning and method: Essays in honor of Hilary Putnam*, ed. G. Boolos, 137–170. Cambridge: Cambridge University Press.

Boër, Steven E., and William G. Lycan. 1986. *Knowing Who*. Cambridge: MIT Press.

Boorse, C. 1976. Wright on functions. *Philosophical Review* 85:70–86.

Burge, T. 1979. Individualism and the mental. *Studies in metaphysics*, Midwest studies in philosophy, vol. 4, ed. P. French, T. Uehling, and H. Wettstein, 73–121.

Burge, T. 1982. Other bodies. In *Thought and object*, ed. A. Woodfield, 97–120. Oxford: Oxford University Press.

Burge, T. 1984. Individualism and psychology. Delivered at the Sloan Conference, MIT, 18 May 1984.

Burge, T. 1986a. Individualism and psychology. *Philosophical Review* 95:3–45.

Burge, T. 1986b. Intellectual norms and foundations of mind. *Journal of Philosophy* 83:697–720.

Burge, T. 1988. Individualism and self-knowledge. *Journal of Philosophy* 85:649–663.

Castañeda, H. N. 1967. Indicators and quasi-indicators. *American Philosophical Quarterly* 4:85–100.

Castañeda, H. N. 1968. On the logic of attributions of self-knowledge to others. *Journal of Philosophy* 65:439–456.

Castañeda, H. N. 1989. Direct reference, the semantics of thinking, and guise theory. In *Themes from Kaplan*, ed. J. Almog, J. Perry, and H. Wettstein, 105–144. Oxford: Oxford University Press.

Cherniak, C. 1986. *Minimal rationality*. Cambridge: MIT Press.

Churchland, P. M. 1979. *Scientific realism and the plasticity of mind*. Cambridge: Cambridge University Press.

Churchland, P. M. 1981. Eliminative materialism and propositional attitudes. *Journal of Philosophy* 78:67–90.

Churchland, P. S. 1980. A perspective on mind-brain research. *Journal of Philosophy* 77:185–207.

Clark, A. 1989. *Microcognition*. Cambridge: MIT Press.

Collet, T. S., and M. F. Land. 1978. How hoverflies compute interception courses. *Journal of Comparative Physiology* 125:191–204.

Cummins, R. 1975. Functional analysis. *Journal of Philosophy* 72:741–765. Partially reprinted in Block 1980.

Cummins, R. 1983. *The nature of psychological explanation*. Cambridge: MIT Press.

Cummins, R. 1989. *Meaning and mental representation*. Cambridge: MIT Press.

Darwin, Charles. 1859. *On the origin of species*. London: J. Murray.

Davidson, D. 1968. On saying that. *Synthese* 19:130–146.

Davidson, D. 1979. Quotation. *Theory and Decision* 11:27–40.

Davidson, D. 1987. Knowing one's own mind. *Proceedings and Addresses of the American Philosophical Association* 60:441–458.

Dawkins, R. 1983. *The extended phenotype*. Oxford: Oxford University Press.

Dennett, D. C. 1969. *Content and consciousness*. London: Routledge and Kegan Paul.

Dennett, D. C. 1978a. *Brainstorms*. Montgomery, Vt.: Bradford Books.

Dennett, D. C. 1978b. The abilities of men and machines. In Dennett 1978a.

Dennett, D. C. 1978c. Intentional systems. In Dennett 1978a.

Dennett, D. C. 1981a. Three kinds of intentional psychology. In *Reduction, time, and reality*, ed. R. Healey, 37–61. Cambridge: Cambridge University Press. Reprinted in Dennett 1987.

Dennett, D. C. 1981b. Wondering where the yellow went. *Monist* 64:102–108.

Dennett, D. C. 1984. Cognitive wheels: The frame problem of AI. In *Minds, machines, and evolution*, ed. C. Hookway. Cambridge: Cambridge University Press.

Dennett, D. C. 1987. *The intentional stance*. Cambridge: MIT Press.

Devitt, M. 1983. Realism and the renegade Putnam: A critical study of *Meaning and the moral sciences*. *Noûs* 17:291–301.

Devitt, M. 1984a. *Realism and truth*. Princeton: Princeton University Press.

Devitt, M. 1984b. Thoughts and their ascription. In *Causation and causal theories*, Midwest studies in philosophy, vol. 9, ed. P. French, T. Uehling, Jr., and H. Wettstein, 383–420. Minneapolis: University of Minnesota Press.

Dretske, F. 1981. *Knowledge and the flow of information*. Cambridge: MIT Press.

Dretske, F. 1983. Author's response to commentaries. *Behavioral and Brain Sciences* 6:82–89.

Dretske, F. 1984. Burge on content. Delivered at the Sloan Conference, MIT, 18 May 1984.

Dretske, F. 1986. Misrepresentation. In *Belief: Form, content, and function*, ed. Radu Bogdan, 17–36. New York: Oxford University Press.

Dretske, F. 1988. *Explaining behavior*. Cambridge: MIT Press.

Drummond, H. 1981. The nature and description of behavior patterns. In *Perspectives in ethology*, vol. 4, *Advantages of diversity*, ed. P. P. G. Bateson and P. H. Klopfer, 1–33. New York: Plennum Press.

Dummett, M. 1973. *Frege: Philosophy of language*. London: Duckworth.

Dummett, M. 1975. What is a theory of meaning? In *Mind and language*, ed. Samuel Guttenplan, 97–139. Oxford: Oxford University Press.

Dummett, M. 1976. What is a theory of meaning? (II). In *Truth and meaning: Essays in semantics*, ed. Gareth Evans and John McDowell, 67–137. Oxford: Oxford University Press.

Dummett, M. 1978. *Truth and other enigmas*. London: Duckworth.

Engel, B. T. 1986. An essay on the circulation as behavior. *Behavioral and Brain Sciences* 9:285–318.

Evans, G. 1981. Understanding demonstratives. In *Meaning and understanding*, ed. H. Parrett and J. Bouveresse. Berlin: deGruyter. Reprinted in Evans 1985.

Evans, G. 1982. *The varieties of reference.* Oxford: Oxford University Press.

Evans, G. 1985. *Collected papers.* Oxford: Oxford University Press.

Field, H. 1972. Tarski's theory of truth. *Journal of Philosophy* 69:347–375.

Field, H. 1978. Mental representation. *Erkenntnis* 13(1):9–61.

Fodor, J. A. 1980. Methodological solipsism as a research strategy in cognitive psychology. *Behavioral and Brain Sciences* 3:63–73.

Fodor, J. A. 1981. *Representations.* Cambridge: MIT Press.

Fodor, J. A. 1985. Fodor's guide to mental representation. *Mind* 94:66–100.

Fodor, J. A. 1986a. Banish dis-content. In *Language, mind, and logic,* ed. Jeremy Butterfield, 1–23. New York: Cambridge University Press. Reprinted in Fodor 1987.

Fodor, J. A. 1986b. Why paramecia don't have mental representations. In *Studies in the philosophy of mind,* Midwest studies in philosophy, vol. 10, ed. P. French, T. Uehling, Jr., and H. Wettstein, 3–23. Minneapolis: University of Minnesota Press.

Fodor, J. A. 1987. *Psychosemantics: The problem of meaning in the philosophy of mind.* Cambridge: MIT Press.

Fodor, J. A. 1989. Information and representation. In *Information, language, and cognition,* ed. Philip Hanson. Vancouver: British Columbia University Press.

Fodor, J. A. 1990. A theory of content. In *A theory of content and other essays.* Cambridge: MIT Press.

Fodor, J. A. 1991. Replies. In *Meaning in mind: Fodor and his critics,* ed. B. Loewer and G. Rey, 255–312. Oxford: Blackwell.

Fodor, J. A. unpublished. On there not being an evolutionary theory of content.

Gettier, E. 1963. Is justified true belief knowledge? *Analysis* 23:121–123.

Godfrey-Smith, P. 1991. Teleonomy and the philosophy of mind. Ph.D. dissertation, University of California at San Diego. See Signal, decision, action, *Journal of Philosophy* 88(1991):709–722.

Goldman, A. 1976. Discrimination and perceptual knowledge. *Journal of Philosophy* 73:771–791. Reprinted in Pappas and Swain 1978.

Gould, S. J. 1980. Return of the hopeful monster. In *The panda's thumb,* 186–193. New York, London: W. W. Norton.

Gould, S. J. 1984. Adaptationism. In *Conceptual issues in evolutionary biology,* ed. E. Sober, 235–251. Cambridge: MIT Press. Reprinted from *The Encyclopedia Einuai,* ed. Milan, 1980.

Gould, S. J., and R. C. Lewontin. 1979. The spandrels of San Marco and the Panglossian program. *Proceedings of the Royal Society of London* 205:281–288. Reprinted in Sober 1984a.

Gould, S. J., and E. S. Vrba. 1982. Exaptation: A missing term in the science of form. *Paleobiology* 8 (1): 4–15.

Hacking, I. 1983. *Representing and intervening.* Cambridge: Cambridge University Press.

Harman, G. 1973. *Thought.* Princeton: Princeton University Press.

Harman, G. 1986. *Change in view: Principles of reasoning.* Cambridge: MIT Press.

Hinde, R. 1970. *Animal behavior: A synthesis of ethology and comparative psychology.* McGraw-Hill.

Holland, A. J. 1977. Scepticism and causal theories of knowledge. *Mind* 86:555–573.

Jackson, R., and P. Pettit. 1988. Functionalism and broad content. *Mind* 97:381–400.

Kaplan, D. 1989a. Demonstratives. In *Themes from Kaplan,* ed. J. Almog, J. Perry, and H. Wettstein, 481–564. Oxford: Oxford University Press.

Kaplan, D. 1989b. Afterthoughts. In *Themes from Kaplan,* ed. J. Almog, J. Perry and H. Wettstein, 565–614. Oxford: Oxford University Press.

Kim, J. 1989. The myth of nonreductive materialism. *Proceedings of the American Philosophical Association* 63(3):31–47.

Kramer, M. 1989. The behavior and natural history of the Florida red-bellied turtle, Pseudemys Nelsoni: An ethological study. Ph.D. dissertation, University of Tennessee.

Kripke, S. A. 1979. A puzzle about belief. In *Meaning and use,* ed. A. Margalit, 239–283. Dordrecht: Reidel.

Kripke, S. A. 1980. *Naming and necessity.* Cambridge: Harvard University Press.

Kripke, S. A. 1982. *Wittgenstein on rules and private language.* Cambridge: Harvard University Press.

Leeds, S. 1978. Theories of reference and truth. *Erkenntnis* 13:111–129.

Lehner, P. N. 1979. *Handbook of ethological methods.* New York, London: Garland STPM Press.

Lepore, E., and B. Loewer. 1989. Dual aspect semantics. In *Representation,* ed. Stuart Silvers, 161–188. Dordrecht: Kluwer Academic Publishers.

Lewis, D. 1979. Attitudes *de dicto* and *de se. Philosophical Review* 78:513–543.

Lewontin, R. C. 1984. Adaptation. In *Conceptual issues in evolutionary biology,* ed. E. Sober. Cambridge: MIT Press.

Loar, B. 1985. Critical review of Saul Kripke's *Wittgenstein on rules and private language. Noûs* 19:273–280.

Loar, B. 1986. Social content and psychological content. In *Contents of thought,* ed. D. Merril and R. Grimm, 99–110. Tucson: University of Arizona Press.

Loar, B. 1987a. Names in thought. *Philosophical Studies* 51:169–185.

Loar, B. 1987b. Subjective intentionality. *Philosophical Topics* 15:89–124.

Lorenz, K. 1950. The comparative method in studying innate behavior patterns. *Symposia of the Society for Experimental Biology* 4:232–233.

LTOBC. See Millikan 1984.

McCulloch, G. 1989. *The game of the name.* Oxford: Oxford University Press.

McGinn, C. 1983. *The subjective view.* Oxford: Oxford University Press.

McGrade, A. S. 1985. Plenty of nothing: Ockham's commitment to real possibilities. *Franciscan Studies* 45:145–156.

Marcus, R. B. 1961. Modalities and Intensional languages. *Synthese* 13:303–321.

Marcus, R. B. 1981. A proposed solution to a puzzle about belief. In *Foundations of analytic philosophy*, Midwest studies in philosophy, vol. 6, ed. P. French, T. Uehling, Jr., and H. Wettstein, 501–510. Minneapolis: University of Minnesota Press.

Marcus, R. B. 1983. Rationality and believing the impossible. *Journal of Philosophy* 80(6):321–338.

Marr, D. 1982. *Vision.* San Francisco: W. H. Freeman and Co.

Matthen, M. 1988. Biological functions and perceptual content. *Journal of Philosophy* 85:5–27.

Millikan, R. G. 1984. *Language, thought, and other biological categories.* Cambridge: MIT Press. Referred to as *LTOBC*.

Millikan, R. G. 1986. The price of correspondence truth. *Noûs* 20:453–468.

Millikan, R. G. 1990. Seismograph readings for *Explaining behavior. Philosophy and Phenomenological Research* 50:807–812.

Millikan, R. G. 1991a. Speaking up for Darwin. In *Meaning and mind: Fodor and his critics*, ed. G. Rey and B. Loewer, 151–164. New York: Blackwell.

Millikan, R. G. 1991b. Perceptual content and Fregean myth. *Mind* 100:439–459.

Millikan, R. G. 1993. On Mentalese orthography. In *Dennett and his critics*, ed. B. Dahlbom. Oxford: Blackwell.

Millikan, R. G. Forthcoming. On unclear and indistinct ideas. In *Philosophical perspectives*, vol. 7 or 8, ed. J. Tomberlin. Atascadero, Calif.: Ridgeview Publishing.

Minsky, M. 1981. A framework for representing knowledge. In *Mind design*, ed. J. Haugland, 95–128. Cambridge: MIT Press.

Moore, G. E. 1899. The nature of judgment. *Mind.*

Nagel, E. 1977. Teleology revisited. *Journal of Philosophy* 84:261–301.

Neander, K. Teleology in biology. Manuscript. Wollongong University, Australia.

Owens, J. 1989. Contradictory belief and cognitive access. In *Contemporary perspectives in the philosophy of language*, vol. 2; Midwest studies in philosophy, vol. 14, ed. P. French, T. Uehling, Jr., and H. Wettstein, 289–316. Notre Dame: University of Notre Dame Press.

Owens, J. 1990. Cognitive access and semantic puzzles. In *Propositional attitudes: The role of content in logic, language, and mind*, ed. T. Anderson and J. Owens, 147–173. Stanford: CSLI Lecture Notes, 20.

Papineau, D. 1987. *Reality and representation.* New York: Blackwell.

Pappas, G., and M. Swain, eds. 1978. *Essays on knowledge and justification.* Ithaca: Cornell University Press.

Perry, J. 1977. Frege on demonstratives. *Philosophical Review* 86:474–497.

Perry, J. 1979. The problem of the essential indexical. *Noûs* 13:3–12.

Perry, J. 1988. Cognitive significance and new theories of reference. *Noûs* 22:1–18.

Pettit, P. 1986. Broad-minded explanation and psychology. In *Subject, thought, and content*, ed. P. Pettit and J. McDowell, 17–58. Oxford: Oxford University Press.

Pinker, S., and P. Bloom. 1990. Natural language and natural selection. *Behavioral and Brain Sciences* 13:707–784.

Purton, A. C. 1978. Ethological categories of behavior and some consequences of their conflation. *Animal Behavior* 26:653–670.

Putnam, H. 1975a. *Mind, language, and reality*. Vol. 1 of *Philosophical papers*. Cambridge: Cambridge University Press.

Putnam, H. 1975b. The meaning of 'meaning'. In *Language, mind, and knowledge*, Minnesota studies in the philosophy of science, vol. 7, ed. Keith Gunderson. Minneapolis: University of Minnesota Press. Also in Putnam 1975a.

Putnam, H. 1978a. *Meaning and the moral sciences*. London: Routledge and Kegan Paul.

Putnam, H. 1978b. Realism and reason. In Putnam 1978a.

Putnam, H. 1980. Models and reality. *Journal of Symbolic Logic* 45:464–482.

Putnam, H. 1981. *Reason, truth, and history*. Cambridge: Cambridge University Press.

Putnam, H. 1983. *Realism and reason*. Cambridge: Cambridge University Press.

Quine, W. V. 1960. *Word and object*. Cambridge: MIT Press.

Sachs, B. D. 1965. Sexual behavior of male rats after one to nine days without food. *Journal of Comparative Physiology* 60:144–146.

Salmon, H. 1981. *Reference and essence*. Princeton: Princeton University Press.

Schiffer, S. 1986. The real trouble with propositions. In *Belief: Form, content, and function*, ed. R. Bogden, 83–118. Oxford: Oxford University Press.

Schleidt, W. M. 1985. In defense of standard ethograms. *Zeitschrift Tierpsychologie* 68:343–345.

Schleidt, W. M., and J. N. Crawley. 1980. Patterns in the behavior of organisms. *Journal of Social and Biological Structures* 3:1–15.

Schleidt, W. M., and G. Yakalis. 1984. A proposal for a standard ethogram, exemplified by an ethogram of the bluebreasted quail (*Coturnix chinensis*). *Zeitschrift Tierpsychologie* 64:193–220.

Searle, J. 1983. *Intentionality*. Cambridge: Cambridge University Press.

Sellars, W. 1956. Empiricism and the philosophy of mind. In *The foundations of science and the concepts of psychology and psychoanalysis*, Minnesota studies in the philosophy of science, vol. 1, ed. K. Gunderson, 253–329. Minneapolis: University of Minnesota Press. Reprinted in Sellars 1963.

Sellars, W. 1963. *Science, perception, and reality*. New York: Humanities Press.

Shoemaker, S. 1975. Functionalism and qualia. *Philosophical Studies* 27:291–315.

Shope, R. 1983. *The analysis of knowing*. Princeton: Princeton University Press.

Smart, J. J. C. 1975. On some criticisms of a physicalist theory of color. In *Philosophical aspects of the mind-body problem*, ed. Chung-yin Chen. Honolulu: University of Hawaii.

Sober, E. 1984a. *Conceptual issues in evolutionary biology*. Cambridge: MIT Press.

Sober, E. 1984b. *The nature of selection*. Cambridge: MIT Press.

Sober, E. 1987. What is adaptationism? In *The latest on the best*, ed. John Dupré, 105–131. Cambridge: MIT Press.

Stalnaker, R. 1981. Indexical belief. *Synthese* 49:129–151.

Stalnaker, R. 1984. *Inquiry.* Cambridge: MIT Press.

Stalnaker, R. 1990. Narrow content. In *Propositional attitudes: The role of content in logic, language, and mind,* ed. T. Anderson and J. Owens, 131–145. Stanford: CSLI Lecture Notes, 20.

Stampe, D. 1979. Toward a causal theory of representation. In *Contemporary perspectives in the philosophy of language,* ed. P. French, T. Uehling, Jr., and H. Wettstein, 81–102. Minneapolis: University of Minnesota Press.

Stich, S. P. 1981. Dennett on intentional systems. In *Mind and cognition: A reader,* ed. W. G. Lycan, 167–183. Oxford: Blackwell.

Stich, S. P. 1983. *From folk psychology to cognitive science.* Cambridge: MIT Press.

Swain, M. 1981: *Reasons and knowledge.* Ithaca: Cornell University Press.

Unger, P. 1968. An analysis of factual knowledge. *Journal of Philosophy* 65:157–170.

Van Fraassen, B. 1980. *The scientific image.* Oxford: Oxford University Press.

Wettstein, H. 1986. Has semantics rested on a mistake? *Journal of Philosophy* 83:185–209.

Wettstein, H. 1988. Cognitive significance without cognitive content. *Mind* 97:1–28. Reprinted in Almog, Perry, and Wettstein 1989.

Wittgenstein, L. 1922. *Tractatus logico-philosophicus.* London: Routledge and Kegan Paul.

Wittgenstein, L. 1953. *Philosophical investigations.* New York: Macmillan Company.

Woodfield, A. 1975. *Teleology.* Cambridge: Cambridge University Press.

Wright, L. 1973. Functions. *Philosophical Review* 82:139–168.

Wright, L. 1976. *Teleological explanation.* Berkeley: University of California Press.

Index

percept, 275
of thoughts, 283
Tracking, 340
Tractatus logico-philosophicus (Wittgenstein), 4, 132
Transcendentalism, 201, 334
Translation, 235
Truth, 71–74, 210, 236. *See also* Beliefs, true; Correspondence theory of truth
analytic, 282
coherence theory of, 193
conditions, 79, 211, 222, 231, 236, 271, 323–324
logical, 283
logically necessary, 282
and meaning, 320
normative ingredient in, 237
redundancy theory of, 193
rules, 211–212, 231–239
theories of, 12
values, 294, 318
Trying to, 23–24
Turing machines, 152–153

Unconscious, 203
Univocity
epistemic givenness of, 287, 294, 304–305, 312, 326, 328, 335
of kontents, 328, 358
psychological law of, 289, 327, 328

Van Fraassen, B., 195
Variable character, 307
Variable names, 308, 330, 333, 336–337, 340–344
defined, 308
mental, 340–341
Verificationism, 12, 94, 211, 212, 231, 232, 238–239, 334, 343
Verification-transcendance, 210
Vrba, E. S., 43–47, 49

Wettstein, Howard, 277
Wittgenstein, Ludwig, 10, 29, 77, 119, 295, 318. *See also* Kripke-Wittgenstein paradox

Philosophical investigations, 29, 310
picture theory of, 4
Tractatus logico-philosophicus, 4, 132, 297, 299
Woodfield, Andrew, 15, 16
Wright, Larry, 15, 16, 24, 25, 26, 33